FATAL WOMEN OF ROMANTICISM

Incarnations of fatal women, or *femmes fatales*, recur throughout the works of women writers in the Romantic period. Adriana Craciun demonstrates how portrayals of *femmes fatales* played an important role in the development of Romantic women's poetic identities and informed their exploration of issues surrounding the body, sexuality, and politics. Craciun covers a wide range of writers and genres from the 1790s through the 1830s. She discusses the work of well-known figures including Mary Wollstonecraft, as well as lesser-known writers such as Anne Bannerman. By examining women writers' fatal women in historical, political, and medical contexts, Craciun uncovers a far-ranging debate on sexual difference. She also engages with current research on the history of the body and sexuality, providing an important historical precedent for modern feminist theory's ongoing dilemma regarding the status of "woman" as a sex.

ADRIANA CRACIUN is lecturer in English and Director of the Centre for Byron Studies at the University of Nottingham. She is the editor of *Zofloya, or the Moor* (1997) and *A Routledge Literary Sourcebook on Mary Wollstonecraft's A Vindication of the Rights of Woman* (2002), and co-editor of *Rebellious Hearts: British Women Writers and the French Revolution* (2001).

CAMBRIDGE STUDIES IN ROMANTICISM

This series aims to foster the best new work in one of the most challenging fields within English literary studies. From the early 1780s to the early 1830s a formidable array of talented men and women took to literary composition, not just in poetry, which some of them famously transformed, but in many modes of writing. The expansion of publishing created new opportunities for writers, and the political stakes of what they wrote were raised again by what Wordsworth called those 'great national events' that were 'almost daily taking place': the French Revolution, the Napoleonic and American wars, urbanisation, industrialisation, religious revival, an expanded empire abroad and the reform movement at home. This was an enormous ambition, even when it pretended otherwise. The relations between science, philosophy, religion and literature were reworked in texts such as *Frankenstein* and *Biographia Literaria*; gender relations in *A Vindication of the Rights of Woman* and *Don Juan*; journalism by Cobbett and Hazlitt; poetic form, content and style by the Lake School and the Cockney School. Outside Shakespeare studies, probably no body of writing has produced such a wealth of response or done so much to shape the responses of modern criticism. This indeed is the period that saw the emergence of those notions of 'literature' and of literary history, especially national literary history, on which modern scholarship in English has been founded.

The categories produced by Romanticism have also been challenged by recent historicist arguments. The task of the series is to engage both with a challenging corpus of Romantic writings and with the changing field of criticism they have helped to shape. As with other literary series published by Cambridge, this one will represent the work of both younger and more established scholars, on either side of the Atlantic and elsewhere.

For a complete list of titles published see end of book.

FATAL WOMEN OF ROMANTICISM

ADRIANA CRACIUN

For Stuart,
whose work is
an inspiration
Adriana

CAMBRIDGE
UNIVERSITY PRESS

PUBLISHED BY THE PRESS SYNDICATE OF THE UNIVERSITY OF CAMBRIDGE
The Pitt Building, Trumpington Street, Cambridge CB2 1RP, United Kingdom

CAMBRIDGE UNIVERSITY PRESS
The Edinburgh Building, Cambridge, CB2 2RU, UK
40 West 20th Street, New York, NY 10011-4211, USA
477 Williamstown Road, Port Melbourne, VIC 3207, Australia
Ruiz de Alarcón 13, 28014 Madrid, Spain
Dock House, The Waterfront, Cape Town 8001, South Africa

http://www.cambridge.org

First published 2003

Printed in the United Kingdom at the University Press, Cambridge

Typeface Baskerville Monotype 11/12.5 pt   *System* LaTeX 2ε   [TB]

A catalogue record for this book is available from the British Library

Library of Congress Cataloguing in Publication data

Craciun, Adriana, 1967–
Fatal Women of Romanticism / Adriana Craciun.
p.   cm. – (Cambridge Studies in Romanticism; 54)
Includes bibliographical references and index.
ISBN 0 521 81668 8
1. English literature – Women authors – History and criticism.   2. Women and
literature – Great Britain – History – 19th century.   3. English literature – 19th century –
History and criticism.   4. Femmes fatales in literature.   5. Romanticism – Great Britain.
6. Women in literature.   I. Title.   II. Series.
PR468.W6 C73   2002
820.9′352042 – dc21   2002067366

ISBN 0 521 81668 8 hardback

for Kari E. Lokke and Jerome J. McGann

There is no knowledge but I know it.
Nick Cave, "Far from Me"

Contents

List of illustrations

Acknowledgments

While working on this book, I have benefited much from the assistance and feedback of many colleagues and friends. Without the support of Marilyn Butler, Linda Bree, and especially James Chandler at Cambridge University Press this book would not have materialized, and so to them I am particularly grateful. Marilyn Butler and my anonymous readers at Cambridge also provided in-depth responses to the manuscript – my thanks to them for their generous and challenging readings.

While working on this book, I received grants from the National Endowment for the Humanities and the University of Nottingham. I would also like to thank the following libraries for permission to publish materials: Ashmolean Library, Oxford; UCLA Library Department of Special Collections; UC Davis Library Department of Special Collections; National Library of Scotland; British Library; The Huntington Library, San Marino, California; Hertfordshire Archives and Local Studies; Edinburgh University Library. Parts of three chapters appeared elsewhere, and I am grateful to those publishers for permission to reprint material here in revised form: " 'I hasten to be disembodied': Charlotte Dacre, the Demon Lover, and Representations of the Body" (*European Romantic Review* 6 [1995]); "Introduction: Charlotte Dacre and the Vivisection of Virtue," *Zofloya; or, The Moor*, by Charlotte Dacre, ed. Adriana Craciun (Broadview, 1997); "Violence Against Difference: Mary Wollstonecraft and Mary Robinson," in *Making History: Textuality and the Forms of Eighteenth-Century Culture*, ed. Greg Clingham (Bucknell University Press/Associated University Presses, 1998); "The Subject of Violence: Mary Lamb, *Femme Fatale*," in *Romanticism and Women Poets: Opening the Doors of Reception*, ed. Stephen Behrendt and Harriet Kramer Linkin (University Press of Kentucky, 1999).

Fatal Women of Romanticism took shape while I worked in several universities, and I want to thank my colleagues for their patience and input as I completed this project. At the University of California, Davis, I benefited from working with Peter Dale, David Van Leer, Marc Blanchard, and Seth Schein; without Rebecca Sammel's support and friendship, graduate school would have been a far less enjoyable enterprise; and without Jane King's pioneering exploration of the women poets found in the UC Davis Kohler Collection, I may never have embarked on this particular project. At Loyola University Chicago, I had the great pleasure of working with Steve Jones, who is everything a Romanticist colleague and friend should be, while, at Nottingham, Máire ní Fhlathúin, Janette Dillon, and Tracy Hargreaves have contributed much, intellectually and materially, to my well-being. Joanna Dodd provided research assistance at critical moments that eased the process of revision. To the exemplary intellectual energy of Frank Cousens at the University of Puget Sound I owe the impetus for joining this profession in the first place.

A number of colleagues and friends provided insights and encouragement while I worked on *Fatal Women of Romanticism*: Andrew Ashfield, C. M. Baumer, Stephen Behrendt, Kevin Binfield, Anne Close, Markman Ellis, Dana Frank, Michael Gamer, Jen Harvie, Ian Haywood, Glenn Himes, Mark Kozelek, Nancy Kushigian, Donna Landry, Cindy Lawford, Harriet Kramer Linkin, Louise Millar, Judith Pascoe, Mary Peace, Orianne Smith, Nan Sweet, Barbara Taylor, Barry Wallis, Susan Wolfson, Duncan Wu. The scholarship of Anne Mellor, Stuart Curran, and Nancy Armstrong in particular provided powerful precedents, and I benefited much from their landmark work on women writers and gender, even where I seem most to disagree. I would also like to thank Anne Janowitz for her generous support and advice, and, equally important, for her help in revising my book's title, much improved from my original.

To my family, who seemed never to give up hope in *Fatal Women of Romanticism* or its author, I owe more than I can say: Magdalena and George Craciun, Rodica and Aurel Dragut, Nan and Bruce Parker. Undoubtedly the longest-suffering of them all is John Logan, whose affection remains my greatest source of happiness. Without John's unwavering support behind the scenes, *Fatal Women of Romanticism* would not have seen the light of day.

My two greatest intellectual and personal debts are to Kari Lokke and Jerome McGann. My conversations with them about Romanticism continually inspire me with new ideas, and their support of my efforts has made all the difference. In gratitude for their generous friendship and imagination, I dedicate this book to them.

The publisher has used its best endeavours to ensure that the URLs for external websites referred to in this book are correct and active at the time of going to press. However, the publisher has no responsibility for the websites and can make no guarantee that a site will remain live or that the content is or will remain appropriate.

Abbreviations

AB	Bannerman, Anne, *Poems. A New Edition*, Edinburgh: Mundell, Doig and Stevenson, 1807
Ainsi	Robinson, Mary, *Ainsi va le Monde, Inscribed to Robert Merry*, 2nd edn, London, 1790
Ashfield	Ashfield, Andrew, ed., *Women Romantic Poets 1770–1830: An Anthology*, Manchester University Press, 1995
Blanchard	Blanchard, Laman, *Life and Literary Remains of L.E.L.*, 2 vols., London, 1841
Bodies	Butler, Judith, *Bodies That Matter: On the Discursive Limits of "Sex"*, London: Routledge, 1993
EC	Landon, Letitia, *Ethel Churchill: or, the Two Brides*, 3 vols. in 1 (1837), ed. F. J. Sypher, Delmar, NY: Scholars' Facsimiles & Reprints, 1992
Hours	Dacre, Charlotte (King), *Hours of Solitude. A Collection of original Poems, now first published*, 2 vols. (1805), New York: Garland, 1978
IR	Robinson, Mary, *Impartial Reflections on the Present Situation of the Queen of France, by a Friend to Humanity*, London: John Bell, 1791
LCML	Lamb, Charles and Mary, *The Letters of Charles and Mary Anne Lamb*, ed. Edwin W. Marrs, Ithaca, NY: Cornell University Press, 1975–78
Letter	Robinson, Mary, *A Letter to the Women of England, on the Injustice of Mental Subordination. A Hypertext Edition*, published by Romantic Circles [signed "Anne Frances Randall," 1799] ed. Adriana Craciun, Anne Irmen, Megan Musgrove, and Orianne Smith (www.otal.umd.edu/rc/eleced/robinson/cover.htm, 1998)

LF	Williams, Helen Maria, *Letters from France*, 8 vols. in 2, Fascimile reprints with an Introduction by Janet Todd, Delmar, NY: Scholars' Facsimiles and Reprints, 1975
LPW	Landon, Letitia, *Poetical Works of L. E. Landon*, Boston: Phillips, Sampson and Co., 1856
Memoirs	Robinson, Mary, *Perdita: The Memoirs of Mary Robinson*, ed. M. J. Levy, London: Peter Owen, 1994
Monody	Robinson, Mary, *Monody to the Memory of the Late Queen of France*, London: T. Spilsbury and Son, 1793
ND	Robinson, Mary, *The Natural Daughter, with Portraits of the Leadenhead Family. A Novel*, 2 vols., Dublin: printed by Brett Smith, 1799
NLS	National Library of Scotland
Nymphomania	Bienville, M. D. T., *Nymphomania, or, A Dissertation Concerning the Furor Uterinus*, trans. Edward Sloane Wilmot (London, 1775); reprinted with Tissot's *Onanism* as *Onanism / Nymphomania*, New York: Garland, 1985.
Passions	Dacre, Charlotte, *The Passions*, 4 vols., London: Cadell and Davies, 1811; New York: Arno Press, 1974
PL	Milton, John, *Paradise Lost*, ed. Scott Elledge, New York: Norton, 1975
Reflections	Burke, Edmund, *Reflections on the Revolution in France* (1790), ed. Thomas Mahoney, New York: Liberal Arts Press, 1955
RG	Mellor, Anne, *Romanticism and Gender*, London: Routledge, 1993
RPW	Robinson, Mary, *Poetical Works* 3 vols. (1806); reprinted, introduction by Caroline Franklin, London: Routledge/Thoemmes, 1996
RR	Landon, Letitia, *Romance and Reality*, 3 vols. (1831); reprinted, ed. F. J. Sypher, Delmar, NY: Scholars' Facsimiles & Reprints, 1998
STC	Coleridge, Samuel Taylor, *The Complete Poetical Works of Samuel Taylor Coleridge*, ed. E. H. Coleridge, Oxford: Clarendon Press, 1912
Tales	Bannerman, Anne, *Tales of Superstition and Chivalry*, London: Vernor and Hood, 1802

VRW   Wollstonecraft, Mary, *A Vindication of the Rights of
               Woman*, 2nd edn (1792); ed. Carol H. Poston, New
               York: Norton, 1975

Walsingham   Robinson, Mary, *Walsingham; or, the Pupil of Nature. A
               Domestic Story*, 4 vols., 1797; Introduction by Peter
               Garside, 4 vols., London: Routledge/Thoemmes,
               1992

WCML   Lamb, Charles and Mary, *Works of Charles and Mary
               Lamb*, ed. E. V. Lucas, New York: G. P. Putnam's
               Sons; London: Methuen, 1903

WL   Landon, Letitia, *Works of Letitia E. Landon*, 2 vols.,
               Boston: Phillips, Sampson, and Co., 1857

WMW   Wollstonecraft, Mary, *The Works of Mary Wollstonecraft*,
               7 vols., ed. Janet Todd and Marilyn Butler, London:
               William Pickering, 1989

Wu   Wu, Duncan (ed.), *Romantic Women Poets: An Anthology*,
               Oxford: Blackwell, 1997

WW   William Wordsworth, *Poetical Works of William
               Wordsworth*, ed. Ernest de Selincourt and Helen
               Darbishire, Oxford: Clarendon, 1947

Zofloya   Dacre, Charlotte, *Zofloya; or, the Moor: A Romance of the
               Fifteenth Century* (1806), ed. Adriana Craciun,
               Peterborough: Broadview, 1997

Introduction

I wish to persuade women to endeavour to acquire strength, both in mind and in body.

Mary Wollstonecraft, *A Vindication of the Rights of Woman* (1792)

Women are what they were meant to be; and we wish for no alteration in their bodies or their minds.

William Hazlitt, "The Education of Women" (1815)

Incarnations of fatal women – the seductress, the mermaid, the queen, the muse – recur throughout the works of women writers, demonstrating that fatal women played an important role in the development of women's poetic identities in the Romantic period. Femmes fatales can be understood as misogynist projections of the "woman within" by male writers, as some scholars have argued;[1] yet such accounts leave little room for women's surprising uses of these figures, other than as reactive critiques. To ask why they used such figments of male fantasy is to ask the wrong question, for it assumes that these figures originate in the imaginations of men. Indeed, part of our problem in mapping the new terrain of women's writing in the Romantic period is of our own making, when we rely on the circular argument that figures such as the femme fatale and the violent woman originate in and appeal to solely the male imagination, something that Romantic-period women writers did not believe.

This book does not trace a continuous tradition of women writers of the Romantic period, nor does it argue that women writers in this era experienced and articulated a distinct, gender-complementary Romanticism in reaction to the canonical Romanticisms of male writers. Feminist literary histories and the anthologies they have produced often attempt to trace such a continuity in women's literature, one that answers Virginia Woolf's need for literary foremothers, and do so by privileging nineteenth-century concepts of literary practice and publication, as well

I

as feminist perspectives that are not particularly useful when applied, for example, to women writing before 1700.[2] According to such feminist literary histories, "anger is an identifying characteristic of the 'female' (biological) reacting to the 'feminine' (socio-cultural)," writes Margaret Ezell (*Writing Women's Literary History*, 25). Ezell's critique is timely and illuminating for those who work on women's writing of the Romantic period, even though her own focus is on pre-1700 women writers. Unlike their later nineteenth-century counterparts, women writers of the Romantic period are just now beginning to be reanthologized and re-canonized by feminist scholars, and therefore present us with an unique opportunity to reevaluate not only Romanticism and gender, but also the meaning and usefulness of a distinct female literary tradition and even of a distinct femaleness.

While the socio-cultural realm of gender has been the traditional focus of feminist literary criticism and literary history in the nineteenth century, this study focuses significant attention on the virtually unexamined realm of "natural" sex, and argues that sex (that is, the sexed body, male and female) is central to the study of Romantic-period women. While not a traditional literary history, *Fatal Women of Romanticism* does contribute to the study of women's literature, but does so while simultaneously interrogating (not dismissing) the usefulness and historicity of such a concept as "women's literature." The category of biological "women" (in addition to that of Woman, which has been closely scrutinized by feminists for centuries) must also be examined, and Denise Riley reminds us "that such a scrutiny is a thoroughly feminist undertaking":

the apparent continuity of the subject of "women" isn't to be relied on; "women" is both synchronically and diachronically erratic as a collectivity, while for the individual, "being a woman" is also inconstant, and can't provide an ontological foundation. (*Am I That Name?*, 2)

To engage these writers and these inconstant categories from our present vantage point is not to project onto the past postmodern fantasies of performative sex and gender, but, rather, to attend to the historically specific and politically interested origins of prevailing modern models of sexual difference.

Feminist literary histories are not properly historical if they fail to examine the history of sex as well as that of gender.[3] Given the wealth of new work on the history of the body and of sexuality,[4] we cannot afford to omit this corporeal history from our reevaluations of these long-neglected writers. Central to my study is an examination of women writers' diverse critiques and interrogations of sexual difference (the "natural" realm of biological sex) as a historically stable and stabilizing reality. I argue that Romantic-period writers not only have questioned the nature of femininity and culturally constructed gender, but that they also questioned the stability and naturalness of sex itself. Modern criticism that focuses on the former instances and ignores the latter does so because the system of natural sexual difference, which was in fact fiercely contested at the turn of the nineteenth century, seems intractable and self-evidently universal two centuries later. What appears self-evident is, of course, ideological and historical: it is recent histories of the body and of sexual difference that have helped restore these women's subtle critiques and questions, and have made them partially visible to our distant eyes. Once we more fully appreciate the diversity of opinion (and the urgency of the debates) regarding "natural" sexual difference among Romantic-period political, philosophical, and scientific thinkers, we should not be surprised that women writers also questioned such purportedly natural categories for their own diverse interests.

Over the last decade, postmodern histories of the body and of sexuality have contested the stability of the sex/gender distinction, and have instead demonstrated that current models of two distinct sexes are culturally and historically specific.[5] This two-sex system of complementary difference gained greater credibility throughout the eighteenth century, supplanting an older one-sex model, in which women's bodies were seen essentially as inferior versions of male bodies. This newer two-sex system established a "powerful alternative" according to Thomas Laqueur, which allowed for "a wide variety of contradictory claims about sexual difference."[6] The two-sex model attempted to ground the ideology of women's passionlessness and domesticity in empirical science, though, as Laqueur shows in *Making Sex: Body and Gender from the Greeks to Freud*, the scientific community was divided over which model to uphold: "It may well be the case that almost as many people believed that women by nature were equal in passion to men as believed the opposite" (152). Despite the growing emphasis on a "biology of incommensurability" and women's passionlessness (which would support current gender-complementary models of Romanticism), the one-sex model's insistence on female sexual desire and on the necessity for female orgasm in conception was not overturned, but, rather, was conveniently downplayed by advocates of sexual difference.

The scientific community's ambivalence regarding which model of sexual difference to uphold, amounting at times to violent disagreement and contradiction, extends to the literary world. Although it is in some ways productive to generalize, as Mary Poovey does in *The Proper Lady and the Woman Writer*, that "[b]y the end of the eighteenth century... 'female' and 'feminine' were understood by virtually all men and women to be synonymous" (6), I find Laqueur's emphasis on the unresolved struggle over both the meaning of the sex "woman," and whether or not such a distinct sex even exists, more compelling. By emphasizing the struggle over the categories of sex and gender, rather than the struggle's outcome (the conflation of gender and sex, of femininity with the "natural" female body), we can give women's diverse perspectives greater visibility. From prominent Enlightenment feminists like Mary Wollstonecraft and Mary Robinson, to poets like Letitia Landon, women writers of the Romantic period always addressed the body when they considered issues of intellect, subjectivity, sexuality, agency, and power.

Gendered studies of the eighteenth century and of the Victorian period have for some time explored the connections between the history of the body and literary history, and have examined the historically contingent nature of embodiment that helped shape notions of cultural gender. Londa Schiebinger's *Nature's Body: Gender and the Making of Modern Science* examines in detail the complex ideological interests that shaped late eighteenth-century and nineteenth-century concepts of sexual difference in nature. Schiebinger's research into botanical, sexual, and racial classification at the turn of the nineteenth century demonstrates that appreciating the contested and thus contingent status of the "natural" order of sex is essential to a full understanding of the evolution of difference, and hence the discourse of political, racial, and sexual equality, in the Romantic period.[7] Interdisciplinary studies of science and literature, specifically of literature and the body, are plentiful for the eighteenth century and earlier periods; these fields have long enjoyed explorations of the carnivalesque, the grotesque, the bawdy, and the perverse that can make nineteenth-century evocations of the body seem impoverished indeed. Drawing on Foucault's interrogations of the Victorian explosion in sexual discourses, and of the relationship of such discourses to legal, penal, medical, educational, and domestic institutions, recent studies of the body in Victorian culture and literature have examined more closely the persistence, and contestation, of sexual difference as a natural and stable category.[8] The emerging consensus among historians of eighteenth- and nineteenth-century medicine emphasizes "that the medical construction of male and female as dichotomous terms had no foundation in 'nature': it was based on ideological oppositions which are deeply entrenched in western thought."[9]

These developments in the history of sexuality and the body, and their impact on literary and cultural studies, are part of the larger theoretical sea change engendered by postmodernism's challenges to traditional Marxist, historicist, feminist, and psychoanalytical critiques. In feminist theory specifically, heated debates over such "constructionist" approaches to gender and especially sex and embodiment often focus on Foucault's influence in these genealogical, deconstructive, and anti-humanist approaches, especially given the elision of gender in his work. Debate on Foucault's usefulness for feminist theory and practice is ongoing, and generally centers on his concepts of resistance and power, which are also central to my study. Foucault's influential theory of power as productive, not merely repressive, of bodies and subjects is seen by some to rob women of the luxury of autonomous, rational subjectivity and agency that many men have enjoyed for centuries under the reign of humanism. Feminist theorists like Elizabeth Grosz, Lois McNay, and Catherine MacKinnon have argued that Foucault's emphasis on ever-present power leaves little room for resistance or agency, and instead intensifies the passivity of (characteristically ungendered) subjects and bodies as they are inscribed, shaped, and punished by "technologies of the self" and corporeal discipline through diet, exercise, work, medicine, hygiene, etc.[10] This well-known critique of the passivity of the Foucauldian subject of power, combined with his failure to acknowledge the historically specific and firmly entrenched domination of women by men, has led some feminists to conclude that "the political experience of women daily subordinated by men, by masculinity, by the social construction of their bodies, makes resistance and change much more complex and problematic than Foucault seems to allow."[11]

But, of course, there are many Foucaults, as there are many feminisms, and a tradition of postmodern feminist theory has refined Foucauldian resistance and found valuable tools in his genealogical method and anti-humanist critique of subjects and bodies. Beyond the utopian promise of "bodies and pleasures" that Foucault enigmatically suggested at the end of the first volume of *The History of Sexuality* as an alternative, posthumanistic strategy of resisting subjection and normalization (as genital, complementary heterosexuality), feminists have also focused on his later writings in which he elaborated his notion of resistance. "There are no relations of power without resistances," writes Foucault: "the latter are all the more real and effective because they are formed right at the point where relations of power are exercised."[12] This is the heart of the matter. Seeing resistance as an effect of power, and power as working discursively from the ground up, robs women of the few epistemological and ontological privileges we have enjoyed. As Biddy Martin summarizes, "[t]he tendency to place women outside culture, to define femininity in terms of an absolute exclusion and consequent innocence with respect to language and ideology reflects an overly simplistic understanding between identity and discourse."[13] But Foucault denies an opposition between "a substance of resistance versus a substance of power," and insists that "power seeps into the very grain of individuals, reaches right into their bodies, permeates their gestures, their posture, what they say, how they learn to live and work."[14] Where then is resistance, collective or individual, feminist or not, and how can such a methodology contribute to our understanding of women's literature of the Romantic period?

If resistance and power are not distinct substances, and there exist no distinct, stable groups that "possess" power (i.e., the middle classes, or men), then resistance must be contextual, localized, and historically specific. Susan Bordo offers two modern examples of how resistance can emerge from normalization, examples that have important precedents in the Romantic period:

the woman who goes on a rigorous weight-training programme in order to achieve a currently stylish look may discover that her new muscles also enable her to assert herself more forcefully at work. Or ... "feminine" decorativeness may function "subversively" in professional contexts which are dominated by highly masculinist norms (such as academia). Modern power relations are thus unstable; resistance is perpetual and hegemony precarious.[15]

In our contemporary context, Bordo argues, celebrations of female "resistance" through the "individual empowerment" of weight loss and exercise are actually mass-produced by "advertisers in the profoundest of cynical bad faith" (*Ibid.*, 198). But Bordo acknowledges the persistent potential for the subversive effects in such marketed "empowerment," despite the exploitative intention of the advertisers (*Ibid.*, 198). This simultaneous, unstable, and contextual slippage between normalization and subversion, read in historical and literary context, is key to appreciating the significance of the corporeal for Romantic-period women writers. Mary Robinson and Mary Hays, for example, continued to celebrate femininity's associations with sensuality and passion at a time when the public intellectual sphere was increasingly masculinized and rationalized. Their use of older associations of women with sensibility to further feminist projects, like Wollstonecraft's advocacy of women's exercise and physical strength, demonstrates early feminism's strategic use of available (and conflicting) gender paradigms to subversive effect. Writing at a time when the bourgeois natural order (grounded in complementary sexual difference and its accompanying gendered spheres) was firmly in place, these writers nevertheless had access to competing, even discredited, cultural models.

Femmes fatales in particular, with their inherent "doubleness" as both feminine and fatal, offer us an especially productive perspective on the development of sexual difference in the Romantic period. This strategy of duplicity, mimicry, or "doubleness of vision" is feminist theory's favorite strategy, one that can account for women's unique "internal exclusion within Western culture, a particularly well-suited point from which to expose the workings of power."[16] Women's writings thus need to be read within this larger field of power, in which resistance is not constituted by "the simple absence or inversion of normative structures," but as a "heterogeneity – the overlapping of competing versions of reality within the same moment of time."[17] Nancy Armstrong describes her Foucauldian feminist history of the novel as aiming for this heterogeneity, a defining characteristic of genealogy as opposed to traditional history, in order to avoid "the linear pattern of a developmental narrative" and instead generate a "productive hypothesis" of "how the discourse of sexuality is implicated in shaping the novel" (*Desire and Domestic Fiction*, 23). Only if we avoid such linear narratives, based on assumptions that women's bodies and texts are simply repressed by patriarchal power, can we see how they are inflected and produced by unresolved, competing discourses.

The constellation of texts, writers, and ideologies known as "Romanticism" currently lacks such gendered studies of literature and culture that also account for the history of sexuality, sexual difference, and the body. The most influential studies of early nineteenth-century women's literature share a commitment to a stable and unchanging relationship between natural sex (the female, which is constant) and cultural gender (the feminine, which is contested); similarly, they also emphasize women writers', particularly women poets', unwillingness or inability, due to cultural constraints, to assert themselves as Romantic poets, as unacknowledged legislators of the world.[18] Gender-complementary studies tend to reread the same increasingly canonical women writers and texts,[19] and to rely on a repressive hypothesis in which (middle-class) women's "authentic" subjectivity is rarely examined as an effect of power, as implicated in regimes of power and oppression. This unresolved problem of women's repressed authenticity, and of their "natural" benevolence and ability to remain outside masculinist socio-economic systems, is thus displaced onto the stable, acultural female body and its liberating promises. Yet, when this bourgeois subject was being enshrined as the stable agent of cultural consumption and production in the middle-class economic and moral order, many alternatives, doubts, and speculations were simultaneously articulated by men and women of diverse interests. If we read for such heterogeneity then we can avoid replicating teleological narratives via "the anticipatory power of meaning" and instead attend to "the hazardous play of dominations."[20] Feminist studies that ignore Foucauldian and postmodern critiques of the subject and the body cannot account for some of the most intriguing and unusual writing by women in the Romantic period, writing that went against the grain of an increasingly hegemonic natural order.

Central to feminist literary criticism on British women writers is the usually unspoken aim to demonstrate that women as a class (that is, as a sex outside of class) eschew violence, destructiveness, and cruelty, except in self-defense or rebellion, like Gilbert and Gubar's imprisoned madwoman in the attic. This faith in women's benevolence, for it is indeed a foundational belief of many modern feminisms, originated in the rise of the bourgeois order itself, which enshrined the maternal, nurturing, and domestic middle-class woman as the protected, private moral center of this new socio-economic order. That Romantic-period middle-class women gained an important new sense of moral, cultural, and economic authority through their domestic identities is undeniable. But should feminist criticism share this same commitment to bourgeois women's special immunity or freedom from masculinist regimes of power, cruelty, or oppression? I want to insist on this connection between contemporary feminist reevaluations of the Romantic period and its normative (but not uncontested) ideology of gender and sex, because current scholarship too often replicates this (gendered) Romantic ideology unproductively.

Rescuing women writers and their female protagonists from charges of wanton cruelty, and capitulation to "masculinist" behavior such as exploitation and objectification, seems to be more the goal of modern gender-complementary criticism than of the writers in question. Aggression, murderousness, sadism, and destructiveness have no room to surface in such accounts of women and women writers, except as responses to masculine injustice and violence. The reception of Mary Lamb's poetry and prose is a case in point: Lamb's critical reception as a writer has consistently been shaped by an implicit desire to efface the violence that remained a part of her life and writings. Nineteenth- and twentieth-century critics alike have struggled to reconcile the violence of Lamb's murder of her mother with her career as a writer of children's literature. Lamb's illuminating reception history and writing invite us to imagine the possibility and consequences of a female subject of violence, something feminist theory has consistently resisted. Such a female subject of violence poses a serious challenge to complementary models of women's writing, women's language, and women's Romanticism, and instead reveals the great extent to which such concepts of women's unique relationships to language, and of "women" in general, rely on an implicit faith in women's nonviolence and moral purity.

Mary Lamb, like many of the women writers represented here, has received little attention in the recent revival of interest in Romantic period women writers. In addition to resisting the temptation to establish prematurely a canon of women Romantic writers, we should also resist the illusion that we can read them from a stance of transhistorical, pure detachment, free from ideological constraints. Rather, these writers would benefit from a (feminist) reading that actively resists feminism's persistent ideology of the consolation of women's natural nonviolence and benevolence, precisely because this ideology has been unable to withstand the critique both of postmodernism, and, more importantly, of Romanticism. In order to attempt new readings of women's relationships to power and violence, and the relationship of power and violence to women's bodies, we need to abandon several a priori assumptions: that women are inherently nonviolent, that cruelty and mastery are in general unnatural (or at the very least culturally masculine, and will be eliminated once women revolutionize all social relations), and that feminist criticism should seek to show how women as a class, throughout history, do not or should not replicate systems of "masculinist" power and violence.

My focus on violent and fatal women in women's writings demonstrates not only that Romantic heroines engaged in extremely unfeminine forms of behavior, but that in women's violence and destructiveness we find the end of woman as a sex, and the end of all the consolations with which woman provides us. Violence "unsexed" women as far back as Lady Macbeth, but my goal is not to trace a rebellious, androgynous human spirit that throughout history has chafed at the cultural constraints on feminine behavior, and occasionally erupted in acts of rebellious, androgynous violence. Rather, I examine women's violence in the contexts of larger political, ideological, and even medical debates specific to the Romantic period, to demonstrate that women's inherent nonviolence was often a necessary feature in arguments for "natural," corporeal sexual difference, and that this two-sex system was by no means universally and unquestioningly accepted as unchanging by either women or men. For example, chapter 2 focuses on the fierce debate over the nature and history of women's physical strength in the context of French women's activism in the French Revolution. Concentrating on the republican feminist tracts of Mary Wollstonecraft and Mary Robinson, I focus on strength and exclude maternity and sexuality because these women themselves isolated physical strength as an area of possible corporeal mutability. In chapter 3 I expand my examination of British women's responses to French Revolutionary women, focusing on a wide range of representations of Marie Antoinette. In Mary Robinson's numerous portraits of Marie Antoinette as both public seductress and private mother, she attempts to fashion a feminism that would allow women access both to the *ancien régime* eroticized body, and to the new bourgeois concepts of rational, maternal domesticity and public citizenship.

The executions of the Queen and other highly visible women like Madame Roland and Charlotte Corday in 1793 mark an important threshold in the history of the sexed body, ostensibly eliminating both the feminine body of the aristocratic beauty and mother, and the masculinized body of the republican assassin from the range of options available to women. Because of this institutionalized exclusion of women from the public political sphere, women writers could use these politicized historical figures to make a wide range of claims to both masculine and feminine spheres of power, and masculine and feminine bodies, increasingly distinct though these categories were. The French revolutionary debates in Britain, and women's little known contributions to them,[21] thus emerge as a key crisis in the history of sexual difference, allowing women a brief window of opportunity in which to imagine daring alternatives to the increasingly rigid definitions and demands of sexual difference.

In misogynist popular accounts, Marie Antoinette was unsexed through her perverse sexuality, just as the republican Charlotte Corday, Marat's assassin, had been unsexed through her unnatural lack of feminine sensibility. "Marat's barbarous assassin," wrote Sade in his elegiac tribute to the radical journalist, "like those mixed beings to which one cannot assign a sex, vomited up from Hell to the despair of both sexes, directly belongs to neither."[22] Unsexed by her violent crime, Charlotte Corday epitomizes the anomalous status of violent women during the 1790s when middle-class political aspirations in Britain (like those of the Jacobins in France) were firmly embodied in the domestic woman and the truth of her sex. These examples of women who belonged to neither sex are related to other indeterminate bodies discussed throughout this study. The unsexed as a category is related to the undead, for both are corporeal categories that fall outside the binary systems that would contain them, and both enjoy none of the consolations of these systems (such as a fixed, natural identity). The unnatural, unsexed, undead, and sometimes inhuman bodies I discuss are all involved with destruction, and it is this unholy marriage to destruction (typically manifested as violence) that ultimately robs these "unnatural" bodies of their cultural consolations. As Angela Carter argued in *The Sadeian Woman and the Ideology of Pornography*, the violent demystification of the womb, and consequently of woman, in Sade's writings marks our final and most painful secularization, for "with the imaginary construct of the goddess, dies the notion of eternity, whose place on this earth was her womb...The last resort of homecoming is denied us" (110). Women writers contemporary with Sade also questioned the sacredness of women and their inherent benevolence and nurturing, at the same time that they engendered modern feminism.

Charlotte Dacre, author of a notorious series of popular Gothic novels, is, in this Sadean respect, the most remarkable writer discussed here. Chapter 4 draws close connections between Dacre's decidedly Sadean displays of female violence and depravity, and the medical treatise *Nymphomania*, in order to demonstrate how far some women writers went to disturb the natural boundaries of bodies. The supernatural femmes fatales in Anne Bannerman's poetry discussed in chapter 5 also demonstrate that women writers have contributed to, not merely critiqued, the fatal woman tradition in Romanticism, and that in some cases they even developed a poetic identity of the poet as magnificent destroyer, a stereotypically masculine figure found throughout Dacre's and Bannerman's works. Dacre's and Bannerman's fatal women consistently fail to embody natural sexual difference, either physically degenerating in the case of Dacre's, or failing to materialize as male readers would have them do, in the case of Bannerman's.

The closing chapter on Letitia Elizabeth Landon examines her use of mermaids and water within the context of public health debates, and identifies a striking materialist critique of Romantic idealism beneath what many modern scholars have characterized as Landon's uneasy embodiment of the ideology of the beautiful. Expanding the parameters of what counts as corporeal even further than previous chapters, and reading in the context of contemporary public health discourse, this chapter shows that psychoanalytical feminist readings, which systematically ally the dead and the corporeal with the repressed, maternal, and female body – i.e., which read solely for gender – underestimate the radically unfemale powers of the dead and the decaying in women's writing.

Thus, while most feminist work on the body in nineteenth-century culture focuses on women's diseases, maternity, sexuality, and hunger, this study is interested in qualities and types of bodies that such sexuality-centered critiques omit: bodies whose strength and size are volatile, even bodies on the threshold between the living and the dead, the real and the phantasmatic. I am interested in these threshold states of "natural" bodies because they demand that we articulate and thereby rethink what counts as corporeal, and, specifically, what counts as evocations of the corporeal in women's writings. Mary Poovey has argued that "by the last decades of the eighteenth century, [for women] even to refer to the body was considered 'unladylike' " (14), yet this is only so if we limit ourselves to sexuality as the defining, or most truthful, indicator of corporeal experience and representation.[23] Once we begin to look for different uses of the corporeal in women's writings, we can explore bodies that bear more than truth. Unsexed and undead bodies are such bodies, sharing an anomalous status between two normative, supposedly fixed categories of truth (male and female, living and dead); they function as a disruptive "third term," which, as Gilbert Herdt has argued in *Third Sex, Third Gender*, embodies not the harmony of the androgyne, but the destruction of all such binary formulations as gender and sex complementarity, and their imagined syntheses in the androgyne.[24] Wollstonecraft and Robinson's speculations on women's strong bodies, and Bannerman's phantasmatic bodies veiled in obscurity, are important examples of women's evocations of the corporeal that are not primarily concerned with sexuality, and that explore bodies between natural categories.

Women's explorations of such unnatural bodies are strategically valuable for feminism's present identity crisis because they contest rather than reinforce the two-sex system on which gender-complementary readings of their works ultimately rely. Isobel Armstrong, Margaret Ezell, and others have argued, and I concur, that feminist literary criticism can no longer read solely for moments of protest, feminist rage, or repressed authenticity, as it typically has done. It seems to me that the postmodern, materialist, and antihumanist challenges to the liberal feminisms of the 1970s and 1980s have yet to be answered in much of the otherwise excellent scholarship on "new" nineteenth-century women writers, and in this respect such criticism is out of step with feminist theory today.

Sexual difference and the feminist value of questioning such difference emerged as one of the key theoretical debates of the latter part of the twentieth century. My project brings to this debate part of its origins in the late eighteenth and early nineteenth centuries, when sexual difference was institutionalized (and contested) according to the familiar two-sex model of incommensurable difference currently under scrutiny and redirection. Throughout this book, therefore, I continue to draw connections between the Romantic-period texts I discuss and current evocations of feminism's identity crisis, because this crisis must be (perhaps can only be) understood in relation to its origins in Romantic-period models of the body and the subject. The identity crisis feminism faces, in which the existence of "real women" is undermined (by feminists and others) and along with it their agency, rights, history, and specificity (some would also add corporeality), was already present in an earlier form in the Romantic period. Mary Wollstonecraft faced it, as did such diverse writers as Mary Robinson, Charlotte Dacre, Letitia Landon, and Anne Bannerman. Their crisis, growing out of the larger political upheavals ushered in by the French Revolution, its nascent promises of human rights, and its redefinition of human nature, is not our crisis. But our crisis is incomprehensible if we continue to ignore the complexity and ingenuousness of their original responses, solutions, and protests, which we too often assume we have ourselves conceived of for the first time.

One question central to this feminist debate surrounding difference is one to which I return throughout this study, as it will no doubt recur in the minds of modern readers. This question concerns the dangers of undermining the stability of "natural" sexual difference. Feminist theorists such as Luce Irigaray, Kari Weil, Elizabeth Grosz, and Gayatri Spivak have reminded us that patriarchy has always benefited from the effacement of woman and her female specificity – the denial of difference. Irigaray famously termed philosophy's denial of difference as a "hom(m)osexual" economy of the same, which excludes woman's distinct voice, body, experience, and language from Western logocentrism. Moreover, male philosophers' appropriation of Woman as the displaced other of this phallogocentric economy has met with great resistance from feminist theorists, and rightly so. Derrida's masquerade as Woman in *Spurs*, Deleuze and Guattari's use of "becoming-woman" in *A Thousand Plateaus*, Foucault's "desexualization of the question," and Nietzsche's figuration of Woman as truth upon which these later philosophers build, have generated feminist resistance to this poststructuralist flirtation with and displacement of femininity.[25] Without delving into great detail here, I wish only to say that my intention is to direct our gaze two hundred years in the past, when women first struggled with this same dangerous choice between, on the one hand, the agency and specificity granted through sexual difference, with its often crippling sacrifices and exclusions, and, on the other hand, the untried promises of liberty and equality that feminists such as Wollstonecraft and Robinson saw in the French Revolutionary ideals of (male) citizenship.

In her illuminating *Womanizing Nietzsche: Philosophy's Relation to the "Feminine,"* Kelly Oliver persuasively argues that when Nietzsche, Freud, and Derrida "attempt to open up philosophy to its others – the body, the unconscious, nonmeaning, even to the feminine – they close off philosophy to any specifically feminine other" (xi). Derrida's celebration of Woman as "undecidability," one of deconstruction's privileged terms, in fact marks women's exclusion:

In the name of undecidability, every sex becomes masculine. Human beings become mankind. Rendering all difference undecidable is not a way of embracing difference. It is yet another way of rendering everything the [same and] we are back within the logic of the proper. (*Ibid.*, 66)

While I agree that this is true of philosophy at the turn of the twenty-first century, it has not always been so. When women and men questioned, blurred, even denied sexual difference in the 1790s, for example, they were not doing so as part of patriarchy's "timeless" effacement of femininity and "woman." When feminists such as Mary Wollstonecraft, Catherine Macaulay, and Mary Robinson speculated in the 1790s that perhaps, with the right exercise, women could become as physically strong as men, and thus erase that specific aspect of "natural" difference and inferiority, they were not attempting to render everything the same, to make women masculine. As I demonstrate in chapter 2, they were in fact historicizing "natural" difference, examining its origins and embodiment in specific institutions and practices, and suggesting alternatives to the two-sex system which, contrary to prevailing modern assumptions, they did not accept as stable and eternal. Attending to women's participation in this particular historical crisis of sexual difference at the turn of the nineteenth century is crucial if modern theoretical debates are to avoid the current tendency to generalize ahistorically about the usefulness of sexual difference and the danger of its displacement.

THE FEMME FATALE AND FEMINIST THEORY

> Would a woman be able to hold us (or, as they say, "enthrall" us) if we did not consider it quite possible that under certain circumstances she could wield a dagger (any kind of dagger) *against us?*
>
> Nietzsche, *The Gay Science*

Nietzsche's question reveals the connection between the violent woman and the femme fatale, the unfemale and the hyperfeminine, that is central to this study. Histories of the femme fatale do not generally acknowledge this connection, but rather resist it. I want to insist on this connection, however, not so as to establish a continuous tradition of destructive female figures, but rather in order to demonstrate the extent to which Romantic-era women writers focused on aggression and destruction as threats to the construct "woman," and the extent to which they helped shape the literary femme fatale traditions usually attributed to male authors.

The femme fatale, writes Mary Ann Doane, is "not the subject of feminism but a symptom of male fears about feminism."[26] As a "functional construct of the male imaginary" and its fear of the feminine, writes Lynda Hart, the femme fatale ultimately upholds the patriarchal sociosymbolic in her eventual destruction.[27] Women who kill, on the other hand, especially those who kill "in cold blood," radically subvert this order by violating the imperative that women remain passive. Hart's illuminating study of the violent woman and her "silent escort," the lesbian, focuses on the core of aggression in representations of these two figures. The violent woman and the lesbian each possess a definitively masculine trait that renders both unfemale: aggression and active desire, respectively, qualities that throw each outside her sex, much like Charlotte Corday and Marie Antoinette. But omitted from this helpful coupling of the lesbian and the violent woman is the femme fatale, the much-maligned hyperfeminine fantasy of heterosexual patriarchy. The femme fatale can exhibit both the active desire of the lesbian and the aggression of the violent woman, and therefore needs to be reintroduced into the nineteenth-century debate on the contested category "woman." If she could not wield a dagger, Nietzsche reminds us with characteristic irony, the enthralling woman could not enthrall.

Prevailing accounts of the literary femme fatale tradition are indebted to Mario Praz and his idiosyncratic *The Romantic Agony*, in which Praz fixes "the starting point" of the *fin de siècle* femme fatale in the Romantic Belle Dame sans Merci, beginning with Matilda in Lewis's *The Monk* (192). Praz's search for a "starting point" for the femme fatale establishes a continuous, canonical, and exclusively male history of this figure to which most studies still limit themselves. Praz further explains that popular focus shifts from the Fatal Man (the Byronic hero) in the first half of the nineteenth century to the Fatal Woman in the second half due to a "chronic ailment" – "The male, who at first tends towards sadism, inclines, at the end of the century, towards masochism" (191, 206). Praz's highly influential account of the femme fatale relies on an androcentric psychological explanation, and virtually all studies of the femme fatale since have accepted his perspective uncritically, even if they locate feminist potential in such male-authored destructive women. Rather than respond with a largely female counter-history, I will introduce women's representations of femmes fatales not as alternative historical "starting points," but as evidence that the femme fatale was an ideologically charged figure that both male and female writers invested with a range of contemporary political, sexual, and poetic significations. She cannot be limited to a fantasy of male masochism, as she is in Praz (and in most accounts which rely on him), nor merely to a nostalgic throwback of the aristocratic "empire of women," which on one level she certainly embodied. Mary Ann Doane's pronouncement that the femme fatale is empty of any subjective intention sums up the femme fatale's role in the male aesthetic of masochism, but it offers us little help when we examine the femmes fatales of Romantic women writers.

My study uncouples the femme fatale from this inadequate (because ahistorical) narrative of male sexual neurosis, and focuses instead on the works of women in their historical, political, and literary contexts. Moreover, the opposition between the (hyperfeminine) femme fatale and the (masculinized) violent woman that most scholars rely upon emerges as a false dichotomy that does not adequately account for the complexity of women's uses of seductiveness and violence in the Romantic period. The first chapter (on Mary Lamb) addresses this false dichotomy in the most direct terms, and this uneasy opposition between femme fatale and violent woman remains relevant throughout this study, particularly when I discuss representations of women who were considered both beautiful and violent, such as Charlotte Dacre's murderous heroines.

Both the republican assassin Corday, an allegory of justice and reason, and Marie Antoinette, the eroticized embodiment of sensual excess, emerge as femme fatale figures in the works of women writers such as Helen Craik, Helen Maria Williams, and Mary Robinson. Too often assumed to be misogynist fantasies, such femmes fatales as Corday[28] and the Queen were actually charged with contradictory political significance in the 1790s, often serving pro-revolutionary or (proto)feminist ends. The familiar images of Marie Antoinette as beautiful seductress, famous in the writings of Burke and Wollstonecraft, are part of a much larger set of speculations on the nature and destiny of women's sexuality and embodiment in the bourgeois public sphere. Throughout her literary career, Mary Robinson returned to the figure of Marie Antoinette and its contradictory significations to fashion her evocative and original feminist vision of the meritocratic "Aristocracy of Genius," in which women would enjoy the benefits of both the aristocratic order of seduction lamented by Burke and the bourgeois natural order championed by Wollstonecraft and Paine. For Robinson, the flamboyant Marie Antoinette came to symbolize women (such as the poet herself) who possessed "transcendent genius" and dared to enter the public sphere on distinctly feminine (and fleshly) terms. By openly celebrating the dangerous associations of femininity with sensuality and the body, and fusing them with the pleasures of intellect and reason, Robinson's Marie Antoinette embodies the "balance of raptures" between reason and passion that Jerome McGann locates in her *Sappho and Phaon*.[29] Women writers' surprisingly positive comparisons between Marie Antoinette and the haughty fallen angel Lucifer, moreover, further illustrate their desire to explore the unstable associations of femininity and female embodiment far beyond the bounds of gender-complementarity and its consolations of natural difference. Robinson's prolific body of work reveals a unique feminist thinker struggling to bridge the growing gap between discourses of difference and equality. Her hitherto unexamined struggle to reconcile these divergent models of sex/gender, like Wollstonecraft's and Craik's, remains instructive to modern feminism.

Femme fatale figures are legion in the poems of Anne Bannerman, a little-known Scottish writer admired by Walter Scott, and they defy the definition "female," being either inhuman or undead, and decidedly destructive. In Bannerman's remarkable poetry, figures such as the mermaid, the revenant, and the prophetess emerge as deadly "women" poets whose voices usher in destruction, not creation, and who are directly linked to femmes fatales in the works of Coleridge, Schiller, and Johnson. Letitia Elizabeth Landon's poetry also challenges the Romantic idealism prevalent amongst male predecessors such as Wordsworth and Keats. Her unexamined numerous fatal women (often supernatural figures such as mermaids, phantoms, and enchantresses) offer an excellent opportunity to investigate how her critique of Romantic idealism, intimately involved with the poetics and politics of the body, is gendered. In chapter 6, I uncover in Landon's poetry and prose a landscape of death and decay that lies in sharp contrast to the sentimental, feminine qualities of her work that traditionally have been emphasized.

Landon's sentimental landscapes, with their nostalgic images of heterosexual romantic love, exist in an uneasy relationship to landscapes haunted by death and disease that echo the growing public concern that urban disease, crime, and moral decay originate from the unhealthy proximity between the living and the dead. This increasingly materialist critique of Romanticism emerges in Landon's later works as a dialogue with, and finally a rejection of, Wordsworth's transcendent imagination and Byron's exoticism. She instead allies her distinctly unfeminine poetics with the body and its often disturbing powers of production, decomposition, and destruction. Landon's materialist "Philosophy of Decomposition" and its radical distrust of the natural is a final example of an increasingly canonical woman writer whose relationship to Romanticism and feminism needs to be rethought once we uncover and theorize the significance of the corporeal in her work. Beyond the *écriture féminine* or doomed essentialism often sought and found in her poetry, we begin to glimpse a novelist, satirist, critic, and poet with far wider intellectual and political scope than she has been given credit for. In this respect, Landon is representative of all the writers reintroduced here, whose evocations of corporeal and subjective experience continue to surprise and inspire.

The contradictory significations of femmes fatales in the 1790s were often distinctly politicized, like much of women's writing in this brief window of opportunity. Reform movements at home and revolutions abroad brought to the fore a wide range of questions about natural rights and abilities, a debate in which women of all political persuasions participated. What we find in later writings such as Dacre's, Landon's, and Bannerman's is an exploration of sex and gender, and nature and culture, that for the most part does not engage with political crises with the same intensity or immediacy as Robinson or Wollstonecraft had done. These early writers, with fellow feminists like Hays and Macaulay, seem to have been aware of the rare opportunity that the French Revolution in particular presented for women seeking larger social and public roles. Their polemical writings were practical attempts to enfranchise women in what they rightly perceived as an increasingly masculinized public sphere. Such early feminist efforts to question the nature of women's physical and intellectual abilities came under increasing attack (as did the authors themselves) once the war with France established a repressive domestic atmosphere enforced by well-known counter-reform measures.

Writing in this more restrictive climate, Dacre, Bannerman, and Landon for the most part did not write polemical critiques like these earlier writers, and, from what little we do know of their politics, they did not support reform.[30] Yet their fatal women are just as valuable for their explorations of embodiment and difference that require us to rethink our assumptions about sex and gender in the Romantic period. At a time when a powerful antifeminist backlash was under way, Charlotte Dacre created femmes fatales with even more destructive and exaggerated ambitions than those in misogynist medical and political writings. Her antiheroines, dismissed by some modern critics as mere reflections of misogyny, rewrote male medical and literary opinion on the nature of women, shocking male critics and thereby illustrating how resistance emerges where power is most concentrated, not where it is absent. Similarly, Anne Bannerman's Gothic poetry is populated by supernatural femmes fatales that intensify the mystification and idealization of women found in the works of male contemporaries like Coleridge and Schiller. Fatal women in her work, as in Dacre's, become figures of intense interest for the writer (and often her audience and reviewers), who offers a perspective that cannot be classified satisfactorily as either inherently subversive or normalizing. Bannerman, Landon, and Dacre are by no means apolitical. Neither are their "radical" or "liberal" political intentions simply veiled through "feminine" strategies of euphemism, deflection, or understatement, though undoubtedly women writers increasingly relied on such strategies, and focused on "appropriate" subjects such as children and religion throughout the nineteenth century. Rather, their explorations of natural and unnatural embodiment ranged beyond the (sexualized) criteria that modern critics typically consider when they examine women's writings on the body.

As Laqueur, Schiebinger, and others demonstrate, the turn of the nineteenth century witnessed fierce debates between competing models of natural difference, resulting in what Schiebinger aptly termed "The

Triumph of Complementarity."[31] *Fatal Women* uncovers the surprisingly broad contours of this struggle in women's writings of the Romantic period, because knowing the outcome of the struggle is not enough. Even knowing the outlines of the polemical struggle of the 1790s, among politically identified women like Hannah More, Wollstonecraft, and Robinson, is not enough. We need to reconsider and expand our criteria for engaging with these women's writings in order to more accurately assess their hitherto ignored perspectives on sex, gender, and embodiment.

CHAPTER I

The subject of violence: Mary Lamb, femme fatale

On 26 September 1796, the *Morning Chronicle* gave the following account of the "fatal catastrophe" that blighted the lives of Mary and Charles Lamb:

On Friday afternoon the Coroner and a respectable Jury sat on the body of a Lady in the neighbourhood of Holborn, who died in consequence of a wound from her daughter the preceding day. It appeared by the evidence adduced, that while the family were preparing for dinner, the young lady seized a case knife laying on the table, and in a menacing manner pursued a little girl, her apprentice, round the room; on the eager calls of her helpless infirm mother to forbear, she renounced her first object, and with loud shrieks approached her parent.

The child by her cries quickly brought up the landlord of the house, but too late – the dreadful scene presented to him the mother lifeless, pierced to the heart, on a chair, her daughter yet wildly standing over her with the fatal knife, and the venerable old man, her father, weeping by her side, himself bleeding at the forehead from the effects of a severe blow he received from one of the forks she had been madly hurling about the room. (*LCML*, 1: 45)

Mary Anne Lamb, the murderer in question, had suffered years of neglect by her mother, and yet, as the newspaper account went on to say, "her carriage towards her mother was ever affectionate in the extreme." As her mother became incapacitated, the responsibility for her care as well as that of her ill father fell disproportionately on Mary Lamb's shoulders; this responsibility, combined with her exhausting labors as a mantua-maker and her mother's coldness towards her, contributed to Lamb's violent behavior. Lamb was spared incarceration and execution because the inquest determined the cause of the murder was "lunacy"; she remained in her brother Charles's care until his death, with periodic incarcerations in private asylums during subsequent violent outbreaks. Remarkably, after the murder Mary Lamb went on to build a career as an author of popular children's literature, in such works as her collection of stories, *Mrs. Leicester's School, or, The History of Several Young Ladies* (1809), her adaptations of *Tales from Shakespeare* (1807), and *Poetry for Children* (1809), all of which also included contributions by her brother Charles.[1]

Mary Lamb's career as a writer might not have been possible had she not murdered her mother. This possibility presents an intriguing problem for any gender-complementary model of writing, and of Romantic-period writing in particular, that would align violence and mastery exclusively with masculinity. Gender-complementary models of Romanticism such as Margaret Homans's in *Women Writers and Poetic Identity* and *Bearing the Word*, and Anne Mellor's in *Romanticism and Gender*, differentiate between women's uses of language and men's, and in many respects offer a welcome correction to earlier ungendered (read androcentric) comprehensive models of Romanticism and poetic identity.[2] Yet such gender-complementary models, while valuable for their gender specificity, often reinscribe the rigid gender boundaries which many women and men of the Romantic period defied. Violence, both rhetorical and physical, presents the greatest challenge to such gender-complementary feminist poetics, in part because it seems so clearly attributable to men and masculine interests.

As I suggested in the Introduction, central to feminist literary criticism on nineteenth-century British women writers in general is the unspoken aim to demonstrate that women as a class eschew violence, destructiveness, and cruelty, except in self-defense or rebellion, like Gilbert and Gubar's madwoman in the attic. This strategy is dangerous (all strategies are) because it leaves unquestioned the "repressive hypothesis" of power, in Foucault's famous formulation, and pursues an ideal of the autonomous female "deep subject" outside masculine power and violence, an ideal which is itself power's most productive effect.[3] Gilbert and Gubar's landmark *The Madwoman in the Attic* (1979) most famously established this reading of nineteenth-century British women writers as engaged in a struggle to release the repressed female self from the grip of male power; *Jane Eyre* is the central text in their reading of repressed female rage and rebellion, as it gives their book its title, and Brontë's novel remains central to much feminist literary criticism of the nineteenth century because it so wonderfully illustrates middle-class women's struggle for intellectual, economic and emotional independence. Michelle Massé has more recently located in *Jane Eyre* woman's triumphant transcendence of the violence central to the "Gothic economy" of patriarchy:

she will not be an accomplice to unjust authority. Jane's testimony as spectator identifies what might overturn the Gothic economy: not eroticizing aggression against one's self and becoming beaten, not repeating the cycle of violence by oppressing others as beater or accomplice, but rather persisting in the search for love *and* independence.[4]

Jane Eyre continues to represent liberal feminism's dream of female love and independence outside power and history; yet, as the compelling critiques of Gayatri Chakravorty Spivak and Nancy Armstrong have shown, this traditional reading of *Jane Eyre* fails to examine its own class and cultural interests in its celebration of the autonomous female subject.[5] Nancy Armstrong and Leonard Tennenhouse, in the volume *The Violence of Representation* (1989), have argued that in *Jane Eyre* we can trace the shift from the earlier order of spectacular violence, to the modern order of violence as representation, of the repressive hypothesis, where Jane's oppositional discourse of self and other produces the deep female subject at the expense of others, such as Blanche Ingram and Mrs. Reed. "So attached to the novel's heroine," Armstrong and Tennenhouse write, "we neglect to see how her descriptive power becomes a mode of violence in its own right."[6] Jane claims a "position of powerlessness" as her source of authority and authenticity, and as such "[s]he is the progenitrix of a new gender, class, and race of selves in relation to whom all others are deficient" (*Ibid.*, 8). Gender-complementary readings of Romanticism and nineteenth-century women's literature in general celebrate and duplicate Jane's claim of "powerlessness," and attempt to speak from and for this place outside power when they banish violence to the domains of masculinity and the male.

The subject of violence with which I am concerned is not, therefore, the elusive autonomous female subject that erupts in rebellious rage against the repressive constraints of male power, as Gilbert and Gubar's monstrous women do, for example. Mary Lamb's writings certainly are rife with images of repressed violence and rage, and her repeated incarcerations in private asylums following violent outbursts throughout her life make it clear that the repression (and production) of her violence was itself a process of actual, not just rhetorical, violence against her self and body. It is significant, however, that Mary Lamb's rage, murderous rebellion, and legal status as madwoman did not warrant her inclusion in *The Madwoman in the Attic*. Mary Lamb's rebellion and rage cannot safely be assimilated in the liberal humanist feminism of Gilbert and Gubar, or in subsequent gender-complementary scholarship, precisely because its violence, lack of provocation, and its female object render its feminist use value low and its destabilizing potential high.[7] The rage and rebellion of the female subject is welcome as long as its violence is that of representation, as is Jane Eyre's, or is a metaphorical rebellion and self-defense, as is Bertha's. The subject of violence itself remains masculine when it is aggressive (not defensive), physical (not metaphorical), sadistic, and/or sexual. Mary Lamb stabbed her mother without immediate provocation after attacking her female assistant; her violence therefore exceeds the functions of rebellion and rage, and demonstrates the precariousness of women's status as reservoirs of bourgeois benevolence and sympathy, qualities necessary to the new social order's claim to moral progress.

"The subject of violence is always, by definition, masculine," though its object may be either feminine or masculine, because violence is engendered through representation; thus argues Teresa de Lauretis in her important feminist response to Derrida's "The Violence of the Letter."[8] Violence cannot escape gender, or the historical power imbalances between men and women: men are responsible for most violent acts, and the victims of their violence are most often women. De Lauretis's critique of Derrida's dangerous eliding of violence's gendering is persuasive and important; yet what, if anything, can we say of the subject of violence who is also a woman? Must the subject of violence be masculine (even if not male)? I suggest that the answer is no, and that, even while we keep in mind de Lauretis' crucial gendering of violence as masculine, we must continue to examine how Lamb's writings explored the possibilities of a female subject of violence.

Subsequent treatments (or lack thereof) of Lamb's violence reveal the inability and unwillingness of gender-complementary criticism to account for violence when it does not fit the model of female metaphorical rebellion or resistance against male domination. Mary Lamb's violence tends to disappear in new critical work on her writing, or is neatly and quickly dismissed as an effect of "mental illness" (as if this explains anything); such acts of exclusion are themselves acts of rhetorical violence, for they displace violence onto an external, perhaps unnatural, source, instead of acknowledging (feminist) criticism's and women's participation in violence.

In order to demonstrate why Lamb's work invites us to revise our assumptions about women, violence, and language, I will first briefly examine Margaret Homans's influential argument regarding women's violent exclusion from the male symbolic order in *Bearing the Word*. Homans's feminist psychoanalytical readings of nineteenth-century women writers have played a significant part in shaping the gender-complementary models of women's writing that emerged in the last two decades. For this reason, and because Mary Lamb's "madness" lends itself to psychoanalytical approaches, I want to look at Lamb's writing through this critical lens in order to explore the limitations of this methodology, and the benefits of engaging women's violence more straightforwardly. I argue that women are necessarily subjects both of language and of violence, and that one reason the Lacanian symbolic order is always gendered masculine in such valuable feminist revisions of psychoanalysis as Homans's is precisely in order to distance women from what Derrida termed the "arche-violence" preceding the violence of writing. Just as we cannot "safeguard the exteriority of writing to speech," as Derrida argued in "The Violence of the Letter," so we cannot safeguard the exteriority of violence to women.[9] Focusing on Lamb's first tale from *Mrs. Leicester's School*, "Elizabeth Villiers: The Sailor Uncle," as well as on her poetry, I go on to argue that Mary Lamb's writing demonstrates women's undeniable participation in the violence of the letter as well as in empirical violence. Modern accounts that overlook this violence ironically do violence to Lamb's work, and by extension to Romantic-period women's writing, by imposing onto it a teleological model of the moral progress of female (and feminist) benevolence.

MARY LAMB AND THE VIOLENCE OF THE LETTER

Death strolls between letters.

Jacques Derrida, "Edmond Jabès and the
Question of the Book"

Mary Lamb presents an intriguing set of problems for feminist scholarship because she embodies irreconcilable qualities of violence and gentleness, assertiveness and self-effacement, and because these irreconcilable differences she embodies are directly related to writing. To a significant degree, Lamb exemplified the "feminine Romantic" subject as Mellor described it in *Romanticism and Gender*: she did not publish under her own name; she was lauded by her friends for being self-effacing, gentle, reasonable, and domestic; she worked in professions typical for women of her time, being a seamstress and later a private tutor; she wrote almost exclusively for children. Wordsworth's well-known description of Lamb is typical: "the meek, / The self-restraining, and the ever-kind."[10] And yet these "feminine" qualities represent only one dimension of Mary Lamb's life and writing, as they represent only one dimension of women's participation in Romanticism. For Lamb was also capable of murderous violence and rage, not only in her actions but also in her writing. It may seem odd for me to order the previous sentence as I did, implying that the greater concern we may have is not with one violent incident when she murdered her mother, but the violence which remained a part of her and her work long after the deed was done. But it is precisely the "violence of the letter," as Derrida termed it, that interests me here, because the violence of the murder is typically and unsatisfactorily explained away as a result of "mental illness," often anachronistically and retroactively diagnosed as manic depressive disorder. I want therefore to focus a consciously feminist inquiry specifically on the Romantic-period woman subject and author, in this case Mary Lamb, in order to question the limits we ourselves place on female subjectivity and authorship, and to reintroduce the transgressive potential of typically "masculine" actions and desires that many Romantic-period women in fact exercised.

Jane Aaron, in *A Double Singleness: Gender and the Writings of Charles and Mary Lamb*, writes of how difficult it was for Lamb to incorporate her violence into her concept of self, and how throughout her life she distanced her "sane" feminine self from her aggressive "insane" self (126); Charles Lamb likewise could not reconcile Mary's gender with her behavior, and as Aaron writes,

appears to have seen the deed as having been committed by a dominant masculine madness, satanic or divine, which had taken possession of his sister... Nurturative female values, embodied very consistently from all contemporary accounts by Mary during her periods of sanity, are thus seen as endangered by aggressive masculine drives.[11]

Mary's violence was so disturbing in a woman that it needed to be displaced onto an inhuman and unfemale source. Her recurring bouts of madness and rage were thus experienced by her brother as possession by masculinity, and she was repeatedly removed from their home to the care of professionals during such periods.

Yet we must be careful not to duplicate this gesture of suppression in our reevaluation of women's position as Romantic subjects and authors. To reduce women such as Lamb to "male-identified," masculinist, or "mentally ill" subjects would be to rely on and reinscribe a circular argument that attributes violence and mastery solely to masculinity. The subject of violence has the power to destabilize such concepts of complementary female subjectivity both in the Romantic period and in our own. Thus, rather than emphasize the virtues of women's exclusion from power and the masculinist symbolic order, I am interested in the feminist possibilities of what I would argue is women's undeniable participation in a symbolic and political order that is admittedly grounded in violence.

In *Bearing the Word*, Margaret Homans, drawing on the work of Nancy Chodorow, locates the origin of the Lacanian symbolic order in the murder and subsequent idealization of the mother by the poet/son:

The symbolic order is founded, not merely on the regrettable loss of the mother, but rather on her active and overt murder. Thus a feminist critique begins by indicating the situation in which women are placed by a myth of language that assumes the speaker to be masculine. (11)

Women are indeed placed in the position of object, listener, or amanuensis of male language; yet I would argue that feminist revisions of Lacanian psychoanalysis highlight and critique this positioning of women as object in part due to the originating violence of the symbolic order, and their desire to deny women as subject of this violence. Mary Lamb's murder of her mother is in fact inseparable from her position as author, and this association between writing and death is a prevalent theme in her works. Thus in this feminist critique, I begin, like Homans, by indicating that in Mary Lamb's myth of language the object of violence and language is indeed female, but, as we shall see, so is the subject.

The most striking connection between women as subject of violence and of writing in Mary Lamb's work occurs in the first story from *Mrs. Leicester's School*, "Elizabeth Villiers: The Sailor Uncle." *Mrs. Leicester's School*, published anonymously in 1809, contains a series of narratives in which young girls tell their life stories to their fellow inmates at a boarding school. Elizabeth Villiers, the heroine of the first tale, tells of learning to read at her mother's grave (see Figure 1):

The first thing I can remember was my father teaching me the alphabet from the letters on a tombstone that stood at the head of my mother's grave. I used to tap at my father's study door; I think now I hear him say, "Who is there? – What do you want, little girl? "Go and see mamma. Go and learn pretty letters." Many times in the day would my father lay aside his books and his papers to lead me to this spot, and make me point to the letters, and then set me to spell syllables and words: in this matter, the epitaph on my mother's tomb being my primer and my spelling-book, I learned to read. (*WCML*, III: 276)

The father not only authorizes but also encourages the girl to read of her mother's death, literally to read her death sentence, thus reiterating

FRONTISPIECE

*In this manner, the epitaph on my mother's
tomb being my primer and my spelling-book,
I learned to read.___ Page 9.*

Figure 1 Frontispiece to Mary and Charles Lamb's *Mrs. Leicester's School* (1809);
the inscription quotes from Mary Lamb's tale, "Elizabeth Villiers: Or the
Sailor Uncle." Courtesy of the Department of Special Collections,
UCLA Library.

her absence and exclusion. Because the girl and the mother share the same name, Elizabeth Villiers, the girl is in fact reiterating her own death. She is initiated into the symbolic order by putting into practice the violent exclusion of the lost referent (the mother, or the female). Thus, Elizabeth's coming to writing is in many respects an ideal example of Homans's persuasive critique of the symbolic order and its sacrifice of the female.

Yet what is curious about this opening scene of instruction is that the subject who is initiated is female. The previous psychoanalytical reading might deny the girl agency in the Lacanian symbolic order because she was instructed by the father to read of the death of her mother, suggesting that the symbolic is ordered by the Law of the Father; and the girl is also absolved of any blame for the mother's death, the violence which sets in motion this order, for this same reason. But we could instead say that one is only authorized as a subject within a system of power that precedes one's existence. Likewise, the subject of language is not an autonomous agent outside that language, but only emerges as a possibility within it. Thus the construction of Elizabeth as female subject of discourse and action is, I would argue, neither the product of a proper external agent (the father, or "power"), nor is it a freely chosen action of the pre-existing self (one who teaches herself to read in a gesture of self-empowerment and self-creation). As Judith Butler explains, the construction of a subject

is neither a subject nor its act, but a process of reiteration by which both "subjects" and "acts" come to appear at all. There is no power that acts, but only a reiterating acting that is power in its persistence and instability. (*Bodies*, 9)

Thus, we see Elizabeth instructed to read by the father, and yet, when her uncle asked who taught her to read, she answers:

"Mamma," ... for I had an idea that the words on the tombstone were somehow a part of mamma, and that she had taught me. "And who is mamma," asked my uncle. "Elizabeth Villiers," I replied ... (*WCML*, III: 276)

The origin of Elizabeth's language is thus not unmediated Nature, nor the authority of the Father, but the repetition of signs. "Elizabeth Villiers" names both mother and daughter of language, the simultaneously self-authorizing and externally authorized female subject.

Derrida, in *Writing and Difference*, articulates the model of language as absence of which Mary Lamb's text is an "ideal" example:

The first book...the eve prior to all repetition, has lived on the deception that
the center was sheltered from play: the irreplaceable...a kind of *invariable first
name* that could be invoked but not repeated. The center of the first book should
not have been repeatable in its own representation. Once it lends itself a single
time to such a representation – that is to say, once it is written – when one
can read a book in the book, an origin in the origin...it is the abyss, it is the
bottomlessness of infinite redoubling. (296)

The repetition of this invariable first name, Elizabeth Villiers, in Lamb's
text effectively replaces the center of original presence, which some theorists claim for women's language, with the abyss of endless deferral.
Both mother and daughter in the text, "Elizabeth" was also mother and
daughter in Lamb's life, being the name of her murdered mother, as well
as of two dead sisters. The death of the first "Elizabeth" predated Lamb's
own birth, her origin, so that her own act of murdering "Elizabeth" is
not, literally speaking, original: it repeats an act of exclusion, and returns
as an echo of an earlier lost "Elizabeth."

Far from being an unmediated female presence, for Elizabeth Villiers's
nature is mediated by language, and both are imbued with death: "the
words on the tombstone were somehow a part of mamma." When re-
flecting on her image of her mamma, the young Elizabeth evokes the
pleasure she gains from nature's presence, yet this living, green presence
is within the grave:

I used to wish I was sleeping in the grave with papa and mamma; and in my
childish dreams I used to fancy myself there; and it was a place within the
ground, all smooth, and soft and green. I never made out any figure of mamma,
but still it was the tombstone, and papa, and the smooth green grass. (*WCML*,
III: 277)

Life and death are here indistinguishable; nature becomes the impossible
living green space within the grave, and her living father and dead mother
share this liminal state. The child cannot experience mother or nature
as presence; rather, the maternal is dispersed throughout her world, and
is experienced through signs (a place within the ground, the tombstone,
the grass).

Percy Bysshe Shelley's account of the poet's desire for mother nature in
Alastor bears a striking resemblance to Mary Lamb's, and yet it is precisely
Shelley's exclusion and idealization of the mother that Homans, quite
rightly I think, uses to exemplify the violence of the dominant Western
myth of language:

Mother of this unfathomable world!
Favour my solemn song, for I have loved
Thee ever, and thee only; [...] I have made my bed
In charnels and on coffins, where black death
Keeps record of the trophies won from thee.

(Poetical Works, 33)

Homans writes that Shelley's hero's ideal female figure in the above quotation "is a figurative substitute for a mother that has been killed... in order to set the poem's chain of signifiers in motion"; "the narrator... makes it clear that it is her association with death – and therefore I would suggest her death itself – that motivates and makes possible his song" (*Bearing the Word*, 10). But we must acknowledge that Mary Lamb's "song" in *Mrs. Leicester's School* is also set in motion by her own murder of her mother Elizabeth, and is repeated in the motherlessness of her female characters.[12]

Jean Marsden has recently also argued that in Lamb's works "learning to read via the mother becomes a complex nexus of death, education, and loss that each child presents as the defining moment of her life."[13] Lamb's allegories "suggest a traumatic induction into a Lacanian symbolic order,"[14] as I have argued, yet it is crucial to insist on the writer's (always limited) agency in this "death" and "loss" at the heart of her language. The mother is not merely lost, she is killed, much as Virginia Woolf argued that women must kill the angel in the house in order to write. If we celebrate Woolf's feminist rage, must we not also, at the very least, accept Mary Lamb's violence, instead of attempting to exorcise it?

The poem "Memory" from Mary and Charles Lamb's *Poetry for Children* (1809) (Mary's authorship of which is uncertain, as will be discussed shortly) celebrates this power of language over nature and history. A "young forgetful" girl desires heightened Memory, and would "travel for her through the earth"; "a female figure came to her," writes Lamb, and advised her:

The only substitute for me
Was ever found, is call'd a pen;
The frequent use of that will be
The way to make me come again.[15]

Mary Lamb understood language's radical separation from nature, and valued it precisely for this reason, since it allowed her to rewrite her own history, and her memory of her mother.[16] Both Aaron and Leslie

Friedman examine in great detail the striking correspondences between the deprivations of Lamb's female characters and of her own life; Friedman notes in particular that the efficient manner in which "unwanted family members can be whisked out of sight in her stories" is characteristic of Lamb's use of writing as mastery: "The power of words and wishes is great, and believing in that power, Mary is able to enact bloodless aggression in the stories" (II: 441). Anne Mellor cites the possibility that "the masculine mind can receive pleasure from the silencing of the female" as one of the most troubling characteristics of masculine Romanticism (*RG*, 19); yet Mary Lamb seems to have derived a similar pleasure from the power of writing as aggression. Mellor herself warns that to assume that "male Romantic writers constructed one kind of self and female Romantic writers another" is to oversimplify and essentialize (*RG*, 168). However, gender-complementary models still associate masculinity with violence and mastery through selective readings, and, I would argue, because the consolations of female pacifism and benevolence are still appealing and therefore are reinscribed. Contrasting Dorothy Wordsworth's building of "refuges" through language with the dominant model of language as violent exclusion of the referent (and the female), as Margaret Homans does, is important, but equally important is questioning why the subject of language's violence is *necessarily* masculine.

Like her female characters who were "unhappy, angry and quarrelsome,"[17] Mary Lamb was far from being a meek and self-effacing woman. Her essay "On Needlework" (1815), a powerful protest against the destructive effects of women's unpaid labor on their intellect and status, is signed "Sempronia," which I believe refers to the classical Sempronia, best known through the Latin historian Sallust, whom the Lambs mentioned by name in another poem.[18] Sallust's Sempronia participated in the Catilinarian conspiracy, and he described her as "a woman who had committed many crimes that showed her to have the reckless daring of a man"; however, he said, despite her sexual promiscuity and recklessness, "her abilities were not to be despised. She could write poetry, crack a joke, and converse at will with decorum, tender feeling, or wantonness; she was in fact a woman of ready wit and considerable charm."[19] Mary Lamb's decision to name herself after such a controversial female figure, especially one known for criminal activity and radical politics, reveals a degree of defiance and assertiveness on her part that did not end with her act of murder.

POETRY FOR CHILDREN

The authorship of the individual poems in Mary and Charles Lamb's *Poetry for Children*, published in 1809 "by the author of Mrs. Leicester's School," remains largely inconclusive and unreliable. We know from Charles Lamb's letters that Mary wrote two-thirds of the 73 poems, yet, because the book was published anonymously, only the authorship of a few of the poems (which were later published elsewhere or claimed in letters) is clear. I want briefly to examine the authorship dispute, which I believe unresolvable given current knowledge, because I will be discussing several poems whose authorship is in dispute, and also, and more interestingly, because the editorial criteria used for attributing authorship is uneasily influenced by Mary's violence. Thus not only is Mary Lamb's critical reception as a Romantic-period poet in significant part determined by our reactions to her violence, but so, to a certain extent, is the very body of her work bound up in and circumscribed by this violence.

Lucas's authoritative edition of the works of Charles and Mary Lamb, published in 1903, supplants earlier editions of their work, such as H. Carew Hazlitt's, and offers different, and speculative, attributions. In his notes to *Poetry for Children*, Lucas writes that:

I have placed against the poems . . . the authorship – brother's or sister's – which seems to me the more probable. But I hope it will be understood that I do this at a venture, and, except in a few cases, with no exact knowledge. (*WCML*, III: 491)

Of the 73 poems, Lucas attributes definitive authorship to only 6; for the remaining poems, he offers conjectural arguments for authorship for a few, but for the majority of the poems we are given a suggested author with no support. We must be wary of accepting these attributions as "most probable," however, not because Lucas may be wrong (because he may very well be right), but because I think his criteria are necessarily informed by a desire to account for and exorcise Mary's violence from the poetry (just as mine would, possibly, be informed by an opposed desire).

More recently, Cyril Hussey suggested a method for assigning authorship based on textual scholarship, internal evidence (Mary's "faulty rhymes"), and, most importantly for my purposes, "the gentle morality one associates with Mary Lamb."[20] Hussey thus articulated the central, unspoken dilemma of most Mary Lamb scholarship – how best to redeem her gentleness in the face of her violence. For example, Hussey clinches

Mary's authorship of "A Birthday Wish" by finally comparing "the nature of the poem itself" (4) (i.e., peaceful) to the nature of Mary Lamb:

> It could be argued that having been through the terrible period of mania when she killed her mother, then the prayer of gratitude to God which the poem embodies, could not have been written by the same person. This does not take into account the gentle and trusting nature of Mary Lamb. (4)

Hussey then goes on to quote at length Gilchrist's account of the murder, and here, significantly, Hussey makes the same move as do virtually all who write on Mary Lamb.

Gilchrist's account in *Mary Lamb*, like the account in the *Morning Chronicle* on which it is based, downplays Mary's agency as murderer not just by repeatedly emphasizing her "frenzy," "insanity," or "nervous misery," but by eliding the scene of violence itself:

> seized with a sudden attack of frenzy, she snatched a knife from the table and pursued the young apprentice round the room, and when her mother interposing, received a fatal stab and died instantly. Mary was totally inconscious [*sic*] of what she had done.[21]

It is Mary who is "seized" by madness, and her mother who interposes and receives a fatal stab – Mary the murderer is nowhere to be found, so that we as readers, perhaps because we desire to, remain as unconscious as Mary is said to have been.

I find it surprising, and disturbing, that virtually all work on Mary Lamb repeats this same violent exclusion of Mary's violence by relying on the accounts of Charles Lamb and the *Morning Chronicle* unquestioningly, to the point of echoing their language and certainly their (sympathetic) refusal to hold Mary responsible for her actions. The *Morning Chronicle* report quoted at the beginning of this chapter offers us only the "menacing" Mary Lamb who "approaches" her parent, and the post-murder discovery: "the dreadful scene presented to him [the landlord] the mother lifeless, pierced to the heart, on a chair, her daughter yet wildly standing over her with the fatal knife." As if inducing in us Mary's unconsciousness, this oft-repeated account reinforces woman's violence as impossible and unrepresentable by violently excising it – simultaneously, of course, making this same violence central.

Charles's letter to Samuel T. Coleridge five days after the murder provides the second oft-repeated strategy of dealing with it: "My poor dear dearest sister in a fit of insanity has been the death of her own mother" (*LCML*, 1: 44). Jane Aaron's excellent study of the Lambs, even while it goes into great depth examining the complex political, social, and personal forces Mary Lamb had to contend with, still echoes Charles's words and their gesture of displacement, abstracting Mary's act of murder to a bringing about of death: "Mary Lamb, in a sudden outbreak of violent mania, brought about the death of her mother" (*Double Singleness*, 97). Pamela Woof's diction in her article on Lamb and Dorothy Wordsworth transforms the murder into an even more ambiguous affair: "If through some notion of saving Mary pain, her friends never mentioned the catastrophe of her mother's murder" (part 1, 50). If one did not already know otherwise, one might imagine from this sentence that someone else had murdered Elizabeth Lamb, not her daughter. Gilchrist's, Ross's, Ashton's, and Davies's studies of Mary Lamb, as well as recent articles such as Marsden's, similarly cushion the impact of her violence by inserting mental illness, insanity, madness as the true agent of the deed.[22] I am not arguing that Lamb's violence was an indication of her "free will," her intentional and transgressive agency as an "autonomous" subject. But neither can I accept modern diagnoses that emphasize her lack of responsibility (the most popular being bipolar or manic depressive disorder), for they represent our current medical and often anestheticizing approach to such disturbing behavior, and in my opinion cannot be offered (as they now are) as helpful explanations; like the explanations of possession, or unreason, or of moral failure, they reveal little about Mary Lamb, and much about the current dominant construction of "mental illness" and its ideological interests.

Certainly such sidestepping and medicalization of Mary Lamb's violence is done today, as it was in her lifetime, "through some notion of saving Mary pain."[23] I have great respect for this sympathetic intention, and my insistence on attending to Lamb's violence is not motivated by a contrasting desire to cause pain. I want to insist that our accounts of this writer accept the violence in her life and writing because her physical, matricidal violence is the most shocking example not of one woman's illness and unconscious actions, but of all women's complex involvement in political, linguistic, and cultural systems that rely on violence. It is precisely because our accounts of Mary's "illness" mirror (with updated diagnoses) those of two hundred years ago so closely (of a possessing, masculine demonic madness, as Charles saw it) that we need to be suspicious of them. Why, we need to ask, is women's violence so dangerous to us? What is so worth preserving that one woman's violence more than two hundred years ago must be expelled from our writings and hers? The answer I want to suggest to these questions is the "woman writer": across race, class, and historical and cultural lines the woman writer shares an ideal prepatriarchal, nurturing, benevolent nonviolent human potential, culturally designated as feminine, which her unjustifiable violence would destroy, or so many accounts of nineteenth-century British women's literature suggest. In our historical moment, as we reexamine Romantic poetics and their complex indebtedness to misogynist practices, the desire to establish a complementary Romanticism, or a female Gothic, seems widespread and sincere, and is in many respects a valuable feminist project. Even today, however, Mary Lamb remains a danger to expectations of a complementary feminine subject, and for this reason all accounts of her murder repeat almost verbatim either the newspaper or Charles's account, interposing a dismissive mental derangement between Mary Lamb and her violence, or obliterating the violence altogether.

Yet Mary Lamb's violence remained a part of her writing, as violence remains a necessary part of all symbolic systems. Jane Aaron among others, has nicely demonstrated how Mary's painful, excessive self-restraint was but an extreme version of the self-restraint expected of all proper women of her time. In Mary Lamb's oft-quoted letter to Sarah Stoddart in 1805, for example, she admonishes herself for the trace of anger in a previous letter:

I wrote under a forcible impulse which I could not at that time resist, but I have fretted so much about it since, that I think it is the last time I will ever let my pen run away with me. (*LCML*, ii: 186)

This is one of many incidents in Lamb's letters where she shrinks from expressing any anger or protest, as Aaron and others have noted; yet it is more than a retraction of her anger. Lamb specifically admonishes herself for being overcome by a "forcible impulse" and expressing anger in a specific way – *while writing*. Her pen runs away with her much like the "fatal knife" had run away with her in 1796, leaving Lamb at once the victim of a demonic power (either of "mental illness," or of language), and a dangerously aggressive writer *and* murderer, who recognizes the dangerous affinity between pen and knife. We cannot separate the writer of children's verse from the murderer, precisely because Mary Lamb tried to do just that for fifty years, and, as in the above letter, found that she could not.

I turn now to several poems from the Lambs's *Poetry for Children* (1809), the definitive authorship of which remains in dispute. It is important to note that, although it is generally assumed that the poets' identities remained unknown for some time, some of the Lambs' contemporaries considered Mary Lamb as the sole author of the poems; the reviewer for

The Monthly Review, for example, made the following startling comment: "We hear that [the poems] are the production of Miss Lambe [*sic*], whose brother published 'Tales from Shakespeare,' and we think that this lady will be entitled to the gratitude of every mother whose children obtain her compositions."[24] The most interesting of the poems in my opinion is "The Beasts in the Tower," which Hazlitt attributed to Mary and Lucas to Charles.[25] Regardless of authorship, this poem clearly engages with the problem of Mary's violence through an allegory of ferocious beasts caged in a tower menagerie (perhaps the Tower of London, which served as a menagerie for such beasts for centuries). In the poem, the narrator warns a young boy about life's destructive forces; the ferocious beasts are described in detail, focusing on their power and beauty while emphasizing their strict confinement: "Within the precincts of this yard, / Each [is] in his narrow confines barr'd" (*WCML*, III: 407). The panther in particular exemplifies the beasts in their deadly beauty: "the fairest beast / ... He underneath a fair outside / Does cruelty and treach'ry hide" (*WCML*, III: 408). The narrator details the killing methods of each beast, warning the child that though the tiger "with ease / upon the tallest man could seize ... and into a thousand pieces tear him," not the smallest infant need fear, for the beast is "cabin'd so securely here." Yet the narrator's sympathy is with the caged beasts: deprived of their "wild haunts" and placed in servitude, "Enslaved by man, they suffer here!" (*WCML*, III: 407).

The precarious nature of the beasts' confinement is emphasized throughout, and on one level is clearly symbolic of the confinement of women to domestic spaces where rage is restrained beneath beauty, yet also exacerbated because of its repression: "Yet here within appointed lines / How small a grate his rage confines!" (*WCML*, III: 409) Women's diminutive or fair outside, the poem suggests, can never wholly contain rage and violence. Lamb's own periodic breakdowns attest that the "unrelenting restraint"[26] she imposed upon herself was only temporary. The poem's closing moral echoes the Lambs's rationalization of their mother's murder as providential:

> This place, me thinks, resembleth well
> The world itself in which we dwell.
> Perils and snares on every ground,
> Like these wild beasts, beset us round.
> But Providence their rage restrains,
> Our heavenly Keeper sets them chains;
> His goodness saveth every hour
> His darlings from the lion's power.
>
> (*WCML*, III: 409)

Both Mary and Charles (and subsequent scholars) absolved Mary of responsibility for the murder, Charles writing to Coleridge that Mary was "the unhappy and unconscious instrument of the Almighty's judgements on our house."[27] A few days after the murder, Mary was "calm and serene," says Charles, and she herself wrote from the asylum where she was confined that "I have no fear. The spirit of my mother seems to descend and smile upon me, and bid me to live and enjoy the life and reason which the Almighty has given me. I shall see her again in heaven."[28] If Providence and its chains alone restrain destructive violence, as Lamb's poem states, then its release is also divinely ordained.

When her murder was attributed to "lunacy" and she was spared execution or incarceration, Mary Lamb effectively surrendered the right to her own rage and violence by placing them in divine hands. She likewise surrendered her public position as author by not publishing under her own name because this name was notorious.[29] And yet her crime was liberatory in two senses – it freed her from the excessive burden of caring for her sick mother (who appears to have been both cruel and neglectful), and marked the beginning of her career as writer, since as far as we know she did not write before the murder. Her dual positions as author of the deed of murder, and author of texts, are thus inextricably bound. Unlike Foucault's Pierre Rivière, who, later in the century, gained notoriety as author both of a murder and of its narrative, Mary Lamb withdrew from public literary attention precisely because her murder in 1796 did not fit into a "historical field" of murder/narratives by women.[30] However, this rage and violence remained a part of her work and life, and, to an important extent, her position as murderer made possible her position as author, despite the fact that publicly she wanted to claim neither position.

MARY LAMB, FEMME FATALE

High-born Helen, round your dwelling
These twenty years I've paced in vain:
Haughty beauty, thy lover's duty
Hath been to glory in his pain.

Mary Lamb, "Helen"

We do have one context in which her position as subject of violence would not be anomalous – the French Revolution and its accounts and allegories of women's aggression. This revolutionary context for Lamb's violence is suggested by Fuseli's sketch of a bacchante, inscribed "Mary Anne" and

"Maria [illegible] 179[–]" by an unknown hand and generally thought to refer to Mary Anne Lamb (Figure 2). Lamb's murder on 22 September 1796 occurred in a context of great English anxiety about revolutionary changes in France and at home. The women's march on Versailles during the October Days of 1789, and other acts of violence committed by women such as Charlotte Corday throughout the Revolution, shocked the British no matter what their political inclinations were, as we shall see in subsequent chapters. Following the Terror in France and its accompanying images of female violence which remain with us to this day, Lamb murdered her mother one day after the fourth anniversary of the Republic.[31]

As Madelyn Gutwirth has shown in *Twilight of the Goddesses: Women and Representation in the French Revolutionary Era*, the image of woman as deadly maenad or bacchante came to represent, with ultimately deleterious effects for women, the destructive potential unleashed by the Revolution as a whole. Yet all such persuasive accounts of female allegory in the French Revolution examine largely the works or representations of men, and we have much work to do in recovering women's own uses of such images. Even the male-authored allegories of women as bacchantes or Liberty served as dangerous examples of real female militancy, as Gutwirth, Lynn Hunt, and others have shown, and, for this reason, were replaced by male allegorical figures such as Hercules. We should not, therefore, accept too easily as stable such allegories of women's violence as misogynist. Instead, as Donna Landry has recently argued regarding the revolutionary Amazon, we must continue to analyze the complex functions of "the Amazon spectrally haunting the figure of the domestic woman" so that we may read "against the grain of much late-eighteenth-century English discourse on womanhood and of many current Anglo-U.S. academic accounts of that discourse."[32]

Reading against the grain, then, I would argue that Henry Fuseli's portrait of a bacchante inscribed "Mary Anne" and "Maria [illegible] 179[–]"[33] is a rare celebration and elevation of Mary Lamb's aggression into political allegory. Philip Martin, in *Mad Women in Romantic Writing*, cites this sketch as an unusual "breach of Romantic decorum" because it portrays the mad woman, Mary Lamb, not as a casualty, but as dangerous (ix). Shown wielding a knife and bedecked with a headdress of grapes to signify her allegiance to Dionysus, god of wine and excess, the woman smiles menacingly at us, holding the leg of what may be a sacrificial lamb or buck, and a knife, Lamb's murder weapon. Like the tiger in "The Beasts in the Tower" who could "into a thousand pieces tear" any

Figure 2 Henry Fuseli, "Woman with a Stiletto, Man's Head with a Startled
Expression" (1810–1820). This drawing bears three inscriptions by an unknown
contemporary hand, two along the upper edge: "Mary Anne" and "Maria[illegible]
179[?]"; the third, "Fuseli," can be seen beneath the man's head. The word after
"Maria" appears either smudged or erased; the "179" is a date, though the final
digit has been cut off by the edge of the paper. These inscriptions and the
incomplete date (possibly 1796, the year in which Lamb murdered her mother)
are generally thought to refer to Mary Anne Lamb. Courtesy of the Ashmolean
Museum, Oxford.

man, the bacchante represents women's allegiance with darkness and excess, and the threat this allegiance poses to male culture, exemplified in the poet Orpheus who was torn apart by the bacchantes.

Though this image of woman as bacchante was used by men during this period, as Gutwirth and Lynn Hunt have argued, to justify restricting women's rights even further, the image of Mary Lamb as destructive bacchante can also serve women's interests. The head of the astonished man to the right of the bacchante is faintly drawn (and inscribed "Fuseli"), and seems to vanish before the fierce gaze of the bacchante, so that her face, her subjectivity, seems to emerge as his recedes in terror. Most importantly, the bacchante's association with the French Revolution contextualizes Mary Lamb's violence within a larger arena of women's violent struggle. No longer an isolated incident of one woman's tragic madness, which contemporary scholars continue to subsume "in a fit of insanity," her violence in the revolutionary context Fuseli's sketch provides gains collective strength while maintaining our sympathy.

Though Mary Lamb certainly never celebrated her murderous violence as liberation from the constraints of domesticity like bacchantes traditionally do, Elizabeth Villiers in *Mrs. Leicester's School* does delight in her freedom at her mother's grave: "I might say anything, and be as frolicsome as I pleased here; all was chearfulness [*sic*] and good-humour in our visits to mamma" (*WCML*, III: 277). Elizabeth's Sailor Uncle proceeds to cultivate in young Elizabeth the "awe and reverence" she should have felt at her mother's grave. The dead mother provides an education both inadequate and dangerous, as Marsden has argued, yet the corrective emotional education she receives from her uncle, who teaches her to see her dead mother as "a real mamma, which before seemed an ideal something," is also dangerous, precisely because it teaches her "to behave like mamma" and acquire the graces of "womanly character":

And he told me that the ladies from the Manor-House, who sate in the best pew in the church, were not so graceful, and the best women in the village were not so good, as was my sweet mamma; and that if she had lived, I should not have been forced to pick up a little knowledge from him, a rough sailor, or to learn to knit and sew of Susan, but that she would have taught me all lady-like fine works and delicate behaviour and perfect manners, and would have selected for me proper books, such as were most fit to instruct my mind. (*WCML*, III: 281)

This fantasy of proper bourgeois motherhood bore no resemblance to Mary Lamb's own experience with her mother; rather, it resembles precisely the model of middle-class domestic maternal education found in the writings of Mary Wollstonecraft, Maria Edgeworth, and Hannah More, a model which, as Jean Marsden and others have argued, Mary Lamb rejects in *Mrs. Leicester's School*. Despite the cultural power of this model of benevolent maternal education, which is often used to contrast the violent symbolic order of the father, we must make room for Mary Lamb's radically different perspective on the mother as educator and of the daughter's coming to writing.

CONCLUSION: BEAUTY IN UNLOVELINESS

To forsake...shelters, to turn away, to unshelter oneself, is...one of the major peripeties of knowledge.

Maurice Blanchot, *The Writing of the Disaster*

The title of this chapter refers to Mary Lamb as femme fatale both because she was, literally, a fatal woman, and, more importantly, because her poetry demonstrates an interest in fatal beauty, that like the beasts in the tower, "underneath a fair outside / Does cruelty and treach'ry hide." One of Mary Lamb's poems, "Salome," focuses on the representation of the traditional femme fatale, the beautiful woman who destroys men with her dangerous sexuality. In Mary Lamb's "Salome" (published in Charles Lamb's *Works* [1818]), Salome demands the death of the rather unsympathetic, "most severely good," John the Baptist, who "preached penitence and tears."[34] Lamb's poem concludes with a meditation on painters' depictions of Salome's "beauty in unloveliness," so that her meditation on the biblical femme fatale becomes a self-referential meditation on her own representation of Salome, and on how her writing continues the ambiguous celebration of the fatal woman at the expense of the "saint" sacrificed for such art:

> When painters would by art express
> Beauty in unloveliness,
> Thee, Herodias' daughter, thee,
> They fittest subject take to be.
> They give thy form and features grace;
> But ever in thy beauteous face
> They show a steadfast cruel gaze,
> An eye unpitying; and amaze
> In all beholders deep they mark,
> That thou betrayest not one spark
> Of feeling for the ruthless deed,
> That did thy praiseful dance succeed.

> For on the head they make you look,
> As if a sullen joy you took,
> A cruel triumph, a wicked pride,
> That for your sport a saint had died.
>
> (*WCML*, v: 35–36)

Lamb referred to her own mother as a "saint," and in this poem we can draw a close connection between her writing and the violence with which it was inextricably intertwined. Lamb questions her own and others' representations of the fatal woman, leaving the woman's true "feeling" about her act unreadable. Salome feels neither remorse, nor pity, nor wicked pride, nor sullen joy – these are all the feelings we as readers and writers of the femme fatale "would by art express," and Lamb leaves her "beholders" with no stable meaning, no tidy moral to take away after gazing on the face of the fatal woman.

In "Helen" (*c.* 1800), Mary Lamb again explored the role of the femme fatale's spectator and poet, speaking as the enthralled lover to his "haughty beauty":

> High-born Helen, round your dwelling
> These twenty years I've paced in vain:
> Haughty beauty, thy lover's duty
> Hath been to glory in his pain.[35]

This femme fatale resembles Elizabeth Lamb, whose neglect of Mary may well have led the poet to lament that: "These twenty years I've lived on tears, / Dwelling for ever on a frown." Yet Lamb also mocks the femme fatale tradition in which the male poet "glor[ies] in his pain" with a tone bordering on bitterness: "I starve, I die, now you comply, / And I no longer can complain." "Helen" is a deeply ironic poem, as is "Salome," and one that similarly questions the artistic construction of beauty and cruelty, or of beauty as cruelty (in short, of two traditional attributes of "woman"), even as it participates in this tradition. While Elizabeth Lamb may serve as Lamb's femme fatale here, the enthralled poet pacing in vain also resembles the restless caged tiger in "The Beasts in the Tower," who "to and fro / Restless as fire does ever go, / As if his courage did resent / His limbs in such confinement pent," and, as such, her poet is a dangerous and powerful figure (*WCML*, iii: 408).

The impossibility of the female subject of violence is precisely what Lamb examines in "Salome": although the poet herself was literally such a subject of violence, her poem is concerned with the construction and representation of this subject, or rather with the limits of its representation. Salome in Lamb's poem represents one instance (of many throughout the Romantic period) of a femme fatale figure in part serving women's interests, and exceeding any misogynist intentions it may have in male-authored texts and their "fear of feminism" or of women. In "Helen," Lamb's poet sings to and worships Helen's portrait, which with its frown and scorn is like that of Salome, a portrait of "beauty in unloveliness" that foregrounds the process of representing women. Yet the futility of the poet's "proudly telling, / Stories of [Helen's] cold disdain" after his ideal has been shattered, suggests that Lamb herself, focusing on cruel and neglectful women in her poetry and in *Mrs. Leicester's School*, is nevertheless keenly aware of the limitations of this femme fatale tradition.

In contrast to Lamb's complex Salome, Bernard Barton in his poem "The Daughter of Herodias" (1828) offers an unambiguous account of Salome's sadistic cruelty, and quotes Mary Lamb's "Salome" in the process:

> More revolting was *thy* part,
> Blending cruelty with art; –
> Girl-hood's grace without its heart,
> Hateful makes the fairest.
> Bard or painter, who would dress,
> "Beauty in unloveliness,"
> Draw from thee: and thus express
> All thy charms have brought thee; –^{36}

Barton's "The Daughter of Herodias" does not pose any questions about how women's cruelty and beauty are represented by painters and "bards," such as Lamb herself. Instead, his Salome is a perfect example of a heartless and hateful beauty, not an example, as she is in Lamb's poem, of how artists *represent* this fatal woman as heartless and hateful. In Barton's "Fireside Quatrains, to Charles Lamb," published in the same volume as "The Daughter of Herodias," he offers a portrait of Mary Lamb that reinscribes an unambiguous definition of "Girl-hood's grace" as both beautiful and loving, in direct contrast with his negative example of Salome. For Barton, Mary Lamb epitomizes "womanhood in all its grace" (line 37), plying "Her sempstress [*sic*] labours," and he notes "The mute expression of her downcast eyes" (line 32). The mute, meek, and feminine seamstress, not the published author (not to mention murderer), is Barton's ideal of womanhood; his ironic quotation from Lamb's conflicted portrait of beauty in unloveliness makes her efforts to explore the possibility of femininity and cruelty coexisting appear even more remarkable.

Nietzsche's question about the enthralling woman illuminates this dangerous affinity between the femme fatale and the violent woman: "Would a woman be able to hold us (or, as they say, "enthrall" us) if we did not consider it quite possible that under certain circumstances she could wield a dagger (any kind of dagger) *against us*?"[37] By "us," of course, Nietzsche means men, the enthralled male lovers of the cruel Belle Dame sans Merci. Yet Lamb's "Salome" is more interested, as was the poem "The Beasts in the Tower," in the "cruel gaze" and "sullen joy" a woman (or "the fairest beast") can take in committing a ruthless deed, the murder of a saint. Lamb emphasizes that it is the painters themselves who "make [Salome] look / As if a sullen joy [she] took" in murder – thus we are left wondering if Salome, and Mary Lamb, did indeed find a sullen joy, a "cruel triumph," in murder. The poem's ironic tone, and its shift at the end to question artists' representations of the murderous woman, suggest the answer "no"; yet simultaneously, by asking the question, and then suggestively leaving it unanswered, she also leaves the answer "yes" as an unspoken and disturbing possibility. Mary Lamb never discussed her murder openly in any surviving records, and I am not suggesting that this poem, or any other, contains her "true intentions" or "private" thoughts, or that she took pleasure in the murder of her mother. I simply want to point out that she did ask the most difficult of questions about women's capacity for cruelty and violence, and hence about the existence of "woman" outside her representations.

Lamb's "Salome" remains a portrait of "beauty in unloveliness," and as such echoes Fuseli's drawing of a knife-wielding bacchante inscribed "Mary Anne." Fuseli's representation of the fatal woman, like Mary Lamb's self-representation in "Salome" (as the murderer of a saint), both connect traditional Romantic femmes fatales with one woman's violent act of murder; both artists thereby invest the representation of the femme fatale with a serious, dangerous significance for real, historical women and their actual and potential violent deeds.

I turn now to Margaret Homans's final questions in her Postscript to *Bearing the Word*:

is it, at the very least, possible to stop excluding and killing the mother for the sake of representation's projects? And can the mother and the linguistic practices she and her daughters can share, tainted as they are by the patriarchal culture with which they are intertwined and by which they come into being, be recuperated for gynocentric, perhaps even for feminist projects? (287)

In response to these most important questions, I would like to pose two others: is it possible to stop overlooking women's killing, violence, and cruelty for the sake of feminist projects? Is it possible to stop seeking the untainted, prepatriarchal feminine, which we imagine as benevolent and just, in our rediscovery of women's writing? I do not believe that it is fully possible, or entirely desirable, but I think that we as feminists must allow such questions to be asked, in addition to (and not instead of) the ones we are now asking. Mary Lamb asked such a question in her explorations of "beauty in unloveliness," and it remains a worthwhile, and unanswered, question.

CHAPTER 2

Violence against difference: Mary Wollstonecraft, Mary Robinson, and women's strength

> Bodily strength from being the distinction of heroes is now sunk
> into such unmerited contempt that men, as well as women, seem
> to think it unnecessary.
>
> Mary Wollstonecraft, *A Vindication of the Rights of Woman*

Women's violence transgresses the boundaries that establish both sex
and gender like no other act can – not only are such women not properly feminine, but they cease to be female. Women's violence was for
many the most shocking of all the French revolution's bloody excesses,
simply because the actors were women. Even Sade found Charlotte
Corday's assassination of Marat disturbing: "Marat's barbarous assassin, like those mixed beings to which one cannot assign a sex, vomited
up from Hell to the despair of both sexes, directly belongs to neither."[1]
Images of Charlotte Corday and of the mobs of armed, enraged Parisian
women are still with us today, a testament to their power to disturb our lingering concepts of women as inherently nonviolent. Because such violent
women are typically described as bestialized or at least as unsexed, it is
too often assumed that such descriptions serve only misogynist ends, and
are found largely in the works of men. Yet, because the violent woman
violates both the limitations and the virtues of natural womanhood so
spectacularly, she is necessarily of interest to us today when feminism's
identity, grounded in the problematic existence of "woman," is in crisis.

In exploring British women writers' representations of such violent
women, we need to avoid two dangers of interpretation. The first is that
these images of aggressive women represent and celebrate unbridled female agency and power. The second, equally dangerous position is that
these images of aggressive women are simply products of male misogyny
internalized by women. Each perspective is insufficient, but together they
produce a constructive tension that I will focus on throughout this book.
In an important sense, my project is in a similar double-bind, as were

47

late eighteenth-century women: Madame de Staël wrote that women's "destiny resembles that of freedmen under the emperors; if they try to gain any influence, this unofficial power is called criminal, while if they remain slaves their destiny is crushed."[2] The autonomous, stable female subject outside history and solely in a negative relationship to power is not, however, the elusive object of my study. Rather, a feminist Foucauldian approach to this double-bind is, I believe, most productive, for the modern subject as both effect and agent of power is most spectacularly illustrated by the violent female subject. As the embodiment of this unresolvable contradiction of women's agency as both produced by and resistant to power, the violent woman manifests this tension on a corporeal as well as subjective level. For, the violent female body, like the subject, neither eliminates its natural corporeal limitations through its violence, nor leaves them intact, but, most significantly, foregrounds their construction and instability.

The mutability of "natural" boundaries which the violent woman foregrounds is best understood if placed in its revolutionary historical context, for such mutability was indeed revolutionary. "During the French Revolution," writes Lynn Hunt, "the boundaries between public life and private life were very unstable."[3] Following the official expulsion of women from the public sphere in 1793, "this line between public and private, men and women, politics and family, became more rigidly drawn" (*Ibid.*, 45). French women's struggle to redefine women's sphere, women's rights, and women themselves during this brief period of radical disorder has been the subject of excellent scholarship in the last decade. Drawing upon these accounts of French women's revolutionary activism, I will examine British women's responses to and characterizations of this uncommonly tumultuous period in women's history. Hunt's focus on "the unstable boundaries of the French Revolution" serves as an excellent starting point for my own inquiry, for I will also examine unstable boundaries – boundaries between masculine and feminine, between male and female, and between these two categories – "cultural" and "natural" – themselves.

THE FRENCH REVOLUTION AND WOMEN

Madelyn Gutwirth concurs with Lynn Hunt and other feminist historians that revolutionary representations of Woman as Liberty, Republic, Maenad, Mother Nature, etc., did not reflect women's power in revolutionary society, but, rather, marked its absence, and ultimately reinscribed male sex-right and misogyny: the "radical Revolution ratified, rather than challenged, male sex-right. This is largely because the French Revolution itself arrived in the midst of a longer and broader struggle to resist women's advancement in society."[4] This struggle for women's advancement connects British women of the Romantic period to their French counterparts. Yet women's own representations of such violent revolutionary women are for the most part left unexamined in both Hunt's and Gutwirth's accounts. Are women's maenads examples of their internalization of male misogyny? Do images of violent and destructive women serve men's interests in maintaining women's oppression? Were the images in question found solely in the works of men, it would be easier, though still not unproblematic, to answer the last question in the affirmative. Yet, once one has begun to see similar images in the works of women, any certainty about the uniform functions of these images, as either misogynist demonizations or feminist celebrations, begins to appear unfounded.

Women and men did not, for the most part, use these images with identical political interests, yet such political differences occurred not merely between men and women, but also within each gender category, especially according to class. The difficulty in aligning women's and men's political interests in the revolutionary period, both in England and France, has been explored by scholars such as Joan Landes and Donna Landry. Olympe de Gouges, probably the most radical feminist of her day, author of the remarkable *Declaration of the Rights of Woman*, was a monarchist, and dedicated her *Rights of Woman* to Marie Antoinette. Mary Robinson, a well-known British republican and a radical feminist, wrote an apotheosis of Marie Antoinette, *Monody to the Memory of the Late Queen of France*, that Burke himself would have been proud to write.

Joan Landes makes a powerful case for such asymmetry in men's and women's political interests vis-à-vis the revolution, arguing that because the new "[r]epublic was constructed against women, not just without them,"[5] class interest often prevailed over that of gender for women. French women's public presence and influence in cross-class salons during the *ancien régime* remained attractive to elite women faced with the new bourgeois public sphere and its demonization of masquerade, performance, wit, stylized speech, luxurious dress – in short, of all things feminine. Under the new doctrine of universal rights, however, women could only be included if effaced by the male universal, or could claim lesser rights and greater moral authority under the sign of difference and exclusion from the universal, which most women ultimately did.

British women's experience parallels this gendering of the public sphere in France, and was influenced by it. Katharine Rogers writes that English male and female observers of the eighteenth century were struck by precisely the "feminine" elements of the *ancien régime* discussed by Landes, and imagined French women to have great influence over political and personal matters through their mastery of witty conversation, flattery, sexual favors, fashion, and affectation. Women such as Elizabeth Montagu and Wollstonecraft celebrated this mingling of the sexes in the public space of the salon, though other British women, such as Frances Burney and Maria Edgeworth, had more reservations regarding French women's relative sexual liberties and their boldness.[6] Thus, the unstable boundaries of the French revolutionary period, destabilized in part by French women's radical and highly visible activism, provide an excellent context in which to trace British women's representations of women who exist between these boundaries of public/private, masculine/feminine.

This chapter focuses on British women's representations of women's sexed bodies as constructed and mutable by reviving the 1790s debate over the nature and history of women's physical strength. While most feminist theorizing of the body has focused on maternity, sexuality, hunger, or disease, throughout this chapter I have intentionally limited my discussion of sexual difference to strength, leaving these more familiar areas untouched.[7] I have done this in order to isolate strength from sexuality and maternity as an independent category, a category that these women themselves isolated and distinguished as an area of possible mutability. While women such as Wollstonecraft critiqued the deleterious effects of maternity as women's sole social outlet, they did not publicly question the centrality of maternity to female experience, which is understandable given the social centrality of maternity to women's lives in the late eighteenth century. My focus on corporeal strength is not intended to detract from the significance of maternity and sexuality in studies of the sexed body; it is instead intended to draw attention to an overlooked, yet central, dimension of the history of the sexed body and of modern feminism.

MARY ROBINSON: "WHY MAY NOT WOMAN RESENT AND PUNISH?"

"The question is simply this," wrote Mary Robinson in 1799: "Is woman persecuted and oppressed because she is the *weaker* creature?"[8] Robinson poses her rhetorical question about the history and mechanism of women's subordination – their supposed weakness – on two levels, mental and physical. Her feminist treatise, *A Letter to the Women of England, on the Injustice of Mental Subordination*, is concerned with both mental and physical subordination, though this corporeal dimension of early feminism's struggle has typically been overlooked, as it was left out of Robinson's own title. Early feminism's critique and revision of physical sexual difference marks a crucial step in the history of the construction of the domestic female body as maternal, yielding, receptive, yet always dangerously susceptible to sexual disorder and excess.

Though feminists such as Wollstonecraft, Robinson, Macaulay, and Williams used the liberal discourse of universal rights and reason to give women equal access to this regime of reason, they always simultaneously addressed the role of the body in the construction of gender. In fact, these women suggest that it is not only women's characters, intellect and manners which need revolutionizing, but also their bodies and bodily limitations. The answer Robinson suggests to her own question is no, women are the weaker sex because they are subordinated and their bodies disciplined: "Let WOMAN once assert her proper sphere, unshackled by prejudice and unsophisticated by prejudice; and pride, (the noblest species of pride,) will establish her claims to the participation of power, both mentally and corporeally" (*Letter*, 2).

Robinson's essay, despite its title, is concerned primarily with women's physical capabilities, responses, and limitations, as they relate to their subordinate social status. "[T]he prominent subject of my letter," writes Robinson, is "that woman is denied the first privilege of nature, the power of SELF-DEFENCE" (73):[9]

Supposing that a WOMAN has experienced every insult, every injury, that her vain-boasting, high-bearing associate, man, can inflict; imagine her, driven from society; deserted by her kindred; scoffed at by the world; exposed to poverty; assailed by malice...she has no remedy...She talks of punishing the villain who has destroyed her: he smiles at the menace, and tells her, *she is*, a WOMAN. (*Letter*, 7–8, orig. emphasis)

This description of women's condition, like Wollstonecraft's *Maria, or The Wrongs of Woman*, locates the fictional conventions of the persecuted heroine popular in late eighteenth-century fiction in women's historical position respective to male law, institutions, and, especially, violence. Richardson's Pamela exemplifies this embattled heroine, and Pamela herself best expresses the widespread belief that women's strength lies in their physical weakness:

I ... have reason to bless God, who, by disabling me in my faculties, empowered me to preserve my innocence; and, when all my strength would have signified nothing, magnified himself in my weakness. (213–14)

Robinson's response to the deplorable condition of this victimized woman is to rouse her from her learned passivity by drawing attention to her body and its self-imposed limitations: "Why may not woman resent and punish? Because the long established laws of custom, have decreed her *passive!*" (*Letter*, 8, orig. emphasis).

Robinson rewrites the ubiquitous seduction plot by offering a counter-example that rejects the equation of women's strength with weakness. When her lover attempted to seduce her before their marriage day, the lady in Robinson's example met him at their romantic rendezvous armed with pistols and a challenge:

"Remember for what infamous purpose you invited me here; you shall never be a husband of mine; and such vengeance do I seek for the offence, that, on my very soul, you or I shall die this hour. Take instantly up the pistol, I'll give you leave to defend yourself; though you have no right to deserve it. In this, you see, *I* have honour, though *you* have none." (*Letter*, 22, orig. emphasis)

The lady's statement draws attention to the disparity between male and female honor, and she claims the right to both kinds – she maintains her chastity (women's honor) by actively defending it in a duel, the quintessential test of male honor. Though (or rather, because) the lover tried to calm the lady using "soft phrases" and blamed her beauty as the cause of his seduction, "she shot him through the heart" (*Letter*, 23). "This short story will prove," writes Robinson, "that the mind of WOMAN, when she feels a correct sense of honour, even though it is blended with the very excess of sensibility, can rise to the most intrepid defence of it" (*Letter*, 23).

Robinson's example is based on the sensational and well-publicized court case of Ann Broderick, who shot her lover in 1794, and was found not guilty by reason of insanity. The presiding judge instructed the jury that, while passion or jealousy were not sufficient grounds for declaring Broderick insane, the fact that she laughed aloud after shooting her lover "was a striking, and almost infallible symptom of insanity."[10] Robinson uses this controversial example of woman's honor to rewrite the seduction plot from *Clarissa* onwards, insisting that women enlarge their understanding of honor and take up arms to actively defend it and themselves. Robinson also extends Wollstonecraft's similar call for "a manly spirit of independence" in *A Vindication of the Rights of Men* (*WMW*, v:16) to women, and, indeed, Robinson saw her essay as a continuation of Wollstonecraft's republican feminist program, calling herself a member of a "*whole legion of Wollstonecrafts.*"

Perhaps the boldest evocation of this "legion of Wollstonecrafts" that Robinson envisaged is found in her 1794 letter to Robert Dundas, the Lord Advocate of Scotland. In January 1794, Dundas had prosecuted the Edinburgh radical reformers (founders of the 1793 British Convention) for sedition, and upheld their sentences of transportation to Botany Bay. Robinson, writing as "Tabitha Bramble," insists that the Scottish radicals Skirving and Margarot were "contending for principles, & certain renovations which every body allows to be founded in Justice."[11] Raising the spectres of the Glorious Revolution and of the French Revolution in her letter, Robinson concludes with a startling threat that Dundas's "sanguinary harsh measures employed against the Reformers" will render him so "perfectly odious" that he will deserve assassination by a new Charlotte Corday:

It will then be reckoned honourable to deprive Society of such a *Pest*. Some Male, or rather more likely some Female Hand, will direct the Dagger that will do such an important Service and Britain shall not want a Female Patriot emulous of the fame of Mlle. Cordet [*sic*].

Corday embodied Justice in the "Female Hand," and through her Robinson imagined avenging her "Country's wrongs." Such a "Female Patriot" was unthinkable both to the French Jacobins and British conservatives; Robinson's support of the British Convention's founders through her feisty Scottish persona of Tabitha Bramble, and using the example of the French republican assassin Corday, is a striking instance of her cosmopolitan politics, and the role that gender played in her ability to undermine the misogyny at the heart of both British conservatism and French radicalism. Corday's physical defense of the republic through political violence lies at the extreme end of the continuum of women's political agency, vilified by French Jacobins and British conservatives alike; yet clearly for Robinson this model of the "Female Patriot" is the logical extension of her claim that women should have the right to "honor," self-preservation, and agency, even the right to resent and punish.

The right to resent and punish is rarely claimed by feminists of the 1790s, since it challenges women's moral superiority and benevolence,

which were increasingly seen as grounded in the middle-class maternal body. Yet, for Robinson, the question of how women's bodies are
constructed as feminine because they are weaker is central to the problem
of their continued political subordination, and Corday's physical agency
serves as a powerful counter-example to the popular claim that women
lack the physical (and mental) strength to engage in public politics. Moreover, if men's oppression of women were understandable given their
"natural" superiority in strength, then women who are physically
stronger than men should likewise be able to oppress men:

In what is woman inferior to man? In some instances, but not always, in corporeal strength: in activity of mind, she is his equal. Then, by this rule, if she is
to endure oppression in proportion as she is deficient in muscular power, *only*,
through all the stages of animation the weaker should give precedence to the
stronger. Yet we should find a Lord of the Creation with a puny frame, reluctant
to confess the superiority of a lusty peasant girl, whom nature had endowed
with that bodily strength of which luxury had bereaved him. (*Letter*, 17)

Robinson argues that, since some women are stronger than some men,
relative strength and weakness are found along a continuum, not necessarily according to sexual difference. Robinson also critiques class and
gender as constructs (as Wollstonecraft did in *Rights of Woman*): luxury
and idleness shape the body of the aristocratic man, much as labor does
that of the "lusty peasant girl." These constructions of peasant and aristocratic body in turn shape the constructions of those classes of subjects,
one thought to require a higher standard of living and more refined
pleasures, the other to be able to bear harsher conditions.

The right to aggressive self-defense, argues Robinson, without being
labeled debased and "unwomanly," would mean the end of woman as
weakness. Robinson reminds women that they perform the most difficult and "laborious avocations" without anyone thinking twice that they
may be too weak for such "household drudgery" (*Letter*, 18). The French
feminist Olympe de Gouges had used a similar argument for women's
full enfranchisement in her 1791 *Declaration of the Rights of Woman*, claiming
that women were due equal positions, honors, and rights because they
materially contribute to society through the "drudgery" and "laborious
tasks" they perform (383). Thus both Gouges and Robinson do not
limit their discussion of women's subordination (and of "woman") to
that of middle-class women's supposed passivity and physical weakness.
Instead of being the cause of women's mental and political subordination,

Robinson argues, (middle-class) women's supposed physical weakness is actually the effect of that subordination. Women's natural difference (i.e., their inferior strength) is thus an *effect* of gender (and of class), to apply Judith Butler's argument, so that "gender is not to culture as sex is to nature; gender is also the discursive/cultural means by which 'sexed nature' or 'a natural sex' is produced and established as 'prediscursive.'"[12] Robinson's novel *Walsingham*, in which a woman successfully masquerades as a man for four volumes, illustrated Robinson's performative model of sex even more dramatically than did the *Letter*.

The body of woman as weakness, hence the body of a "real woman," is revealed as phantasmatic not only in works of feminists who urged women to surpass the identity of woman as weakness, but, as we shall see, also in works of conservative writers who urged submission to the physical inferiority ascribed to women within the ideology of sexual difference. Both conservative and progressive thinkers of the period knew that disciplining the body and controlling its practices simultaneously materialized both political subjects and politicized bodies. Feminist criticism needs to acknowledge this problematic status of the female body even in the late eighteenth century when the cult of proper femininity had such force, and an excellent place to begin is in antifeminist works of both women and men that ground their critique of women's behavior in the supposedly natural female body.

Female and male writers on the condition of women, regardless of their ideological commitments, never failed to address women's corporeal state, and the dangers or potential they saw grounded in women's bodies. As with the Romantic era's debate on women's reason and rights, which so much scholarly work has already addressed, the debate on women's bodies and bodily limitations also spanned a continuum of political interests and agendas. Mary Wollstonecraft's work embodies the entire range of approaches to the female body and the call for its reformation; she argued for greater physical strength both in the interests of domestic motherhood (strength as domestic forbearance, and necessary for raising healthy citizens) and in the interests of revolutionary feminism (strength as the final barrier of inequality holding women back from full participation in the public sphere and its rights).

This range of approaches to women's corporeal potential also includes more conventional women writers such as Hannah More, Maria Edgeworth, Lucy Aikin, and Priscilla Wakefield, and conservative male writers on women such as Thomas Gisborne, Thomas Taylor, and

Richard Polwhele. For example, the Quaker feminist Priscilla Wakefield, in *Reflections on the Present Condition of the Female Sex* (1798) argued that:

There is no reason for maintaining any sexual distinctions in the bodily exercises of children; if it is right to give both sexes all the corporeal advantages which nature had formed them to enjoy, let them both partake of the same rational means of obtaining a flow of health and animal spirits, to enable them to perform the stations of life. (20)

However, Wakefield is concerned with how women can best perform the duties in each of the four classes (noble, wealthy, middle class, and laboring poor), and thus does not advocate a revolution, though she does want increased access for women to traditionally male professions. She also advocates dress reform, but debates the use of leather bodices and whalebone stays in terms of their effects on women's labor productivity: "far from these unyielding machines affording support to the wearer, and assisting her to perform laborious employments with greater ease, they are a painful impediment to the motions of the body, and prevent the full exertion of her strength" (*Ibid.*, 26).[13] Thus, like Wollstonecraft's earlier, more conservative works (*Education of Daughters, Original Stories*), Wakefield's work on the woman question emphasizes the physical requirements of women's domestic duties; yet this consistent focus on the female body and its construction indicates that writers of this time were consciously aware that the "natural" features and abilities of the female body were vulnerable to fierce contestation.

Lucy Aikin, Anna Laetitia Barbauld's niece, was known primarily for her historical works and her children's literature. Like Robinson and Wollstonecraft, Aikin explicitly identified women's physical inferiority as the basis of men's ability to enforce their domination. But both Wollstonecraft and Aikin, despite their political differences, put this natural immutability of bodily constitution in conditional terms – "as long as," "if it is true that," "it seems that," etc., thus inviting the (at least speculative) possibility that this problem of unequal constitution has a history – that it will not always exist, or that it has not always existed. Aikin, like her more radical feminist contemporaries, also grounds her claim for women's rights in the discourse of spiritual equality through reason. In *Epistles on Women* (1810), she rejects Pope and Milton's "blasphemous presumptions" that women's intellect is nonexistent, and believes that men's dominion over women is grounded in their ability to physically harm others (vi). Men's power over women, however, is "no tyranny, being founded not on an usurpation, but on certain unalterable necessities" (*Ibid.*, v). Aikin does not advocate changing this "unalterable" state of women's oppression as Robinson does, though she may put it in conditional terms:

As long as the bodily constitution of the species shall remain the same, man must in general assume those public and active offices in life which confer authority, whilst to woman will usually be allotted such domestic and private ones as imply a certain degree of subordination.
    Nothing therefore could, in my opinion, be more foolish than the attempt to engage our sex in a struggle for stations that they are physically unable properly to fill; for power of which they must always want the means to possess themselves. (*Ibid.*, v–vi, emphasis added)

Though she begins her Introduction by renouncing "entirely the absurd idea that the two sexes ever can be, or ever ought to be, placed in all respects on a footing of equality," she also reflects on the change which brought about women's inferiority by rewriting Milton's account of Adam and Eve: "Alike the children of no partial God; / *Equal* they trod till want and guilt arose, / Till savage blood was spilt, and man had foes" (*Ibid.*, v, 12). Aikin thus writes of a prelapsarian equality in which violence and physical strength, not women's moral weakness, brought about the fall into difference and tyranny.

The descent into (male) violence marks the irreversible descent into difference for Aikin. Perhaps then we could say that the descent into *female* violence marks the end of difference. The mutability of the female body into monstrous, unfemininely large, and violent possibilities marks women's indifference to men's natural dominion. Though Aikin did not leave such a possibility open, she shares with Robinson, and, as we shall see, with Wollstonecraft, an awareness that the sexed body is a key site for political struggle. Aikin believes that the struggle is lost before even attempted: "Nothing therefore could...be more foolish than the attempt to engage our sex in a struggle for stations that they are physically unable properly to fill" (*Epistles*, vi). But not all women, or men, dismissed women's struggle to transgress or transform the boundaries of their sexed body and subjectivity. Women's violence and the physical mutability it signals are part of a larger tradition of resistance to Enlightenment taxonomy and bourgeois class and gender differentiation. Terry Castle has argued convincingly that, throughout the eighteenth century, masquerade, carnival and travesty created a subversive "culture of travesty" in which the oppositional differences on which Enlightenment ideology depended were destabilized, and anomalous, monstrous, or fantastic bodies were temporarily celebrated: "it was the very fluidity of carnival – the way it subverted the dualities of male and female, animal and human, dark and light, life and death – that made it so inimical to the new 'atomizing' sensibility that heralded the development of modern bourgeois society."[14]

And, of course, not only women violated the Enlightenment's normalizing categories – the Chevalier/e d'Eon's celebrated, decades-long performance as a man pretending to be a woman who dressed as a man destabilized sexual dimorphism by foregrounding the "fluid, mutable, and elastic" distinctions among sexed bodies; as Gary Kates persuasively argues:

D'Eon was then neither a transvestite, nor a transsexual, nor for that matter was he a "homosexual" anymore than he was a "heterosexual," or even a "man" nor "woman." The fact is that contemporary theorists of gender identity cannot help us understand d'Eon because d'Eon does not fit into any of the categories used by modern psychology.[15]

The physically aggressive women in Robinson's essay and Wollstonecraft's works are similarly at odds with traditional binary models of gender and sex. Being an "unsexed" Woman, as Wollstonecraft herself was in conservative eyes (i.e., a hermaphroditic "hyaena in petticoats" according to Horace Walpole), is not the same as being male. The unsexed female is *unfemale*, a third term in an anomalous position outside the two-sex binary, that, like the Chevalier/e d'Eon, attests to the limitations of modern sexual dimorphism. Modern feminist rejections of such unsexed females as simply masculine, merely inverting patriarchal gender polarity, attest to the limitations dimorphism and identity politics place on liberal feminism in particular.[16] But because these women writers lived in a time when sexual dimorphism was still in competition with an older one-sex model, as Thomas Laqueur has demonstrated in *Making Sex*, we need to revise our models in order to engage these writers productively. Their placement of biological sexual difference in conditional, historical terms would otherwise continue to remain below our threshold of interest, and thus we would fail to recognize these early origins of a feminist critique of the sexed body.

MARY WOLLSTONECRAFT AND THE BODY

I find that strength of mind has, in most cases, been accompanied by strength of body.
          Mary Wollstonecraft, *A Vindication of the Rights of Woman*

Mary Wollstonecraft's "deep ambivalence about sexuality"[17] in *A Vindi-cation of the Rights of Woman* has become an accepted and much lamented fact, argued most eloquently by Cora Kaplan and Mary Poovey. Such a reading of Wollstonecraft's strategic repression of women's passions, however, threatens to conflate sexuality with corporeality. This reduction of the corporeal to its sexual dimensions makes possible the exaggerated further assertion that Wollstonecraft offered women a disembodied sub-jectivity, and that on the female body she offered only warnings against the passions, setting up nineteenth-century feminism's "heartbreaking conditions for women's liberation – a little death, the death of desire, the death of female pleasure."[18] While I share Kaplan and Poovey's observa-tion that Wollstonecraft suspected "that female [sexual] appetite might be the precipitating cause of women's cultural objectification," I do not believe we can say that this distrust of sexuality "helps account for her vehement disgust with female physicality" in general.[19] Wollstonecraft, like Mary Robinson, offered women much more on the subject of the body than warnings about the need to suppress it in order for women to gain access to equal political rights as rational citizens.

Throughout *Rights of Woman*, Wollstonecraft links physical strength with mental strength, and repeatedly urges women to pursue both. In her critiques of soldiers and coquettes, she also connects her critique of each group's character (and of the ideology they embody) to the state of their bodies and the way their bodies are acculturated and disciplined. In fact, Wollstonecraft's sensitivity to the impact of bodily discipline on subjectivity has been pointed out by Susan Bordo as an example of a pre-Foucauldian feminist history of the body:

neither Foucault nor any other poststructuralist thinker discovered nor invented the "seminal" idea . . . that the "definition and shaping" of the body is "the focal point for struggles over the shape of power". *That* was discovered by femi-nism, and long before it entered into its recent marriage with poststructuralist thought – as far back, indeed, as Mary Wollstonecraft's 1792 description of the production of the "docile body" of the domesticated woman of privilege.[20]

Wollstonecraft, drawing on Macaulay, went further than observing how women's characters and their minds are disciplined and formed through the body, however. She urged women to resist actively this normalization by altering their bodies, thus leaving open the possibility that physical sexual difference (as well as gender) is not natural but constructed, and therefore can be shaped.

Wollstonecraft's pronouncement that "It is time to effect a revolu-tion in female manners" is implicitly grounded in a revolution in female corporeal normalization and discipline (*VRW*, 45). Thus her suggestion that we "make [women]... as part of the human species, labour by re-forming themselves to reform the world" should be taken literally as well as figuratively – women can and must literally re-form themselves, physically and mentally, for "dependence of body naturally produces dependence of mind" (*VRW*, 45, 43).

The risk in thus engaging Wollstonecraft's project of reform on both mental and physical grounds, is that of exacerbating the mind/body binary split by yet again highlighting it. Yet feminism's historical struggle to undermine this binary opposition, as well as all such binaries, was central to eighteenth-century feminism's self-conscious resistance against the Enlightenment's explicit gendering of reason (masculine) and the passions (feminine). Thus Wollstonecraft's repeated calls to strengthen the mind *and* body, and my own attention to these instances, represent more than a recapitulation to masculinist binary categories. Wollstonecraft and Robinson destabilized these two distinct categories, mind and body, not only by insisting on women's mental equality to men, thus resisting the Enlightenment's masculinization of reason, but also by focusing on the connections between mind and body as they relate to women's oppression. Their resistance against the ideology of incommensurable difference suggests a possibility for physical equality as an additional means for gaining political equality, while grounding political and philosophical critique of female oppression in the body.

By urging women to re-form themselves on two levels, physical and mental, Wollstonecraft is going beyond her period's increasingly aggressive demand that women's political agency be limited to the private domain, to the cultivation of a feminine self. According to this new ideology of domestic femininity or "republican motherhood," which in many ways Wollstonecraft articulated,[21] women's political agency, their power of social reform, is localized and personalized in their identities as mothers and educators of future public citizens, their sons. Poovey in fact isolates Wollstonecraft's tendency to revolutionize solely women's private characters, instead of their public roles, as one of her project's greatest shortcomings: "Women are simply to wait for this revolution to *be* effected, for their dignity to *be* restored, for their reformation to *be* made necessary. The task is primarily men's, and it involves not confrontation but self-control."[22] Women's subjectivity, even for Wollstonecraft, is then synonymous with their subjection to a regime of self-regulation, according to this ideology of domestic femininity that successfully established cultural hegemony during the late eighteenth century. And yet Wollstonecraft's interest in corporeal reform exceeds this purpose of self-regulation and normalization, even while it relies on the mind/body split that makes this ideology of women's disembodied and depoliticized subjectivity possible.

The key to grasping Wollstonecraft's subtle evocations of a re-formed female body lies in her much-acclaimed "double-voiced" discourse in the *A Vindication of the Rights of Woman*. Gary Kelly credits Wollstonecraft with creating a "revolution in discourse" in order to articulate women's interests in the late eighteenth-century middle-class cultural revolution: Wollstonecraft's "argument has elements of rational, general, abstract and 'philosophical' method, but is formulated in terms of 'women's sphere' of common, quotidian, domestic life, and expressed in what would be seen by many as a 'woman's voice.' "[23] Because Wollstonecraft uses what Kelly terms "feminine" discourses (conduct books, romances, familiar letters) and "masculine" discourses (philosophical treatises, polemics), her usage of certain key terms, most notably strength and virtue, confounds the gender difference upon which the terms normally rely and leaves open a possibility for women to take on masculine physical and mental characteristics. Using both masculine and feminine notions of strength and virtue, simultaneously and ambiguously, Wollstonecraft can claim to leave certain "natural" distinctions in place (such as men's superior strength), even while her language works against such natural distinctions by describing women with the same "masculine" terms.

Central to Wollstonecraft's *Rights of Woman* is a debate on the nature of strength and weakness:

I wish to persuade women to endeavour to acquire strength, both in mind and in body, and to convince them that the soft phrases, susceptibility of heart, delicacy of sentiment, and refinement of taste, are almost susceptible with epithets of weakness. (*VRW*, 9)

Wollstonecraft repudiates traditional *ancien régime* femininity as an unnatural effect of women's oppression; weakness of body and mind has been constructed and should be reconstructed, she argues throughout. We are accustomed to focusing on her "strength" as mental or moral – yet what does she mean by physical strength? The strength to regulate the passions? The strength to endure injury and abuse? The strength to remain impregnable under attack? The strength to labour in any profession? The strength to retaliate, attack, or kill? The strength to grow larger?

Clearly these different senses of strength are gendered; self-regulation was by this time almost exclusively associated with women;[24] strength as impregnability or resistance against pain also are important qualities of the domestic woman. Strength as the ability to perform physical labor is best understood in terms of its function to distinguish the classes; strength belonged to laboring women as a sign of their inferior refinement and proximity to a state of "barbarism,"[25] and to men in general due to their masculinity (part of the circular argument of natural difference). Strength as the ability to grow larger is characteristically masculine, since women were praised for diminutive stature during this time, and monstrous women were typically monstrous because "abnormally" large.[26] Aggression also remained a quality of masculine strength, of masculine virtue as virility. And the gender conflict within "strength" also arises in the word "virtue," because the realm of virtue, for so long a masculine domain of virility and courage through the etymological root "vir" (man), had become by this time domestic womanhood's quintessentially feminine personal and social mission, identical with sexual purity.

Throughout Wollstonecraft's *Rights of Woman*, "strength" and "weakness" oscillate between these long-standing masculine and feminine connotations, so that a curious subtext of women's possible physical reformation emerges. Because strength refers simultaneously to masculine force and feminine forbearance, the term endows strong women with an ambiguity extending to their biology. "In the government of the physical world," writes Wollstonecraft in her Introduction, "it is observable that the female in point of strength is, in general, inferior to the male. This is the law of nature; and it does not appear to be suspended or abrogated in favour of woman. A degree of physical superiority cannot, therefore, be denied" (*VRW*, 8). She thus first establishes strength as a physical and masculine quality, governed by immutable laws in favor of men. Yet in her next treatment of strength, which I quoted earlier, when she calls on women to "acquire strength, both of mind and body" (*VRW*, 9), this use of strength overlaps with feminine ones of forbearance and self-control, for this strength is contrasted with the "weakness" in behavior, sentiment, and taste which women resort to in order to gain men's pity and love.

In the section of *Original Stories from Real Life* (1788) titled "The Benefit of Bodily Pain: Fortitude the Basis of Virtue," Wollstonecraft, quoting Rousseau, likewise collapsed physical strength into the stoic, and, in her context, feminine, virtue of forbearance: " 'The term virtue, comes from a word signifying strength. Fortitude of mind is, therefore, the basis of every virtue, and virtue belongs to a being, that is weak in its nature, and strong only in will and resolution.' "[27] The (female) body's strength is, in other words, the strength of the mind to control the body. Wollstonecraft erases the androcentric origin of virtue in order to apply it to women, and in so doing she duplicates the historical gender shift "virtue" underwent. Yet this earlier, more conservative usage is contrasted with many instances in the *Rights of Woman* when women's physical passivity (forbearance) in the face of male injustice is challenged: "A frail being should labor to be gentle. But when forbearance confounds right and wrong, it ceases to be a virtue" (*VRW*, 34). Thus for Wollstonecraft the issue of self-defence becomes, as it did even more dramatically for Robinson, the threshold where women cross over into physically active beings, where passive feminine "virtue" is destabilized by virtue's older, masculine associations.

Following her concession in the Introduction to the *Rights of Woman* that a "law of nature" renders women inferior to men in physical strength, she continues to make this concession, yet, curiously, in conditional terms. But it is not clear why such conditionals should be necessary if a natural law were in operation – "acknowledging the inferiority of woman, according to the present *appearance* of things"; "their *apparent* inferiority with respect to bodily strength"; "bodily strength *seems* to give man a natural superiority over woman."[28] Wollstonecraft places the natural law of male superior strength in conditional terms precisely because she knows it is not natural. Like so many of the other rhetorical concessions in the *Rights of Woman*, physical incommensurability is an assurance to her readers that her argument for women's advancement has limits.

Wollstonecraft's advocacy of a disembodied (because desexualized) feminism has been overstated, especially since her contemporary critics objected to the apparently limitless potential for female physical reform that they saw in her works. As she herself regularly paired corporeal and mental strength, so did Richard Polwhele and Thomas Taylor in their critiques of *Rights of Woman*. In *The Unsex'd Females* (1798), Richard Polwhele is particularly disturbed by Wollstonecraft's call for women to violate the laws of nature by increasing their strength and abandoning their empire of beauty. Wollstonecraft, says Polwhele, calls on women to discard "each little artifice... / No more by weakness winning fond regard," and instead urges them to "nobly boast the firm gymnastic nerve." He clarifies this last statement with a footnote: "Miss Wollstonecraft seriously laments the neglect of all muscular exercises, at our female Boarding-schools." The list of "unsex'd women" who answer Wollstonecraft's call in the poem are compared to Spartan women trained for military battle, since they engage in "corporeal struggles mix'd with mental strife."[29]

Thomas Taylor also foregrounds Wollstonecraft's ideas on altering women's corporeal abilities in his parody of *Rights of Woman* titled *A Vindication of the Rights of Brutes* (1792). Taylor ridicules Wollstonecraft and Paine's critique of gender and class distinctions, respectively, by extending their arguments of equality to nonhuman animals, an idea he trusts readers will find absurd. According to Taylor, Wollstonecraft's call for women's equality, like his for the equality of all animals, "will perhaps appear to many too abstracted and refined, and as having a tendency to destroy those distinctions of society, which seem to have been pointed out by nature herself" (14). Yet he, of course, proceeds to destroy such "natural distinctions" between human and nonhuman animals, citing Wollstonecraft's assertion of equality in physical strength as his (presumably absurd) precedent:

this sublime doctrine [of universal equality] is daily gaining ground amongst the thinking part of mankind . . . Mrs. Woolstonecraft [*sic*] has indisputably proved, that women are in every respect naturally equal to men, not only in their mental abilities, but likewise in bodily strength, *boldness*, and the like.[30]

Robert Bisset in *Modern Literature* (1804) similarly ridiculed Wollstonecraft's supposed advocacy of men and women's equal physical strength: women "were to be coachmen, postillions, blacksmiths, carpenters, coal-heavers, &c" and Wollstonecraft "trusted the time would soon arrive when the sex would acquire high renown in boxing matches, sword and pistol."[31] In the United States, Benjamin Silliman warned that Wollstonecraft

recommends an early initiation of females into the athletic sports, and gymnastic exercises of boys and young men. She would have them run, leap, box, wrestle, fence and fight, that the united exertion of bodily and mental energy may produce, by mysterious cooperation, that amazing force of character, of which she supposes her sex to be capable.[32]

Like Taylor and Bisset, Silliman identifies equality in physical strength as the potential nadir of Wollstonecraft's radical feminism: Wollstonecraft "boldly pronounces them [women] equal to the rougher sex in every thing but bodily strength; and even imputes their deficiency, in this particular, principally to a falsely refined education" (22). Of course, Wollstonecraft had not argued that women are equal in bodily strength to men, but had called for increased female strength while conceding a natural (and conditional) male superiority, the rhetorical nature of which seems to have been clear to conservatives like Taylor, Polwhele, Bisset, and Silliman.

Wollstonecraft's assurance of "naturally" superior male strength is not only placed in conditional terms, but, as her critics realized, leaves open the disturbing possibility that women may continue to push the limits of corporeal distinctions to such a degree that the sexual order itself would be threatened on its supposedly most incontestable ground, that of natural corporeal difference. For, when she assures her audience that "Men have superior strength of body," she immediately proposes: "Let us then, by being allowed to take the same exercise as boys, not only during infancy, but youth, arrive at perfection of body, that we may know how far the natural superiority of man extends" (*VRW*, 85). For all her assurances to the contrary, then, Wollstonecraft does leave open the possibility of an ever-receding limit to women's corporeal strength, and thus an eventual end to men's "natural superiority." This stance is similar to Godwin's on physical perfectibility in *Enquiry Concerning Political Justice*, yet readings of Godwin (as of Wollstonecraft) have traditionally emphasized the idealism and aversion to physicality in his concept of the mind which can transform and even eliminate the limits and desires of the body.[33] Despite her own belief in human moral perfectibility, influenced by Richard Price's ideas, this charge of disembodied perfectibility cannot be leveled at Wollstonecraft unless one reduces her argument on women's bodies to a warning on the dangers of sexual passion (a warning that she did give). Even when she wrote of women's minds, Wollstonecraft consistently employed the physical metaphor of size, urging women to "Strengthen the female mind by enlarging it" (*VRW*, 24), thus drawing together mind and body in a physically grounded philosophy that called for an end to the limits on the size and strength of women.

Wollstonecraft, in arguing that "genteel women are, literally speaking, slaves to their bodies, and glory in their subjection" (*VRW*, 43–44), is far from anticipating Foucault's famous reversal in *Discipline and Punish* that the soul is the prison of the body. Wollstonecraft's enlightenment discourse of liberty still relies on a negative model of power, precisely the model overturned by Foucault in his model of power as productive and normalizing even as it is repressive. Yet what is most important is that Wollstonecraft and other feminists of her time had a clear sense that the female body is an ideological construct, and that they urged women to adopt exercises, sexual behavior, adornment, and diet[34] that would offer them increased political and intellectual opportunities. These feminists returned to the issue of corporeal practice and construction, going against the grain of their reliance on immutable "natural" characteristics such as sympathy, reason, or benevolence with which we are more familiar.

THE BEGINNING AND THE END OF DIFFERENCE

Modern feminist theory has done much to problematize and historicize the construction of the female body, especially as it relates to weight management, reproduction, sexuality, and disease. Physical strength remains associated with masculinity, however, and calling for women to become stronger, as Wollstonecraft and Robinson do, is dismissed by some as an end to femaleness and an absorption of the female body by the male universal, sometimes disguised as the androgynous body. One might argue that my reading of strong bodies reinscribes a masculinist model of strength and power in which autonomous, stable subjects and bodies possess power over others, a naive model of power overturned by both Foucault and feminism. Could these early feminists' interest in strong bodies simply be dismissed as an unfortunate result of their acceptance of the (masculine) gendering of power, and of women's exclusion from "power" in the domestic sphere? Foucauldian feminist studies of this period, such as Nancy Armstrong's *Desire and Domestic Fiction*, focus on precisely the domestic sphere of power that has historically been defined as disempowered, silent, and exiled, and reveal the class interests which bourgeois domestic women articulated and benefited from as part of this private sphere. A Foucauldian model of power exercised through technologies of the self, then, has proven invaluable to feminist critiques of what constitutes women's power and influence. And yet these feminist revisions of power do not exclude the possibilities of power in strength, nor the reduction of strength to masculinity; rather, it is these associations (of strength with masculinity) themselves which have been the objects of Foucauldian and feminist scrutiny, and should not therefore be passed over as transhistorically stable and stabilizing.

Wollstonecraft and other feminists did maintain an interest in a negative model of power, in which the autonomous, stable self must conform to external power while exercising a similar control over its internal hierarchy of sentiment and appetites. Yet Wollstonecraft's interest in women's increasing physical strength, activity, and size is much more than a rejection of femaleness as the price for becoming fully enfranchised citizens with "masculinized" selves and bodies. She found feminist potential in stronger and larger bodies because they could transform the very ground of the sex/gender system. The strong female body transforms gender, which early feminists such as Wollstonecraft, Robinson and Macaulay knew to be culturally constructed, by transforming "natural" sexual difference itself, which they suspected could be altered. Physical strength was central to these women's conception of the political order and men's dominion in it; thus despite their simultaneous interest in women's cultural power as republican mothers, they pursued inquiries into women's cultural and political power through manipulating and controlling hierarchical biological difference, the possibility of which threatened their cultural authority as republican mothers. Thus even in the beginnings of modern Western feminism do we find the end of difference, the identity crisis modern feminism is confronting anew.

But is this interest in minimizing biological difference by increasing strength and size the end of "femaleness"? Certainly in early twenty-first-century Western culture the idealization of women's slenderness and youth amounts to a normalizing standard best met by the preadolescent male body. In *Unbearable Weight: Feminism, Western Culture and the Body*, Susan Bordo persuasively argues against the "empowering" images of strong, self-disciplined, and slim bodies as used in advertising. Thus in this modern Western context, the influence of the diet and fitness industries and of the mass media on the production of women's desires for strong and "healthy" bodies would problematize any resistance such "strength" would provide. But, in the late eighteenth century, representations of women's physical strength were not yet a means of normalization, and were not co-opted by industries through advertising. Pat Rogers has traced the beginning of weight management to this period, however, and specifically to the novel, arguing that the body, both male and female, as natural given began to be replaced by a notion of the body as malleable.[35] The connection between weight management and strong bodies lies in this concept of mutability and of the body as site and agent of cultural production. Women's own representations of the mutable female body cannot be dismissed as misogynist depictions of the dangerous animality or disease-prone instability of women's bodies; these representations are examples of women's own contributions to the prevailing medical and political models of sex and gender which they are too often assumed simply to have received (from masculinist power) and either absorbed or rejected. We cannot afford to ignore these early feminists' own doubts as to the naturalness, and even the value, of "femaleness" as distinct corporeal difference.

Wollstonecraft, Robinson, Macaulay, and Aikin all suggested that an inequality in power (political, intellectual, economic, and/or physical) predated and constituted corporeal difference, understood in the limited aspect of a gendered inequality of physical strength. The question of the nature of the relationship between power, sex, and gender is thus simply moved back in time and still unanswered, for the nature of the "original" power that allowed men to enforce political domination of women through physical violence, and enabled the construction of "the weaker sex," is placed in a prehistorical and prelapsarian void. And it is not clear that "man" and "woman" existed before this power imbalance. We can understand this gesture of placing sexual indifference "outside" history as an utopian one, parallel to the nostalgia for the precultural, prepatriarchal feminine, and one that has remained a part of certain feminisms to this day. But it is not as such a nostalgic gesture that I wish to examine women's visions of undifferentiated or mutable bodies, for as Butler has argued:

The postulation of the "before" within feminist theory becomes politically problematic when it constrains the future to materialize an idealized notion of the past or when it supports . . . the reification of a precultural sphere of the authentic feminine. (*Gender Trouble*, 36)

One could read these women's speculations on the origins of sexual differentiation, and the possibility of a lost precultural and prelapsarian sexual equality, as part of a larger Romantic project of imagining and pursuing a unified, authentic, and androgynous body and self. The androgynous bodies and selves dreamed of by Percy Bysshe Shelley and William Blake, for example, are typically read as an eclipse of the feminine by the masculine universal in its quest for self-sufficient totality.[36] Yet the concept of androgyny as lost authenticity, while accurate for Shelley and Blake, is not precisely what these women's representations of increased strength suggest. As Wollstonecraft described her relationship to Rousseau, it is he who looks for lost authenticities, while she seeks them in the future: "Rousseau exerts himself to prove that all *was* right originally: a crowd of authors that all *is* now right: and I, that all will *be* right" (*VRW*, 15).

Masculinization and sexlessness, rather than idealized lost androgyny, were the terms in which Wollstonecraft ultimately considered the future transformation of sex and gender. Wollstonecraft (like Hays) specifically denounced women who were masculinized in a certain respect – in taking up blood sports,[37] and by extension all violent activity, as her demonization of the October Days marchers shows. She clearly did not want women to replicate a system of violence by becoming agents of that violence; yet this rejection of violence is, of course, also a rhetorical strategy: "because I am a woman, I would not lead my readers to suppose that I mean to violently agitate the contested question respecting the equality or inferiority of the sex" (*VRW*, 8). What is most interesting is that Wollstonecraft's feminism allowed for the possibility of a continuum of biological difference despite a simultaneous belief in binary sexual difference. In *Equivocal Beings*, Claudia Johnson has also argued that for Wollstonecraft "manliness and liberty are virtually synonymous" (31), and has demonstrated the extent of Wollstonecraft's anxiety over men's and women's growing physical and mental effeminacy:

Rights of Woman is premised on the possibility that the virtue of manliness is accessible to female as well as to male minds and bodies, but the evidence seems to be that if sex can be separated from gender in women's case, it can in men's as well, and that the "natural" masculinity she is idealizing may only be a construction too. (45)

But I think we can and should go further. I think Wollstonecraft fully realized that this natural "manliness," which I have considered in terms of strength, was in fact a construction; she saw strength as a quality that both established and destabilized boundaries between sex and class, making it both dangerous and potentially revolutionary, and thus absolutely central to her project.

Wollstonecraft's emphasis on women's revolution and re-formation, and her belief in human moral perfectibility, contributed to her suspicion that sexed bodies have changed and will continue to change, and that, in her historical context, it was imperative that women, increasingly defined by their "weakness," struggle to grow stronger and to enlarge their mental and physical faculties. Her concept of the "sexless" mind and soul, like that of the strong body, is thus not parallel to male Romantics' originary androgyny and its cannibalization of the phantasmatic (female) Other.

WOLLSTONECRAFT AND SADE

Active evil is better than passive good.

William Blake

Wollstonecraft's conception of sex and gender connects her not to Romantic androgyny, but to Sade's concept of social hierarchy in which power and not sex is the ordering principle. During the Reign of Terror, Wollstonecraft wrote in "A Letter on the Character of the French Nation" that she had lost the "perspective of the golden age" where benevolence and reason are the order of the day, and, losing thus in part my theory of a more perfect state, start not, my friend if I bring forward an opinion, which at the first glance seems to be levelled against the existence of God! I am not become an Atheist, I assure you, by residing at Paris: yet I begin to fear that vice, or, if you will, evil, is the grand mobile of action, and that, when the passions are justly poised, we become harmless, and in the same proportion useless. (*WMW*, vi: 444–45)

If we connect Wollstonecraft's confession that she fears evil is the prime mover of action to her much-criticized call for revolution that does not advocate for women's agitation and public activism, we can infer the cost she is not willing to pay for women's revolution – women's violence. The women who marched on Versailles were demonized by Wollstonecraft (and conservative writers) because their violence and mobilization signified a corporeal disruption, a violation of the system of sexual dimorphism:

a multitude of women by some impulse were collected together...The concourse, at first, consisted mostly of market women, and the lowest refuse of the streets, women who had thrown off the virtues of one sex without having power to assume more than the vices of the other. (*WMW*, vi: 196–97)

Wollstonecraft depicts the bodies of these violent women as the grotesque body of the crowd, characterized by a lack of proper boundaries between sexes and classes, and most importantly by a lack of unified purpose, since they were gathered "by some impulse": "such a rabble has seldom been gathered together; and they quickly showed, that their movement was not the effect of public spirit" (*WMW*, vi: 197).

Wollstonecraft's emphasis on the unpredictable and radical mobility of this mass body of women is most significant for our discussion. It is the women's emotional and physical violence, or in Wollstonecraft's terms, "evil," that effects radical political change. As these women assume a public, militant position, their distinct bodies degenerate and they throw off their feminine subjectivity (the virtues of their sex). It is precisely such a violent sexual revolution that Wollstonecraft's texts momentarily consider and push to the margins; the price of this revolution, the dissolution of the proper (middle-class) female body and its virtues, is simply too high for (middle-class) women to pay, as Wollstonecraft saw it.

Yet such a concept of mobility and change driven by destruction and not creation finds an interesting parallel in Sade, and one which helps us better understand the radical potential of violence against difference in Wollstonecraft's time at which she hinted but from which she drew back. Wollstonecraft's fear that "evil" drives the universe was precisely

Sade's point, and one which he celebrated with unequaled ferocity in all his works. In *Philosophy in the Bedroom*, Sade wrote:

The primary and most beautiful of Nature's qualities is motion, which agitates her at all times, but this motion is simply a perpetual consequence of crimes, she conserves it by means of crimes only; the person who most nearly resembles her, and therefore the most perfect being, necessarily will be the one whose most active agitation will become the cause of many crimes; whereas...the inactive or indolent person...the virtuous person, must be in her eyes...the least perfect.[38]

Sade's female libertines, most notably Juliette, like the "lowest refuse of the street" which Wollstonecraft had condemned, proliferate agitation and crime through their exuberant actions. This criminal motion and agitation lead not only to social disorder, as in the case of the women's march on Versailles, but to sexual disorder, as these agents of crime throw off their sex and assume that of a monstrous mass body which transgresses the boundaries of the proper bourgeois body. Sade's female libertines, like Wollstonecraft's market women, also disturb the boundaries of a two-sex system through their agitation, possessing phallic clitorides while engaging in sexual acts that degenitalize the body, drawing pleasure from indiscriminate objects and bodily sites. These libertines still live in a two-class system, but the classes are strong and weak, or master and slave, and women, though largely in the weak class, can move into the class of masters by perpetrating crimes and causing the suffering of others. Sade's system of master and slave classes has been the focus of much feminist debate, and some (such as Simone de Beauvoir, Alice Laborde, and Angela Carter) argue that his model of power, because it unmasks the violence that underlies all sexual and social relations, serves the interests of feminism, especially since (admittedly exceptional) women like Juliette can move from one category to the other, something the two-sex system ostensibly disallows. Although Sade's female libertines are dismissed by other feminists as token women in masculinist institutions, it is clear, on the other hand that, as Angela Carter argues, these token women are simultaneously "engaged in destroying those high places all the time that [they are] enjoying the pastimes they offer."[39] It is ultimately as agents of destruction (as opposed to traditionally feminine creation) that they are valuable to feminism.

In *Literature and Evil*, Bataille linked Sade's appreciation of destruction and radical disorder to Blake's Romantic celebration of transgressive energy (embodied in his infernal proverb, "Exuberance is beauty").

Wollstonecraft and Robinson also acknowledge the connection between radical political transformation and violence, specifically in the case of women, but ultimately could not advocate a sexual revolution based on this connection because it would mean the overthrow of woman's virtues as well as of her chains. Thus Wollstonecraft abandoned her original project on the French Revolution after reaching the disturbing conclusion during the Terror that "evil is the prime mobile of action," and instead began her *Historical and Moral View ... of the French Revolution* which limits itself to the early, less problematic years of the revolution, although it was written during the Terror. Wollstonecraft's telling omission of the violence that surrounded her and her text affirms the dangerous centrality of that violence, specifically women's violence, to feminism's landmark texts and authors. Wollstonecraft's negative account of the market women's march on Versailles, quoted earlier, depends on a speculation, shared with conservative male writers, that women cannot move themselves to violent political action, but must be the unwitting dupes of conspiratorial (male) agitation:

That a body of women should put themselves in motion to demand relief of the king, or to remonstrate with the assembly respecting their tardy manner of forming the constitution, is scarcely probable; and that they should have undertaken the business, without being instigated by designing persons ... is a belief which the most credulous will hardly swallow. (*WMW*, vi: 207)

In *The Cenci*, Percy Bysshe Shelley's Beatrice Cenci embodies his similar uncomfortable conclusion that all action implicates one in "evil" and cruelty, even if one is oneself a victim of cruelty. As Stuart Curran has argued: "Within the perverse framework of this tragedy, to act is to commit evil. The tragic premise admits of a second and less obvious reading: an evil act can only be met by another evil act. Good is by its nature fundamentally passive."[40] Beatrice's descent into evil is more disturbing than even Curran admits, I believe, for, rather than representing "Everyman," Beatrice more precisely represents Everywoman: a victim of sexual violence and injustice who responds with orchestrating violence herself, thus confounding the difference between victim and aggressor. Women's action, such as Beatrice's or that of the Versailles mob, is implicated in active evil, which in turns threatens to destroy the very foundation of "natural" femininity, maternity and its life-affirming consolations. This demystification of the maternal body and its benevolence is, according to Angela Carter, the most dangerous price for women's emancipation for "it represents the final secularization of mankind."[41]

Women's public violence thus threatened Wollstonecraft's revolutionary project as much as their private subjugation did, and her texts move to suppress this violence. Wollstonecraft's explanation of "moral progress" as the repression, not elimination, of public vice is a similar move to distance violence: "Are not...many of the vices, that formerly braved the face of day, now obliged to lurk, like beasts of prey, in concealment, till night allows them to roam at large" (*WMW*, VI: 112). The nature of these vices among the ancients is not specified, though previous examples of vices given are sadistic torture and killing by tyrants, as well as a reference to the Romans' "unnatural vices," probably referring to the public visibility and acceptance of certain forms of male homosexuality. This aversion to "unnatural [sexual] vices" may account for Wollstonecraft's further enigmatic comments on moral progress: "And the odium which now forces several vices, that then passed as merely the play of the imagination, to hide their heads, may chase them out of society, when justice is common to all." The progress of moral justice thus requires the suppression of violence, and of transgressive "unnatural" sexualities – the public activities of market women and of the French queen are thus alike unacceptable because they make visible women's violence and sexuality, respectively.

The "beasts of prey" Wollstonecraft urges underground are those she witnessed during the Terror, and those which Sade and even Blake ushered into the open as agents of a destructive energy which, in Bataille's words, "incarnates revolutions." Women who incarnate revolution through physical violence are in the process of destroying the two-sex and two-gender system that gives them their identities as women, and provides us with the consolations of "natural" feminine nurturance and benevolence. Carter values Sade precisely because his "invention of Juliette is an emphatic denial of this entrancing rhetoric" of the sacredness of women.[42] Feminism's crisis of identity has in fact always been with us, and the challenge that poststructuralism has posed to feminism's identity politics began to emerge two hundred years ago, if we consider Sade in conjunction with Wollstonecraft, the father of poststructuralism and the mother of modern feminism.

Wollstonecraft's works hinted at a Sadean world, one in which sex was more or less an effect of power, and in which women's Revolutionary violence revealed not so much that women's nature is inherently violent, but that it is nonexistent, or rather that it is a necessary illusion. The consequences of women adopting such a Sadean perspective were considered in more direct terms by Robinson:

Supposing women were to act upon the same principle of egotism, consulting their own inclinations, interest, and amusement only, (and there is no law of Nature which forbids them; none of any species but that which is framed by man;) what would be the consequence? The annihilation of all moral and religious order. So that every good which cements the bonds of civilized society, originates wholly in the forbearance, and conscientiousness of woman. (*Letter*, 86–87)

Robinson was prepared to accept women's nature as a necessary illusion, necessary for nothing less than maintaining all moral and religious order. Even politically conservative writers of the late eighteenth century feared that women's inferiority in strength, to which they ascribed men's ability to enforce their dominance, was a product of history and not of nature, and that "woman" herself, on the corporeal level, was, in Butler's words, "a term in process, a becoming, a constructing."[43] Though it may be disturbing at times, as Wollstonecraft's horrified reaction to the Parisian market women demonstrates, we can no longer afford to ignore women's and feminism's active role, and undeniable interest, in destroying the very consolations of difference on which modern feminism is based.

That Wollstonecraft actively tried to forget the possibility that women can be and are as violent, cruel, and "evil" as men, that they can in short stop being women altogether, is precisely why we should remember it. Anne Grant of Laggan, whose poetry and prose on Scottish Highland superstitions were well known in the Romantic period, criticized Wollstonecraft's *Rights of Woman* in her *Letters from the Mountains* (1794) "as every way dangerous" precisely because she saw that Wollstonecraft's desired "revolution in female manners" would undermine women's, and humanity's, precarious benevolence:

I think the great advantage that women, taken upon the whole, have over men, is, that they are more gentle, benevolent, and virtuous. Much of this only superiority they owe to living secure and protected in the shade. Let them loose, to go impudently through all the jostling paths of politics and business, and they will encounter all the corruptions that men are subject to, without the same powers either of resistance or recovery...

What, as I said before, has she [Wollstonecraft] done? shewed [*sic*] us all the miseries of our condition; robbed us of the only sure remedy for the evils of life, the sure hope of a blessed immortality; and left for our comfort the rudiments of crude, unfinished systems, that crumble to nothing whenever you begin to examine the materials of which they are constructed. (II: 270, 273)

Grant's lengthy discussion of Wollstonecraft accedes that the natural benevolence so central to "woman's nature" is culturally constructed, and that this uncomfortable truth is the logical conclusion of

Wollstonecraft's radical feminism, even before she had published her works on the French Revolution. Grant's impassioned reaction demonstrates that Wollstonecraft's contemporaries, like Wollstonecraft herself, feared that the consequences of a feminist revolution would mean the end of women's essential benevolence, and of an essential "human nature" itself.

It is not by ignoring and unremembering Wollstonecraft's Sadean speculations, or feminism's antihumanist inheritance, that feminist critical practice best serves women and women writers. The affinities between Charlotte Dacre and Sade have been commented on for over a century; one could argue that perhaps Dacre is merely the sole British woman writer with the distinction of being symbolically relegated, like Félicité de Choiseul-Meuse in France, to *l'enfer*, the infamous pornographic section of the Bibliothèque Nationale.[44] But the centrality of power, not sexuality, in Sade's work is not unique to it, and is found to different degrees in works of Romantic-era women writers from Austen to Dacre and beyond. Such Sadean affinities are another important example of how the very ground of sexual difference can and will be displaced by other important differences within women's writings and within "women."

CHAPTER 3

"The aristocracy of genius": Mary Robinson and Marie Antoinette

Yet with an unconquerable enthusiasm, I shall ever pay homage to the FIRST of all distinctions, – the ARISTOCRACY OF GENIUS!
Mary Robinson, *Sight, the Cavern of Woe, and Solitude* (1793)

RECUPERATING MARIE ANTOINETTE

Much as Charlotte Corday had been made an example of unacceptable female political violence by the Jacobins who executed her in 1793, Marie Antoinette was made an example of the *ancien régime*'s corrupt "empire of women." Feminist historians have demonstrated that the public vilification of Marie Antoinette in political pornography, contemporary accounts, and in her treason trial was part of a larger campaign by the Jacobins to excise and demonize all feminine elements in the new republic.[1] This violent purge of women from the public sphere was presaged in August 1793 by the replacement of Marianne, the figure of female Liberty, by Hercules, a symbolic shift which Lynn Hunt has shown indicated that "[i]n the eyes of the Jacobin leadership, women were threatening to take Marianne as a metaphor for their own active participation; in this situation, no female figure, however fierce and radical, could possibly appeal to them."[2] Corday's assassination of Marat in July 1793 was precisely the kind of identification with Marianne that the male Jacobins began to repress in publicly active women. In turn, Robinson's identification with Corday as a "Female Patriot" in her threatening letter to Dundas represented one of the British government's greatest worries, of a British revolutionary fervor allied with publicly active feminism and French republicanism. A few months after Corday's death, Marie Antoinette's execution in October 1793 signaled the official exclusion of all women from the French public sphere, formalized two weeks later by the outlawing of all women's political clubs. Two of the best-known women of the Revolution, the monarchist Olympe de Gouges and the Girondin Mme. Roland, were executed the following week.

British women's accounts of Marie Antoinette reveal their awareness that it was the Queen's gender itself that was under attack, and that, as modern historians agree, her trial "was staged virtually as a morality play on the evil impact of women on the body politic."[3] Mary Wollstonecraft's work on the French Revolution addresses women specifically only in her discussion of the Queen and the women of the October Days; in the latter example, "Wollstonecraft dismisses the march to Versailles in an almost Burkean fashion."[4] Her silence on the radical women activists is telling, for, as Joan Landes argues, "While the Society [of Revolutionary Republican Women] is not mentioned in her 1794 history of the Revolution, Wollstonecraft could not have failed to notice its rise and banishment – coming as it did directly upon the guillotining of the queen and Mme Roland, whose circle Wollstonecraft joined."[5] Wollstonecraft, like Helen Maria Williams, was herself identified with French women radicals in the British press; for example, one contributor to the *Anti-Jacobin* wrote that "Mrs. W[ollstonecraft] as well as many other revolutionary heroines have attained [the notoriety of shameless vice]," specifying in a footnote that the other revolutionary heroines include Theroigne de Mericourt and Helen Maria Williams.[6] Mericourt, a former courtesan who according to popular legend had participated in the taking of the Bastille, was notorious for her supposed dramatic leadership, armed with two pistols, of women in the October Days march on Versailles; she was exactly the type of militant radical from which Wollstonecraft distanced herself on the basis of class (at least in her writings), yet with which British conservatives associated her on the basis of gender.

These "paradoxes of feminist thought," as Landes terms them, where gender and class interests conflict, are crucial to understanding the construction of "woman" and "woman poet" in this period, and the history of feminism since. The Society of Revolutionary Republican Women from which Wollstonecraft distanced herself had no systematic program for addressing women's concerns in particular, and, in fact, it was their violent clash with market women which led to their banishment from public society. Yet their struggle represented a "scenario of gender politics"[7] since they, like their market women opponents and feminists like Wollstonecraft, were competing to define the terms of women's public presence. The Society had publicly denounced Corday after she assassinated Marat, and the feminist royalist Olympe de Gouges described Corday as a "monster," evidence that women of this period had class and political differences that are too often overlooked by scholars who hope to trace a homogeneous female tradition in literature or politics. Marie Antoinette, then, is part of the same "scenario of gender politics" as were the female revolutionaries, and British representations of the Queen's body and political influence are thus crucial to understanding contested female subjectivity and poetic identity in the Romantic period.

MARIE ANTOINETTE, FEMME FATALE

The Queen endangers the masculine public sphere, argues Hunt, because she is "the emblem (and sacrificial victim) of the feared disintegration of gender boundaries that accompanied the Revolution."[8] This threat to gender distinctions was felt beyond the borders of France and beyond political discourse, being central to the male Gothic imagination, according to Joseph Andriano. Andriano, in *Our Ladies of Darkness*, argues that the powerful femmes fatales in Gothic fiction such as *The Monk* threaten male subjectivity with a breakdown in gender distinctions which masculinity cannot survive. Marie Antoinette was the most notable femme fatale of the period, described as the "Austrian she-wolf," depicted as a vampyre in satirical cartoons, and compared at the beginning of her trial to a host of historical femmes fatales, as in this British account of her trial:

like Messaline, Brunchant, Fredigonde, and Medicis, who were formerly qualified with the titles of the Queen of France, whose names have ever been odious, and will never be effaced from the pages of history – Marie Antoinette, widow of Louis Capet, has, since her abode in France, been the scourge and the blood sucker of the French . . . having squandered the finances of France . . . in a dreadful manner, to satisfy inordinate pleasures, and to pay the agents of her criminal intrigues.[9]

The comparison to other notorious femmes fatales such as Brunchant, Frédégonde, and Catherine de Medicis (as well as Semiramis, Messalina, and Agrippina) was commonplace in pornographic satires of Marie Antoinette, as well as in accounts of her trial like the one quoted here. The charges against the Queen – "Promiscuity, incest, poisoning of the heir to the throne," etc., all reflect, argues Hunt, "a fundamental anxiety about queenship as the most extreme form of women invading the public sphere."[10] This anxiety was focused on the Queen's body, depicted as sexually insatiable, vampyric ("blood sucker of the French"), perverse (rumored to have indulged in orgies and lesbian relationships), bestialized, and incestuous. These charges of the Queen's alleged sexual transgressions, characterized in such sensationalistic terms, flourished in many accounts of her trial and execution published in Britain.

The *Anti-Jacobin Review* in 1806 acknowledged with regret the persistence of femmes fatales and the empire of beauty in post-revolutionary French public consciousness and literature. "It is in vain," wrote the *Anti-Jacobin* in its review of the English edition of *Le Plutarque des Jeunes Desmoiselles*, "that we look in French books for any information of those women who have attained that masculine command of their passions... Such persons are only found in England."[11] The reviewer objected in particular to the "purely fabulous" Semiramis and Frédégonde being included in *Le Plutarque*'s list of illustrious women, because these notorious queens had been inextricably linked to Marie Antoinette in Jacobin attacks. Frédégonde (d. 597 CE) was queen of Neustria and came to power through murder, and Semiramis, who had Babylon built in a year, was a queen who used a combination of sexual allure and murder in order to rule. Along with the Roman Agrippina and Messalina, these queens became archetypal figures of women's corrupting political influence, which always operated in part through their flamboyant sexuality. Here the *Anti-Jacobin* wants to distinguish between these notorious examples of women who used their sexuality to destroy and control, and Marie Antoinette, a symbol of just monarchy whom the Jacobins had unjustly maligned by comparing her to these earlier femmes fatales:

The whole history and perhaps too the very existence of Semiramis, is a very fable. The same character may be applied to the account of Fredegonde, supposed to have become a Gothic princess in the fifth century, by her intrigues and horrible atrocities. This Gothic tale ... first became popular at the commencement of the revolution, when every means were used to render the unfortunate Queen odious, and has since been repeatedly the subject of many sapient reflections in the Moniteur, on the effects of *female* influence and government. (orig. emphasis; 476)

At once defending the "unfortunate Queen" and attacking her political influence, the *Anti-Jacobin* nevertheless reinforces the associations between Marie Antoinette and these femmes fatales, Semiramis and Frédégonde, because the counter-revolutionary journal shares the Jacobins' "fundamental anxiety about queenship as the most extreme form of women invading the public sphere."[12] Thus, the reviewer continued:

It is, indeed, an unquestionable fact, that France has been from the earliest times to the present hour, uniformly *governed* by women! Robespierre was led by his mistress, and the present tyrant [Napoleon] is equally influenced by his, who has more historical knowledge and much greater talents, than he himself possesses. (orig. emphasis, 476)

Burke's defense of Marie Antoinette in *Reflections*, like the *Anti-Jacobin's* in its above review of *Le Plutarque des Jeunes Demoiselles*, similarly illustrates the dangerous slippage to which Marie Antoinette's symbolic significance was subject in the 1790s. Burke himself had been accused by those sympathetic to the Revolution (including Wollstonecraft and Catherine Macaulay, as we shall see) of falling under the sexual influence of this Messalinan femme fatale, a charge he firmly denied in this 1790 letter to Philip Frances:

I really am perfectly astonished how you could dream, with my paper in your hand, that I found no other cause than the beauty of the queen of France (now, I suppose, pretty much faded) for disapproving the conduct which has been held towards her ... I know nothing of your story of Messalina.[13]

Even for British admirers like Burke and the *Anti-Jacobin*, "the age of chivalry" that Marie Antoinette embodied could always slip into its twin "order of seduction," wherein women like Messalina reigned as tyrants over their enthralled male subjects.

Of course, this order of seduction also worked against its female supporters like Robinson, who, like Marie Antoinette, was accused of relying on her beauty to earn the praise of her literary admirers. For example, the *Gentleman's Magazine*, in its review of Robinson's 1791 *Poems*, suggested that:

without at all detracting from the merits of her publication, we are inclined to apprehend that, had she been less distinguished by her personal graces and accomplishments, by the impression which her beauty and captivating manners have generally made, her poetical taste might have been confined in its influence, and might have excited the complacent approbation of her friends, with little attention, and with less reward, from the public. (560)

This courtly order of seduction, in which women's public influence was grounded in their sexuality, was roundly denounced by republicans like Wollstonecraft and Catherine Macaulay (and the Jacobins), and conservatives like Hannah More and Matilda Hawkins, women of great political differences who similarly found little value for women in such an aristocratic, often misogynist, model of seductive influence, and instead advocated (albeit different) bourgeois models of women's virtuous influence and rational education.[14] Yet Marie Antoinette's imprison-ment, widowhood, and execution transformed the French queen into precisely such a vision of idealized bourgeois motherhood for many British observers in the 1790s (though not for Wollstonecraft and Macaulay), so that during this decade she enjoyed a curious, contra-dictory symbolic value, embodying both the worst excesses of the *ancien régime* and the best virtues of the new bourgeois moral order.

Mary Robinson valued aspects of the order of seduction lamented by Burke, and of the new bourgeois order of rational motherhood cham-pioned by Wollstonecraft and More, in whose academy she had been educated. While the *Anti-Jacobin* had denounced *Le Plutarque*'s "illustri-ous characters" such as Ninon de l'Enclos as "daring prostitutes," it was precisely such public women who had not attained "a masculine com-mand of their passions" that Robinson had lauded in her 1799 *Letter to the Women of England on the Injustice of Mental Subordination*. Robinson's boldly feminist *Letter* included two notable lists: a list of living eminent women writers, and a list of eminent historical female figures, largely ed-ucated women from classical times through the Middle Ages who were paragons of virtue. To this impressive list of historical female figures, excerpted from Vossius's seventeenth-century Latin *Philology*, Robinson added controversial modern French women, such as Madame de Maintenon, Madame de Berry, Charlotte Corday, Madame de Genlis, and Marie Antoinette. For Robinson, the royal mistresses de Berry and de Maintenon, like Marie Antoinette, exemplified feminization not as corruption of the French court (as Wollstonecraft, More, and the *Anti-Jacobin* would have it), but rather as its refinement, making possible its appreciation of women's intellect and wit, as well as of their physical beauty.

WOMEN WRITERS AND MARIE ANTOINETTE

Wollstonecraft's description of Marie Antoinette as Circean enchantress ruling an emasculated court and indulging in "messalinan feasts" is well known, and virtually indistinguishable from unabashedly misogynist at-tacks.[15] As a champion of republican motherhood and bourgeois wom-anhood, Wollstonecraft is, of course, using the Queen to embody the corrupting excesses of the *ancien régime*, and in *A Vindication of the Rights of Woman* applies a similar critique to British women of leisure who rule by beauty and cunning. Like Wollstonecraft, fellow republican feminist Catherine Macaulay was also not seduced by the Queen's charms, and in her pamphlet *On Burke's Reflections on the French Revolution* (1790) also accused Burke of attempting "to *enslave* our affections" rather "than to *lead* our judgment":

The high colouring given by Mr. Burke to those scenes of regal distress, will, I doubt not, captivate the imagination of the greater number of his readers, in a degree equal to the effects produced on the author by the *charms* of the Queen of France. (53, orig. emphasis)

In contrast, Ann Yearsley, also a supporter of the early Revolution,[16] did not condemn Marie Antoinette in the same moralistic tone as did Wollstonecraft, or resist her charms in the name of rational republicanism as did Macaulay. Instead, Yearsley eulogized the Queen as persecuted femininity, so that, as Donna Landry argues, "one is tempted to conclude that Yearsley has conflated her own recent public victimization as wife and mother with the French queen's."[17] Yearsley's conflation of her own role as public woman (a published poet) with the Queen's is, like Robinson's, evidence that "the queen represents a vexed instance of gender politics playing with and against national politics,"[18] and one which we cannot appreciate if we take Wollstonecraft's and Macaulay's accounts as representative of feminist interests in the 1790s.

Yearsley, a working-class poet who according to Landry posed as the figure of "British Liberty" for her frontispiece to *The Rural Lyre* (1796),[19] recognizes that the death of the French Queen poses a threat to the woman poet:

> O'er her pale Beauties, Hist'ry stands amaz'd,
> The pencil trembles as she draws her Lines,
> While MARIE, on whom Crowds with Pleasure gaz'd,
> On the cold Bosom of her Lord reclines.[20]

The figure of the Queen as unnatural spectacle, as she appeared in Wollstonecraft and in political pornography, here appears as the figure of the (implicitly endangered) poet herself in a moment of self-referentiality, "as she draws her Lines." The spectacular Queen and the woman poet are intimately connected in Yearsley's poem, and, as we shall see, this connection is even more explicitly established in Robinson's extensive poem on Marie Antoinette.

In *Monody to the Memory of the Late Queen of France* (1793),[21] Mary Robinson attempts precisely what the emergent bourgeois ideology of the proper woman, and Wollstonecraft's feminism, resisted with increasing vigor – to allow women access to both republican and *ancien régime* definitions of woman. Robinson, a well-known actress and writer, as well as an object of public vilification in satirical writings,[22] identified with the Queen's position as a public female figure in an era when this position was sexually suspect, and increasingly defined as dangerous and unnatural. Robinson's poem, even while it insists on the Queen's unappreciated bourgeois maternal qualities, never fails to celebrate the voluptuous femininity for which Marie Antoinette was infamous. Robinson's celebration of this waning *ancien régime* femininity is due in part to her own controversial experiences that were more acceptable in *ancien régime* France than late eighteenth-century Britain: her affairs with the Prince of Wales and other public figures, and her career in the theater. Throughout her life, her clear aristocratic aspirations (visible in her extravagant carriage and clothing) sat uneasily with her struggle to earn her living as a professional writer. The precariousness of her own class position explains in part her attempts to bridge the aristocratic and bourgeois regimes of gender that were in transition in the Romantic period. Yet this precariousness (or even this family romance) perhaps also granted Robinson a perspective, one which Wollstonecraft, Hays, and Macaulay could not have shared, from which she could find value in aristocratic femininity and all it represented. Certainly her Della Cruscan poetics of sensibility, with their emphasis on poetic language as sensual artifice, remained better suited to the *ancien régime* than to the bourgeois natural order's emphasis on language's clarity and sincerity (which accounts in part for her posthumous critical neglect as a writer).[23]

Robinson's visit to Marie Antoinette's court in 1783 deeply impressed her and influenced her subsequent portraits of the Queen. She was clearly flattered by the attentions paid to her by the French, often contrasting their "liberal kindness" with the harsh treatment she received from both the British public and the British royalty. Robinson visited Marie Antoinette immediately after the end of her painful financial battle with the Prince of Wales, and in her *Memoirs* both the Duc d'Orleans and Marie Antoinette serve as sexual rivals to the Prince of Wales who had recently rejected her. Robinson is received in Paris with a fête in her honor, "amidst a magnificent illumination, [where] every tree displayed the initials of *la belle Angloise* [*sic*]" (122), an introduction to French society similar to Helen Maria Williams's exhilarating experience upon her arrival in Paris in 1790. Robinson is pursued by the "libertine" Duc d'Orleans, but it is Marie Antoinette herself whom she finds sexually attractive, and with whom she has a suggestive exchange:

A small space divided the Queen from Mrs. Robinson, whom the constant observation and loudly whispered encomiums of her Majesty most oppressively flattered. She appeared to survey, with peculiar attention, a miniature of the Prince of Wales, which Mrs. Robinson wore on her bosom, and of which, on the ensuing day, she commissioned the Duke of Orleans to request the loan. Perceiving Mrs. Robinson gaze with admiration on her white and polished arms, as she drew on her gloves, the Queen again uncovered them, and leaned for a few moments on her hand. The Duke, on returning the picture, gave to the fair owner a purse, netted by the hand of Antoinette, which she had commissioned him to present, from her, to *la belle Angloise*. (*Memoirs*, 123)

In Robinson's *Memoirs*, the two notorious libertine figures, the Duc d'Orleans and the Prince of Wales, are reduced to objects of the female gaze and of exchange between two women; one becomes a messenger and the other an object – a brooch that directs the Queen's eyes to Robinson's bosom. This mutual desire between the two women, while it is triangulated through the Prince and the Duke, is never disguised, and instead Robinson's account dwells on the beautiful arms of the Queen, and her suggestive display of them that Robinson's admiring gaze initiates. Robinson briefly becomes one of the Queen's spellbound subjects in this episode, something that Wollstonecraft, with whom Robinson strongly identified, would have found highly objectionable.

Robinson's appreciation of the homoerotic aspects of women's interactions in this order of seduction stands in significant contrast to Wollstonecraft's anxiety in *Rights of Woman* over the sensual dissipations of aristocratic women, and over the physical intimacy of working- and middle-class girls in boarding schools. Rumors of Marie Antoinette's supposed lesbian affairs with such intimate friends as the Princesse de Lamballe and Yolande de Polignac were in circulation from the 1770s onward, and surfaced most dramatically in the antiroyalist pornography discussed by Lynn Hunt and Chantal Thomas. Yet Terry Castle has documented how women writers themselves reinforced the "recurrent association between Marie Antoinette and female homoeroticism," transforming the Queen into a "code figure for female homoeroticism, even a kind of proto-lesbian heroine."[24] "There is something bizarrely liberating, if not revolutionary, about the transmogrification of Marie Antoinette into [a] lesbian heroine," writes Castle of the twentieth-century lesbian writers who fantasized about encounters with the Queen's ghost:

It is true that there is a nostalgic element in her cult: women who thought they "saw" her ... were in one sense flagrantly retreating into the past, into a kind of psychic old regime. But in the act of conjuring up her ghost, they were also, I think, conjuring something new into being – a poetics of possibility. (*Ibid.*, 31)

Castle's illuminating account of the liberatory possibilities of Marie Antoinette's rumored lesbianism remains instructive when applied to the 1790s, because it reminds us that the misogynist, male-authored images of the Queen as lesbian or as perverse, as a femme fatale or a whore, were always subject to women writers' unique redirections.

Some women, of course, shared in the vilification of the Queen's reputed lesbianism, and in doing so confirm the circulation of these rumors in Robinson's Britain. Hester Thrale Piozzi recorded her disgust with Marie Antoinette's lesbian relationships in her diary in 1789: "The queen of France is at the Head of a Set of Monsters call'd by each other *Sapphists*, who boast her example; and deserve to be thrown with the He Demons that haunt each other likewise, into Mount Vesuvius."[25] Robinson's appreciation of the Queen's (homo)erotic fascinations is an important early example of how she used the Queen to fashion her own "poetics of possibility": not the exclusively lesbian world of intimacy envisioned by twentieth-century writers, but a world in which women enjoyed considerable seductive and corporeal pleasures, in addition to increased intellectual and political power. Like Castle's twentieth-century examples, Robinson's account of her intimate encounter with Marie Antoinette in her *Memoirs* "seems to dramatize a movement away from masculine sexuality toward a world of female–female love and ritual"[26]: from the Prince Regent to the waiting arms of Marie Antoinette. It was Robinson, we must remember, who aspired to be the "English Sappho."[27]

Despite her appreciation for the voluptuous femininity and (homo)eroticism associated with Marie Antoinette, however, for the frontispiece of her *Monody to the Memory of the Late Queen of France*, Robinson selected a portrait of a matronly Marie Antoinette in mourning to combat the often pornographic popular images of the Queen as monster or whore. Robinson's Marie Antoinette is a devoted mother and benevolent ruler even while she surrounds herself with opulent excess:

> MORE LUSTROUS THAN THE MORN, thy BEAUTY rose!
> When all was pleasure, adoration, ease;
> For POW'R was temper'd, by the WISH TO PLEASE;
> Where all around thee, charm'd the dazzled view,
> For ever splendid, yet for ever new;
> Adorn'd with gems, to GALLIA'S SONS UNKNOWN,
> DOMESTIC VIRTUES, glitt'ring round THE THRONE! (5)

Descriptions of Marie Antoinette characteristically indulge in such a
"fetishistic, delirious profusion of words."[28] Robinson's excessive praise
of the Queen's domestic virtues perturbed even contemporary reviewers:
the *Monthly Review* objected to "that exuberance of fancy, that glitter of
ornament" of Robinson's language, which, the reviewer acknowledged,
is "the prevailing taste of the age."[29] The *Critical Review* similarly complained that Robinson's portrait owed too much to "fancy":

We only wish the fair author had confined her praise to the attractions, and her
sympathy to the sorrows of Antoinette, without claiming for her the wreath of
domestic virtues, without speaking of the *wonders of her mind*, of *her peerless virtues*, and
enumerating among those virtues her truth and sincerity.[30]

The reviewer objected to Robinson's confusion of two incompatible definitions (and discourses) of women, and did not want to grant Marie
Antoinette the same domestic virtues and sufferings of a proper bourgeois wife and mother. In this regard, the reviewer represents the new
bourgeois ideology's valorization of virtue, truth, transparency, and its
vilification of masquerade, appearance, affectation. Robinson's representation of Marie Antoinette occupies the threshold between old and new
gender regimes, showing the Queen as both public and private woman.

 Using the rhetoric of women's private virtue against itself, Robinson
claims that "Gallia's sons" did not know of the Queen's private virtues
precisely because they were private:

> OH! I have seen her, like a SUN, sublime!
> Diffusing glory on the wings of TIME!
> And, as revolving seasons own its flight,
> Marking each brilliant minute with DELIGHT!
> Yet not to pleasure ONLY was she prone;
> She made the mis'ries of mankind her own!
> No ostentation lessen'd pity's meed–
> UNSEEN she GAVE! and SILENCE seal'd the DEED!
> She sought no plaudits from obsequious pride!
> She paid HERSELF – for NATURE was her guide!
>   (10–11)

In this remarkable passage, quoted in several reviews, the figure of the
Queen stands in for an impossibly contradictory series of signifieds. The
enlightenment metaphors of sun, illumination, and sublimity, typically
masculine associations of glorious culture, are combined with the invis-
ible, silent, self-effacing, and all-giving status of women as nature. She
is in fact both a sun king and his consort, the moon, to which she is

often compared: "Pre-eminent she shone! – each lesser light / Shrunk from HER radiance, in the glooms of night" (13). The Queen's luminous and sublime qualities, her gems and splendid surroundings, coexist with the sphere of the beautiful and the domestic which Robinson insists has remained unseen. While Robinson consciously renders the Queen as the sublime and typically masculine sun (as she had also rendered Sappho in *Sappho and Phaon*), she also consciously alludes to Burke's famous description of the Queen "glittering like the morning star" in his *Reflections on the Revolution in France*. Robinson knew Burke, and, despite their political differences and their different symbolic uses of the Queen, she clearly valued his defense of Marie Antoinette's "high rank, great splendour of descent, great personal elegance and outward accomplishments."[31]

Here we must remember that chivalry and romance had two contradictory political inflections in the French Revolutionary era, both counter-revolutionary and revolutionary, for Burke's and Robinson's portraits of the romance of the Queen illustrate these dual aspects of the genre. "The confrontation between these two myths," writes David Duff in *Romance and Revolution*, "between the counter-revolutionary romance of Burke and the revolutionary romance contained in the writings of his opponents – is one of the most interesting features of the so-called 'pamphlet war' of the 1790s" (9). Robinson's neglected contribution to the pamphlet war also focuses on Marie Antoinette, and like the rest of her writings on the Queen, values both republican politics and *ancien régime* femininity. Her prose *Impartial Reflections on the Present Situation of the Queen of France*, signed "A Friend to Humanity," was published in 1791 by John Bell; Bell had also published her republican poem *Ainsi Va Le Monde* (1790), dedicated to the controversial Robert Merry ("Della Crusca"), a prominent member of the republican British Club in Paris. *Impartial Reflections* contains the germ of her longest meditation on Marie Antoinette, *Monody to the Memory of the Late Queen of France*, published after the Queen's execution, and uses some of the same language and imagery. It is an important document in the evolution of Robinson's politics and poetics, and a remarkable one in the context of the pamphlet war's use of romance for both revolutionary and counter-revolutionary ends, because it incorporates both political aspects of romance in a single text.

Robinson's *Impartial Reflections* addresses the National Assembly with the express purpose of bringing about the Queen's release from prison, where she remained on the Assembly's orders following the royal family's flight to Varennes in June 1791. The "Friend to Humanity" is clearly republican: "that the Revolution is the most glorious achievement in the annals of Europe, is universally felt and acknowledged," she writes (*IR*, 8).[32] Appealing to the National Assembly's sense of manly reason and justice, Robinson offers a stern critique of the French "COURT where despotism had usurped uncontrouled dominion" (*IR*, 14) worthy of Wollstonecraft or Paine. Robinson denounces the "courtly sycophants" for "feeding on the vitals of a groaning people, reveling in the luxuries wrested from the helpless million," and accuses these "propagators of evil" of "profit[ing] by the darkness of fanaticism" (*IR*, 16, 17, 16). Appealing to reason and against the "strong fascinations [found] in the tinsel blandishments of worldly superiority" (*IR*, 7), Robinson stands with Paine and Wollstonecraft against Burke's sentimental and reactionary defense of aristocratic privilege, mystification, and tradition in his 1790 *Reflections*. Paine's and Wollstonecraft's responses to Burke had rejected "the *Reflections* as a sentimental fiction in which Burke figures as a feminized man of feeling whose exquisite sensibility works to deflect attention from the defects of established political systems."[33] Burke's own *Letter to a Member of the National Assembly*, published earlier in 1791, had been written to an aristocrat with the express purpose of defending "the original gentlemen, and landed property of a whole nation" (3). In contrast, Robinson's letter contains her *impartial* reflections, from one friend of humanity to another, the National Assembly. Hers is a reasoned public address that rises above such particular, class-based and emotional interests as Burke's, and instead assumes the rational detachment characteristic of a male citizen of the public sphere:

THERE is not a doubt that all good men, whatever their *political* sentiments may be, feel deeply interested in the fate of the captive Queen. Every *impartial* eye has a tear for her sufferings and looks forward to a DECISION, that, it is to be hoped... will add dignity to the French nation. (*IR*, orig. emphasis, 30–31)

Identifying not with the victimized Queen, as she would in her *Monody*, but as her public republican defender, Robinson's "impartial" reflections attempt to appeal to the French National Assembly's sense of justice, beyond the "political sentiments" and indiscriminate rage which, she contends, had imprisoned the Queen in the first place.

Nevertheless, after tactfully quoting Rousseau in her concluding remarks, Robinson also quotes Burke's lament in his *Reflections*: "It is now in the power of that august Tribunal [the National Assembly] to prove, that '*the Days of Chivalry*' are not '*at an end*;' that as they have given innumerable testimonies of their patriotism and judgment, they also cherish the laudable and dignified sentiment of justice and humanity!" (*IR*, orig. emphasis 27). Robinson's savvy appropriation of a public, impartial voice remains inseparable from her appreciation of aristocratic femininity, even in this appeal to the revolutionary tribunal. She does not resist the temptation to fetishize the Queen through familiar celestial metaphors: "every inferior constellation in the courtly circle, borrowed radiance from the refulgence of her superior brightness! What is she now? A forlorn and mournful CAPTIVE; immured within the walls of a palace, but a short time since the scene of domestic joy, and splendid festivity!" (*IR*, 28). While not a rhetorically wise allusion, Robinson's use of Burke's chivalric defense of the Queen in her public appeal to the National Assembly does set out the unique course her feminist politics would follow for the next decade: a feminist and increasingly radical politics, as her spirited defense of the "British Convention" shows, that claimed both romance and revolution as allies. Neither a triumphant transcendence of politics, nor an unworkable and confused contradiction, Robinson's mixture of aristocratic and bourgeois politics (and poetics) place her on a historical threshold, a turning point where early feminists like herself could briefly imagine new possibilities, conflicted and ephemeral though these were. The ambivalent figure of Marie Antoinette is central to Robinson's feminist project, providing her a symbolic discourse on gender and politics that transforms the era's most notorious femme fatale into a bourgeois mother, a persecuted wife, and as we shall see, the embodiment of female Genius.

THE ARISTOCRACY OF GENIUS

In the closing of *A Monody to the Memory of the Late Queen of France*, Robinson draws a comparison between the misunderstood Queen and the poet herself, assuring the immortality of each through the other:

> Immortal GENIUS! let the votive line,
> The MUSES LAUREL, and her FAME, be THINE!
> For THOU shalt LIVE, when PRIDE's indignant eye,
> Clos'd in eternal solitude, shall lie![...]
> THOU SHALT SURVIVE!   (26)

Though she here refers to the Queen's genius, Robinson is also alluding to her own, given their shared fate as victims of "INFERIOR souls." Her vocation as woman poet exposes her to the venom of "reptiles" and "insects," yet it also elevates her to a similar nobility:

Then, GENIUS, let the toilsome task be THINE,
TO LABOUR in the dark precarious MINE;
And if, amidst the *chaos*, thou *shouldst* find
One great, one beauteous attribute of mind,
To twine round MERIT's brow the wreath of FAME,
And give *Nobility* A LOFTIER NAME!" (26)

Robinson displays a powerful sense of poetic self-consciousness and elevation. She does not hesitate to place the wreath of fame on Marie Antoinette and the laurel wreath on herself: the nobility to which she elevates herself is that of Romantic poet. Robinson's dedication to John Taylor in her poem *Sight* (1793), which celebrates the visionary power of "glorious SIGHT! sublimest gift of God," makes it clear in what esteem she holds her poetic vocation: "Yet with an unconquerable enthusiasm, I shall ever pay voluntary homage to the FIRST of all distinctions, – the ARISTOCRACY OF GENIUS!" (*Sight*, 8, iii–iv). Charlotte Smith made what is on the surface a similar gesture in *The Emigrants* (1793), when she asserted that "worth alone is true Nobility" (1. 240), echoing *Pamela*. Yet Robinson's "Aristocracy of Genius" is not so much an equalizing gesture as is Smith's, but, rather, one that implicitly elevates the (woman) poet above others, rather than leveling class privilege altogether.

Robinson, like Yearsley and Smith, draws on the popular eighteenth-century concept of untaught genius, yet her concept of Aristocracy of Genius goes further: she explicitly genders the Romantic genius as female, essentially recuperating the effeminacy associated with the aristocracy, and connecting it to the likewise maligned sensibility embodied in the female body, specifically the hypereroticized body of Marie Antoinette. Jerome McGann has argued that, in *Sappho and Phaon*, Robinson celebrates sensibility's "largest philosophical and social claims," and elevates this feminized source of poetical power to the "preeminent intellectual force, and the emblem of whatever social and philosophical advancement the present age can claim for itself."[34] The "balance of raptures" McGann eloquently locates in Robinson's prophetic vision of Sappho and Phaon, reason and passion, is also embodied, with more overtly political implications, in her numerous reflections on Marie Antoinette.

Robinson's personal identification with Marie Antoinette, found throughout her novels, prose, and poetry, is grounded in Robinson's own painful experience as a woman punished for her sexuality, profession, and ambition, as well a woman who had been imprisoned because of her husband's crimes, experiences which she evoked in increasingly politicized terms throughout her career. And, as Judith Pascoe has shown, Robinson derived "a sense of her own spectacular power" as eroticized public figure through this "act of identification" with Marie Antoinette.[35] For Robinson, the treason trial of the French Queen came to represent the public persecution of all women who dared enter the public sphere. More specifically, the Queen represented women of genius, such as Robinson herself, who dared enter the Republic of Letters on distinctly feminine terms, by celebrating the dangerous associations of femininity with sensibility, sensuality, and the body.

Thus the treason trial of the Queen is also the trial of embodied female genius, from Sappho, the founding matriarch of this persecuted lineage, to modern poets such as Robinson. In Robinson's masterpiece *Sappho and Phaon*, Sappho is the victim of envy and prejudice, an important predecessor for modern women poets "who, unpatronized by the courts, and unprotected by the powerful persevere in the paths of literature, and enoble themselves by the unperishable lustre of MENTAL PRE-EMINENCE!" (*Wu*, 187). Modern professional female writers, who figure prominently in Robinson's fiction, inherit both Sappho's "mental pre-eminence" and her trials. Thus the semi-autobiographical heroine of Robinson's novel *The Natural Daughter* (1799) is an actress (and writer) figuratively on trial because of the sexual stigma of her public profession: "She stood before the tribunal of the public on the basis of her own talents: but it was undermined by arts which even the most transcendent genius cannot always counteract" (*ND*, 1: 248). Robinson knew that the fates of Sappho and Marie Antoinette before this public tribunal were dangerous precedents for the modern woman poet.

As a figure of the Aristocracy of Genius, Marie Antoinette embodies, paradoxically, Robinson's desired feminist meritocracy, a concept that she used throughout her works to critique distinctions based on wealth and class. In direct contrast to Burke's "natural aristocracy,"[36] Robinson reminds us in *The Natural Daughter* that "the aristocracy of wealth had little to do with the aristocracy of genius" (1: 249). Thus this Aristocracy of Genius is characterized by a suggestively republican "unconquerable enthusiasm" (*Sight*, 8), and evokes the older Greek meaning of aristocracy – the rule of the best citizens – in opposition to other contemporary usages of the term (by the British) to mean the nobility or (by French republicans) to mean counter-revolutionary.[37] That the outspoken republican Helen Maria Williams would later use the same phrase as a compliment in a letter to a friend substantiates the democratic associations that the expression carried: M. de Nivernois "had a double claim" to the protection of Providence, wrote Williams, "uniting the aristocracy of genius with that of birth."[38]

That such a figure of excessive wealth as the Queen could stand in for Robinson's critique of distinctions attests to the complexity of Robinson's gendered poetics and politics, as well as to the contradictory significations of Marie Antoinette in the 1790s. Robinson's controversial *Walsingham; or the Pupil of Nature* (1797), like *The Natural Daughter* and *Letter to the Women of England*, had attacked distinctions based on birth and in their place advocated the equal "rights of man," a critique that one reviewer described as "distorted by very false notions of politics."[39] Moreover, in *Walsingham*, Robinson had specifically linked the French Revolution to what would be accurately described as the Rights of Genius: "The ears of princes in the atmosphere of Versailles were deaf to supplicating merit... Every neglected man of genius became the enemy of despotism; every exalted son of illustrious intellect flew to the standard of tremendous retribution" (III: 262).[40] French and English princes and courts are conflated in Robinson's condemnation of aristocratic despotism, as her contemporaries would have immediately understood, given her well-publicized attempts to obtain the Prince Regent's promised financial settlement. The *Anti-Jacobin* predictably complained in its review of *Walsingham* that "[l]ike Charlotte Smith, she has conceived a very high opinion of the wisdom of the French philosophers" Voltaire and Rousseau, and urged her to "abstain from attempting political philosophy" (161, 164).

Robinson's critique of the aristocracy of birth, central to *Walsingham*, is expanded in *The Natural Daughter* to include a more extensive celebration of the aristocracy of genius. In *The Natural Daughter*, both the heroine, who struggles to survive through a series of tenuous professions such as strolling actress, poet, novelist, and teacher, and the heroine's aristocratic patron are allied with the Aristocracy of Genius that Robinson associated with Marie Antoinette, attesting to the class mobility of the term as she used it. Upon seeing Georgina, Duchess of Chatsworth (Robinson's idealized benevolent female patron, the Duchess of Devonshire) her heroine Martha's "heart bounded with ecstasy; for what heart that feels the pressure of sorrow does not bound at the name of this enchanting woman? who that has seen her smile, that has heard her voice, can forbear to own the magic of their power"? (II: 164). Martha, whom the *British Critic* reviewer had denounced as "of the Woolstonecraft [*sic*] school," is a strong critic of class distinctions, prompting the journal to complain that "it is of little use to lament or censure the French revolution, if the morals and manners which tended to produce it, are inculcated and held up for imitation" (321).[41] Yet, despite her critique of class distinctions, Martha responds romantically and even chivalrously to this aristocratic figure of female sensuality and beauty; Robinson writes that Martha bows before the duchess "because she felt that species of adoration which warms the Persian's bosom when he beholds the rising sun, the source of all his zeal and all his blessings" (II: 165). Not the feminine moon but once again "the Sun sublime" is Robinson's metaphor for radiant female beauty and its diminishing power.

The anonymous author of "Verses, Addressed to a Female Republican," published in *The European Magazine* (1799), also connects a critique of distinctions with French (female) republicanism, and with the feminist claim to women's pre-eminence:

> If what you say be just and real,
> That all distinction is ideal,
> Pray stem this mighty evil;
> Destroy your own pre-eminence,
> In wit, accomplishments, and sense,
> And join our humble level.   (46)

Both this radical critique of distinctions and the claim for female "mental pre-eminence" were characteristic preoccupations of Robinson's later works, and it is quite possible that the female republican addressed is Robinson. The "Verses, Addressed to a Female Republican," when considered as directed toward Robinson's kind of republicanism (unusual and unpopular in 1799), if not directly to Robinson, associate republicanism with the overthrow of several orders, in addition to that of the *ancien régime*:

> To reign, by beauty's soft controul,
> The Sovereign of the captive soul,
> Would then be public treason;
> The Queen of Love herself might dread
> To lose her throne, perhaps her head,
> In our new "Age of Reason."

Echoing Burke's lament that "[a]ll the pleasing illusions which made power gentle and obedience liberal ... are to be dissolved by this new conquering empire of light and reason," the warning voiced by the "Verses" against disrupting the sexual as well as the political and religious orders is the conventional conservative response to Wollstonecraftian feminism and republicanism (*Reflections*, 87). Like Burke, the "Verses" author embodies this age of chivalry in the Queen of Love, Marie Antoinette, who, as the poem acknowledged, was tried in public for treason because of her alleged political influence over the King (in addition to her supposed sexual crimes). Again we can see how the chivalric sexual order Burke and the "Verses" author mourned was always dangerously close to slipping into the corrupting order of the empire of women, of women's dangerous preeminence through beauty. Robinson's unique perspective on the role of beauty in this empire of women identifies women's beauty not simply with Love (whether domestic or excessive), but with Genius. Thus, in the figure of Marie Antoinette, the female republican Robinson on the one hand, and the conservative Burke and the "Verses" author on the other, each locate very different versions of the empire of women.

Robinson fashions Marie Antoinette into an imaginary figure of the Aristocracy of Genius, her distinctly feminized allegory of a Rights of Genius who is paradoxically at once a flamboyant femme fatale and a republican mother, a spectacular Queen and a genius toiling in obscurity. Unlike Wollstonecraft, who saw no value in the "mistress system" and court culture that the Queen epitomized, Robinson, a former royal mistress and hence, perhaps, a potential future queen, saw aristocratic women's public influence in the *ancien régime* as one valuable avenue for women's access to and refinement of public sphere politics. Thus, in *A Letter to the Women of England*, while advocating that women gain access to greater economic, political, educational and physical liberties, Robinson nevertheless celebrates the woman-centered salon culture for which *ancien régime* France was notorious in British eyes, and claims that women's influence had helped bring about the French Revolution:

Women soon became the idols of a polished people. They were admitted into the councils of statesmen, the cabinets of princes. The influence they obtained contributed greatly towards that urbanity of manners which marked the reign of Louis the Sixteenth. The tyrants of France, at the toilettes of enlightened WOMEN, were taught to shudder at the horrors of the Bastille: which was never more crowded with victims, than when bigotry and priestcraft were in their most exulting zenith. (*Letter*, 61–62)

Robinson's insight into this systematic exclusion of women from French and British public politics throughout the 1790s presents her readers with a different solution, perhaps a more viable one, than did Wollstonecraft in her wholesale rejection of feminine influence and the order of seduction.

For the staunchly middle-class Wollstonecraft, "aristocracy" carried only negative connotations, both sexual and political (most famously in her lengthy critiques of the aristocracy's excesses and effeminacy). She also theorized the aristocracy of sex in *Rights of Woman*, where she named the misogyny at the heart of Rousseau's Rights of Man a "male aristocracy" that unlawfully monopolized the rights due both sexes: "The *rights* of humanity have been thus confined to the male line from Adam downwards. Rousseau would carry his male aristocracy still further" (*VRW*, 87). Wollstonecraft shares with Robinson this feminist understanding of the "rights of humanity," but the two friends part ways when it comes to the "aristocracy of genius," and French women's historical preeminence in this aristocracy.

Robinson's feminism in *Letter to the Women of England* is at least as bold as Wollstonecraft's, and bravely allies itself with her recently deceased friend, whose reputation had recently suffered an irreparable setback after Godwin's unwise publication of her *Memoirs* in 1798: "it requires a *legion of Wollstonecrafts* to undermine the poisons of prejudice and malevolence" proclaimed Robinson (*Letter*, 2, orig. emphasis). Robinson's central aim in her *Letter* is identical to Wollstonecraft's: to "establish her [woman's] claims to the participation of power, both mentally and corporeally" (2). As we saw in chapter 2, Robinson's feminist treatise takes Wollstonecraft's corporeal argument even further, insisting on women's right to physical self-defense, even violence. She also maintains alongside Wollstonecraft's republican feminism an affinity and nostalgia for the salon culture of Enlightenment France, and a lasting appreciation of the warmth of manners and the public interaction of the sexes found in continental Europe, where she had lived for a time.

French men, Robinson wrote, "found by experience, that society was embellished, conversation enlivened, and emulation excited, by an intercourse of ideas" between the sexes (*Letter*, 61). Ultimately, aristocratic French women's influence meant that "the republic of letters had more ornaments of genius and imagination" (*Letter*, 61). In Britain, in contrast,

we hear of no public marks of popular applause, no rank, no title, no liberal and splendid recompense bestowed on British literary women! They must fly to foreign countries for celebrity...where genius...is still honoured *as* GENIUS, one of the best and noblest gifts of THE CREATOR." (*Letter*, 64–65, orig. emphasis).

French women's influence in Enlightenment salon culture had helped bring awareness of the *ancien régime*'s abuses and had helped usher in the Revolution; thus their contributions to the Republic of Letters helped bring about the actual republic, a feminist anticipation of Habermas's influential argument that "the Republic of Letters made possible the political republics of the late eighteenth century."[42] Tom Paine, in *Rights of Man* (1791–92), had similarly allied genius and the Republic of Letters with the meritocratic political republic: "As the republic of letters brings forward the best literary productions, by giving genius a fair and universal chance; so the representative system of government is calculated to produce the wisest laws."[43] Robinson's complaint that such a republic of letters does not currently exist for women in Britain is another instance of her critique of the British political and literary establishments that is at once republican, feminist, and cosmopolitan.

The Republic of Letters that Robinson wants to recreate in her *Letter to the Women of England*, centered around self-educated and respected *salonnières*, had already vanished in France in the 1780s, replaced by the self-consciously masculinized culture of political clubs and *musées*.[44] It had never existed for women in Britain. The bluestocking salons earlier in the century were not comparable to the French salons that Robinson wanted to emulate, because of Robinson's insistence that women's participation in these salons have an impact on public politics. In an essay published in 1800, Robinson complains that "Political restrictions have been enforced" against the Republic of Letters, but that, despite this censorship and the lack of public patronage of the arts, "the tree of knowledge has flourished spontaneously."[45] For Robinson, the problem remains that "[t]he cabinets of our statesmen are closed against the aristocracy of genius."[46] The bluestockings had indeed celebrated an aristocracy of genius, and throughout the later eighteenth century had been maligned for their intellectual ambitions; yet, as a 1794 satire suggests, the bluestocking salons relied on class distinctions: their society "originated in a laudable resolution amongst certain *fine* ladies to establish an Aristocracy in the Republic of Letters."[47] The bluestockings's emphasis on propriety and their "consciousness of the *just* deference due to their rank and fortune," as the satirist elaborated, were precisely the qualities of this earlier formulation of the Republic of Letters that Robinson, as an outsider to rank, fortune, and sexual propriety, wanted to reform.

Robinson, like other writers of her generation, struggled against such restrictions, and, like other prominent feminists, was rejected by other women writers because of her controversial life and writings. As a consequence, she wanted to foster a more inclusive and overtly politicized Republic of Letters, one in which women could seek a wider sphere of power: "How powerful might such a phalanx [of enlightened women] become," she reflected in 1800, "were it to act in union of sentiment, and sympathy of feeling."[48] Robinson was right that the French Republic of Letters, "whose relations were structured by reciprocity and the equality it implied,"[49] had been central to the Enlightenment's challenge to the French monarchy. By implication, then, her own open letter to British women attempts to revive and extend this intellectual and political republic, with its accompanying critique of class and sex privilege, to England – a radical claim, whose potential was cut short by Robinson's death in 1800.

In its British literary context, Robinson's seeming paradox of the Aristocracy of Genius in the Republic of Letters shares a similar conflict as that experienced by contemporaries such as S. T. Coleridge and William Wordsworth, for whom "populist aspirations existed alongside an evident longing for a discourse beyond the ordinary" in an uncomfortable "intersection of elite and mass culture."[50] Thus Annette Wheeler Cafarelli warns that "[w]e must be wary of simply concluding from the testimony of their ambivalence that the Romantics merely endorsed an intellectual aristocracy in place of the old forms of patronage, or that they did not practice what they preached."[51] But perhaps Robinson is not so much ambivalent as she is ambitious. She did not share Wordsworth's anxieties over "public taste," but instead placed great faith in print culture's liberating and democratizing potential.[52] Her simultaneous desire for an intellectual aristocracy and an egalitarian meritocracy develops in part from her increasingly feminist understanding that, historically, deserving women have been systematically denied the opportunities and rewards of authorship. In other words, unlike Wordsworth and Coleridge (and the bluestockings), and like the plebeian population in general, they have been denied access to both the intellectual aristocracy *and* the Republic of Letters. It is understandable, then, that Robinson wants access to both.

A Letter to the Women of England marks Robinson's ongoing evolution as an increasingly radicalized and professionalized writer, qualities inextricably bound to her likewise increasingly vocal feminism. She envisioned that this role would be fully realized in a "Republic of Letters," and simultaneously in an "Aristocracy of Genius," in which women were fully enfranchised and embodied public citizens. That Robinson would return to the figure of Marie Antoinette throughout her career is no surprise once we take into account the subtlety of her insights into the gendered politics of the French Revolution debates, the likewise multivalent significations that the image of the Queen carried throughout the 1790s, and Robinson's own precarious social standing.

HER SATANIC MAJESTY: "AN AWFUL LESSON
FOR EACH FUTURE AGE"

Robinson repeats a call for poetic immortality throughout her *Monody to the Memory of the Late Queen of France*, enacting through the power of her verse the immortality of both the poet and her heroine, thus elevating herself to the highest honor to which a Romantic poet can aspire:

> ILL-FATED QUEEN! then let the tribute just,
> The POET'S NUMBERS, consecrate THY dust! [...]
> YET, 'midst the desolating gloom descry
> TRANSCENDANT CHAPLETS that shall NEVER DIE!
> The WONDERS OF THY MIND shall HIST'RY own.
>
> (27)

The transcendent wreath is that of poetry, and it is through the "wonders" of Robinson's own mind, inscribed on "TRUTH's recording page" (27), that the history of the Queen, the symbolic last vestige of the *ancien régime*'s "empire of women," will survive.

Robinson's prophecy of Marie Antoinette's recuperation is realized in the current feminist histories of the Queen's image and the role of women in the French Enlightenment. Robinson's status as significant Romantic poet has also only recently been reestablished. This reassessment of women Romantic poets in general is deeply invested in understanding the profound shifts in gender and class which, ostensibly, made poet incompatible with woman in the nineteenth century. Robinson is but one example of many women Romantic poets who boldly identified themselves as poets, and saw themselves as part of a long poetic tradition (in Robinson's case, often figured as a royal dynasty), as well as a present poetic community, as their many dedications to fellow women poets reveal. That Robinson (like Yearsley) attains the status of poet of history by immortalizing the "AWFUL LESSON" (27) illustrated by Marie Antoinette's execution is no coincidence. Marie Antoinette represented "the menace that the feminine and the feminizing presented to the republican notions of manhood and virility."[53] Likewise, the woman poet represented this same threat of feminization to male Romantic poets.[54]

The "awful lesson for each future age" that Marie Antoinette illustrated for Robinson, and Robinson in turn illustrated for future readers,
was not the familiar lesson of excessive pride and power humbled, nor
Burke's lesson of anarchy loosed upon the world when the organic family
and "natural aristocracy" are overturned. These more familiar lessons,
particularly Burke's vision of Marie Antoinette as persecuted femininity,
abounded in British poems about the execution of Marie Antoinette.
For example, in Thomas Campbell's "Verses on Marie Antoinette," the
Queen is seen solely as martyred wife and mother in her "lone captivity,"
enduring through "scenes of [her] sad sequestered care"; likewise, in
John Wolcot's "The Captive Queen," the Queen is virtue in distress
in her Gothic dungeon, awaiting "the blow that sinks that beauteous
frame / [and] Gives all the virtues to the tomb."[55] Margaret Holford,
author of an epic about an archetypal bad mother and power-hungry
queen, *Margaret of Anjou*, in her poem on Marie Antoinette is less sentimental than Campbell or Wolcot. Her poem focuses instead on the
Queen's "[d]ominion, beauty, pomp" swept away in "one rude whirlwind"; even the Queen's grief, the focus of most of her contemporaries'
poetry, is for Holford "[t]ired with its own excess." "Yet trace these faded
lines," advises Holford, and see "[w]ith what enduring bliss the world's
fair smile is fraught!" (*Poetical Album*, 255–56). Robinson's *Monody*, *Letter
to the Women of England*, and her poem "Marie Antoinette's Lamentation
in Prison" offered similar sentimental visions of the Queen as virtue in
distress and persecuted motherhood, and did so to excess, as the *Critical
Review* had complained. Robinson's fusion of the domestic mother and
the spectacular Queen is unique, and crucial for understanding the
Queen's other "awful lesson" for Robinson: the fate of persecuted but unabashedly proud female genius, "hurled from the most towering altitude
of power" (*Letter*, 27).

For Robinson, this awful lesson, one that she repeated throughout her
later works, is that women are continuously, often violently, excised from
history and from the public sphere. Thus the real lesson of her *Monody* is
not a conciliatory Christian one extolling pity, or offering the consolation
of Marie's celestial reunion with Louis, even though this consolation is
central to the *Monody*'s surface narrative, that of the rise and fall of Marie
Antoinette. Parallel to Robinson's sentimental apotheosis of the Queen,
and to her attempt to characterize the Queen as both the epitome of
aristocratic beauty and bourgeois motherhood, Robinson's larger lesson
is one for the woman writer, amounting to a distinctly Satanic claim to

> the proud supremacy of WORTH;
> Its blest dominion vast and unconfin'd,
> Its CROWN ETERNAL, and its THRONE THE MIND!
> That persecution's agonizing rod
> Should boldly smite THE "NOBLEST WORK OF GOD!"
> That RANK should be a CRIME, and GENIUS hurl'd
> A mournful wand'rer on the pitying world!
>
> (*Monody*, 23)[56]

Hurled from the skies like Lucifer, the morning star, Robinson's "Genius" here complicates Burke's morning star description of Marie Antoinette to which Robinson had alluded in her *Monody* (and which the "Verses to a Female Republican" had also used to transform Antoinette into the "Queen of Love," Venus). The planet Venus was both the morning star and the evening star, the latter traditionally associated with Aphrodite, the Goddess of Love, and the former with Lucifer because it defied the sun by remaining in the sky and rivaling the star in its brightness.[57]

For Burke, Marie Antoinette's beauty rivaled that of the sun, hence he effectively combined the morning and evening star in his vision of the Queen as Venus, the queen of love. In contrast, Robinson's vision of the Queen as outcast genius evokes the morning star's political and Romantic overtones of proud rebellion and defiance, familiar to modern readers in the poetry of Blake, Byron, and Percy Bysshe Shelley. Charlotte Smith had also echoed Milton's Satan in 1791, when she elevated her own transcendent poetic perspective to that of "a spirit conscious of superior worth, / In placid elevation firmly great."[58] Both Robinson and Smith allude to the unrepentant Satan's high self-worth, a bold claim to a Miltonic inheritance:

> Satan, whom now transcendent glory raised
> Above his fellows, with monarchial pride
> Conscious of highest worth, unmoved thus spake.
> 'O progeny of heav'n, empyreal Thrones,
> With reason hath deep silence and demur
> Seized us, though undismayed: long is the way
> And hard, that out of hell leads up to light.'
>
> (*PL*, II. 427–33)

Rallying the outcast angels to seek their original splendour and power, Satan suits undismayed feminists like Smith and Robinson who similarly urged women, as the progeny of heaven, not to "labour in the dark precarious mine" but instead to seek the public sphere of the "sun sublime."[59]

The "supremacy of worth" that Robinson celebrates in Marie Antoinette is thus at once Miltonic and overtly revolutionary (and in keeping with reformers' allusions to Milton's republicanism), a meritocratic concept that she had also used in her outspoken 1790 poem on the French Revolution, *Ainsi va le Monde, Inscribed to Robert Merry*. There she opens the poem by lauding Merry's "superior worth," and goes on to celebrate that in France, Freedom "Strangles each tyrant Phantom in its birth, / And knows no title – but superior worth" (*Ainsi*, 1, 9). The republican Robert Merry, Marie Antoinette, and Milton's Satan are thus part of the same revolutionary (and admirably inclusive) Aristocracy of Genius.

Monody to the Memory of the Late Queen of France concludes with an extended metaphor of a cedar tree for this undismayed "radiant KNOWLEDGE" of genius that the Queen embodies: " 'Midst the wild winds, the lordly CEDAR tow'rs," writes Robinson, echoing Milton's description of Satan, who "above the rest / In shape and gesture proudly eminent / Stood like a tow'r" (*PL*, 1. 589–91). Defying the storm that topples inferior trees, "the proud TREE its verdant head rears high, / Waves to the blast, and seems to pierce the sky" (*Monody*, 24). Like the fallen angels whom Milton likened to the scorched "forest oaks, or mountain pines," that "with singèd top their stately growth though bare" remain standing "on the blasted heath," Robinson's cedar continues "to climb / SUPREMELY GRAND, and AWFULLY SUBLIME!"[60] Ranging far from the iconography traditionally associated with Marie Antoinette, Robinson's "BOLD USURPER of that HEAV'N-TAUGHT POW'R" of genius is the same Promethean figure of liberty as Milton's bold usurper, who would "Through all the coasts of dark destruction seek / Deliverance for us all."[61] The perseverance of female genius, initially embodied in the Queen in Robinson's *Monody*, is in the poem's conclusion metaphorized as the lordly cedar and as Prometheus, figures that, like Satan, grant Robinson's feminism an impressive boldness, one that transforms the preeminence of the fallen aristocracy into that of feminized outcast genius. It should come as no surprise, then, that in her poetic tribute to Robinson, Charlotte Dacre would apply Robinson's biblical allusion of the towering cedar to Robinson herself, making explicit Robinson's implicit comparison of herself to the French Queen. For Dacre, Robinson is an "angel… forlorn," "Like a cedar amid the rude desert high soaring," an extension of Robinson's vision of Marie Antoinette as fallen angel (*Hours*, 1: 131).

Charlotte Smith had also explicitly allied the imprisoned Marie Antoinette with the fallen Satan in 1793: in *The Emigrants*, the imprisoned

Marie Antoinette is at once a suffering mother to be pitied, the victim of a corrupt system, and the fallen angel:

> Ah! much I mourn thy sorrows, hapless Queen!
> And deem thy expiation made to Heaven
> For every fault, to which Prosperity
> Betray'd thee, when it plac'd thee on a throne
> Where boundless power was thine, and thou wert rais'd
> High (as it seem'd) above the envious reach
> Of destiny!   (11. 154–60)[62]

"But eminence / Of misery is thine," writes Smith, anticipating Byron, and echoing Satan's complaint that "[t]he lower still I fall, only supreme / In misery."[63] Smith, unlike Robinson, was an outspoken critic of the French monarchy, yet she nevertheless found in the Queen's "eminence of misery" and in her own consciousness of "superior worth" a powerful link to the original outcast, Milton's Satan. Both Smith and Robinson use the Romantic Satan to elevate the beauty of the femme fatale, Marie Antoinette, to the level of the sublime, simultaneously allying female Genius (and implicitly themselves) with the ostensibly masculine model of the heroic outcast.

For Helen Maria Williams also, Marie Antoinette's "haughty indignant spirit" after the King's execution resembled Satan's. In *Letters from France*, Williams speculated that if Marie Antoinette herself were faced with execution,

her haughty indignant spirit, which preferred the chance of losing empire and life to the certainty of retaining any thing less than absolute dominion, would probably meet death with becoming dignity, feeling, that "to be weak is to be miserable, doing or suffering." (*LF*, 1. 4: 3)

Williams, like Smith, had little sympathy for the French monarchy, and in fact her controversial statement that "History will . . . condemn Lewis the sixteenth" appears in this same letter in which she imagines the Queen agreeing with Satan that "to be weak is to be miserable" (*PL*, 1. 156–57). Yet she clearly admired the Queen's "becoming dignity" and pride, as she admired the stoicism of other female victims of the guillotine such as Charlotte Corday and Madame de Roland. This Satanic inheritance, and the prideful and resolute strength it evoked for women, necessarily emboldens these writers' laments over the fate of women with an explicitly dangerous and unfeminine undercurrent of revolutionary anger.

Revolution and romance meet in the republican Satan, the first revolutionary and hence the beloved of Shelley, Byron, and Blake, much to the chagrin of Miltonists.[64] Robinson and Smith also clearly admired Satan's "monarchial pride," which like the "Aristocracy of Genius," was easily incorporated, perhaps even necessary, to the revolutionary, often republican, struggle their feminism engaged in: "long is the way And hard, that out of hell leads up to light." It was Wollstonecraft herself who, with her characteristic dry wit, had resisted Rousseau's fetishization of Edenic domesticity in Satanic terms: "Similar feelings has Milton's pleasing picture of paradisiacal happiness ever raised in my mind; yet, instead of envying the lovely pair [Adam and Eve], I have with conscious dignity, or Satanic pride, turned to hell for sublimer objects" (*VRW*, 25 n. 3). The Satanic overtones of this moment of crisis in the history of feminism (the execution of the Queen and its symbolic significance for British women) have not yet been incorporated into readings of the Queen's significance for women writers, or into accounts of women writers of the Romantic period. The defiant "monarchial pride" and "conscious dignity" ascribed to Marie Antoinette, and by extension to themselves, by republican sympathizers like Robinson, Smith, and Williams attests to the boldness of these women writers' poetic identities, as well as to their explicitly feminist alliance with what is erroneously assumed to be one of the most masculine aspects of Romanticism, Satanism.[65] These portraits of Marie Antoinette also reveal how the era's most infamous femme fatale shares with the "fatal man" of Walpole, Radcliffe, and Byron, a similar origin in the sublime villain of *Paradise Lost*.

Robinson's recasting of the morning star metaphor in defiantly Satanic terms was not the only such contemporary politicization of this trope: one contemporary had used Burke's morning star comparison to republican ends in "Ode on Liberty," recited in London in honor of the French Revolution on July 14, 1792:

> Hail! more refulgent than the morning star,
> Fair QUEEN OF BLISS – fair daughter of the sky,
> We woo thee, LIBERTY, and hope from far
> To catch the brightness of thy raptur'd eye![66]

The poet celebrates the "sacred love" of Liberty's "radiant form divine," and urges true patriots "[t]o live in thine embrace, or in thine arms expire!" Marie Antoinette and French republican Liberty are here conflated in one image of femininity both seductive and powerful, an image echoed in Robert Southey's and Adam Lux's visions of Charlotte Corday as a republican femme fatale at whose altar they wished to be sacrificed.[67] Robinson herself was described in a similar fashion by a poetic admirer in 1794, who praised how "Wisdom's stern Goddess," Pallas Athena, who "presided over arms and arts," is united in Robinson with the goddess of love, Venus.[68] These 1790s portraits of female figures who unite the discordant spheres of public and private reveal a rare window of opportunity for redefining gender that Robinson was particularly attune to.

Robinson is not content, unlike many of her contemporaries and most Victorians, to recuperate Marie Antoinette as a vision of the newly normative bourgeois wife and mother seen only in her domestic tranquility or captivity.[69] Rather, Robinson expands the Queen's significance to include both public and private spheres of power, both republican and aristocratic visions of femininity. Her examples of the French nobility are not rendered more sympathetic, as they are in Smith's *Emigrants*, by being portrayed as exiled mothers and clergy, even though Robinson does strip Marie Antoinette of her aura of perversity. Instead, Robinson rewrites the claims of the French nobility for her own purposes as a Romantic poet: the nobles, and implicitly the poet, unrepentantly continue to claim their "CROWN ETERNAL, and its THRONE THE MIND." Economic "RANK" is characteristically conflated with "GENIUS" because each is criminalized, and, like Milton's Satan, "hurl'd / A Mournful wand'rer on the pitying world." The contrast with *The Emigrants* is once again instructive, for Robinson, unlike Smith, does not try to elicit pity for these aristocratic female wanderers, but instead suggestively allegorizes an unrepentant (and here ungendered) Aristocracy of Genius as that first revolutionary and proud outcast who chose to reign in hell rather than serve in heaven. A Satanic Genius here enjoys a "dominion vast and unconfin'd" enthroned in the mind, via its elusive and dangerous power, quintessentially Romantic, to make a heaven of hell, and of its confined (private) sphere a vast dominion. This is Robinson's unique contribution to the Romantic construction of genius and the femme fatale, transforming both into Satanic over-reachers, at once feminine and beautiful. Byron and Shelley clearly owe much to Robinson.

The true lesson of Robinson's *Monody to the Memory of the Late Queen of France* would, then, more fruitfully be described as a Monody to Genius, and in fact the poem echoes Robinson's earlier "Ode to Genius," in which the poet repeatedly chants, as she did in the *Monody*, "I have seen thee!" and celebrates Genius, "dressed in awful pride," in sublime terms identical to those which had described Marie Antoinette:

Of thee I'll sing. – Illustrious Maid!
In peerless majesty array'd!
Who, all creative, all sublime,
First sprang from the ethereal clime,
To bid enraptur'd fancy trace
The bright infinity of space,
Where FAME of pure celestial birth
A starry wreath prepares to crown IMMORTAL WORTH!
Blest GENIUS! pow'r divine!
Now shall the votive song be thine!   (*RPW*, I: 91)

The lesson, like the figure celebrated, is also identical: "I've seen thee
stamp each name / On the UNPERISHABLE ROLLS OF FAME! And,
smiling o'er the consecrated page, / ANTICIPATE the BOAST of MANY
A FUTURE AGE!" (*Ibid*). This anticipated boast survived the execution
of female Genius, as Robinson predicted, but the "awful lesson" remains worth remembering in the present, when too many accounts
of women's Romantic-era poetry overemphasize these poets' supposed
"anxiety of authorship," or their hesitancy to proclaim themselves vi-
sionaries, geniuses, unacknowledged legislators, or even Satanic over-
reachers. Robinson anticipated, even boasted of, her fame in future ages,
and history has proven her correct.

Robinson's *Monody to the Memory of the Late Queen of France* is valuable as
a site of a Romantic poet's self-creation, as a meditation on the condition
of women, and as an attempt to alter that condition by contesting the
definitions of proper femaleness and femininity that the new bourgeois
order instituted. Robinson's lament of Marie Antoinette is a lament of the
larger exclusion of women from public discourse, and of women poets
from due public acclaim. As she wrote in *A Letter to the Women of England*:

The embargo upon words, the enforcement of tacit submission, has been productive of consequences highly honourable to the women of the present age.
Since the sex have been condemned for exercising the powers of speech, they
have successfully taken up the pen: and their writings exemplify both energy of
mind, and capability of acquiring the most extensive knowledge. The press will
be monuments from which the genius of British women will rise to immortal
celebrity: their works will, in proportion as their educations are liberal, from year
to year, challenge an equal portion of fame, with the labours of their classical
male contemporaries! (orig. emphasis, 90–91)

Robinson is probably alluding to the 1778 prohibition against women
listening to the debates in the House of Commons, and to their lack of
the right to speak or be represented in government.[70] More abstractly,

she refers to the silencing of women, such as the French Queen, as public speaking subjects in the new ideology of domesticity and difference. Robinson knows that women have resisted this ideology, have contested their positions as objects of male knowledge and imagination, and have used the written word to participate in the continuing ideological struggle to define their sex and gender. She in fact presents an early version of Foucault's concept of power as productive of resistance, and demonstrates, as Jana Sawicki and other Foucauldian feminists have argued, that strategies are never inherently oppressive or subversive.[71] Thus, women's exclusion from the public sphere and its powers of speech, argues Robinson, ironically contributed to the explosion in the literary marketplace and the unprecedented opportunities, as writers, readers, and consumers, that this print culture offered so many women. Robinson confirms that for women, as for radical reformers, "[c]onfidence in a free press became a frankly polemical position," and that feminists, like the early nineteenth-century reformers Kevin Gilmartin has discussed, "were convinced that the press necessarily promoted liberty and reform."[72]

Mary Robinson's "Aristocracy of Genius" and its consciously feminized prophecy would be realized in Letitia Landon, whose influential poetic career *Fraser's Magazine* compared to Marie Antoinette's reign of beauty:

Letitia Elizabeth Landon! Burke said that ten thousand swords ought to have leaped out of their scabbards at the mention of Marie Antoinette; and in like manner we maintain, that ten thousand pens should leap out of their inkbottles to pay homage to L.E.L. In Burke's time, Jacobinism had banished chivalry – at least, out of France, – and the swords remained unbared for the queen; we shall prove, that our pens shall be uninked for the poetess.[73]

It is not Robinson's Satanic majesty, but Burke's embattled beauty that is transformed into the sentimentalized poetess, without a trace of Robinson's conflicted portrait of the Queen. *Fraser's* portrait of Landon ignores the ironic gendered contradiction embedded within its own allusion, for, while Marie Antoinette never wielded a sword, Letitia Landon certainly wielded a pen, thus confounding *Fraser's* portrait of the woman poet as endangered femininity in need of chivalric literary defense. *Fraser's* goes on to praise Landon's supposedly exclusive focus on love, asking: "Is she to write of politics, or political economy, or pugilism, or punch? Certainly not. We feel a determined dislike of women who wander into these unfeminine paths." Robinson, of course, had walked these unfeminine paths (as had Landon), and her model of the woman Romantic poet, unlike *Fraser's* portrait of Landon as fragile poetess/queen, encouraged other women to do the same. For Robinson, Marie Antoinette could and did embody both of these masculine and feminine, bourgeois and *ancien régime*, private and public, regimes of power. By the time Landon was enshrined as "poetess" three decades after Robinson's death, the dangerous, public powers associated with Marie Antoinette and the Aristocracy of Genius had become even more suspect, and were increasingly difficult to evoke.

The public and private spheres which Robinson had uneasily united in Marie Antoinette had become increasingly distinct in the early nineteenth century, and the empire of beauty which she had defended had lost its credibility as a means of women's empowerment, even amongst the aristocracy. This domesticization of the aristocracy was crystallized in "the mirror image of Marie-Antoinette's execution in France, the trial of Queen Caroline" in 1820.[74] Queen Caroline was defended as "a blameless British woman," the epitome of chastity and restraint, and as a woman married to the epitome of licentiousness – an inverse image also of Marie Antoinette's marriage (*Ibid.*, 268). Queen Charlotte, her granddaughter Princess Charlotte, and Queen Victoria were also part of this new vision of royal women as domestic mothers and wives; the nineteenth-century domesticization and feminization of the British monarchy was complete with Victoria's coronation in 1837.

Robinson in her portraits of Marie Antoinette as the distinctly feminine Aristocracy of Genius had imagined something very different from these British monarchs who embodied a domesticated femininity. Yet all these royal female figures, and the uses their examples were put to by middle- and working-class women, nevertheless represented women's ongoing assertion of their power, whether this power was a stabilizing and domesticating one, as it was for Hannah More, or a more far-reaching and ambitious power imagined by writers such as Mary Robinson, Charlotte Smith and Mary Wollstonecraft.

FEMINIST THEORY AND THE ORDER OF SEDUCTION

> The reign of philosophy succeeded that of the imagination.
> Mary Wollstonecraft, *A Historical and Moral View of the French Revolution*

> Nothing can be greater than seduction itself, not even the order that destroys it.
> Jean Baudrillard, *Seduction*

Baudrillard's paean to seduction is part of poststructuralism's romance with the figure Woman, most famous in the works of Derrida, Lacan, Deleuze, and Guattari, and their forerunner Nietzsche. Feminist theory has been suspicious (and rightly so) of male theorists' celebrations of Woman's inessentialness, her masquerade, her identification with surface and style, and of their alliance of poststructuralism with these feminine properties. Yet as we have seen in the "awful lesson" of Marie Antoinette, the vilification of precisely these feminine elements of the aristocracy cost many French women their lives, and most women the option of identifying themselves with such qualities.

Baudrillard's celebration of seduction, like Burke's, locates the overthrow of this feminine order of seduction in the bourgeois revolution and its creation of a natural order:

The eighteenth century still spoke of seduction. It was, with valour and honour, a central preoccupation of the aristocratic spheres. The bourgeois Revolution put an end to this preoccupation... The bourgeois era dedicated itself to nature and production, things quite foreign and even expressly fatal to seduction.[75]

Yet, the natural order of truth and latent depth is continually and fatally disrupted by seduction and its free play of indeterminateness, masquerade, and style; as Baudrillard assures us, "nothing can be greater than seduction, not even the order that destroys it" (2). Robinson's *Walsingham, or the Pupil of Nature*, with its crossdressing hero/ine, had dramatically illustrated the order of seduction's performative model of gender as masquerade, revealing the protagonist's "true" sex only after four volumes. Yet in this denouement, as Chris Cullens has argued, "the novel does indeed undeniably contribute to the construction of a social discourse in which the natural body and sexual otherness become the defining standard," a new order which is fatal to seduction and which inscribes "material inequalities" within nature itself.[76]

Feminist historians have confirmed this violent movement against masquerade and seduction in the new eighteenth-century bourgeois order. What is perhaps surprising is the extent to which the order of seduction persisted in the works of women as well as men long after the *ancien régime*. Not to deny the moral power granted to middle-class women in the new domestic order, the persistence of the seductive order's attractions remained a significant part of the debate on the nature of women's power, and the nature of women. The seductive order and its mythic reign of beauty still enchanted some women (and men) despite its overthrow, and, rather than being a nostalgic vestige of an *ancien régime*, it haunted, and continues to haunt, this reigning natural order of truth. Marie Antoinette's transformation into a twentieth-century lesbian heroine is one such example of the order of seduction's function as a "poetics of possibility" in women's interests. In the nineteenth century, Marie Antoinette would resurface in figures of the unnatural female monarch such as Margaret Holford's *Margaret of Anjou*, and in enchantress figures who rule through beauty and sexuality, such as Mrs. Ross's *The Marchioness*, M. E. Braddon's Lady Audley, and Charlotte Brontë's Cleopatra in *Villette*. In the decade after Robinson's death, the Satanism, sensuality, and criminality associated with Marie Antoinette would be amplified in the novels of Robinson's admirer, Charlotte Dacre, to a new level of self-consciousness and explicitness. Thus, despite Wollstonecraft's hope that the philosophical order had supplanted that of seduction, seduction and the reign of beauty mark an ongoing tradition of gender critique that flourished in the works of Romantic-period women such as Mary Robinson and Charlotte Dacre.

CHAPTER 4

Unnatural, unsexed, undead: Charlotte Dacre's Gothic bodies

INTRODUCTION: DACRE'S LITERARY TRADITION
AND RECEPTION

Montague Summers's Fortune Press edition of Charlotte Dacre's Gothic novel *Zofloya*, published in 1928, brought to a crisis the pornographic reputation that had shadowed Dacre's novel since its initial publication in 1806. Summers is well known to scholars of the Gothic for his early studies, *The Gothic Quest* and *A Gothic Bibliography*.[1] What is not generally known is that, in 1934, Summers's Fortune Press translations of Sinistrari's *Demoniality* (1927) and *The Confessions of Madeleine Bavent* (1933) were seized and condemned under England's Obscene Publications Act. A total of eighteen Fortune Press texts were ordered destroyed in 1935, including Summers's above-mentioned translations, the well-known *Don Leon* erroneously attributed to Byron, and novels by Huysmans and Louÿs. The magistrate who ruled the books obscene declared that:

The majority of the books which came before me are of a kind which no publishers of reputation would dream of associating with their names. I regard the action of the police in this case as a public duty, and I think they would be doing a public service if they keep an eye on similar publications.[2]

It seems that *Zofloya* was not one of the eighteen books destroyed, though it may very well have been among the more than one hundred "books, papers, writings, prints, pictures and drawings" seized during the raid.[3] What is certain is that *Zofloya* is at home among the heretical and perverse assemblage published by the Fortune Press, and in particular among Montague Summers's encyclopedic taxonomies of demonology, sadism, and the Gothic.[4] The magistrate's tone of moral outrage in 1935 is identical to that of Dacre's sternest critics in 1806, and is not unrelated to the impatience or dissatisfaction on the part of some modern critics with her work's contradictory moral codes. Yet what wonderful company to be among the decadent Louÿs and Huymans for a writer like Dacre, so clearly at ease in the decadent and surrealist traditions, which themselves hearken back to the works of Sade and Lewis.

We need to read Dacre in this (ostensibly male) tradition of pornographic and sensationalist literature, a tradition in which she consciously situated her works, in order to appreciate the full significance of her fatal women figures and her focus on corporeal pleasure and destruction. The femme fatale characters in Dacre's best-known novel, *Zofloya; or, The Moor*, and in her last novel, *The Passions* (1811), are unique in women's writing of the Romantic period, and yet have much in common with the heroines of Sade and Lewis. Dacre herself chose as her pen name "Rosa Matilda," a clear reference to the femme fatale of Lewis's *The Monk*, Rosario/Matilda, a novel that Dacre admired and revised in *Zofloya* with a female protagonist. Her conscious and public alliance with Lewis's demonic woman complicates any unproblematic reliance on the moralistic elements throughout her works, where she urges readers to follow sexually conservative and even misogynist prescriptions in order to avoid the dangers of sexual indiscretion. Even Sade in his introduction to *The Crimes of Love* (1800) half-heartedly declared his purpose to be morally edifying: "I wish people to see crime laid bare, I want them to fear it and detest it, and I know no other way to achieve this end than to paint it in all its horror."[5]

Dacre's unusual life offers us some insights into the controversial female characters throughout her works. Charlotte Dacre[6] (b. Charlotte King, *c.* 1772–1825) was the daughter of the famous Jewish self-made banker, writer, and supporter of radical causes Jonathan King (1753–1824), and his first wife, Deborah, whom he divorced in 1785 to marry a countess. Known as the "Jew King," John King was a visible figure in London society, "had direct dealings with Godwin, Byron and Shelley," and "displayed a long record of political opposition."[7] Interestingly, John King also had financial dealings with Mary Robinson's husband, and was rumored to have had an affair with her.[8]

John King's financial involvements and lawsuits were well publicized throughout the 1790s, meaning that his daughter had first-hand experience of the print media's considerable power. In works such as *Oppression Deemed No Injustice* (1798?) and *Mr. King's Apology; or, a Reply to His Calumniators* (1798), King detailed his lawsuits for libel, bankruptcy, and other financial misdealings with a passionate sense of the injustices committed against him by opportunists and blackmailers. King's sense of utter alienation as a Jew in London, "alone, isolated and abandoned" after his publicized bankruptcy, must have fueled his daughter's ambition (and indeed necessity) to become financially independent, and to obtain the "privileges of citizenship." "The rights of nativity and the privileges of citizenship afford no advantage of alleviation," he wrote; "like a being of another nature, the dignity of humanity is lost."[9] Dacre's writing would be peopled with such figures, "beings of another nature" who have moved beyond human dignity and into extreme emotional and physical states.

Dacre must have been accustomed from an early age to scandal and controversy, not least because of her father's radical political associations. King had financially supported the defendants in the 1794 Treason Trials, and had been an early ally of Fox and Paine, though he recanted his Paineite republicanism and associations with radicals like Holcroft in subsequent writings.[10] In 1798, the year in which Charlotte and her sister Sophia began publishing their volumes of poetry and novels, John King was charged with sexually assaulting two women.[11] Charlotte and Sophia King's volume of verse, *Trifles from Helicon*[12] appeared in the spring of 1798, shortly before the sex scandal broke but after King's bankruptcy had already made his name notorious. In that same year, he had confessed that he "was obliged to write for bread," another lesson which it seems his daughters learned through adversity.[13] Charlotte and Sophia dedicated their volume to King, thanking him for the education with which he had provided them, and demonstrating their allegiance to their embattled father. Yet in July 1798 they had to endure another scandal, this time charges that King had sexually assaulted two prostitutes, who later withdrew the charges in a storm of controversy. 1798 was the last year in which Charlotte published under her father's name. No doubt the sex crime scandal was the final straw, leading her to assume the pseudonyms Charlotte Dacre and Rosa Matilda, the names by which she was best known to her contemporaries. Yet scandals would continue to follow Dacre, partly of her own making because of her writing's overt eroticism, and her risky self-promotion as a writer of such morally questionable and profitable literature.

Dacre's novels and poems often take up the theme of women abandoned by unfaithful partners, as it appears her mother was by her father, yet Dacre's own marriage in 1815 appears to have occurred after a lengthy affair with a married man. Charlotte King, "spinster," married the Tory editor of *The Morning Post*, Nicholas Byrne,[14] in 1815, yet their children seem to have been born long before this date.[15] Charlotte Byrne died in 1825 at the age of 53, thus placing her birth in 1771 or

1772, ten years earlier than what her own prefatory remarks indicated in her 1805 volume of poetry, *Hours of Solitude*, when she gave her age as 23.

Placing Dacre on a political spectrum, given her texts and what little we know about her life, yields conflicting results. Her father's scandals and (inconsistent) radical politics, her own status as outsider because Jewish, and her long-term illicit relationship might suggest sympathy for liberal politics and political outsiders (and, indeed, she published many poems in the radical *Telegraph* in the 1790s). Yet later poems such as "On the Death of the Right Honorable William Pitt" (1806),[16] in which Pitt is elevated to "a Saint in Heaven," and passages in *The Passions* which attack contemporary feminists such as Wollstonecraft, suggest that Dacre was politically conservative and no feminist. Yet, as we have seen in previous chapters, class and political differences within the category woman often mattered much more than the category of gender itself, thus Dacre's rejection of liberal and reformist politics in the public sphere need not (and does not) coincide with an acceptance of the ideology of women's domesticity and passionlessness.

Rather than lament our lack of access to Dacre's "true" intentions, I suggest we use her relative anonymity as a test case for examining how gendered readings, especially gender-complementary ones, to a large extent depend on an author's biography and their sex, and therefore in a sense reproduce a circular argument as to what constitutes a woman's text (or a "female Gothic"). How would we read *Zofloya*, for example, if we did not know the sex of the author, much less whether or not she identified herself as a (proto)feminist? I believe that readers of Dacre's novel, past and present, would have assumed the author to be male if *Zofloya* had been published anonymously or with a male pseudonym, as readers had done with more famous examples such as *Frankenstein* and *Wuthering Heights*.

In its review of *Zofloya*, *The Annual Review* was distressed by this dissonance between the sexual content of Dacre's novel and Dacre's sex, lamenting that the "principal personages in these wild pages are courtezans of the lewdest class, and murderers of the deepest dye," and concluding that

[t]here is a voluptuousness of language and allusion, pervading these volumes, which we should have hoped, that the delicacy of a female pen would have refused to trace; and there is an exhibition of wantonness of harlotry, which we would have hoped, that the delicacy of the female mind, would have been shocked to imagine. (5 (1806), 542)

Not surprisingly, *Zofloya* sold well, not despite but probably because of its "voluptuousness of language" and "exhibition of wantonness," reaching two editions and inspiring a pirated chapbook, *The Daemon of Venice* (1810), as well as a French translation.[17] *Zofloya* also influenced Percy Bysshe Shelley's Gothic romances, *Zastrozzi* and *St. Irvyne*, and Medwin wrote that Dacre's novel had "quite enraptured" the young Shelley.[18]

Dacre's first novel, *The Confessions of the Nun of St. Omer* (1805), had been dedicated to Mathew Lewis, and reveled in the scandalous style and subject matter for which he was notorious. *Zofloya* took this association even further, rewriting *The Monk* into a woman's "outsider narrative," to use Kate Ferguson Ellis's term for the male Gothic's central preoccupation. Dacre's third novel, *The Libertine*, similarly focused on erotic adventures and parental irresponsibility, reached three editions and a translation, and was roundly denounced as "prurient trash" appealing solely to the "depraved" and "warped."[19]

Yet, later in the century, Algernon Swinburne admired Dacre's prose precisely because of the pornographic elements reviewers had disapproved of. Swinburne compared favorably "the remarkable romance of Zofloya" to Sade's *Justine* and *Juliette*:

> The action of the three volumes [of *Zofloya*] is concerned wholly with the Misfortunes of Virtue in the person of "the innocent Lilla" ... and the Prosperities of Vice in the person of "the fiendish Victoria," who ultimately succeeds in accomplishing the vivisection of virtue by hewing her amiable victim into more or less minute though palpitating fragments. (*Swinburne Letters*, V: 174–75)

The "Misfortunes of Virtue" and the "Prosperities of Vice" are, of course, the subtitles of Sade's novels *Justine* and *Juliette*, respectively. Swinburne clearly saw in Dacre's "remarkable work" a fusion of Sade's two novels: the libertine heroine Victoria, like Juliette, dismembered her "sister" Lilla in a Sadean "vivisection of virtue." And it is only fitting that *Zofloya* has continued to accumulate such pornographic associations, culminating in its republication by the controversial Fortune Press.

Following Swinburne's example of more than a century ago, I suggest that, rather than rely on our knowledge of Dacre's gender (as her reviewers had done) or her feminism – in other words, on our assumptions of what makes a "woman's" text or a "female Gothic" text – we recontextualize Dacre within the tradition she was writing in and against, namely that of Lewis and Sade, in order to configure a more complex relationship between women writers and "masculine" discourses. For, although her antiheroines may fail by traditional feminist standards (e.g., they are punished, and do not establish a stable, subversive subject position), they do succeed in Sadean terms, as Swinburne says of Victoria: she "ultimately succeeds in accomplishing the vivisection of virtue."

Ultimately, then, it is not any subversive intention in Dacre's work that is of interest, but the subversive effect in the pleasure she clearly takes, and her fatal women clearly take, in the vivisection of virtue. Dacre, like Austen and Wollstonecraft, clearly warns her readers against the dangers of excessive sensibility in women, a task that R. F. Brissenden argues Austen shares with Sade.[20] Yet, unlike Austen and Wollstonecraft, Dacre does not attempt to persuade through reason or moral example, but rather to demonstrate a doctrine of destruction strikingly similar to Sade's. The critical difference between persuasion and demonstration is delineated by Deleuze in *Masochism: Coldness and Cruelty*, where he successfully disconnects the mechanisms of sadism and masochism, and rejects the complementary hybrid "sado-masochism" which has been anachronistically misapplied to Sade and Sacher-Masoch. Deleuze writes that, if we understand Sade correctly, we expect no instruction from him, because

the intention to convince [in Sade] is merely apparent, for nothing is in fact more alien to the sadist than the wish to convince, to persuade, in short to educate. He is interested in something quite different, namely to demonstrate that reasoning itself is a form of violence, and that he is on the side of violence, however calm and logical he may be ... The point of the demonstration is to show that the demonstration is identical to violence. (18–19)

Dacre by no means demonstrates, in Adorno and Horkheimer's words, "the identity of domination and reason"[21] that Sade obsessively pursues. However, she abandons persuasion for the morally questionable task of describing in erotically charged terms irrational, vicious, and violent behavior in women: Dacre demonstrates the identity of passion and destruction, and the pleasures found in both.

CHARLOTTE DACRE'S POETRY

And if it is in death that the spirit becomes free, in the manner of spirits, it is not until then that the body too comes properly into its own.

Walter Benjamin, *The Origin of German Tragic Drama*

Charlotte Dacre's work is unusual in its excesses, even among Gothic writers, but it shares with the other women writers we have seen thus far a powerful resistance to gender-complementary models of Romanticism and the Gothic. Specifically, Dacre's use of the demon lover motif throughout her two-volume collection of poetry, *Hours of Solitude*, demonstrates that women writers of the Romantic period held more complex and positive views of the body and sexuality than modern readers might assume, and that they imagined heroines with desires as dark as any Gothic villain's.

All work on the demon lover in the Romantic period shares the often tacit assumption that the demon lover is a preoccupation of male writers. But, because Charlotte Dacre's work has more in common with the dark imaginations of Lewis and Sade than with those of other women writers, her demon lovers resist this assumption, and the circular argument on which it is based: namely, that women were not interested in the demon lover because this figure, whether male or female, represents an essentially masculine obsession with male punishment of defiant women, or with the danger posed to men by the otherness of femininity.[22] Rather than limiting the demon lover to such sociological or psychological functions, I suggest that we also recontextualize the demon lover within late eighteenth-century competing discourses on the body and on imagination, and on the ability of each to deform the other.

In Romantic-period discourses warning of corporeal deformation – in the animated undead body, the unsexed body, and the nymphomaniacal body – we can also glimpse the era's realization that bodies are not immutable or naturally fixed. In each of these discourses on the body (whether undead, unsexed, or diseased), women are typically assumed to be the objects or victims of male imagination and knowledge, never the subjects. Charlotte Dacre's poetry in *Hours of Solitude* offers an important example of women writers' subtle evocations of bodies that may escape our modern criteria of how human bodies and sexualities are typically represented. In Dacre's poetry we can glimpse an imagined potential for corporeal transformation in the above-mentioned misogynist discourses on deformation.

Dacre's demon lovers and revenants in these poems are remarkably diverse, ranging from the ghost of Mary Robinson that the speaker summons to haunt her, to sensual explorations of love beyond the grave, to a female revenant who returns not to destroy but to warn the future female victim that her lover is a vampyre. The "self-conscious fleshliness" of Dacre's poetry, to use Jerome McGann's apt description, associated her with the earlier Della Cruscan school of poetry that had come under attack as excessively effeminate and sensual (and republican).[23] Byron's famous attack of Dacre's poetry as "prose in masquerade" in *English Bards and Scotch Reviewers*, and of her as a late Della Cruscan "straggler," are examples of how her contemporaries associated her with this discredited group.[24] *Hours of Solitude* contains numerous such amorous poems, some in an exchange between "Rosa Matilda" and a "gentleman" named "AZOR," intended to revive the Della Cruscan tradition of erotic poetic correspondences. Yet the Azor poems are most likely Dacre's own (Azor is Rosa said in reverse), a sign of her self-conscious approach to her poetic predecessors. Her supernatural poems also display a similarly canny approach to poetic traditions, with Gothic ballads written "in humble imitation of the soaring flights of some legendary and exquisitely pathetic modern Bards" like Coleridge and Lewis – imitations of imitations.[25] Dacre's numerous poems of demon lovers and revenants include: "Death and the Lady," "The Skeleton Priest; or, the Marriage of Death," "To the Shade of Mary Robinson," "The Lover's Vision," "The Power of Love," "The Doubt," "The Musing Maniac," "The Apparition," and "The Aerial Chorus; or, The Warning." *Hours of Solitude* also includes an unusual series of poems about anthropomorphic natural forces, which are given emotional, sometimes erotic, properties: "Fog," "Will-O'-Wisp," "Mildew," "Wind," "Frost," "Thaw." But her most evocative Gothic poetic texts are the two versions of "The Mistress to the Spirit of Her Lover," one in Ossianic prose and the other in verse, both of them uncanny precursors of *Wuthering Heights*.

Undead bodies

In *Perils of the Night*, Eugenia DeLamotte argues that "the central dilemma of Gothic romancers" is exemplified in the way "their images of transcendence have a disconcerting way of reverting to images of mortality even as one contemplates them" (141). Though DeLamotte is concerned with boundaries of the self in her study, one can also consider this oscillation between transcendence and collapse of boundaries in terms of boundaries between and within bodies. By bodies and their boundaries I mean more than bodies as naturally occurring, coherent entities which symbolize social or psychological relations between distinct subjects (e.g., the penetration of the villain's body into the heroine's representing his violation of her integrity, rights, safety, etc., a worthwhile and often-examined theme). Rather, I want to consider the social construction of materiality itself, keeping in mind that "what constitutes the fixity of the body, its contours, its movements, will be fully material, but materiality will be rethought as the effect of power, as power's most productive effect" (*Bodies*, 2). The unstable and indefinable body of the demon lover will in fact illustrate Judith Butler's contention that "materialization is never quite complete, [and] ... bodies never quite comply with the norms by which their materialization is impelled" (*Bodies*, 2).

The material instability of demon lovers and revenants (especially in the latter's decay) can be read as a symbol of the inability of the transcendent Romantic imagination to grasp the supernatural and the noumenal. But we can just as easily focus on the *ability* of these beings to transform themselves, most significantly their bodies, rather than on their inability to maintain material cohesion, and thus look at corporeal transformation as more than a metaphor for failed spiritual transcendence. Rather than embodying the noumenal, the supernatural demon lover or revenant embodies the phenomenal nature of all bodies, and this is most clear in the disturbing ease with which these mysterious figures change their shape, their size, and their sex. Thus, in addition to being an allegory of the "soul's immensity" and its desire to transgress all boundaries, as DeLamotte would argue,[26] the demon lover is also the embodiment of the radical potential of all *bodies*, not just selves, to lose cohesion, organization, and even materiality as it is usually understood (as a naturally occurring, fixed state), and to perform material transformations. The decomposition of the living corpse, the immateriality of the phantom lover, and the often elemental composition (e.g., made of water or mist) of the demon lover, all attest to the volatile nature of bodies as they verge from degeneration to regeneration in an ongoing process of transformation.

The demon lover can grow immense, a transformation often read as an allegory of spiritual transcendence, though in the anonymous poem "The Bleeding Nun," based on the episode in *The Monk*, we have an opportunity to read this physical transformation literally, that is, corporeally.[27] Raymond, thinking he speaks to his lover, unintentionally binds himself to the reanimated corpse of the Bleeding Nun with his vow that "Thou art mine, and I am thine, / Body and soul for ever!" The supernatural nature of the materialized Bleeding Nun is beyond the threshold of Raymond's perception because he imagines her to be his living lover, Agnes. Thus he easily "bore her in his arms away," and yet, when he finally becomes aware of her supernatural, "ghastly, pale, and dead" nature, she is suddenly "A form of more than mortal size." The horrifying outcome of Agnes' masquerade as a murderous and sexually transgressive ghost attests to the ability of all women's bodies to metamorphose into unnatural (because unfemininely large) bodies through the enactment of unnatural desires. Raymond is paralyzed with fear as his lover's body, no longer the diminutive object of his desire, becomes the monstrous subject of its own unnatural desires. The touch of the living corpse with its rotting fingers introduces decay and impotence[28] into Raymond's body, making the danger of the undead and demonic decidedly corporeal. Raymond's horror is indicative of the age's anxiety over (and also delight in) the disruptive potential of bodies, and women's bodies in particular, to exceed the boundaries of the natural.

The story of the Bleeding Nun is also, of course, symbolic of male fear of women's sexual agency and aggression. The sexually transgressive behavior of revenants, vampyres, and demon lovers, because they are typically incestuous, necrophilic, sadistic, or homosexual, is noted by all who write on the subject as an expression of the writer's dissatisfaction with the sexually repressive legacy of Christianity.[29] But like the reading of the ability to grow immense as a spiritual allegory, the reading of the demon lover solely as fantasy of sexual transgression ignores the corporeal dimensions of transgression. Thus, the Bleeding Nun's immense size, like the unusually large and unfeminine size of the female creature in *Frankenstein* and of Dacre's antiheroine Victoria in *Zofloya*, is not a metaphor for but a *materialization* of her unnatural, because unfeminine, desires and actions. And, as Robert Miles notes, "Victoria's career is a rewriting of the story of the Bleeding Nun,"[30] thus connecting Dacre's portrait of a murderous woman even more closely to the corporeal anomaly her textual ancestor embodies. The Bleeding Nun (and Dacre's Victoria) achieves the stature of Burke's sublime, becoming "vast in [her] dimensions," and inspiring "Strength, violence, pain, and terror,"[31] in Burke's words, much like a revolutionary heroine or a Robinsonian feminist who insists on the right to resent and punish.

Sexed and unsexed bodies

The physical metamorphoses enjoyed by demon lovers in Gothic texts should be considered in the larger context of late eighteenth-century theories of natural difference. While the two-sex model of complementary difference between men and women gained credibility throughout the eighteenth century, this epistemological shift did not eliminate the older one-sex model. Given the unresolvable conflict between the one-sex and two-sex models that Laqueur has delineated, Polwhele's *The Unsex'd Females*, typically read as evidence of the era's deterministic insistence on natural sexual difference, could be read as testimony to the instability of the two-sex model. To unsex a woman as Polwhele did Wollstonecraft and Hays, is not to make her a man by simply reversing rigid gender polarities. To be an unsexed female, a monstrous "hyaena in petticoats"[32] like Wollstonecraft, is to be notfemale. The notfemale is neither male nor a utopian androgynous third sex, but like the hermaphrodite suggested by the hyena, the notfemale points to the limits of the two-sex model even within the minds of its most passionate advocates. The unsexed, like the undead, remain undefinable in the natural order, making all distinctions between the sexes and between living and dead problematic.

The Enlightenment had naturalized sexuality, seeing it not so much as part of a religious moral economy, but as part of "the economy of Nature."[33] Anomalies such as the unsexed and the hermaphrodite fascinated Enlightenment taxonomists because of the challenge they posed to this natural order. Despite an increased tolerance for "natural" sexual expression (reserved for the most part for straight men), Enlightenment sexuality was restricted in its very naturalness, since nature was typically imagined as benevolent, beautiful and ordered. Hence the sexuality of working-class people, servants, homosexuals, and children, because it often exceeded the boundaries of the decorous and (re)productive, often figured (in medical or conduct literature, for example) as potentially threatening to this "natural sexuality" enjoyed with unprecedented openness by many straight men. But women's sexuality became increasingly disruptive of the bourgeois social order during this time precisely because it threatened to disturb this "natural" order within the individual bourgeois subject herself, and within her supposedly natural body. Dacre's evident interest in extreme states of passion, bordering on madness, and her exploration of women's unnatural and supernatural experiences, need to be examined within this larger cultural debate regarding natural desire, its function, and its perversion.

As Dacre understood, "the *source* of sexual feeling" for women, and hence the entry point of disorder, was imagination.[34] Bienville's *Nymphomania, or, A Dissertation Concerning the Furor Uterinus*,[35] the first medical treatise devoted to this condition, insists that the imagination is the source both of female sexual pleasure and disorder, and devotes an entire section to the subject: "Observations on the Imagination, As connected with the *Nymphomania*." According to G. S. Rousseau, *Nymphomania* is significant because "Bienville rejects an entirely mechanistic view of the nervous system and... argues that the brain and imagination influence each other in some reciprocal but unspecified way."[36] Bienville warns throughout his text that, because "the imagination is the source of [the nymphomaniac's] disorder" (and the perusal of novels frequently the catalyst), it must also be the source of the cure: "there are cases which will admit of a cure from a simple attention to the imagination; but there are no cases (or, at least, scarcely any) in which physical remedies can alone effect a radical cure. There is no constitution without a germ of this natural generative fire" (*Nymphomania*, 112, 160).

Bienville's text, like Dacre's works as a whole, encompasses the contradictory claims regarding sexual difference that Laqueur described. Bienville argues that women's sexuality is natural (and that "Marriage alone cures" nymphomania) and that its suppression is "capable of... causing a revolution, and disorder in the physical system of their nature," while simultaneously emphasizing "the fragility of [women's] nature," their greater vulnerability to their distinctly sexualized body, and even the inhuman and sinister qualities of their bodies (he compares the cervix to a dog's muzzle and the womb's ligaments to bat wings) (*Ibid.*, 107, 160, vii). Thus, despite his assurance of the naturalness of women's sexuality, the competing claims of difference compel Bienville to exclaim that "these monsters in human shape abandon themselves to an excess of fury" (*Ibid.*, 37).

Nymphomania combines medical discourse with sensationalistic case histories, and is directed not to other physicians, but to parents and educators of young women, whom Bienville enlists as "secret physicians." Bienville appealed to a lay middle-class audience, and, judging by his subsequent influence on literary reviewers of the Gothic, he seems to have reached this audience, as we shall see. The mixed medical/literary nature of his own discourse bridges the gap between medical and literary discourses with which modern readers are more familiar.[37] Dacre's literary reworking of such misogynist medical discourse offers an instructive example of how women's imaginative representations of bodies can transcend the passionlessness or reticence often ascribed to them by modern critics.

Bienville describes nymphomania in lurid detail as an "incredible... metamorphosis" that "can debase, afflict, and as it were unhumanize" women, and, like Foucault (who discussed his work), argues that the ultimate danger in nymphomania is social disorder through corporeal disorder: "it is from this general overthrow of all their relations to each other, that a delirium arises to destroy the order of ideas, and impels the person afflicted to affirm what she had denied, and to deny what she hath affirmed" (*Nymphomania*, 136, 186, 70). The "revolution... in the physical system" of women will thus lead to a revolution in female manners, to recall Wollstonecraft's expression (*Ibid.*, 160). In the third, "desperate" stage of nymphomania, which is accompanied by sexual aggression and violence toward men, the nymphomaniac "sinks into a state of perfect reconciliation with the powers of her body" and the body itself undergoes a physiological transformation, the brain's fibres becoming lax and penetrable by sensual desires, the clitoris growing "larger than in discreet women," and the reproductive organs swollen and infested with tapeworms, tumors, or abscesses (*Ibid.*, 70, 74, 80).

The nymphomaniac's physical metamorphosis shares with the undead body's animated decay a surrender of the proper subject to the power of the body. This body is not a proper, organized body, but a body without proper boundaries, like that of the revenant Alonzo the Brave in Lewis's ballad, through which "The worms they crept in, and the worms they crept out."[38] Women's imagination, unrestrained by reason and indulged by the "fatal rage of *Masturbation*,"[39] materializes as the hysterical, penetrable body that Foucault described as lacking a "*moral* density; the resistance of the organs to the disordered penetration of the spirits is perhaps one and the same thing as that strength of soul which keeps the thoughts and the desires in order."[40] Thus, the disorder experienced by the hysterical body in Dacre's writings is not the (Platonic) "revolution of the depths to the heights but a lawless whirlwind in a chaotic space,"[41] an apt description of the demon lover's body as it penetrates the body of its lover and begins to proliferate disorder.

In the prose version of Dacre's "The Mistress to the Spirit of Her Lover," the Mistress specifies that it is the imagination which allows her to give the spirit of her lover an ephemeral material cohesion. The absence initially encountered by her imagination bears a synecdochic relationship to the absence of all natural bodies:

Sometimes thy features seem to waver – it must be in the twilight, when all has a dubious shade; but I cannot always catch those loved features – *it appears to me as though they were fading wholly away; but suddenly, by an effort of the imagination, I again identify them*, and secretly determine never more to look off of them.[42]

Dacre's emphasis on imagination, transcendence, and the sublime (consistent themes throughout her works) is evidence that women Romantics did concern themselves with philosophical and poetic issues central to canonical Romanticism. But Dacre's use of the imagination, in this

corporeal context, falls outside the categories of Enlightenment imagination as dangerous illusion, and Romantic imagination as redemptive
vision.

The Mistress's imagination can be seen as a destructive, sexualized illusion that draws her to her death, much as one woman in Bienville's narrative admitted to being "seduced by the illusions of the imagination."[43]
At the same time, however, her imagination creates cohesion and syn-
thesizes identity. Imagination's relation to disorder is thus paradoxical,
taking place on the threshold of the Romantic redemption of Enlightenment imagination. G. S. Rousseau argues that, because Enlightenment
science's "promise of an organic marriage of the spiritual (imagination)
and the material (animal spirits, fibres, nerves)" was thwarted, "powerful minds like Coleridge [and] Wordsworth" were responsible for providing a "new phenomenology": "The diseased imagination was...ro-
manticised, endowed with an aura of glory it had never known."[44] But
Rousseau neglects to gender his assessment of the new Romantic ideology of the visionary imagination, for the diseased imagination remained
feminized, even in the works of feminists like Wollstonecraft.

The Mistress's imagination embodies the conflicted nature of Romantic imagination because of its debt to Enlightenment diseased imagination, and the poem foregrounds the role of gender in this conflict. Dacre's
poem is Romantic and visionary, yet the female gender of the speaker
allows for the possibility of reading the poem as an example of women's
diseased imagination. This contradictory reading is precisely why we
must resist any gender-complementary reading that would neatly resolve
the conflict (i.e., by arguing that women writers rejected a monolithic
"Romantic imagination").

Demonic bodies

The Mistress senses within her Lover the "lawless whirlwind in a chaotic
space" that Foucault ascribed to the hysterical body:

> That aerial form, which no atoms combine,
> Might dizzily sport down the abyss of death,
> Or tremble secure on the hazardous line.
> (*Hours*, 11: 34, 36)

The dizzying indeterminateness of the Lover threatens to engulf the
Mistress herself, yet she desires to share her Lover's remarkable ability

to tremble secure on the line between ostensibly distinct states, to enter and emerge from the abyss. In its subtitle, the Ossianic prose version of "The Mistress" provides us with a straightforward explanation for the Mistress's passionate visions of her dead Lover: "The Mistress to the Spirit of her Lover, Which, in the phrenzy occasioned by his loss, she imagined to pursue continually her footsteps." The Mistress has gone mad, a possibility she herself considers in the verse version of the poem: "Oh! Lover illusive, my senses to mock– / 'Tis madness presents if I venture to think." But we can do more than cite the Mistress's excessive desire for her lover as the cause of her madness. If we read passion according to Foucault, "as a chance for madness to penetrate the world of reason," then the Mistress's passion is more than a clinical explanation for her "delusion," since passion

laid...man open...to the infinite movement that destroyed him. Madness, then, was not merely one of the possibilities afforded by the union of body and soul; it was not just one of the consequences of passion. Instituted by the unity of soul and body, madness turned against that unity and once again put it into question.[45]

The apparition of the Lover puts into question the unity of body and soul, for the Lover may be a reanimated body without soul, an immaterial soul, or neither. In the figure of the Lover, the Mistress glimpses the fragility and insufficiency of this unity, and of each half of the unity. Body and soul become stable entities in their own right, and only momentarily, through the effort of her imagination. She attempts again and again to fix the true nature of her Lover, either body or soul or both, while experiencing him in an impossibly contradictory series of senses: corporeal, immaterial, aural, imaginary, celestial, demonic, elemental.

The most remarkable aspect of the Lover is his liminal quality. Appearing at twilight, when the Gothic's powers to disturb Enlightenment clarity are at their height, the figure of the Lover is in a constant state of flux and inhabits a threshold:

> Ah! wilt thou not *fall* from that edge of the steep?
> The pale moon obliquely shines over the lake;
> The shades are deceptive, below is the deep,
> And I see thy fair form in its clear waters shake.
>
> (*Hours*, II: 35)

The Lover trembles and hovers above the hills and beneath the water, "speaks in a low murmuring voice": he is the embodiment of perpetual motion and indistinctness. Dacre's poetry contains many similar supernatural figures, usually male and made of mist, rain, shadow, fog, or light, which have a characteristic physical indistinctness that deliberately invokes the sublime.[46]

The Mistress, rather than fearing this fatal lover drawing her toward destruction, desires this indistinctness and the indistinguishable pain and pleasure that his presence brings her: "Follow me, follow me over the earth; / Ne'er leave me, bright shadow, wherever I rove.... / Thou formest my pleasure, thou formest my pain" (*Hours*, ii: 34). In the prose version, the Mistress's description of her dead Lover as a "Vision of beauty" celebrates his physical beauty: his "heavenly form" is "habited in robes of mist, and his silvery hair undulates upon the gale" (*Hours*, ii: 31). He has a distinctly Luciferan air, being both "luminous" and "celestial," yet having a "shadowy form" that leads the Mistress to ask, "Art thou from earth or from heaven exil'd?" She finds this dangerous mixture irresistible even though, or perhaps because, his beauty carries the taint of death and physical decay which connects his materiality to natural forces: "sometimes me thinks upon my glowing cheek I feel thy breath, but it is cold and damp" (*Hours*, ii: 32).

She desires to mingle her living body with his (undead) body, and draws his body into her own in a demonic version of inspiration: "I respire eagerly the bleak breeze that passes over thy dubious form; I inhale it with ardent, melancholy delight, for it is impregnated with thy spirit" (*Hours*, ii: 32–33). The demonic nature of their physical interpenetration lies not merely in his "dubious" nature, alluding to the infernal origin of traditional demon or revenant lovers. The bleak breeze carrying the spirit of the dead is an allusion to the physical and social threat that the decomposing body brings to the living, which is one basis of traditional vampyre and revenant legends. What is remarkable about the Mistress's response is that she respires eagerly the pestilential air, inviting the disorder of the plague into her body in order to share the indeterminate undead state of her Lover. She both recreates and maintains his incoherent physical presence outside her by an effort of the imagination, and draws this mingled Life-in-Death into herself, becoming "impregnated" by an immaterial spirit in order to bring about the eventual destruction of her own physical integrity as she nears the edge of the abyss. Their passionate union will in fact bring about dissolution of all "natural" unities.

Thus, their final embrace in the verse version is much more than the Mistress's symbolic self-destruction – it is self-transformation. In the embrace of the living and the undead is the possibility of transforming the "natural" living body into a supernatural body:

> Lo! see thy dim arms are extending for me;
> Thy soul then exists, comprehends, and is mine;
> The life now is ebbing which mine shall set free;
> Ah! I feel it beginning to mingle with thine.
>
> (Hours, ii: 36)

Traditionally, the fatal lover draws the hapless heroine toward death, which is one possible reading of the poem's conclusion. Yet it is the Mistress who desires to mingle with the Lover in an embrace suggestive of both necrophilia and sexual ecstasy, and it is her own generative imagination that empowers the Lover to take shape and beckon to her. Dacre's poem "Edmund and Anna" contains a more traditional version of a heroine's suicide upon the death of her lover, which ends, however, in an even more explicitly sexual embrace of death: "'Dear Edmund, I come,' She stretches her arms out, and dies!" (*Hours*, ii: 140). It is as such a unity of eros and thanatos that most critics characterize the demon lover's transgressive erotic power, but this eros/thanatos unity is typically thought to appeal solely to the male imagination, and to function as a threat in women's imaginations. Yet this unnatural mingling of the living and the undead is on one level also a coded version of female sexual pleasure and agency, for, as in *Zofloya*, the Mistress herself conjures up the object of her affection, the demon lover, and urges him to pursue her, reversing the familiar trajectory of male desire.

The Mistress has little in common with the trusting victims of the demon lover ballads who are horrified to discover their lovers' supernatural state.[47] Like "Rosa Matilda" who took the name of the era's most famous demon lover, the Mistress identifies with the demonic figure itself. The Mistress' despair is clearly due to her inability to be certain of her Lover's material or spiritual presence; yet part of her pleasure in seeing him arises from his very indistinctness, and her pain from her own increasing desire to become like him, rather than for him to become like her. Thus her cry to this "wild spirit" is one both of despair and envy:

> Oh! vain combination! – oh! embodied mist!
> I dare not to lean on thy transparent form;
> I dare not to clasp thee, tho' sadly I list –
> Thou would'st vanish, wild spirit, and leave me forlorn.
>
> (Hours, ii: 35)

In "To the Shade of Mary Robinson," Dacre makes this same gesture of identification toward the spirit of the poet she admired, asking "why not, sometimes, in thy form light and airy, / Deign in the deep wild my

companion to be?" (*Hours*, 1: 132). Conscious of Robinson's influence
on her own poetry, Dacre also uses the demon lover as poetic muse (as
male Romantics did), celebrating Robinson's poetic talents in a poem
that also reads as the lover lamenting and invoking the beloved to, "when
I wander in sadness, Glide distant before me" (*Ibid.*).

Dacre's fascination with the indistinct or unbounded nature of bodies
is not limited to supernatural figures. In Dacre's poem "Tu es beau
comme le desert, avec toutes ses fleurs et toutes ses brises," the speaker
describes her male lover much as the Mistress described her phantom
lover:

> Thy perfect form, of atoms pure combin'd,
> Fair habitation for a lovely soul,
> Seeming too much for mortal clay refin'd,
> Such bright effulgence mantles thro' the whole.
>
> (*Hours*, 11: 71–72)

Dacre's work resounds with such subtly erotic celebrations of the
beloved's body, which emerge from the poetry if one begins to read
for different types of natural bodies, not just human bodies. Comparing
the "perfect form" of the male beloved to a natural body – a desert full
of flowers and scents – is not a euphemistic or hesitant gesture, but one
that breaks down barriers between types of bodies and explores their
interconnections. As the speaker contemplates the body of her beloved,
she identifies with and is drawn into him much as the Mistress had been:
"from me my impassion'd soul does steal, / As anxious to identify with
thine!" Though clearly on one level a coded reference to sexual ecstasy
(being literally outside oneself), this process of identification with the
lover is also a process of transformation through the agency of scent and
wind:

> Ambrosial air doth ever thee surround
> Thy proper atmosphere – its pow'r I feel
> With such strange influence as persuades me well,
> *Near* me thou com'st, tho' sight may not reveal.
>
> (*Hours*, 11: 72)

As with the Mistress' supernatural lover, this lover's "strange influence"
emanates beyond the boundaries of his body, and in fact draws the
speaker outside the boundaries of her own. His physical presence is not
bounded by the visible outline of his body, for she senses the power of
his physical presence even when she cannot see him. The light ("bright
effulgence"), scent, and air that emanate from the male beloved are also

found in supernatural figures, and thus both natural and supernatural bodies in these poems share a similar fluidity and ability to transcend ostensibly natural boundaries.

If in our rediscovery of writing by women Romantics we wish to read for their thoughts on the body and on sexuality, we need thus to begin to read differently, to allow for representations of bodies that may be beyond the threshold of our current assumptions of what constitutes the corporeal. We would do well to apply to women Romantics' representations of bodies the advice the Wandering Jew gave to Raymond about the Bleeding Nun's body: "Though to you only visible for one hour in the twenty-four, neither day nor night does she ever quit you."[48]

"I hasten to be disembodied": Dacre and Wuthering Heights

The body is more than the acultural object of the mind's repression and discipline; as Foucault argued, the sexed body is a constructed "artificial unity [of] anatomical elements, biological functions, conducts, sensations, and pleasures,"[49] both a product and an agent of power, as well as a site of resistance. Dacre's redirection of male medical discourse is a good example of Foucault's point that resistance is "formed right at the point where relations of power are exercised,"[50] not where power is "absent." The Romantic period's conflicted notions of the imagination represent a particularly complex understanding of the interplay within the mind/body binary, in which bodies are both objects of repression and production, as well as agents in their own right. The imaginative faculty can in fact productively alter the shape, nature, and powers of the body, and can therefore in a sense materialize. But the body can therefore also dematerialize and rematerialize as it performs actions and acquires qualities that place it outside the threshold of normative materiality, and as different criteria of corporeal coherence are applied. And, as Bienville warned, the degeneration of the body completes the vicious circle as the body sinks into unbridled pleasures and further exacerbates the imagination.

The degeneration of the nymphomaniac's internal organs parallels the decay of the living corpse – both bodies are in the process of rematerializing as something else. The primacy and identity of each category, mind and body, are therefore impossible to sustain, as is the stable relation between them. Even when the Mistress determines that the apparition does possess her lover's true soul, exclaiming that, "Thy soul then exists, comprehends, and is mine," she is no longer in possession of her own soul. The act of mutual possession is one of mutual displacement, as in the case of Raymond and the Bleeding Nun, and Heathcliff and Cathy; if his soul is hers, then her soul must be his.

Heathcliff makes the same gesture forty years later in *Wuthering Heights* when he is no longer able to live with his soul in the grave. Indeed, Dacre's poem bears an uncanny resemblance to Brontë's novel. The Mistress's affinity for the demon lover is shared by Cathy, for, as Peter Grudin argues in *The Demon-Lover*, "[a]s Catherine and Heathcliff exchange roles, it is she who assumes that of the demon-lover," and this role exchange "symbolizes the final dissolution of the barriers between insider and outsider" (142, 152). Heathcliff's desire to be haunted by his lover is identical to the Mistress's, and the last lines of Dacre's prose poem are prophetic of Heathcliff's necrophilic attempt to mingle with Cathy's decomposing body, and of the legend of the two lovers haunting the moors:

Soon will... *my* soul too be free. My body, which is of concentrated atoms, shall lie by thine in the narrow grave, which it will not deny me to share with it; and then together shall our spirits wander over the mountains, or re-visit the scenes of our youth. (*Hours*, II: 33)

J. Hillis Miller argues that what haunts the center of *Wuthering Heights* is not the presence of original union between lover and beloved, but the absence of this union, an argument that applies to Dacre's poem as well:

This ghostly glimpse [of an original union between lovers] is a projection outward of a oneness from a state of twoness within. This duality is within the self, within the relation of the self to another, within nature, within society, and within language. (*Fiction*, 68)

I would add to this list the lack of unity within the body, and within the relation of the mind or soul to the body. Thus the Mistress's dream of disembodied spirits reunited, and united in themselves, functions like the traces of original union in *Wuthering Heights* – they are a manifestation of the absence of such a natural unity in experience. The Mistress, like Heathcliff, sees in the dubious form that haunts her "a faint resemblance unto the charms of my beloved," a trace of his presence in a world where presence is always mediated and constructed "by an effort of the imagination."

Like the Mistress, the speaker in Dacre's "Song of Melancholy," as in many of the demon lover poems, is clearly suicidal: "I come, I come, gloomy shadows! I hasten to be disembodied!" (*Hours*, II: 65–67). Yet we can also say that their desire to be disembodied, like Heathcliff's, speaks of more than the soul being liberated from the prison-house of flesh. To be disembodied from the "natural" body leaves open options other than being an immortal soul. The speaker who hastens to be disembodied, whose "days are a dim mist," could share the indeterminate threshold state of an unsexed female, of the "unhumanized" nymphomaniac. These bodies, like Dacre's supernatural figures which her narrators embrace,[51] are defined by what they are not, they are placed at the boundaries of the human or the female. The very persistence of unsexed, undead, or otherwise unnatural bodies is a reminder that the nature of bodies is never stable. Whether feared or desired, and they are usually both, bodies outside the natural order attest to the supernatural powers that all bodies possess.

THE PASSIONS AND ZOFLOYA

Hopes at once dangerous, and absurd are, by these writings, instilled into her mind, and all her thoughts are fixed on sensuality.

Bienville, *Nymphomania*

Dacre's reformulation of corporeal discourses on female sexuality continues throughout her novels. *The Passions*, in particular, represents an expanded version of one of Bienville's narratives from *Nymphomania*, keeping the name of the protagonist Julia, while also connecting Bienville's story to Rousseau's *Julie, ou La Nouvelle Héloïse*. Dacre characteristically focuses her attention not on the innocent "victim" Julia, but on the corrupting antiheroine of the text, Appollonia, giving her Satanic aspirations and soliloquies that rival those of a Byronic hero, and leave her misogynist origins in Bienville and Rousseau far behind.

This unique "vivisection of virtue" that Dacre undertakes with such zeal in *Zofloya* and *The Passions* is conducted to an important extent on a corporeal level. In *The Confessions of the Nun of St. Omer* and *The Libertine*, Dacre explored the dangers of excessive sexual passion in titillating detail. I am particularly interested in *Zofloya* and *The Passions*, however, because in these novels Dacre takes the femme fatale figure to new heights of erotic explicitness and cultural significance. In both *Zofloya* and *The Passions*, Dacre uses a similar and popular narrative device of two complementary female characters, much like Sade's Justine and Juliette; most significant for the purpose of this discussion, however, is the degree to which these two types are embodied differently and, most interestingly, how one type of body, that of the proper woman, can degenerate into an unsexed, unfemale, and unnatural body through physical and emotional violence (passion being a form of inner violence).[52] Both the virtuous and the vicious body, Dacre repeatedly demonstrates, are dangerously mutable, and the catalyst for their degeneration is most often female sexual desire. Her portraits of destructive women leave neither vice nor virtue intact, but show how both categories, not just the "unnatural" one, are socially constructed, and similarly destroyed, through the infectious power of literature.

Because Dacre deals so often with complementary doubles, and because her femmes fatales could be interpreted as female versions of masculinist or misogynist stereotypes of improper women, we need to begin our discussion by examining the feminist debate regarding the questionable subversive value of such travesties of proper womanhood. I use the term travesties deliberately, because the debate regarding the value of the destructive female double overlaps with the debate over female transvestitism, and even hermaphroditism, in literature, and whether such gender inversion constitutes any meaningful subversion of gender polarity.[53]

The binary structure of this problem, with its either/or limitations (either subversive or normalizing) is itself a product of the binary system responsible for gender and sexual normalization. In contrast, my emphasis on the unresolvable conflict between the one-sex and the two-sex system as described by Laqueur, and between the healthy and diseased body in Bienville, attempts to establish a continuum of sexed bodies and subjects, which materialize and rematerialize, to use Butler's rather Gothic terminology, according to historically specific and shifting categories. This continuum also exists on a literary level, with writers like Dacre sharing more ground with Sade and Lewis than with other women writers, a phenomenon that I believe makes the labels "subversive" or "normalizing" unproductive for many women's writings of this period, as long as the status of gender (and sex) itself is left unexamined and assumed to be monolithic and stable. Thus, as previous chapters resisted the either/or choice regarding the subversive qualities of the femme fatale or the violent woman, this chapter will continue to critique this binary formulation itself.

Terry Castle's *Masquerade and Civilization* offers an excellent example of how criticism engaging with the subversion question can (and should) subvert the binary terms of the debate itself. Castle argues that masquerade and the carnivalesque were subversive for reasons specific to the Enlightenment and its privileging of hierarchically ordered categories, and cites contemporary opposition to the masquerade's "antitaxonomic energy" as evidence. Castle maintains that the ambiguity, not the simple role reversal, within masquerade is what was truly disturbing:

The masquerade...predicated the hallucinatory merging of self and other; it set up magical continuities between disparate bodies. Miraculous transmogrifications were symbolically enacted; the metamorphoses of dream and folklore became a temporary reality. (*Masquerade*, 101–2)

Though the atomizing ideology of bourgeois individualism was persistent and the ambiguity of the masquerade temporary, we should not underestimate the force of such ambiguity. Similarly, though the proper "natural" woman emerged as a distinct, pervasive norm by the end of the eighteenth century, we find in Gothic literature of the period countless examples that she existed alongside temporary anomalies, monsters, and phantoms. And the Gothic's preoccupation with decay and disintegration, so often read on a psychological or political level (like the demon lover), should also be read in terms of the anomalies that persisted after the sexes and genders had been supposedly fixed according to a binary model. Like eighteenth-century masquerade, Gothic literature was the focus of intense cultural monitoring, visible in the omnipresent turn-of-the-century debates about the socially subversive potential of women's reading, especially their reading of Gothic romances; the real danger presented by the Gothic's temporary anomalies (like masquerade's) is visible in the anxieties of its critics.

Castle qualifies her argument by emphasizing the temporary nature of masquerade's subversion; similarly, my argument for the subversive potential of Dacre's femmes fatales is qualified by the temporary success she allowed such transgressive characters, who are nonetheless punished at the narrative's end. Yet the exploits of such women momentarily reveal (to a large female audience)[54] the violent disorder of female subjectivity, and its violent repression by demonic masculinity, an accomplishment which according to Robert Miles lifts *Zofloya* "into the realm of critique" (*GW*, 188). Moreover, the outcomes of Dacre's narratives do not reestablish normative bourgeois morality, because most of her characters do not survive. The innocent and the guilty are alike destroyed, as the chapbook version of *Zofloya*, called *The Daemon of Venice* (1810), emphasized in its closing sentence: "Thus the precipice was the grave of two, the innocent Agnes [Lilla] and the wicked Arabella [Victoria]."[55] These temporary reversals of natural order and morality, and the lack of any moral restoration in the conclusions, were precisely what reviewers were anxious about when they dismissed her novels as prurient trash, capable of warping readers.

The contagious potential of Dacre's critique lies in the process of reading itself, in its controversial function in the production (and destruction) of subjects and even bodies. The danger of reading sentimental and Gothic fiction is a ubiquitous theme in the Romantic period, and it is a theme central to all of Dacre's novels, as well as to Bienville's *Nymphomania*. In fact, in 1802 the *Scots Magazine* had alluded directly to Bienville's treatise in its essay "On Novels and Romances," paraphrasing Bienville in its warning against "luxurious and voluptuous" Gothic romances such as *The Monk*:

If any thing further were required, in support of what is here said to be the consequences which result from an indiscriminate perusal of such books, the opinions of an author of a medical treatise lately published, might be referred to. While attending to the influence which the affections and passions of the mind are found to have on our system, he does not hesitate to say, that among the mournful passions, must be included an extravagant degree of love, and into which he says, young females particularly, are precipitated, merely, by reading improper novels.[56]

The *Literary Journal* had similarly warned in medical terms that Dacre's imagination (like the nymphomaniac's) is both diseased and infectious:

this malady of maggots in the brain is rendered still more dreadful by its being infectious. The ravings of persons under its influence, whenever they are heard or read, have a sensible effect upon the brains of a weak construction, which themselves either putrify or breed maggots, or suffer a derangement of some kind.[57]

The medical context this reviewer provides, albeit satirically, highlights Dacre's own exploration of the dangerous properties of imagination, and of nymphomania, in *Zofloya*. Dacre's "extravagant language," her "overwhelming all meaning in a multitude of words,"[58] marks an important intersection of medical and poetic discourses of passion and imagination. The extravagance of her language allows us to understand how these extreme states are experienced physiologically, psychologically, socially, and even supernaturally, and why they are both pleasurable and dangerous.

Significantly, Dacre gives her readers access to the pleasure felt by her vicious heroines as they set out to seduce and destroy; the narrator of *Zofloya* details the exquisite torments of passion, thwarted desire, and sadistic cruelty Victoria experiences, and the epistolary format of

The Passions allows us, like Rousseau's original text, to read the first-hand accounts of adulterous passion, and more importantly, of the Satanic Appollonia's passion to destroy. Such destructive female protagonists are rare in women's writing of this period (though they are, of course, common in this study), and represent an early female equivalent of the Romantic criminal artist figure later popularized by Byron, DeQuincey, and Percy Bysshe Shelley. More importantly, Dacre's critique exacerbates the contradictions both of fixed bourgeois subjectivity, more precisely women's subjectivity, and of corporeal stability. Through their revisions of already controversial works (*The Monk* and *La Nouvelle Héloïse*), Dacre's texts instruct women readers not only that women's sexual desires are capable of destroying both self and others, a conventional and often misogynist concept, but that the naturally asexual and domestic woman held up as the alternative ideal is as unnatural as her "degenerate" double.

Though the antiheroines in both Dacre's *Zofloya* and *The Passions* are punished and denounced as improper models for female behavior, both novels simultaneously and ambiguously instruct readers how to reach such depths of depravity. Thus, not only are such disturbing examples of female behavior allowed to flourish temporarily, but Dacre's novels celebrate the powers of the poisonous texts they claim to warn against. The prohibitions against novel reading in Dacre's own novels make transparent, or demystify, how normative sexuality and the normal female body are constructed through the exclusion of negative examples.

Dacre's dire warnings against Rousseau, that "sentimental luxurious libertine," are ultimately as prescriptive as they are prohibitive,[59] for Dacre rewrites Rousseau's text in even more lascivious terms, focusing in minute detail on Appollonia's decidedly sexual pleasure in destroying the virtuous Julia, as well as on Julia's and her lover's adulterous desires. For example, the antiheroine Appollonia celebrates her sexual corruption of the happily married Julia through the "sovereign poison" of books in such a way that Dacre's implicit warning against such novels, occurring in precisely such a voluptuous novel, amounts to an endorsement. The warning ensures that readers will, if they have not already done so, immediately seek out a copy of Rousseau's novel:

I know that there is not in the world a more subtle poison than that which is extracted from and administered by books...there is not in my estimation a more dangerous work extant, or one better calculated for the purposes of seduction [than *La Nouvelle Héloïse*]: for I defy the female, however pure in her heart, however chaste in her ideas she may be, *before* reading this book, to remain wholly unaffected, and unimpressed by its perusal. I aver that it is utterly impossible so many highly-coloured and voluptuous images as are there depicted, can be permitted to take their passage through the mind, and leave no stain behind. (*Passions*, 1: 207, 209–10)

One might argue that in deploying this familiar argument against women reading sentimental novels, Dacre perpetuates a misogynist concept of women's sexuality as dangerous, much as Bienville had done when he repeatedly warned against the "venomous" power of novels to unleash nymphomania in women: "The perusal of a novel, a voluptuous picture . . . soon excite those emotions, of which but the moment before, she seemed herself the mistress" (76).[60] Yet because Dacre, unlike Bienville, is precisely the sort of novelist she warns us against, her narratives of sexually transgressive women who destroy properly asexual women and are themselves punished are, in fact, sophisticated accounts of the discursive construction of *both* natural and unnatural women and their sexuality. In Dacre's novels, the asexual feminine ideal is produced only by isolating the young woman from corrupting social influences such as novels and fashionable society; yet Dacre, like Radcliffe and Wollstonecraft, insists that such an "ideal" woman is artificial, vulnerable, and destined for destruction precisely because of her isolation in the domestic sphere.

The Passions

Passions are spurs to action.
Mary Wollstonecraft, *A Vindication of the Rights of Woman* (1792)

What are passions, but another name for powers?
Mary Hays, *The Memoirs of Emma Courtney* (1796)

Women's sexual desires are clearly and spectacularly the central concern of Charlotte Dacre's writings, and of much of the Gothic as a whole. Though distrusted by writers such as More and Edgeworth, and regarded ambivalently by Wollstonecraft, sexual passion remained a dangerous possible outcome of the cult of sensibility that middle-class women were urged to embrace. Associated with the violent enthusiasm of the French Revolution, and with the sexual promiscuity the British considered to be a French export (especially through Rousseau), excessive sensibility had been soundly discredited by Dacre's time as a danger to both proper femininity and masculinity.

In *The Passions*, Charlotte Dacre undertook a task similar to Joanna Baillie's in her celebrated *Plays on the Passions* (1798), where Baillie devoted each play to one passion, and resolved that her tragedies would trace the progress of "those strong and fixed passions": "There is, perhaps, no employment which the human mind will with so much pursue, as the discovery of concealed passion, as the tracing the varieties and progress of a perturbed soul" (86, 73). Dacre's novel focuses not on a single passion, but on the progressive effects of passions on women's physical and mental stability. Her plot is a familiar one, distilled from *La Nouvelle Héloïse* and one of Bienville's narratives, and in it she demonstrates how the proper domestic woman and her lascivious libertine complement are alike destined, to use Bienville's terms, for the "impending wreck" of mental and corporeal disintegration.

Bienville had been similarly obsessed with uncovering the private passions of young women, and like Rousseau and Richardson, supplied voyeuristic readers with the intimate details of young women's "private" letters and secrets. One of Bienville's tragic examples of nymphomania involved a young innocent woman, Julia, "initiated into the secrets of Venus" by a "voluptuous procuress of lascivious pleasure," her young friend and waiting-woman, Berton (*Nymphomania* 165). Berton initiates Julia in illicit novels, erotic infatuation, and masturbation, precipitating her into nymphomania and eventual incurable madness, though Bienville offers us no motive for Berton's destructive manipulations. Dacre in effect focuses on this minor character Berton, giving her the ambition and intellectual aspirations of Satan, and setting her against the domestic, Eve-like ideal of Rousseau's Julie. Dacre's Appollonia not only destroys the emotional and sexual tranquility of Julia's domestic isolation, but she destroys all but one of the characters in the novel, and is herself a victim of the fatal passions she inspired.

Struggle and subjectivity

Who fights against whom? We all fight against each other. And there is always within each of us something that fights something else.
Michel Foucault, *Herculine Barbin*

According to Dacre, a struggle for mastery underlies all interactions, both within and between subjects and bodies. Like the corporeal disintegration experienced by natural and supernatural bodies in her demon lover poems, the struggle underlying subjectivity dissolves boundaries between proper and improper, natural and unnatural. While I may emphasize the struggle between distinct subjects, especially in Appollonia's quest for revenge, it is critical to keep in mind that this level of struggle is always in Dacre undercut by a simultaneous and even more violent struggle within. For this reason Foucault and Nietzsche's models of subjectivity as produced, not just repressed, through a network of power relations is most relevant. Mellor and Homans, in contrast, both rely on Chodorow's psychoanalytic model of subjectivity to construct a gender-complementary women's Romanticism for writers such as Mary Shelley and Dorothy Wordsworth.[61] In order for their models to function, femininity must remain essentially outside power, a strategy shared by Romantic-period advocates of both reason and sensibility, but one challenged in distinct ways by the fatal women represented in this book. Whether they are betrayed women in duels, revolutionary heroines, or haughty queens, these fatal women invite us to question the definitions of woman that we imagine Romantic-period authors relied on.

Dacre's model of subjectivity as struggle engages (without resolving) the larger cultural struggle over the term "woman," and raises to a more disturbing, even pornographic, level the parody Barker-Benfield (like Brissenden) locates in Austen's *Sense and Sensibility*:

The alternatives offered to women in the 1790s – the approved vision of mindless sensibility or the outlawing bogey of the strong-minded Amazon – can be seen as a parody of the conflict represented by Marianne and Elinor Dashwood. As Wollstonecraft recognized, the conflict existed both within women, and between women and the surrounding male and female authorities, telling them what it was to be female. (*Culture of Sensibility*, 382)

The unique value of Dacre's doubles lies in their process of degeneration, in the way they experience increasingly perverse gradations of pleasure and pain as they reach the parodic extreme. In *The Passions*, Dacre isolates two contemporary models of female subjectivity at their most extreme and shows how easily one "natural" type can degenerate into the other, thereby undermining the possibility for fixed identity. The narrative of *The Passions* is set in motion by the Countess Appollonia Zulmer's desire for vengeance against the man who rejected her, Count Weimar, and this vengeance is directed at the object of his love, his new bride Julia. Weimar presents Appollonia as the *ancien régime* model of femininity that is actively sexual, aggressive, and intelligent:

The Countess Zulmer . . . does not endeavour gently to steal into the heart, but attacks it by storm, as able generals strive to carry all by a *coup de main*. Sensible of her power in conversation, whatever the topic, she takes a part, and enters freely; she obtains admiration, astonishment – but not love ... fearless, regardless of prejudice, an ardent spirit and daring intellect, she discusses opinions, combats errors, exposes systems, detects folly; in each and all she appears great; in every act of her character, full of power. Her fierce and penetrating eyes seem to look into the heart, with a glance so quick, so piercing, that other eyes are unable to meet them, and are cast down, as with a feeling of conscious guilt. Soaring, and eccentric in her flights, she leaves her wondering sex far behind. (*Passions*, 1: 27–28)

Like Corday, whose "mixture" of male and female qualities had "raised her infinitely above the general character" of other women, Appollonia soars above her sex's limitations. A conflation of Wollstonecraftian feminism, bluestocking intellectualism,[62] and *ancien régime* flamboyance, this negative representation of Appollonia is further complicated by the identity of the letter-writer, Weimar, who is an even more unflattering figure than Rousseau's own Wolmar. Lacking in any warmth, Weimar allows his estranged wife to suffer in order to save his pride, and ultimately is utterly unable to fathom human emotion. Thus the above allusions to Medusa ("astonishment"; "her fierce and penetrating eyes") like the multiple references to classical femmes fatales (e.g., Messalina, bacchante, Circe, Calypso) throughout the novel, do not have a stable (i.e., antifeminist) meaning or intent, given the novel's epistolary format and individualized perspectives (in particular the unsympathetic Weimar's).

Appollonia is a fascinating contradiction, possessing a bold and articulate intellect, and exercising this intellect in the public sphere, seeking admiration above all else, even love: an outrageous Charlotte Corday, if Craik had been a committed counter-revolutionary. She clearly embodies the Burkean sublime, being consistently described as great, soaring, powerful, dazzling, and fierce. Like Wollstonecraft, Dacre highlights the gender-specific nature of Burke's sublime, but does so in a way Burke could scarcely have imagined: by exploring the sublime dimensions of the violent female body and subject. Patricia Yaeger has identified precisely such a forbidden appropriation of violence as one feminist possibility for a new "female sublime of violence that needs, again and again, to be rewritten."[63] Burke's sublime, though (or because) ostensibly a means of transcending the corporeal, relies on gender-specific physical qualities (e.g., roughness, loudness, vastness, strength). It follows that women, who in order to be beautiful must be small, smooth, and submissive, can therefore become sublime by becoming "vast in their dimensions," exercising power, and inspiring terror through their crimes, for crime is always "triumphant and sublime" according to Sade. Dacre rewrites the

Burkean sublime in her novels, creating sublime antiheroines who are made to be admired, not loved. "I admire the Countess [Appollonia] Zulmer," says Weimar in *The Passions*, "in some respects you may even esteem her, but love her you cannot, for she is not made to be loved." Weimar has read his Burke:

There is a wide difference between admiration and love. The sublime, which is the cause of the former, always dwells on great objects, and terrible; the latter on small ones, and pleasing; we submit to what we admire, but we love what submits to us.[64]

Appollonia's embodiment of the sublime enacts a critique of the Burkean gendered sublime worthy of Wollstonecraft, even though Dacre's conscious intention may have been to caricature feminists such as Wollstonecraft. In her desire for admiration and power, not love, Appollonia emerges as yet another Satanic femme fatale who rewrites the sexual plot of the fallen woman as that of the fallen angel.

Like Milton's Satan (and unlike Shelley's Prometheus), Appollonia is trapped in a cycle of destruction which leaves the idea of free will (or of feminist subversion as autonomy) out of reach: "I [will] now...sell myself to destruction to destroy him...Toppled from my high eminence, I will not singly fall, others shall be dragged down, and struggle with me in the depths of my despair" (1: 282–83). Again we see that Satanic Romanticism appealed to women writers in surprising ways, allowing them to imagine dangerous and ambitious possibilities for women's physical action and agency.

Julia, Appollonia's rival, is at first passive, submissive, and asexual – the ideal woman according to Weimar:

Behold my picture of a perfect woman: – chaste simplicity, retiring charms – diffidence, modesty, reserve; tender sensibility, yet strong reason...a heart, formed for love – but to love only *one*, to seek after marriage no pleasure after beyond the sphere of her duty, or the wish of her husband; to be ever, under every ill, his tender consoler, not an imperious reprover; to have no passion, or excess in aught, but *love for him*. (*Passions*, 1: 31, orig. emphasis)

Weimar's narcissism is abundantly clear in Dacre's novel, and his Rousseauesque ideal is submitted to a simple test – can it survive even the slightest contact, say, a novel, from outside its domestic confinement in the Alps? Dacre foregrounds the masculine literary origins of this normative model of ideal femininity, beginning with the first letter in *The Passions* where Weimar retreats to the sublime Alps, his "ethereal essence elevated and purified." Weimar's effusions upon his return to nature and natural man are shown by Dacre to be a double return, a return to the textual origins of the natural:

I am delighted with the inhabitants of Switzerland: with the utmost simplicity of manners, they combine ... a degree of native genius ... The rudest mountaineer among them is not ignorant; it is nothing uncommon to see a herdsman with a volume of Voltaire or Rousseau in his hand. They are universally benevolent, kind-hearted, and hospitable; their women are handsome, modest, and reserved. I do not think I shall very soon quit a spot where I appear to tread more proudly; where, in the midst of these primitive people of the vast solitudes which surround them, I feel more independent, and seem to breathe more freely than in the busy world. (*Passions*, 1: 12–13)

Dacre reveals how such idealized purity and autonomy come at the expense of others, the "primitive" laboring class and women, who are themselves naturalized to suit this popular Romantic fantasy of nature. *The Passions* leaves no such natural or desirable model of subjectivity intact. All the women in the novel are destroyed – the libertine Appollonia, the degenerate Julia, the completely passive Amelia (wife of the man Julia falls in love with) – leaving no viable position for any woman, subversive or not, in a world regulated by such Rousseauesque definitions of the natural.

Weimar's inability to understand the two women in his life, his wife Julia and his would-be mistress Appollonia, belies precisely the approach to subjectivity (as fixed and expressive of natural differences) that Dacre will prove wrong:

the points of difference in the character of each are so strong, that it is morally impossible they should ever assimilate; as well could Appollonia acquire the virtues and softness of Julia, as Julia the animation and bold independence of Appollonia. Nature formed them in different moulds; they may associate with as little danger of combination as any two opposites in existence. (*Passions*, 1: 144)

Dacre proceeds to prove Weimar's assumptions about natural differences wrong, focusing on active (and adulterous) sexual desire as the means of Julia's transformation beyond the "natural" category of proper femininity, into a sexual, enchanting, and independent woman who eventually abandons her family, contemplates murder, and loses all stability through madness and death.

Appollonia destroys the domestic tranquility of Weimar and Julia by awakening Julia's sexuality in the same terms that Milton's Satan seduced Eve:

I will initiate you! I will shew [*sic*] you the extent of your dominion, and how infinitely you are sovereign over the fate of him you obey... The secret of your slavery must be unfolded to you. You must taste of the tree of knowledge. (*Passions*, 1: 173)

Appollonia's motivation for revenge is thus elevated above unrequited love to a Luciferan power struggle between men and women:

the pride and vanity of man – in other words his *self-love* causes him to *dread superiority in woman*, he bears no rival near the throne! Why else this endless despotism? why this alarm? this unceasing watchfulness over the female mind, to arrest it in its first, least step towards knowledge if it is not from a servile dream, that their eyes should become opened! – that perceiving their equality in the scale of existence, they should (rebelling) throw off the iron yoke of slavery and never more consent to wear it! (*Passions*, 1: 169–70, orig. emphasis)

Appollonia's Miltonic speech evokes the sexual and intellectual revolution associated with the Fall; as Samuel Johnson argued in "A Dissertation on the Amazons," the "revolt of the Amazon against the male warrior" is "an evil analogous with the Christian myth of the fall."[65] But, by the same token, her sexual struggle is a political struggle like that of any Promethean Romantic hero, to which she overtly and repeatedly compares herself, so that she emerges as an unique Satanic heroine:

Oh! what are the... punishments of the damned in their fabled hell? What are the tortures of Tantalus, the labours of Sisiphus, the miseries of Ixion, the agonies of Prometheus; what are they all, compared to the new species of suffering devised by my evil genius for me? (*Passions*, 1: 40–41)

It is thus Appollonia's own sadistic pleasure in causing the suffering and death of all those close to Weimar that generates the narrative of *The Passions*; the supposedly active male (i.e., Julia's married lover) is relegated to an object between a triangulated female exchange, as Appollonia claims, quite rightly, that it was "*I*, who seduced her heart from [Weimar]...*I* bade her give the reins to loose illicit love and pleasure!" (*Passions*, IV: 85, orig. emphasis).

Appollonia's Satanism can be read as either an endorsement of the masculine Romantic model of autonomous heroic subjectivity, or as a literal demonization of Wollstonecraftian feminism, since Wollstonecraft was popularly associated with sexual corruption of young women.[66] Yet the most productive reading would reject both pure subversion (Appollonia as autonomous hero) and pure normalization (Appollonia as demonized and defeated feminist). Instead, like Milton's Satan and Barbauld's woman in "The Rights of Woman," Appollonia embodies the conflicted status of a subject who is necessarily subjected: "Thou mayst command, but never canst be free," wrote Barbauld in her important response to Wollstonecraft (*Ashfield*, 18). Appollonia (and, as we shall see, *Zofloya's* Victoria) thus takes her place beside Marie Antoinette as an allegory of women's ambition and fall from power, an allegory that clearly intrigued Romantic women writers, and inspired a hitherto unacknowledged Satanic Romanticism deeply concerned with the war between, even within, the sexes on earth.

The enactment of female sexual desire, voracious and sadistic, and not reflective of a primary male libido, is the greatest threat to "natural" femininity, as Weimar's friend warns him:

such a woman as Appollonia Zulmer is calculated to do more mischief to her sex than the most abandoned libertine of ours, the most avowed profligate of her own. She is an enchantress – a Circe; and her arts enable her to conceal her deformity under the mask of the most seducing beauty. (*Passions*, 1: 149–50)

Appollonia's monstrousness, which is increasingly emphasized as the novel progresses, her vaguely phallic "deformity" (suggestive of lesbianism and nymphomania, which Bienville claimed were accompanied by a large clitoris), and her masculine associations (Apollo, Apollyon (the angel of death), Satan, Prometheus) all contribute to the indistinctness of her sexual identity, to the indistinctness of the truth of her sex. The sadistic capacity of sexual desire, which Dacre suggests is part of a larger and pervasive will to power, when exercised by women takes them outside their age's sexual categories and into the sublime states of madness, monstrousness, the supernatural, and, eventually, violent death.

The suggestions of Appollonia's lesbianism, since she does indeed "seduce" Julia, are clearly homophobic, as they were in attacks on Wollstonecraft's influence on young women, and in pornographic satires of Marie Antoinette. *The Passions*, however, illustrates that the female homosocial continuum was not as stable and unproblematic in the Romantic period as we might assume. Julia's degeneration into heterosexual adulterous passion is, as stated earlier, a triangulated one, the conflict and attraction existing most dramatically between the two women. Julia's degeneration might then be termed a spectacular, perhaps unique, illustration of female homosexual panic, but I am skeptical of such a reading. Rather, I take Julia's degeneration into nymphomania, for that is what Dacre is clearly dramatizing, as illustrating a larger cultural anxiety over women as sexual subjects, whether straight or gay. Fear of excessive female sexual intimacy, especially across class lines, was pervasive in conduct and sentimental literature (and in medical literature such as Bienville's, where the corrupting lesbian influence is predictably the servant). Even Wollstonecraft lamented young women's initiation into illicit sexual practices by other women : "A number of girls sleep in the same room, and wash together... I should be very cautious to prevent their acquiring nasty, or immodest habits; and as many girls have learned very nasty tricks, from ignorant servants, the mixing them thus indiscriminately together, is very improper" (*VRW*, 127). The homophobia Appollonia inspires in her male observers thus attests to the intensely homoerotic connection between women of this time, as this description of Appollonia's effect on women demonstrates:

The moment Appollonia appears, the dullest party is enlivened. Frigid matrons, and women of profound virtue... are delighted in her society... Hence these dignified females simper at the approach of the Countess, who like a fair Euphrosine, advances towards them – the goddess of mirth and smiles. (*Passions*, 1: 148)

Here "frigid matrons" are aroused by the presence of another woman, an evocation of the homosocial continuum (what Adrienne Rich termed the "lesbian continuum") among women, in which men might appear as peripheral observers, if at all, and female sexuality might operate outside the heterocentric exchange of women.[67] My intention is not to efface lesbian specificity in the above instances by insisting on the larger issue of "female sexuality." I think that Dacre and Wollstonecraft did have lesbian sexuality in mind when they worried about the dangerous effects of women's intimacy, and I think they simultaneously feared other types of illicit sexuality, such as solitary masturbation and promiscuous heterosexual activities, that were the products, in their minds, of such homosocial intimacy. In the context of our discussion of femmes fatales, Appollonia's suggested lesbianism, like Marie Antoinette's, attests to the femme fatale's dangerous ability to evade sexual classification, and her affinity with other transgressive figures such as the eighteenth-century "Sapphist."[68]

Of course, the sexual behavior of such "commodities among themselves" is often under the shadow of the male gaze, much as in Sade's orgies, where one is never able to extricate completely the desires and interests of the female libertines from their male counterparts.[69] Appollonia's sexual exploits above are related by Weimar's philosophical adviser, Rozendorf, yet she, too, as we have seen, boasts of the pleasure she finds in sexual enchantment. At one point in *The Passions*, Rozendorf attempted to fix with a "piercing glance" the truth of Appollonia's character, much as Apollonius had tried to transfix and unmask the "truth" of Lamia's identity in Keats's poem. While all women are enchanted with Appollonia (especially Julia, who says "She is like a bright star" (1: 137)), Rozendorf is troubled that, while Appollonia is to be admired for her intellect and independence,

she is not made to be loved. – She has a rare *assemblage*, but not a *union* of fine qualities; she has more dazzling accomplishments than solid ones, and her character is so various, there is no point, as it were, round which affection could rally. (*Passions*, 1: 143, orig. emphasis)

Appollonia's lack of a central "point," one which would clearly define her as female (i.e., "made to be loved") is actually shared by all of Dacre's male and female characters, as it is by Keats's Lamia, who may have inherited much from Dacre's femmes fatales.

In addition to this incident in *The Passions* which I believe is echoed in *Lamia* when Apollonius detects Lamia's secret identity, there are echoes in *Lamia* of both *The Passions* and *Zofloya*, in particular their use of sexual enchantment. Appollonia's enchantment of Julia is emphasized throughout the novel, and, in *Zofloya*, it is Zofloya's enchantment of Victoria that also bears some resemblance to Lamia's enchantment of Lycius, and vice versa. In *Zofloya*, for example, Victoria says of Zofloya, that "Strange mysterious being" whose celestial shape and voice she cannot resist: "yet am I now so bound, so trammelled to thee (by what magic arts I know not)" (237). In *Lamia*, Lycius contemplates "How to entangle, trammel up and snare Your soul in mine, and labyrinth you there" (1. 50). *Lamia* is admired for its intricate and unresolvable ambiguities regarding Lamia's and Lycius's mutual enchantment and deceptions, as in the above quote where the "enchanted" Lycius desires to ensnare Lamia's soul. Dacre's use of enchantment and supernatural (or even "unnatural") seduction throughout her novels and poetry manifests the same degree of subtlety and ambiguity as does Keats's poem. While Appollonia, Zofloya, and Victoria are not sympathetic characters in any straightforward sense, Dacre's portrayal of passion and sensual enthrallment is more complex than most modern critics appreciate, especially when they focus largely on the author's supposed moral intentions and outrageous plots.

The overdetermined Gothic landscape Dacre unfolds is always self-consciously a psychological landscape, wherein subjectivity is experienced as a violent clash between and within wills. Here stability, as in

Weimar's case (the sole survivor of *The Passions*), is merely a temporary Nietzschean mastery of a commanding will over an obeying will:

mine is a fearful struggle. I oppose myself to myself... By turns conquering and conquered, I am the sport of sensations... My heart is as a land which is the seat of war, the rival powers combat, but vanquish which may, the wretched land is ravaged and destroyed. (*Passions*, IV: 18)

Thus, sanity and self-control for Dacre are not synonymous with a harmonious psychic integration, or a balance between reason and passion. Rather, subjectivity, in particular women's subjectivity, is figured as the continual fragmentation and reconstruction of a field of struggle. In such a volatile landscape, female subjects and bodies, even the most virtuous ones, can always harbor a secret "deformity." Dacre's fatal women in both *The Passions* and *Zofloya*, along with Keats's Lamia, Coleridge's Lady Geraldine, and Lewis's Matilda, are examples of the Romantics' fascination with and fear of women who defied the age's insistence on sexual difference as a "natural" ordering principle, and instead revealed the hidden disorder within.

Zofloya; or, The Moor. A Romance of the Fifteenth Century

Most modern commentary on *Zofloya* agrees with the reviewer for the *New Annual Register*, who in 1806 described *Zofloya* as "a stimulating novel after the manner of The Monk – the same lust – the same infernal agents – the same voluptuous language. What need we say more?"[70] We need to say that this "same" lust, violence, and voluptuousness is that of a young woman, Victoria, who has more in common with the ruthless heroines of Sade than the embattled heroines of Radcliffe or Smith. Dacre's revision of *The Monk* in *Zofloya* challenges delineations of the Gothic along gender lines in such works as Kate Ellis's *The Contested Castle*, William Patrick Day's *In the Circles of Fear and Desire*, Diane Hoeveler's *Gothic Feminism*, and Anne Williams's *Art of Darkness*. These works elaborate a "female Gothic" that centers on a reactive and entrapped heroine, and distinguish this from a male Gothic such as Lewis's, which focuses on a rebellious hero (masculine because exiled from the domestic sphere, according to Ellis, and because he seeks to control rather than adapt to his world, according to Day).[71] Dacre's heroine Victoria is exiled, seeks to master her world and those in it, and is decidedly sadistic, tormenting, and murdering for the pleasure of exerting her will; she is thus neither within the female or male

Gothic traditions but somewhere in between. While such "negative" female characters do exist in women's literature of the period, they are typically secondary characters, dark doubles of the central heroine whose destructiveness must be expelled from the text before the heroine can reach her desired goal (examples include Maria de Vallerno in Radcliffe's *A Sicilian Romance*, Laurentini in her *The Mysteries of Udolpho*, and, most famously, Bertha in *Jane Eyre*).

Reviews of Dacre's novels consistently expressed disgust with the excessively sexual language of her prose, and one review noted the singular inappropriateness of a woman novelist knowing, much less using, medical terminology for female sexuality:

Here the language in general is bombastical; new words are introduced, such for example, as *enhorred* and *furor*, the latter of which is certainly used in the language of medicine, but in a sense which delicacy will not permit us to explain.[72]

The *furor* the reviewer (and *Zofloya*) refers to is the *furor uterinus*, or nymphomania, medical language fit for a misogynist medical treatise such as Bienville's, intended to demonstrate women's "imbecility" (*Nymphomania* vii), but absolutely "odious and indecent" in a woman writer's Gothic romance.

As Ambrosio's sexual and moral liberation is inspired and perhaps directed by the infernal influence of Matilda in *The Monk*, Victoria's sexual and moral liberation is influenced by Lucifer in the form of the seductive Moorish sorcerer Zofloya. But Dacre goes even farther than Lewis did in questioning the external origin of Ambrosio's violent desires, for, unlike in *The Monk*, the infernal agent enters *Zofloya* midway through the novel, after Victoria has begun her seductions. The reviewer for *Monthly Literary Recreations* found Satan's superfluousness indicative of the novel's "disgusting depravity of morals," since Victoria is depraved before Satan arrives: "The supernatural agent is totally useless, as the mind of Victoria, whom Satan, under the form of Zofloya, comes to tempt, is sufficiently black and depraved naturally, to need no temptation to commit the horrid crimes she perpetrates." As many critics argue, Matilda's influence is in effect a projection of the pious monk's own unspoken destructive desires; Zofloya's influence on Victoria, urging her on to increasingly violent crimes, is similarly a projection of her own destructive desires. Thus the submission of the protagonist to the infernal agent, through the selling of the soul, is in both texts a liberation of repressed desire.

Yet Dacre also deliberately describes Victoria's eventual submission to Zofloya's will as a marriage, and his attempts to convince her to depend on him are expressed in the language of romantic courtship. Here Dacre highlights the subjecting (not liberatory) function of heterosexuality and its central institution, marriage, since, as Foucault reminds us, the promise of "liberated" sexual desire is power's most attractive ruse. The story of Victoria's downfall is thus also the story of the loss of social identity, mobility, and independence that a woman suffers in marrying her lover, who then becomes her legal master after having acted the part of her devoted and enthralled servant:

"Now then, Victoria!" cried the Moor, but not in the gentle voice in which he had been wont to address her – "now then, thou art emancipated from falling ruins, from hostile guards, from fear of shame, and an ignominious death... I have watched thee, followed thee, and served thee until now: – If, then, I save thee for ever from all future accidents – all future worldly misery – all future disgrace; say – wilt thou, for that future, resign thyself entirely to me?... wilt thou unequivocally give thyself to me, heart, and body, and soul?" (*Zofloya*, 253)

Thus, unlike Ambrosio, who is destroyed through liberating the excesses of his own desires, Victoria is destroyed through her submission to another, a husband, who ends her existence as mistress of her own will by gaining her wifely submission through the false promise of protection.

Dacre's contradictory accounts of Victoria's "evil" render any moralistic pretenses the novel may profess dangerously unconvincing, as critics from the early reviewers to Robert Miles have observed:

Four discourses offer competing explanations for the origin of Victoria's evil: a religious one of fallen nature and satanic temptation; a sentimental, libertarian one of nature/nurture; its Sadean variant ("Is not self predominant through animal nature?")... and one of paternal and class responsibility. Typically, these explanations are left in contradictory and irresolute condition. (*Gothic Writing*, 181)

Victoria's violence cannot be neatly explained by any of these models of "evil," and, though the bad example set by her mother is repeatedly cited by the narrator as the cause of Victoria's "love of evil," the narrator contradicts herself repeatedly by also offering competing explanations, which leads Gary Kelly to describe the novel as "hopelessly self-contradictory on the causes of the evil."[73] Yet as the *General Review* pointed out in 1806, "Zofloya has no pretension to rank as a moral work." *Zofloya's* resistance to rank as a moral work is formidable, and goes against the grain of most women's novels of the Romantic period, inviting us instead to read her in the amoral tradition of Lewis and Sade.

Zofloya celebrates Victoria's capacity for sexual desire and pleasure; her desire for Zofloya is itself transgressive, not because it is blasphemous as is Ambrosio's desire for Matilda (who modeled for the portrait of the Madonna) in *The Monk*, but in part because it grows as the novel progresses and Zofloya grows more demonic. Unlike the conventional woman in a demon lover ballad who is horrified to see her lover revealed as infernal, Victoria, like several of Dacre's poetic narrators, finds his supernatural and infernal origins arousing:[74]

Never, till this moment, had she been so near the person of the Moor – such powerful fascination dwelt around him, that she felt incapable of withdrawing from his arms; yet ashamed, (for Victoria was still proud) and blushing at her feelings, when she remembered that Zofloya, however he appeared, was but a menial slave, and as such alone had originally become known to her – she sought, but sought vainly, to repress them; for no sooner (envelopped in the lightning's flash as he seemed, when it gleamed around him without touching his person), – did she behold his beautiful and majestic visage, that towering and graceful form, than all thought of his inferiority vanished, and the ravished sense, spurning at the calumnious idea, confessed him a being of a superior order. (*Zofloya*, 227)

Victoria's desire for a black servant who was once a slave "crosses class and racial taboos,"[75] but her desire grows as does Zofloya's class status (and stature, literally), undercutting the subversive charge and highlighting the novel's racist and orientalist dimensions. Dacre may have read an earlier novel, *Zoflora, or the Generous Negro Girl* (1804), transforming the persecuted female slave Zoflora to the persecuting former slave Zofloya, thus offering an unsympathetic and unsentimental portrayal of a black slave in the year preceding the passage of the anti-slave trade bill.[76]

Reviewers amplified *Zofloya*'s questionable racism (casting the devil as a black man, and vice versa): the *General Review* thus parodied the novel's faint attempt at moralizing: "if the devil should appear to them [young ladies] in the shape of a very handsome black man, they must not listen to him."[77] The *Literary Journal* made the connection between Zofloya's race and his evil origins even clearer: "Satan...had the decorum to lodge himself in a black body, so as to be something in character."[78] But the irresistible beauty of Zofloya's body, of his eyes and voice (reminiscent of Othello's), is emphasized throughout the novel, so that, while

Victoria's desire for him cannot be separated from the racism and exoticism implied in conflating a black man and the devil, neither can her desire be reduced to racist dimensions. Moreover, Dacre's *Hours of Solitude* contains sentimental images of black men in such poems as "The Poor Negro Sadi" (an abolitionist poem) and "The Moorish Combat," the latter featuring a sympathetic Zofloya-like Moor in a tragic romantic interlude with a blonde, knife-wielding woman (1: 108–12). Thus, Dacre exploited both negative and sentimentalized images of black male sexuality and subjectivity available to her.

Zofloya's greatest value lies in its complex and conflicted femme fatale heroine. The novel traces the progress of Victoria and her brother Leonardo, who are exiled from a superficially "idyllic" patriarchal family because of their mother's adultery and her abandonment of them. Victoria is the novel's protagonist, actively pursuing her desires for wealth and power, never submitting, and seldom wavering in moments of personal danger. Possessing an "unflinching relentless soul" filled only with "ambitious, the selfish, the wild, and the turbulent" sensations, Victoria's ability to "inflict pain without remorse" and revenge her own injuries likens her to Sade's Juliette, as Swinburne suggested. Her brother is overshadowed in the narrative by his lover, Megalena Strozzi, who like Victoria derives her pleasure from mastering others. As in *The Passions*, the women in *Zofloya* strategically use their sexuality to enchant or command men, and it is this process of mastery itself that is the source of their pleasure. The language of erotic pleasure in these novels is thus that of domination and submission, not of affection. In the following passage Dacre indicates through male seminal metaphors that women's sexual agency (initiating and manipulating "pure" men into "voluptuousness") disrupts the categories of natural sexual difference, since Megalena is temporarily masculinized through the husbandry image and Leonardo is feminized as pure and fertile:

> her triumph: she had sown (as she believed) the first germs of love and passion in a pure and youthful breast; she had seen those germs shoot forth and expand beneath the fervid rays of her influence, and she enjoyed the fruits with a voluptuous pleasure. (*Zofloya*, 123)

Because Megalena performs actions uncharacteristic of proper women (sexually initiating a man, plotting to murder, deriving pleasure from others' pain) she is metaphorically masculinized in this passage, since the categories of natural sexual difference, supposedly well in place by Dacre's time, simply cannot account for such a subject being a woman.

But Megalena is always simultaneously and consciously acting the part of a "true" woman, feigning devotion and dependence in order to maintain her control.

It is Victoria who violates the natural difference between the sexes to such an extent that her body itself is transformed through her increasingly cruel and violent actions into a larger and decidedly masculine form. Victoria's increasingly physical masculinization reveals the anxiety (and hope) of Dacre's age that perhaps the two sexes themselves (and not merely the gender identities they supposedly establish) are not fixed or natural. According to Foucault, the eighteenth century's fascination with hermaphrodites and the question of their "true" sex is indicative of modern Western society's pursuit of the truth of sex.[79] The truth of Victoria's sex (and of Appollonia's) becomes increasingly unclear as she proceeds to seduce, dominate, torture, and murder. Her body, no longer a "natural" unity, is redesignated as unnatural according to her actions, in an enactment of Judith Butler's (and Foucault's) problematization of the supposedly stable distinction between "natural" sex and "cultural" gender: "Gender is not to culture as sex is to nature; gender is also the discursive/cultural means by which 'sexed nature' or a 'natural sex' is produced and established as 'prediscursive.' "[80] Dacre illustrates exactly how sex is a product of gender, and not the other way around.

When we first see Victoria at age fifteen, she is "beautiful and accomplished as an angel," with a "graceful elegant form," yet already of "an implacable, revengeful and cruel nature" (*Zofloya*, 40, 59). After seducing her first lover, Victoria's angelic beauty begins its decline, a clear parallel to Satan's increasingly tarnished beauty in *Paradise Lost*: she is described as possessing a countenance "not of angelic mould; yet, though there was a fierceness in it, it was not certainly a repelling, but a beautiful fierceness" (*Ibid.*, 96) After committing two murders and attempting to seduce her affianced brother-in-law Henriquez, Victoria is described as possessing a "masculine spirit" (*Ibid.*, 190), whereas previously her spirit had been consistently described as bold, independent, and inflexible, without explicit reference to gender. After this degeneration of her feminine "spirit," it is her body that is suddenly masculine when compared to that of her rival, Lilla, Henriquez' fiancée whom Victoria has kidnapped and will soon murder. No longer a "graceful" and "elegant" beauty, in comparison to Lilla Victoria is now not feminine and perhaps no longer female, as if a hidden deformity similar to Appollonia's had emerged:

"He would have loved you [said Zofloya] had you chanced to have *resembled* Lilla."

"Ah! would," cried the degenerate Victoria, "would that this unwieldy form could be compressed into the fairy delicacy of hers, these bold masculine features assume the likeness of her baby face!" (*Zofloya*, 211, orig. emphasis)

It is the fluidity of corporeal identity that is significant, for Victoria will indeed transform her body into that of the absent and ideally feminine Lilla. Henriquez, drugged and spellbound, will believe Victoria to be his Lilla and will make love to her under this spell, thereby temporarily granting the masculine Victoria the "fairy form" of the properly feminine and unquestionably female Lilla.

In addition to growing larger and more masculine, Victoria's body seems also to have grown darker, so that one can also read her corporeal degeneration as a sign of miscegenation. Her darkness is increasingly emphasized, particularly in contrast to the milk-white Lilla, as in this scene where Henriquez awakes after having slept with Victoria while drugged, and is repulsed by her appearance: "those black fringed eyelids, reposing upon a cheek of dark and animated hue – those raven tresses hanging unconfined – oh, sad! oh, damning proofs! – Where was the fair enamelled cheek – the flaxen ringlets of the delicate Lilla?" (*Zofloya*, 217). Victoria's and Zofloya's increasingly large bodies, like their darkness, also owe something to the discourse of miscegenation, for, as H. L. Malchow has argued: "By the end of the early nineteenth century, popular racial discourse managed to conflate... descriptions of particular ethnic characteristics into a general image of the Negro body in which repulsive features, brutelike strength and size of limbs featured prominently" (*Gothic Images*, 18). Yet darkness and "more than mortal" size and strength also belong to other competing discourses of the period, among them medical and supernatural.

That a degenerate, "unwieldy," and "dark" woman such as Victoria can resemble and become the fragile and fair Lilla suggests the primacy of performance over fixed essence. Judith Butler's concept of performative gender, and of sexual difference as one of its ongoing productions, can thus be effectively applied to female subjectivity in Dacre:

woman itself is a term in process, a becoming, a constructing that cannot rightfully be said to originate or to end. As an ongoing discursive practice, it is open to intervention and resignification ... Gender is the repeated stylization of the body, a set of repeated acts within a highly rigid regulatory frame that congeal over time to produce the appearance of substance, of a natural sort of being. (*Gender Trouble*, 33, orig. emphasis)

Dacre reveals how her women characters enact such an ongoing process of self-creation and self-destruction as they take whatever actions and roles are necessary for survival, which in their eyes is synonymous with increased power. In constantly drawing attention to the desire to master shared by Victoria, Megalena, and Appollonia, Dacre offers a version of female subjectivity that is not complementary to male subjectivity, but which dissolves the boundaries that her contemporaries, or modern critics, would like to fix between genders and between sexes.

If a fixed feminine subjectivity (and female biology) was and remains crucial to a larger ideological process of naturalizing a rational and benevolent bourgeois identity, then Dacre effectively deprives her readers of the consolations of femininity and benevolence. Wollstonecraft and Robinson each faced a similar loss (of the consolations of femininity) when they contemplated the logical conclusion of women's violence. While their texts confronted explicitly the political contexts and consequences of this violence, Dacre's sexually and psychologically focused exploration offers us a similar look inside some of early feminism's most compelling self-examinations.

Dacre insists that female and male subjects are driven by a will to power and possess an infinite sadistic capacity, which in her age translates into a "love of evil." In the last line of *Zofloya*, Dacre poses the novel's central question regarding this "love of evil" in such as way as to suggest that the widely held and supposedly "reasonable" faith in human benevolence is in fact as reasonable as believing that "infernal influence" is the cause of crimes "dreadful and repugnant to nature":

Either we must suppose that the love of evil is born with us (which would be an insult to the Deity), or we must attribute [such crimes] (as appears more consonant with reason) to the suggestions of infernal influence. (*Zofloya*, 254–55)

Yet the world Dacre's characters inhabit never operates according to reason; on the contrary, the unreasonable "love of evil" is shown by Dacre to be neither "repugnant to nature" in general, nor to women in particular, but rather to constitute the ongoing struggle for power which is both constructive and destructive. Poised at the transition between the eighteenth century and its fascination with masquerade, coquetry, transvestism, and hermaphrodism, and the nineteenth century's cultivation of a "proper femininity" enshrined in bourgeois motherhood, Romantic female subjectivity was, as it still is, a site of intensified struggle. While writers such as Mary Shelley and Dorothy Wordsworth may have idealized a feminine subjectivity outside power, Dacre had no such utopian outlook, instead creating heroines like Victoria, who could proclaim that "there is certainly a pleasure...in the infliction of prolonged torment."

CONCLUSION

> I think that pleasure is a very difficult behavior. It's not as simple as that to enjoy one's self...I would like to and hope I'll die of an overdose of pleasure of any kind...Because I think that the kind of pleasure I would consider as *the* real pleasure would be so deep, so intense, so overwhelming that I couldn't survive it.
>
> Michel Foucault, "The Minimalist Self"

The value of Dacre's Victoria and Appollonia is ultimately not as subversive models of female subjectivity, for they are as much products of normative discourses of femininity as their tamer complements. The value of these femmes fatales lies in the dialectical relationship they have with their "innocent" victims, Julia and Lilla, for Dacre ultimately makes these asexual martyrs as repugnant and inhuman as their destroyers. Angela Carter's insights into *Justine* and *Juliette* apply just as well to Dacre's novels: "Justine is the thesis, Juliette is the antithesis; both are without hope and neither pays any heed to a future in which might lie the synthesis of their modes of being."[81]

The true subversive potential of Dacre's heroines lies in their mutual annihilation, and in the pleasure Appollonia and Victoria found in such destruction. Destruction and its accompanying violent sublime have historically been neglected by scholars of women's literature in favor of creation, nurture, and the "female" sublime. Dacre's most important contribution to the critique of the proper woman of her time is not in creating a new vision of female subjectivity (as Wollstonecraft had done with the rational woman, for example), but in destroying the possibility of a stable subject identity, and even of a natural corporeal identity. Charlotte Dacre presents women characters who systematically perform actions "unnatural" for women (such as dominate, assert, desire, aggress, and kill), thereby destabilizing the categories "feminine" and "female." Thus, like Sade's Juliette, her femmes fatales do not seek to recreate the world, but to destroy it.

Dacre's femmes fatales belong in a Sadean world but remain in and are limited by the English Gothic and sentimental traditions; yet, even in their self-destructive, melodramatic outbursts we see a radical critique of the subject that is remarkably similar to Sade's:

Oh! for ten thousand scourges, applied at once – for the stings of knotted scorpions – for any species of corporeal suffering, that for a single instant might divert to it the superior and unspeakable agony of my soul – that for a single instant one might be swallowed up in the other. – But, no, it may not be; I am sadly free from physical pain – all, all is soul, the nerve of mind. (*Passions*, 1: 41–42)

In this remarkable passage, Appollonia comes close to articulating Sade's (and Foucault's) desire that the self be swallowed up in the body, and that the body no longer be subjected to the self. Appollonia echoes Olivia's speech in *The Italian*: "What are bodily pains in comparison with the subtle, the exquisite tortures of the mind! Heaven knows I can support my own afflictions, but not the view of those of others when they are excessive" (*Italian*, 127). But Dacre transforms the "generous purpose" of Olivia's desire for self-denying martyrdom into a questionable desire for a literal annihilation of the self (not a suicide) and the annihilation of others. Appollonia's desire is not part of the moral economy of sympathy, which allows Olivia to weigh the suffering she knows she can endure against the unbearable spectacle of another's pain.[82] Dacre is interested in something very different here, a destruction of self and body based on excess and not exchange, akin to the destruction envisioned by Bataille, Sade, and Foucault (in the epigraph to this conclusion).

Like the Mistress, Victoria, and the nymphomaniac, who are drawn into the demonic body and into death, Appollonia "sinks into a state of perfect reconciliation with the powers of her body" (*Nymphomania*, 70). When the self is "swallowed up" by, or is "reconciled" with, the body, its destruction is both violent and suggestive of violence to others. Much as for Foucault the ultimate pleasure is a deadly one, Appollonia's "passion, that unfortunate but violent passion" (1: 43) she succumbs to, is a marriage of pleasure and destruction, the literalization of her own conflicted status as femme fatale.

Dacre's works, like Sade's, are potential examples of "pornography in the service of women."[83] Her femmes fatales are unacknowledged precursors of the heroines of sensation novelists such as Mary Braddon and decadent writers such as Vernon Lee (and Swinburne). We could begin to construct from Dacre's femmes fatales a submerged countertradition in nineteenth-century women's writing, a tradition which for too long has been overshadowed by the realist novel and its heroines. Simultaneously, however, we need to consider how Dacre's strong Sadean affinities and pornographic subject and style challenge the notion of a "woman's tradition," and of gender-complementary readings of Romanticism and the Gothic in particular. At the very least, Dacre's imaginative excesses and spectacular femmes fatales have helped widen the field of possibilities for women writers, a worthy accomplishment for any writer.

CHAPTER 5

"In seraph strains, unpitying, to destroy": Anne Bannerman's femmes fatales

Like Charlotte Dacre, the Edinburgh poet Anne Bannerman (1765–1829) situated her writing in the tradition of Mathew Lewis, in this case the Gothic ballads included in *The Monk* and *Tales of Wonder*. Dacre had associated her fiction with Mathew Lewis's for maximum sensational effect, leading to high sales and notoriety of name. Dacre's success in the "school of Lewis" came not without scandal, though it seems clear that Dacre herself, familiar with controversy throughout her childhood, had skillfully channeled critics' outrage into publishing success, in part through her sexually charged authorial persona. While Dacre's writing reveled in the sexual and blasphemous excesses of Lewis's writing, Bannerman was interested in different qualities of the Gothic, choosing instead to intensify the obscurity and ambiguity characteristic of Lewis's supernatural poetry and Radcliffe's novels. Perhaps these contrasting qualities of the Gothic, its erotic explicitness and its studied ambiguity, help account for Dacre's publishing success as a novelist, and Bannerman's commercial failure as a poet.

Bannerman's first volume, *Poems* (1800), published by Mundell in Edinburgh and Longman in London, was dedicated to the influential scholar Dr. Robert Anderson. *Poems* was highly praised in reviews and contained a series of extended poems such as "The Genii" and "The Nun," original odes and sonnets, and two sonnet series based on Petrarch and *Werther*.[1] Her second volume, the Gothic ballad collection *Tales of Superstition and Chivalry* (1802), was published anonymously by Vernor and Hood, and received less favorable reviews. Both volumes were revised and reprinted in an 1807 volume, *Poems, A New Edition*, dedicated to Lady Charlotte Rawdon and published by subscription in the hope of earning enough to allow the income-less author to live off the interest. These three volumes, and a substantial amount of periodical poetry, represent the bulk of Bannerman's literary production.

Bannerman's critical obscurity is the effect of a complex set of forces, which this chapter examines in detail: the material circumstances of her books' production; their critical (mis)timing and reception; her precarious position in an important (and masculine) Edinburgh literary circle that included Robert Anderson, Thomas Campbell, John Leyden, and Bishop Percy; and, last but not least, as Bannerman herself put it to her publisher, her poems' "peculiarity of subject," because of which "it was not to be expected that they could please generally."[2] This "peculiarity" refers both to the gender and the genre of her subjects, and thus gender and genre must figure prominently in any discussion of Bannerman's work and of her importance to us today. It was the peculiarity of her female figures, and the opulently Gothic manner in which she wrote, that led the poet herself to expect a small audience and a fleeting one.

Before appreciating the peculiarity of her subject, especially in her unusual femme fatale figures, we need first to place this remarkable poet in the context of her immediate literary publishing circle, which revolved around the eminent editor Dr. Robert Anderson. This chapter next examines the "peculiarity of subject" of Bannerman's poetry, and the Gothic excesses of its style and labyrinthine structures, focusing on three poems and their femmes fatales: "The Dark Ladie," "The Prophetess of the Oracle of Seäm," and "The Mermaid." A minor publishing scandal involving one of the engravings in her volume of ballads, and the sexual dynamics and hierarchies of publishing in Edinburgh at the turn of the nineteenth century, will illustrate why Bannerman stopped publishing poetry in 1807 to become a governess, while her friends Campbell and Leyden went on to enjoy professional literary careers.

What little we know about Bannerman's life we know largely through Dr. Robert Anderson's letters about her, detailing his efforts to help her publish, and her destitution and depression after the deaths of her brother (a surgeon with the East India Company, who drowned off the coast of Africa) and mother, which left her impoverished, alone, and "inconsolable." Her father had been a "running stationer," a street merchant authorized to sell and sing broadside ballads.[3] Bannerman's familiarity with the ballad tradition, both literary and oral, is evident in her strongest work, *Tales of Superstition and Chivalry*. Anderson, the editor of the influential 13-volume *Complete British Poets* (1792–95), sent his literary friends copies of Bannerman's first volume, *Poems*, along with Thomas Campbell's first volume (*The Pleasures of Hope*), warmly praising both poets' first efforts. Anderson marveled at the "splendor & energy" of her poetry, and declared that "[s]o opulent a mind at such an age is a phe-nomenon."[4] He also put her in contact with Joseph Cooper Walker (the Irish scholar of Italian and Gaelic-Irish literature, who was also a friend of Charlotte Smith), and organized her 1807 edition of poems by subscrip-tion as a means of relieving her impoverishment, an effort which largely failed, for the publisher had trouble getting the 250 subscribers to take the volume. Her 1800 *Poems* continued to sell at least until 1806, when, according to the Longman archives, of the 160 copies on hand in 1803, 32 more had sold. The death of her mother in 1803 had left Bannerman without any income or family, and by 1804 she was also without a home. Thomas Percy, the Bishop of Dromore and editor of *Reliques of Ancient English Poetry* (1765), was another admirer of Bannerman's poetry, and in 1804 sent her 10 guineas via Anderson.[5] In 1805 Bannerman, with Lady Charlotte Rawdon's support, appealed to Lord Melville for a pension, which was not granted. Thomas Park was successful in his application to the Royal Literary Fund on her behalf, and she was awarded £20 that same year.

Anderson's letters from 1800 to 1807 show his growing disapproval of Bannerman's efforts at self-education (she taught herself Italian) and a literary career. He consistently recommended that she renounce the hope of becoming a serious and self-supporting writer, and urged her to become a governess, which she eventually did in 1807 for Lady Beresford of Exeter, earning £60 per annum. For example, Anderson wrote that: "My ideas of moral duty have inclined me, from the beginning, to give the preference to the scheme of tuition as the means of living a livelihood by the diligent & honourable exertions of her own talents & personal in-dustry." "Being born to the prospects of no pecuniary provision, this was her original" destiny, wrote Anderson, and the consequence "of her receiving an education above her condition."[6] By 1818, she was living in Edinburgh again, and visited the writer Anne Grant in 1824, who commented on Bannerman's progressively worse illness, "high intellec-tual powers," and "her little irritations [which] never disturbed me but on her own account."[7] In her final years, Bannerman was surviving at least in part on donations from her former pupil and Lady Beresford. In September 1829, Bannerman died, an invalid and in debt, in Por-tobello, a small marine town on the outskirts of Edinburgh. Baroness Caroline Nairne, the well-known ballad writer and Jacobite, lived in Portobello from 1806 to around 1838, and Scott frequently visited the Portobello beach while writing *The Lay of the Last Minstrel* in 1802.[8] After Bannerman's death, Lady Beresford paid £22 towards Bannerman's debts, and urged a mutual friend to destroy all of Bannerman's letters, adding enigmatically that "They cannot be in safer hands than yours."[9]

THE PALPABLE OBSCURE

Bannerman's championing of Gothic obscurity[10] serves as a touchstone throughout this chapter, associating her with a feminized and critically maligned Gothic poetics. Relying on labyrinthine narrative structures and enigmatic veiled figures, Bannerman's poems resisted the attempts of readers and critics to unveil their meaning. In thus resisting a will to truth, a desire for absolute truth and vision, Bannerman's veiled femmes fatales resisted the emergent Romantic poetics of the ideal as unveiled truth, and of the ideal woman. This (proto)feminist resistance to ideals of femininity and feminized ideals, like her related Gothic obscurity, contributed to her critics' and male patrons' disaffection with her work. Anne Bannerman's obscurity, then, has much to teach us about the specific circumstances and necessities that women poets faced in the first decade of the nineteenth century. Moreover, by taking into account more than her poetry's unusual thematic content (i.e., more than gender content), this chapter makes a case for the significance of the materiality of texts, and how these social factors should be taken into account in any reevaluation of Romantic-period women writers.

Anne Bannerman's siren speaker in her poem "The Mermaid" (1800) declares that "Mine was the choice, in this terrific form, To brave the icy surge, to shiver in the storm," challenging the popular generalization that femmes fatales are figments of misogynist fantasy. Bannerman did not use the ostensibly male-inspired figure of the femme fatale simply to critique male writers' objectification of women, though she did make this critique powerfully and repeatedly. Bannerman also simultaneously, and paradoxically, used this seductive figure both to evoke and critique Romantic idealism, while submitting this critique of Romantic ideology to a further, (proto)feminist critique. Embodying the dangerously seductive powers of poetry as illusion, Bannerman's femmes fatales thus shared in Romanticism's powerful (self-)critique of a poetics of presence, and simultaneously foregrounded how this poetics of presence is gendered. The femme fatale is not a preoccupation of misogynist fantasy, a symptom of men's fears; but neither is she simply a reaction to women's exclusion from literary history, a symptom of women's anger. As we have seen, the femme fatale can be both a subject of feminism and of Romanticism.

The existence of femmes fatales in women's writings of the Romantic period does not serve as a mere supplement to our necessarily incomplete literary histories. Bannerman's use of femmes fatales to both suggest and deny a Romantic poetics of (feminized) ideals, and ideals of femininity, is significant today as another early gendered critique of Romantic ideologies of the imagination and the will to truth. Bannerman's praise of obscurity runs counter to the growing spirit of revelation, truth and simplicity found in the works of contemporary poets such as William Wordsworth, a sensibility she shares with the early Coleridge and Lewis, whose works she knew well.

The distinctive feature of her *Tales of Superstition and Chivalry* is the cultivated obscurity of its narratives, as her contemporary reviewers consistently observed:

the author has heard that obscurity is one source of the sublime, and has therefore veiled his [*sic*] sublimity in impenetrable darkness. (*Critical Review*, 1803)

The language is in a high degree poetical, and the incidents well imagined. One fault, however, runs nearly through the whole of the volume. It is obscurity. (*Poetical Register of 1802*)[11]

Her poetry seduces but does not satisfy, complained the *Critical Review*: "The beginning of every poem excites expectations of something very great" (111). In five of her ten *Tales of Superstition and Chivalry*, these unresolved narrative expectations are embodied in female figures that are never satisfactorily unveiled: "The Dark Ladie," "The Prophetess of the Oracle of Seäm," "The Penitent's Confession," "The Prophecy of Merlin" and "The Festival of St. Magnus."[12] Thus Anna Seward complained, in a series of harsh letters published during Bannerman's lifetime, of "the palpable obscure" of her poetry, which Seward dismissed as "laboured imitations of the Della Crusca school" and "stilted abortions."[13] Remarkably, Seward had also asked their mutual friend Thomas Park to deliver a long letter to Bannerman in which Seward attacked her work in unaccountably vicious terms (i.e., as "stilted abortions") after receiving a copy of *Tales*. Park refused to send the letter to Bannerman, and was shocked at Seward's harshness, particularly toward a "sister poetess," in publishing similar letters attacking Bannerman.[14]

Seward's attack reveals her antipathy toward Bannerman's poetry's unacceptable flaunting of the conventions of femininity, as well as a larger cultural unease with both the eroticism of the Della Cruscans and the anticlosural obscurity of the Gothic.[15] Seward had also dismissed *Tales of*

Superstition as a parody of Coleridge's "Rime of the Ancyent Marinere" (1798), "which is itself a fine original wild thing," but likewise "its faults are too much obscurity of purpose, & of moral."[16] Thus Coleridge's dangerous Gothic excess is, according to Seward, taken to an unacceptably self-conscious level in the "satiric mirror" of *Tales of Superstition* (*Ibid.*). Seward's disingenious dismissal of Bannerman's ballads nevertheless reveals an important link between Bannerman and Coleridge in the minds of their readers, one which highlights Coleridge's seminal role in the development of Gothic poetics (a poetics which, as he and Bannerman understood, eschews originality and authenticity for a different set of effects). The Della Cruscan comparison was another common critical insult at that time, leveled most often at women poets, like Robinson and Dacre; in Bannerman's case, the comparison is presumably based on her "opulent" style and on her two sonnet series that focused on erotic passion, re-workings of Petrarch and of Goethe's *Werther*. But reviews of the 1800 *Poems*, which had contained the two sonnet series, were very positive, even in a conservative journal such as the *British Critic*, and reviews typically focused on the sublimity of the volume's original odes, not on the passionate sonnets. Seward's charge of obscurity was directed specifically at the Gothic *Tales of Superstition*, and thus her impatience with Bannerman's obscurity demonstrates an important point of contact between Della Cruscan and Gothic, as two devalued and excessively feminine genres that by 1802 were frequently maligned by critics and established poets such as Seward and Wordsworth, even as they continued to exert considerable influence on both writers and readers.

Bannerman's femmes fatales, who seduce but do not satisfy, hold a special place in literary histories of the femme fatale, written as they were between those of Coleridge and Keats. Mario Praz's *The Romantic Agony* is by far the most influential account of the femme fatale, and before diverging from his focus on male sexual neuroses, I will first place Bannerman's femmes fatales in relation to those of her male contemporaries. According to Praz, although in Romanticism "there is no established type of Fatal Woman in the way that there is an established type of Byronic hero," "[n]evertheless a line of tradition may be traced through the characters of these Fatal Women, right from the beginning of Romanticism" (191). Within this male Romantic tradition of the fatal woman, Keats's "La Belle Dame sans Merci" holds special significance because she possesses many of the qualities of the late nineteenth-century fatal woman, and Praz traces Keats's La Belle Dame one step further, to Coleridge's "Introduction to the Tale of the Dark Ladie."[17]

Between Coleridge's Dark Ladie and Keats's La Belle Dame, however, we have already located a wealth of femmes fatales in the works of women writers. In three of Anne Bannerman's poems – "The Dark Ladie" (1800), "The Prophetess of the Oracle of Seäm" (1802), and "The Mermaid" (1800) – we encounter surprisingly destructive and seductive female characters that stand in stark contrast to the domestic, rational female characters that dominate much of women's literature of this period. Bannerman shared the work of developing the Romantic tradition of the femme fatale with Coleridge, Keats, and Lewis, yet, significantly and perhaps surprisingly, her femmes fatales are even more destructive than those created by her male counterparts.

Bannerman's poems respond directly to Coleridge's "Introduction to the Tale of the Dark Ladie," Johnson's *Rambler*, and perhaps Schiller's "The Veiled Image of Saïs," Coleridge's and Schiller's works forming part of Praz's canon. But Bannerman's use of the femme fatale amounts to much more than a critique of male Romanticism's representation of Woman, though it certainly is that; Bannerman also uses the radical alterity of the femme fatale to explore the concept of the (female) poet as prophet. She does so by appearing to allow her supernatural femmes fatales to inhabit the acultural space beyond language, the myth of the pure (feminine) presence beyond the veil. Her Dark Ladie and Sibylline Prophetess are familiar to us as Romantic Muses, yet they are themselves (simultaneously and impossibly) also inspired poet figures whose female gender highlights the double-bind in which women poets of Romanticism found themselves: that is, women may be either the object or Muse of Romantic inspiration, but not its subject. Bannerman does not offer a tidy solution to this long-standing problem of women and language. She could, for example, have unveiled the veiled female presence in "The Prophetess of the Oracle of Seäm" and allowed her to speak in her original "language strange." She could have traced to her Prophetess's cave the origin of women's exiled cultural and poetic power, but instead she confronts us with "terrible" doubt. In "The Prophetess," discussed in detail below, we only glimpse this enigmatic female figure through an unreliable third-hand account of a priest's ordeal:

> For he had said the veil was drawn
> That hid the sacrifice within;
> That his eyes had seen the Prophetess
> At that uncover'd shrine;

> But whether his knee had bended there
> Was buried with him in the grave:...
> He felt that doubt more terrible
> Than the terrors of the cave.
>
> (*Tales*, 33, orig. ellipsis)

Mary Shelley similarly resisted an essentializing gesture (of "woman" speaking in her true, authentic voice) in her Introduction to *The Last Man*, where her narrator hints at the fragmentary, mediated nature of even the Sibyl's divinely inspired rhapsodies, the basis of the novel's narrative: "My only excuse for thus transforming them, was that they were unintelligible in their pristine fashion" (4). Bannerman's female prophetesses and veiled supernatural figures like "The Dark Ladie" are, in fact, ruthlessly demystified, not through the explained supernatural preferred by Radcliffe, but through the poems' stubborn resistance to narrative clarity, what is in fact an excessive and opulent mysticism that draws attention to itself as such.

Bannerman's female prophets offer only destruction, the consequence of objectifying women as absent ideals; they are examples of the poet as destroying demon, cursed and exiled like the Ancient Mariner, and simultaneously, of Muses who withhold their "gift" of inspiration and instead inspire only terror by demonstrating language's radical lack of originality and referentiality. By terrifying the men they encounter into either stunned silence or uncontrollable repetition, figures like Coleridge's Mariner only without any pretense of Christian penance, these dark ladies mercilessly disabuse their readers of any faith in language as redemptive, and in absolute unveiled (female) presence as retrieved wholeness.

Walter Scott's praise of Bannerman's poetry in his "Essay on Imitations of the Ancient Ballad" (published in 1830, the year after Bannerman's death) identifies precisely the evocative quality of her poetry:

Miss Anne Bannerman likewise should not be forgotten, whose *Tales of Superstition and Chivalry* appeared about 1802. They were perhaps too mystical and too abrupt; yet if it be the purpose of this kind of ballad poetry powerfully to excite the imagination, without pretending to satisfy it, few persons have succeeded better than this gifted lady, whose volume is peculiarly fit to be read in a lonely house by a decaying lamp. (16–17)

Bannerman's poems are indeed "too mystical and too abrupt," and, as Scott recognized, their genius lies in their consistent thwarting of their reader's will to truth. By exciting our desire to unveil the feminized ideal, without pretending to satisfy this desire, Bannerman foregrounds the power and centrality of this feminized ideal in Romantic poetry, and simultaneously foregrounds the power of the poet in so expertly seducing her readers. Her poetry enacts a merciless critique of poetic mysticism, and yet through this very process exercises and glorifies poetry's seductive powers.

"THE DARK LADIE"

Women must always see things through a veil, or cease to be women
Maria Edgeworth, *Letters for Literary Ladies* (1795)

The close relation of Bannerman's "The Dark Ladie" to Coleridge's "Introduction to the Tale of the Dark Ladie" places Bannerman firmly in the canonical femme fatale tradition with which modern readers are more familiar. Coleridge's "Introduction to the Tale of the Dark Ladie," first published in the *Morning Post* (1799) and the *Edinburgh Magazine* (1800), and later in the *Lyrical Ballads* (1800 onwards), slightly altered, as "Love," was composed between parts 1 and 2 of "Christabel."[18] As Praz noted, Coleridge's poem contains a prototype of La Belle Dame sans Merci, and Coleridge's narrative of "the cruel scorn, / that craz'd this bold and lovely Knight" is told by a poet to his beloved in order to seduce her by appealing to her mercy (*STC*, 11: 1056). Coleridge's poem uses the Belle Dame figure as valuable pawn in a masculine sexual economy, a fantastic "beautiful and bright" Fiend whose pride the poet makes an example of in order to seduce his virginal beloved, also a figure of male fantasy, for she is described in terms that echo the beautiful and bright fiend: "And so I won my Genevieve, / My bright and beaut'ous bride" (*STC*, 11: 1059). His seduction complete when his lover swoons into his arms, the poet in Coleridge's ballad illustrates the Romantic appropriation by which "romance as a medieval genre is transformed into romance as amorous fantasy."[19] The poem concludes with a promise that will remain unkept for over thirty years: "I promis'd thee a sister tale / Of man's perfidious cruelty: Come, then, and hear what cruel wrong / Befel the Dark Ladie" (*STC*, 11: 1059). Coleridge's "The Ballad of the Dark Ladie" was indeed apparently written in 1798, but only published in 1834. It is a traditional ballad of a woman who has been betrayed by a knight to whom she gave what she "can ne'er recall" (*STC*, 1: 294), and ends with her fantasy of their wedding day which we know shall never be.

Anne Bannerman published her own "sister tale" of the Dark Ladie in her 1802 volume of supernatural ballads, *Tales of Superstition and Chivalry*. In fact, she first published "The Dark Ladie" in the *Edinburgh Magazine*, with a footnote directing readers to Coleridge's "Introduction to the Tale of the Dark Ladie," published in the same journal one month earlier.[20] Bannerman's "Dark Ladie" is remarkable, and remarkably dissimilar from the version Coleridge eventually published, for several reasons. Bannerman focuses on the Ladie's terrifying revenge upon the Christian crusaders who took her from her home in the Holy Land, providing not another tale of women's victimization but of one woman's revenge. Second, Bannerman's supernatural ballad resists the covert misogyny of the Romantic idealization of women found in Coleridge's "Introduction to the Tale of the Dark Ladie." While Coleridge's balladeer tells his tale of women's cruelty in order to seduce both the listener (his idealized beloved) and the reader, in fact producing another potential Dark Ladie in his beloved, Bannerman's multiple male narrators compulsively tell the tale of the Dark Ladie's seduction because, like the Ancient Mariner, they are cursed to do so. Her poem thus replies to Coleridge's call for a sister tale by avenging the seduction in his own poem, and its seductive misogyny that promised a lamentable tale of yet another fallen woman. Third, Bannerman's poem is a high Romantic exploration of imagination, and its pursuit of the ideal. The Dark Ladie is a veiled female figure who can never be unveiled, ostensibly the embodiment of Romantic idealism, yet her destructive influence and her resistance to this very role subvert the idealist tradition she embodies.

Bannerman's Dark Ladie imprisons her captor and a succession of men like him in the very castle in which he sought to imprison her, by compelling these knights to repeat the tale of her seduction and destruction, precisely the traditional tale of women's sexual victimization Coleridge introduced. But Bannerman's Dark Ladie, unlike Coleridge's, forces the knights to repeat this predictable narrative in order to destroy them, not simply to elicit their pity. Bannerman's poem begins with the return of the crusading knights to celebrate their military victories at the castle of brooding Sir Guyon, named for the Knight of Temperance in Book Two of Spenser's *Faerie Queene* who "successfully" resisted Acrasia's temptations in the Bower of Bliss. In Bannerman's revision of this classic scene of the dangers and pleasures presented by femininity, the Circean Dark Ladie pledges the questing knights herself with a glass of wine. Unlike Spenser's Ladie, she offers them no temptation and no bliss, only

a curse that they repeat her story, leaving them almost certainly trapped
in the entirely masculine House of Temperance.

The Dark Ladie's spectacular entrance into this excessively masculine
scene is significant, and I therefore quote it at length:

> A Ladie, clad in ghastly white,
> And veiled to the feet:
>
> She spoke not when she enter'd there;
> She spoke not when the feast was done;
> And every knight, in chill amaze,
> Survey'd her one by one:
>
> For thro' the foldings of her veil,
> Her long black veil that swept the ground,
> A light was seen to dart from eyes
> That mortal never own'd.
>
> And when the knights on Guyon turn'd
> Their fixed gaze, and shudder'd now;
> For smother'd fury seem'd to bring
> The dew-drops on his brow.
>
> But, from the Ladie in the veil,
> Their eyes they could not long withdraw,
> And when they tried to speak, that glare
> Still kept them mute with awe!
>
> [....]
>
> And to the' alarmed guests she turn'd,
> No breath was heard, no voice, no sound,
> And in a tone, so deadly deep,
> She pledg'd them all around,
> That in their hearts, and thro' their limbs,
> No pulses could be found.   (*Tales*, 5–7)

After this terrifying visit of the Dark Ladie, which the poet implies occurs
each night, each knight is haunted by her veiled form in his sleep, and
the reader eventually hears of her story through a succession of accounts,
one knight telling the others how he too is still haunted by her story:

> "But O! that Ladie! Huart cries, ...
> That Ladie, with the long black veil,
> This morn I heard! ... I hear it still,
> The lamentable tale!

"I hear the hoary-headed man,
I kept him till the morning dawn,
For five unbroken hours he talk'd,
With me they were as one!
(*Tales*, 11, orig. ellipsis)

Bannerman implies that this hoary-headed Mariner figure, like Sir Guyon, is a prisoner of the Dark Ladie's narrative because he too remains in this isolated castle, and is compelled to tell her story to visiting knights: "peace...he never had, since he saw the Dark Ladie!" But the Ladie herself transforms the old man into this Mariner figure through her piercing gaze which itself resembles the Ancient Mariner's: "It glared for ever on his sight, / That fixed eye, so wildly keen! Till life became a heavy load; / And long had heavy been" (*Tales*, 14). The reader is left wondering if these knights too will waste away in the castle, held in thrall like Keats's "pale kings and princes" by the Ladie's lamentable tale.

Bannerman's poem ends with the knight Huart recounting a tale which the hoary-headed man himself heard from an unnamed source, through which we learn that she had been taken from her husband, child, and home in the Holy Land after Guyon and his knights had murdered the "infidels" "beneath the blessed Cross." The knight's account of the Ladie's tale, like the hoary-headed man's tale on which it is based, is enigmatic and unreliable, and leaves unresolved for the reader (as for the knights) the truth of the Ladie's death, and the truth of who or what she actually is, since she cannot be unveiled. The knight concludes the poem with a series of questions that are unresolved and unresolvable, ending with, "why it cannot be remov'd / That folded veil that sweeps the ground?"

The Ladie's veils, which allow her to look out but prevent the knights from looking in, frustrate the Romantic desire for the ideal, a desire which the veils, of course, simultaneously represent and in fact generate. All who see the Dark Ladie are struck by the unearthly eyes that penetrate her veils from the inside out, and the corresponding engraving in Bannerman's volume illustrates precisely such a moment (Figure 3). She is thus an impossibility – a feminine, exoticized object that not only resists and foregrounds her objectification through her multiple veils, but returns it by reducing the (male colonial) subjects of the gaze to silent and immobile objects: "But, from the Ladie in the veil, / Their eyes they could not long withdraw, / And when they tried to speak, that glare / still kept them mute with awe!"

Figure 3 MacKenzie after E. W. Thomson, "The Dark Ladie," from Anne
Bannerman's *Tales of Superstition and Chivalry* (1802). Courtesy of the Department
of Special Collections, University of California, Davis.

The Dark Ladie is not once but doubly veiled, which, in addition to signaling the Ladie's racial and religious otherness as a Muslim, also recalls Coleridge's Ladie. She wears the white wedding veil, for, as in Coleridge's poem, she was cheated out of marriage, and the black veil which here signifies death, for the poem suggests that the Ladie is a revenant returned for revenge. The double veil suggests more than double resistance to unveiling – it suggests endless veils, the impossibility of depth and its latent meanings. "The veil is the place of any voided expectation" in Gothic writing, writes Eve Kosofsky Sedgwick, because it "very often hides Nothing, or death, or in particular, some cheat that means absence and substitution."[21] The absence the Dark Ladie embodies and unleashes on the knights is the absence of Woman herself, and, by extension, the absence of the Romantic ideal. If Coleridge's "Introduction to the Tale of the Dark Ladie" relies on two traditional stereotypes of Woman (the Beloved and the Dark Ladie, or the bride and the fiend), then Bannerman's Dark Ladie embodies both these extremes, literalized in her veils of pure light and pure darkness. She proceeds to use this double construction against these very men, or poets, who proliferate such images of women through the seductive tales they tell.

According to Bannerman's response to Coleridge, then, the tales men tell of the Dark Ladie, of femmes fatales in general, originate not in the fantasies of male speakers/poets, nor in the "true" voices of oppressed women, but in a model of narrative as a powerful curse to which narrators and poets are alike subject (albeit in different ways), and in which all language is repetition. Behind such tales of the femme fatale, significantly, Bannerman also often locates an act of sexual violence, so that her Dark Ladie provides a much-needed gendered perspective. Yet for Bannerman this resistance to Romantic misogyny accompanies a simultaneous fascination with the femme fatale as a demonic poet, cursed like the Mariner to a life of utter alienation, yet also, like the poet of "Kubla Khan," possessing a dangerous and seductive gift in her unearthly song that "came forth, dull, deep, and wild, / and O! how deadly slow!"

Her work also shares with Coleridge's early poetry its antipathy to narrativity, particularly in "Christabel." "Christabel" was composed in 1797 and 1800 and pulled from the *Lyrical Ballads* largely due to William Wordsworth's frustration with the expectations of narrative closure that it initiates but does not satisfy.[22] Published much later in 1816, "Christabel" generated critical hostility and popular parodies, and thus has much in common with the fate of Bannerman's *Tales of Superstition* as a whole.[23] We should remember, too, that the same journals that complained of Bannerman's obscurity and narrative confusion also dismissed Coleridge's "The Rime of the Ancyent Marinere" as "a rhapsody of unintelligible wildness and incoherence," a "confusion of images," and an unconnected series of stanzas that are "absurd or unintelligible,"[24] leading Wordsworth to remove it from its position as the opening poem in *Lyrical Ballads*. Thus, both the early Coleridge and Bannerman paid a price for their Gothic antinarrative poetics. Paul Magnuson has recently argued that such an antinarrative and extravagant poetics is implicitly politically radical, and was received as such at the time, accounting in part for Coleridge's (and by extension Bannerman's) poor reception: "That which is a rhapsody, or obscure, or unintelligible, or extravagant in the 1790s is highly suspicious and dangerous to the civil peace."[25] The "Ancyent Marinere" in particular was "to many of its readers...a Jacobin poem of violated boundaries and errant wandering" (*Ibid.*, 109). Yet Magnuson's argument does not seem to account for the conflicting Burkean associations of the obscure, and the related emphasis on clarity and demystification found in radical rhetoric of the 1790s. Bannerman's obscurity, like Coleridge's, reveals the characteristic slipperiness of the Gothic that make its politics difficult to categorize comfortably, particularly by modern feminist criteria, and consequently makes such criteria visible.

"THE PROPHETESS OF THE ORACLE OF SEÄM"

> I have passed from the outermost portal
> To the shrine where a sin is a prayer
> > Algernon Swinburne, "Dolores"

Bannerman's remarkable ballad, "The Prophetess of the Oracle of Seäm" (1802), like "The Dark Ladie," provides an antinarrative that centers on a female figure that cannot be unveiled. The poem builds on a brief note from Drayton's *Polyolbion* about the mythical isle of Seäm in the English Channel where nine virgin priestesses were said to tend an oracle and possess supernatural powers.[26] More significantly, she may be combining this obscure reference with Schiller's "The Veiled Image of Saïs," which she may have read since, although his poetry was not as widely known as his drama, fugitive translations had appeared in British periodicals which also included Bannerman's poems.[27] In Schiller's poem, an Egyptian youth penetrates beyond the veil in the temple of Isis in order to see the truth unveiled, and pays with his life, being afterward stunned into silence. Nietzsche's reading of Schiller's poem exemplifies his radical attack of idealism's will to truth:

one will hardly find us again on the paths of those Egyptian youths who endanger temples by night, embrace statues, and want by all means to unveil, uncover, and put into a bright light whatever is kept concealed for good reasons. No, this bad taste, this will to truth, to "truth at any price," this youthful madness in the love of truth, have lost their charm for us: for that we are too experienced, too serious, too merry, too burned, too *profound*. We no longer believe that truth remains truth when the veils are withdrawn; we have lived too much to believe this. Today we consider it a matter of decency not to wish to see everything naked, or to be present at everything, or to understand and "know" everything.[28]

Like Nietzsche and Percy Bysshe Shelley in "[Lift Not the Painted Veil]," Bannerman counsels against lifting the veil, because, like Nietzsche, she too does not "believe that truth remains truth when the veils are withdrawn." Yet her Prophetess of Seäm does not wait, like Schiller's Isis, for young men to seek her out and violate her temple – she destroys passing ships with her voice and selects specific men – priests – to bring behind the veil. Bannerman's critique of the Romantic will to truth is a proto-feminist one (unlike Nietzsche's), for her priestess of the oracle is active, not an ideal and absent female object of male pursuit. And, significantly, Bannerman never reveals the priestess either, so that we do not know what it was, if anything, that the priest saw behind the veil of the shrine, only that its presence, or absence, shattered his faith and reduced him to a living phantom.

Bannerman is fascinated by moments of unveiling, which are repeated and deferred through narrative frames in many of her poems. Like Tennyson in "The Lady of Shalott," Bannerman knows that the most powerful (and difficult) evocation of poetry in a poem is not the moment of revelation – the unveiled truth – nor the moments of searching for this truth, but the acts of veiling and unveiling. The process itself of making "truth," not the product made, is one way of defining a poet as maker, one who produces. Blanchot writes:

The poem is thus the veil which makes the fire visible, which reveals it precisely by veiling it and concealing it. The poem shows, then; it discloses, but by concealing, because it detains in the dark that which can only be revealed in the light of darkness. (*Space of Literature*, 230)

Yet Bannerman's poetics of veiling offers an unique gendered perspective, for in her work the poem that is the veil is also a female figure (the phantasmatic embodiment of woman as truth/poem). Moreover, Bannerman makes this figure a poet herself, exiled to an undersea cave, to the light of darkness. Her Prophetess is thus both the Romantic *poète maudit*, and a distinctly female poet. Mary Browne made a similar, though conventional, point in her poem "The Poetess" (1828):

> Oh! Woman's heart is like
> The silent ocean cave,
> Where sunbeams never strike
> Through the pure wave. [...]
> And, as the sunshine ne'er
> Down to the sea cave came,
> So never pierceth there
> The light of fame.[29]

Browne's poetess simply waits in obscurity to be unveiled, however, whereas Bannerman goes far beyond this unproblematic (though sympathetic) lament over the invisibility of women poets.

Bannerman consciously frames her ballads of the Dark Ladie and of the Prophetess of Seäm through a series of narrative repetitions that signal the endless deferral of ideal presence on which poetic language depends. She also draws inspired poetry dangerously close to a curse, for the men who encounter the Dark Ladie and Prophetess are never happy again, and, like Coleridge's wedding guest, leave haunted by what they have heard. Yet this deferral and repetition, while negating poetry's power to speak the truth, simultaneously affirms the power of poetry to curse. Curses, or more generally incantations, are of course popular Romantic enactments of poetry's performative power, yet they are rarely discussed in relation to women's writing. Bannerman (and Landon, as we shall see) in this respect offers an important precursor to Barrett Browning's vigorous poetic persona in later works such as "A Curse for a Nation" (1860).[30]

Bannerman's "The Prophetess of the Oracle of Seäm" uses a complex and deliberately disorienting series of narrative frames, or more precisely cycles, to undermine the possibility of narrativity itself. The ballad "begins" on a doomed ship with a priest, Father Paul, repeating the legend of the Prophetess who destroys passing ships like a siren, as he heard the tale told by the sole survivor (another priest) of such a shipwreck:

> "And he told them of the Prophetess
> And the Oracle below!

"He told the tale of Seäm's isle,
He told the terrors of its caves,
That none had passed them with life
When that sleep was on the waves !

"He told them, when the winds that roar'd
Around that isle had ceas'd to breathe,
Was the fated night of sacrifice
In the gloomy vaults beneath.

"He told them, he remember'd once
A father of St. Thomas' tower,
Who never had bow'd before the cross
Till he touch'd his dying hour.

"That then he named to the priest
What he had seen in Seäm's caves,
For he had reach'd them in a ship
When that calm was on the waves !

"Thro' the sleepless nights of thirty months,
He had listen'd to that shriek of woe;
But he never had seen the Prophetess
Of the Oracle below!

"Till that chilly night, at the equinox height,
When the thirty months were gone,
As he listen'd, in the outer cave,
To that unbroken groan,

"A hand, he saw not, dragg'd him on,
The voice within had call'd his name !
And he told all he witnessed
At the Oracle of flame !

"But when he came to tell, at last,
What fearful sacrifice had bled,
His agony began anew,
And he could not raise his head!

"And he never spoke again at all,
For he died that night in sore dismay:
So sore, that all were tranc'd for hours
That saw his agony!   (22–25)

As in this tale that Father Paul tells the sailors, their ship is destroyed
and he alone is taken beneath the sea to the oracle.

The "central" story of the Prophetess at Seäm's shrine is this reiteration and continuation of the story Father Paul himself had heard from the previous priest, a member of his order (St. Thomas' Tower at Einsidlin).[31] The third-person narrator shows us how, when Father Paul himself encounters the Prophetess' oracle, he is in fact remembering it, by recounting the stories he had heard from past priests, so that his own account of the truth behind the veil, like all such accounts, is mediated:

> Like a dream it flitted o'er his brain.
> That miserable hour!
> When the father died, in agony,
> In the cell of St. Thomas' tower;
>
> For he had said the veil was drawn
> That hid the sacrifice within;
> That his eyes had seen the Prophetess
> At that uncover'd shrine;
>
> But whether his knee had bended there
> Was buried with him in the grave:...
> He felt that doubt more terrible
> Than the terrors of the cave....
>
> (*Tales*, 33, orig. ellipsis)

The poem "ends" within this cycle of repetition, when, forty years later, a new priest encounters the ghostly Father Paul, who like the poet (and preacher) in Shelley's poem, "strove [f]or truth, and...found it not."[32] Upon Father Paul's return on Pentecost (which celebrates the descent of the Holy Spirit on the disciples) to his order at Einsidlin, he creates another silent and haunted figure in the new priest presiding at the altar: "It awed the priest of Einsidlin, / And he could not speak at all!" (36). This newest victim of the presence behind the veil remains immobilized at the altar-rail in his church, so that the Prophetess' shrine imagined in the depths of the sea mirrors the Christian altar, where the faithful remain enchanted by a Holy Spirit which may or may not exist, enduring a "doubt more terrible / Than the terrors of the cave."

One possible explanation for Father Paul's despair is that he may have "bent his knee / At Seäm's dark, unhallow'd shrine" (25), putting aside his crucifix and worshipping another deity, a distinctly female one. This is precisely Swinburne's deepest desire in "Dolores," to pass "from the outermost portal / To the shrine where a sin is a prayer," overturning Christianity's empire by worshipping the older chthonic goddesses of the underworld. Bannerman's Christian priests enter this shrine, though she never resolves for us what precisely their sin is, or if they even commit one, or what divine or infernal deity, if any, inhabits the shrine. She leaves all possibilities open, so that we readers are in the same position as those who listen, spellbound, to the legendary tale of the powers of this oracle. All priests (and faithful readers) collapse into one another in this poem, and the mystical revelation at the heart of each of their narratives emerges as an effect of the endless creation, pursuit, and deferral of divine presence in readings of poetry that search for truths (readings frustrated by Bannerman's obscurity, such as Scott's, Seward's, and the *Poetical Register's*). This perpetual suspension of presence is also, of course, the high Romantic poem in its making and unmaking.

Bannerman's oracular poetry does not ultimately offer any visions or truth, nor does it answer for us the question, what use are poets in times of distress?,[33] but instead directs us, again and again, to "the answer's absence," in Blanchot's words:

the more the world is affirmed as the future and the broad daylight of truth, where everything will have value, bear meaning, where the whole will be achieved under the mastery of man and for his use, the more it seems that art must descend toward that point where nothing has meaning yet, the more it matters that art maintain the movement, the insecurity and the grief of that which escapes every grasp and all ends. (*Space*, 247, fn. 8)

Bannerman's praise of obscurity and her Gothic excesses are instances of a decidedly Gothic negation of truth. Because she unveils the gender-specific (in this case misogynist) aspect of Romantic imagination in "The Dark Ladie" and "The Prophetess," Bannerman offers us a (proto)feminist critique of a Western metaphysics of presence, specifically Romanticism, and its often violent exclusion of women. Yet, and this is crucial, Bannerman simultaneously celebrates this same poetics, descending again and again to that point where poetry "escapes every grasp and all ends," including feminist ones.

This descent itself is significant, for unlike the prophetic moments of ascent in the works of Coleridge and William Wordsworth, Bannerman's prophetic descents accomplish what Tilottama Rajan argues Shelley's "Mont Blanc" accomplishes: "a deconstruction of the visionary idealism associated with epiphanic ascent and with modes, such as prophecy, that rhetorically simulate ascent."[34] Both Shelley's and Bannerman's poems play at uncovering that "each to itself must be the oracle" of truth,[35] only to completely undermine such faith in the human heart, the "true voice of feeling," and imagination. As a woman poet, Bannerman had an additional reason to question her own sense of language as the true voice of feeling: namely, that, during the Romantic period, women's sphere, particularly that of women poets, was increasingly reduced to that of the emotions and their transparent expression (as Letitia Landon's Improvisatrice lamented, "The echoes of the broken heart, / Were all the songs I now could sing").

SPIRITS OF THE STORM

Unlike the ballads of "The Dark Ladie" and "The Prophetess of the Oracle of Seäm," which used complex narrative cycles, "The Mermaid" sustains a first-person, high prophetic voice that is both feminine and fatal. Her ode begins where Johnson's "Anningait and Ajut" left off in the *Rambler* – a fictional native Greenland woman, whose lover has not returned from the sea, sets out in search of him. Some say, according to Johnson, that her lover "was seized by the Genius of the Rocks, and that [she] . . . was formed into a *Mermaid*, and still continues to seek her lover, in the deserts of the sea."[36] But, as with the Dark Ladie, Bannerman does not give us the sympathetic figure that Johnson (or John Leyden in his "The Mermaid") preferred – the mermaid forever in search of her beloved without whom she is incomplete. Anne Penny's poem "Anningait and Ajut" (1771) similarly sentimentalizes Anningait into a bereaved woman devoted to "Constancy and Love."[37] Rather than seek her lover, Bannerman's bereaved woman transforms herself into a mermaid in order to destroy: "Mine was the choice, in this terrific form, To brave the icy surge, to shiver in the storm" (*AB*, 21). In the "unbounded waste of seas" the mermaid celebrates the destructive power of her song:

> I pour the syren-song of woe; . . .
> Firm on the rent and crashing mast,
> I lend new fury to the blast;
> I mark each hardy cheek grow pale,
> And the proud sons of courage fail;
> Till the torn vessel drinks the surging waves,
> Yawns the disparted main, and opes its shelving graves.
>
> (*AB*, 22–23)

In *The Rambler* tale that Bannerman cites, the narrative is a familiar one of a cruel and beautiful woman who refused to reciprocate the affection of her long-suffering lover before he disappeared, despite his many attempts to please her. As in "The Dark Ladie," then, Bannerman again revises the male-authored femme fatale, not into a sympathetic character, the abandoned woman who laments her fate, but into a more spectacular destroyer whose chief weapon is her song.

Bannerman's poem celebrates the demonic, not the divine, source of poetry, beginning with a terrifying evocation of the correspondent breeze: "Blow on, ye death-fraught whirlwinds! blow, / Around the rocks and rifted caves; / Ye demons of the gulf below!" (20). "The Mermaid" is a supernatural ode sung by a siren poet whose very existence as poet figure challenges any assumption that the demonic or Satanic poet is consistently male, and that mermaids are simply objects of male fear or desire. Here the mermaid is both female poet and pitiless destroyer who aids the "avenging ministers of wrath," an intriguing vision of the Romantic woman poet:

> To aid your toils, to scatter death,
> Swift, as the sheeted lightning's force,
> When the keen north-wind's freezing breath
> Spreads desolation in its course,
> My soul within this icy sea,
> Fulfills her fearful destiny.
> Thro' Time's long ages I shall wait
> To lead the victims to their fate;
> With callous heart, to hidden rocks decoy,
> And lure, in seraph-strains, unpitying, to destroy.
> (*AB*, 24)

Though Bannerman's mermaid embodies the familiar concept of women as treacherous sexual predators, her mermaid cannot be reduced to such male anxieties. Her siren poet consciously manipulates the sailors' expectations by singing the pitiful lament that Johnson, like Coleridge, expected her to sing: "To lure the sailor to his doom; / Soft from some pile of frozen snow / I pour the syren-song of woe." Like the Dark Ladie, then, the mermaid repeats the familiar narrative, but with a deadly difference.[38]

Because Bannerman links sublime destruction and poetry, the magnificent destroyer and the visionary poet, she develops an elusive, and, as yet unaccounted for, model of the woman Romantic poet. In her poem "The Spirit of the Air" (1800), Bannerman assumes a prophetic voice similar to Shelley's in "Ode to the West Wind," and, as in Shelley's poem, her poet's voice ushers in the apocalypse: "The herald of impending fate; / I speak – the suffocating blast descends / In clouds of fluid fire; and Nature's conflict ends" (*AB*, 7). Like Shelley's "West Wind" which raged against the Peterloo massacre (more subtly than he had done in "Mask of Anarchy") earlier that year, Bannerman's "The Spirit of the Air" is also on one level a political poem, for her Spirit of the Air destroys the "men of blood" off "Afric's bleeding shore," slave traders:

> I come, on viewless winds reclin'd
> To cheer the wretch, whom fetters bind,
> To crush the oppressor's giant crest,
> To hurl destruction on his breast,
> Amid the spoils his abject soul adores;
> While trembling earth recoils along her utmost shores.
>
> (*AB*, 4)

In several of Bannerman's poems, the poet speaks in the voice of a tempest, the longest and most remarkable being "The Genii," and her poetry aspires to the dangerous heights of a "Mont Blanc," allying herself, like Shelley was to do, with the questionable poetic power found in "A desart peopled by the storms alone" ("Mont Blanc," III. 67).

Bannerman's evocations of storms are significantly different from those of other women poets, for example, Felicia Hemans's "The Voice of Spring" (1823), where the poet summons "the children of gladness" and vows to seek them "in a world where there falls no blight."[39] Hemans's voice of the spring wind ushers in life, even while it acknowledges the power of death over such a seemingly blightless world. In contrast, Bannerman's voice of the storm is relentlessly destructive and clear about poetry's role in this destruction. Bannerman's natural and supernatural destroyers often prey on patriarchal Christian institutions, those of chivalry and superstition, as her volume's title indicates. At the end of her sonnet "The Watchman" (1800), for example, the lighthouse watchman, like Coleridge's Mariner and the priest in the "Prophetess of Seäm," is engulfed by a storm precisely when he invokes divine assistance: "he... calls on Heav'n: – The billows urge their way, / Upheave the rooted base, and all is swept away" (*AB*, 95). The destruction of the watchman is the occasion of the poem's creation, for the narrator had entered the poem midway, in time to see and recount the destruction: "I mark, between the blasts infuriate fits, / The gleaming taper's solitary ray, / And fancy wanders where the watchman sits" (*AB*, 95). The arrival of the poet's wandering "fancy" on the scene coincides with the obliteration of the scene itself, the watchman, and the poem – all this through fancy's invocation, and ruthless negation, of the power of invocation itself.

Bannerman's poems repeatedly demonstrate what Steven Goldsmith argues Shelley's *Prometheus Unbound* unwillingly demonstrates, that "the liberation of creative imagination occurs only in conjunction with the release of destructive power."[40] Goldsmith argues that "the violence of Shelley's apocalyptic imagination" was at odds with his political and poetic idealism (*Ibid.*, 225); the violence of Bannerman's imagination is similarly at odds with her own political and poetic idealism, which often and self-consciously seeks refuge from injustice and war in moments of transcendence. Her "Verses on an Illumination for a Naval Victory" (1800) is typical of her conflicted response to scenes of violence; the poem denounces both sides of the battle, the "uncultur'd savage" and "the Sons of Europe" (58–59), and seeks Peace "in some sequester'd, solitary dell" where "The lone Enthusiast, wrapt in trance sublime, / Might soar, unfetter'd by the bounds of time" (*AB*, 61). "Such were the dreams, that sooth'd the pensive breast," writes Bannerman, and moves on to scenes of decay, disappointment, and judgment, ending with an apocalyptic "illumination" that effectively parodies the public fireworks celebration of war which occasioned her poem. Apocalyptic endings are common in Bannerman's poetry, and are linked to poetic imagination, as in her poem "The Genii" (1800), where she traces the "sublime career" of the destructive "dark Genii," who like the poet of "Kubla Khan" build "transparent temples high in air" with their "piercing, and sublime" powers (135):[41]

> To rule supreme, your daring souls aspire;
> As fancy wills, you rear the pillar'd dome,
> In earth's deep caverns, or in ocean's foam,
> Hang your transparent temples high in air,
> Or to the realms of flame, your glory bear.
>   (*AB*, 116)

The Genii are figures of Romantic genius that repeatedly reveal scenes of sublime destruction and desolation, "The polar night alike, and tropic blaze" (*AB*, 125). As in poems like "Spirit of the Air" and "The Mermaid," her first-person speakers find distinct pleasure in the violence unleashed by such destructive storms, and through this motif Bannerman examines the connection between imagination and destruction.[42] Bannerman's dialogue with Coleridge's early poetry, like Robinson's, establishes a significant thread of influence, or, perhaps more importantly, of affinity, that deserves further investigation.[43] Through Bannerman and Coleridge (and Robinson, Lewis, and Dacre) one could trace an alternative line of inquiry in studies of the Gothic and of Romanticism, beyond female and male complementarity. This is what David Moir suggested in 1851, when he grouped together such writers as Bannerman, Lewis, Radcliffe, Leyden, Coleridge, and Scott as "the supernatural school."[44]

In addition to using the popular folk motif of storms, Bannerman similarly used Scottish legends of mermaids to critique the most pressing political issue of her day: Britain's involvement in the slave trade. And, because Bannerman's spirits of the storm are consciously feminized, even while inhuman, she simultaneously offers a protofeminist revision of the traditional associations of destruction with masculinity, as well as yet another vision of woman's association with the "powers of darkness," and of the woman poet. It is then, perhaps, tempting to focus on the feminist use value of Bannerman's violent sublime,[45] so that the violence of her imagination can be contained by a larger, socially productive goal of ending patriarchal injustice in all its guises. But such a harmonizing and anachronizing (and Romantic) interpretation would rob Bannerman of the most dangerous qualities of her imagination: a fascination with the sublimity of destruction, and of poetry's relationship to this destruction. Her poet/destroyers are social figures, but they are fundamentally asocial at the same time, because of the ease with which they sweep away the innocent and the guilty alike. And even the social dimensions of Bannerman's violent sublime (like Dacre's) do not consistently conform to modern liberal or feminist politics: while she wrote against slavery in several of her poems, like many opponents to the slave trade, she also spoke out against the French Revolution, as in the anonymous verse *Epistle from the Marquis De La Fayette to General Washington* (1800) generally attributed to her, which celebrated the sublimity of paternal power in distinctly Burkean terms.[46]

While Bannerman's poetry does not demonstrate an interest in the artist as criminal[47] or the sublime crime, it most definitely is concerned with the violence of representation itself and with the sublimity of this violence, two quintessentially masculine preoccupations that we have already encountered in Dacre and Lamb. Bannerman's poetry rehearses the most self-tortured and self-indulgent examinations of Romantic ideology we typically find in the "second generation" of Romantics, further evidence that our narratives of Romantic generations and genealogy are untenable now that we have reintroduced women poets into the period. I am not suggesting that Bannerman is representative of a submerged tradition of Romantic women writers who share the philosophical preoccupations and "masculinist" excesses of their male contemporaries. On the contrary, I do not believe Bannerman's work to be representative of any dominant tradition, male or female, and it is for this reason that she should be read and taught: to remind us of the limitations of our literary histories, and of the persistence of heterogeneous writers and writings that these histories cannot and should not safely appropriate.

We can cite at least one poet directly influenced by Bannerman's work,[48] Jessie Stewart, a member of Bannerman's literary circle who published as "Adeline." Stewart published numerous poems in periodicals which in some cases are indistinguishable from Bannerman's. Stewart's poems such as "The Seraph: An Ode," "The Spirit of the Storm," "Verses on the Sea Shore," as well as numerous sonnets, share with Bannerman's odes and storm poems a fascination with speaking in the voice of tempests, an unusual quality for women poets. Thomas Park noted with approval that Stewart had "watched the bold flights of Miss Bannerman with the eye of a parnassian eaglet."[49]

In addition to her public acknowledgement of Coleridge, Bannerman also saw her poetry as following in Joanna Baillie's footsteps, expanding Baillie's theory of dramatic composition in her influential "Introductory Discourse" to the *Plays on the Passions* (1798) by applying it to the sonnet. She explained in *Poems* that "an attempt has been made in the 'Sonnets from Werter,' to delineate the progress of a single passion . . . In this manner a *unity* may be communicated" (orig. emphasis, *AB*, 220). Bannerman sent Baillie a presentation copy of her *Poems* in 1800, and Baillie replied that "[t]o be thought well of by my country women, and remembered in the land which I love, will always be to me the most gratifying reward of my labours."[50] Thus, while her sonnets followed in the traditions of Charlotte Smith, Anna Seward, and Helen Maria Williams through her translations from Rousseau, Goethe, and Petrarch,[51] it was to Baillie, that "priestess of the tragic muse" as she called her, that Bannerman returned to in her final published volume.

In "Verses to Miss Baillie, on the Publication of her First Volume of Plays on the Passions" (1807), after comparing Joanna Baillie to Shakespeare, Bannerman consciously elevated herself to this visionary company:

> Yes! tho' these lines the feeble effort own,
> The soul that stamps them bears another tone!
> Thro' realms of beauty, and thro' darkest night,
> That soul hath trac'd thee in thy towering flight.
>
> (*AB*, 110)

The fearlessness and self-aggrandizement, the repeated, chanted "I" which resembles the excesses of the most egotistical male Romantics, are characteristic of Bannerman's poetic speakers. Early reviews of Bannerman's *Poems* had admired precisely "the sublimer and more energetic" qualities of her writing, typically "the productions of a *masculine spirit*":

Anne Bannerman's Odes may be quoted as an irrefragable proof that the ardour, whatever be its gender, which gives birth to lofty thought and bold expression may glow within a female breast.[52]

These same qualities of a "masculine spirit" also troubled her male patrons even while they intrigued them, and they had difficulty assimilating these qualities into their models of the female poetess of sensibility. Robert Anderson, the editor of the 13 volume *Complete British Poets* (1792–95), one of the first national anthologies, praised her poetry along with the work of Campbell and Leyden in letters to publishers, noting her characteristic sublimity:

Her poems are the production of no common mind. They are brilliant, if not highly finished effusions; more distinguished perhaps by strength & ... splendor & energy of expression than tenderness of sentiment ... So opulent a mind at such an age is a phenomenon.[53]

But her poetry's "strength," "splendour" and "energy" also clearly disturbed Anderson, for he made it clear in these same letters that he disapproved of her pursuing writing as a career, and blamed her ambition on "her having received an education above her condition."[54] Not surprisingly, he did not include any women in his *Complete British Poets*. Bannerman held out until 1807, four years after her mother's death had left her without income and without a home; she stopped publishing after her last volume sold poorly, and became the governess Anderson thought her destined to be, "which does her more honour than all her poetry," he wrote.[55]

It is no coincidence that an "opulent" poet of such unconventional *femmes fatales*, who ultimately and atypically leave their readers' desires unsatisfied, was discouraged from continuing to publish, even though as I have shown, her poetry received warm praise in the private correspondence of highly respected and influential male literary figures, and in early reviews.[56] Perhaps it was not in spite but because of Bannerman's poetry's strength and splendour that it has all but disappeared. Her femme fatale as a poet /destroyer "exulting in immortal might"[57] nevertheless emerges as one possible version of the Romantic woman poet, one which clearly lost out in the end to the self-sacrificial poetess, the poet figure favored by Victorian editors and critics. Like Elizabeth Bath who proclaimed, "Give me the mind where genius sits alone, / Creating worlds and kingdoms of her own,"[58] Bannerman is one example of many women poets of the Romantic period, among them Charlotte Smith, Letitia Landon, Mary Robinson, and Maria Jewsbury, whose unabashed celebrations of sublimity, genius, and transcendence can no longer be overlooked in re-assessments of the period and of British women's literature in general.

In the apocalyptic conclusion of "The Spirit of the Air," the poet tries to transcend the material and historical limits of her time and place ("O'er me nor cold, nor heat, prevails, / Nor poison from malignant gales") in a moment of egotistical triumph: "I smile at Danger's threat'ning form; / I mock Destruction on his tow'ring seat, / And leave the roaring winds, contending at my feet." Her sublime self-presence is similar to that of Byron's and Campbell's speakers in their apocalyptic visions (the "Last Man" poems), and in direct contrast to Mary Shelley's *The Last Man*, according to Steven Goldsmith: "When these poems [of Byron and Campbell] bypass the annihilation of consciousness and round back upon their own creative agency, their capacity for self-generation, they do so *explicitly* at the expense of the feminine" (*Unbuilding*, 272). Perhaps this is what Anne Bannerman did too, also explicitly at the expense of the feminine, making her difficult to classify according to gendered models of Romantic writing.

Bannerman as a poet fits neither the current model of Romantic poetesses we have inherited (at least in part, through the exclusion of women from early national anthologies such as Anderson's and Park's), nor the model of self-present, transcendent poetic speaker she explored (and critiqued) in her poems.[59] But her anomalous status, according to either current gender-complementary or ungendered models of Romanticism, is precisely what makes her a fascinating writer, one who tried to destroy the ideal of the proper poetess under which women poets labored, and replace her with the femme fatale.

"THE QUEEN OF BEAUTY"

The brief scandal caused by the fourth and final engraving ("The Prophecy of Merlin") in *Tales of Superstition* offers a final insight into the sexual politics of publishing that Bannerman and other women poets contended with, and an important example of why any re-assessment of women writers of the Romantic period should account for more than the gender content of their works. Bannerman had intended to illustrate *Tales of Superstition* with woodcuts, presumably to evoke a Gothic atmosphere, but her publisher was unable to secure woodcutters, and instead hired engravers.[60] She was also to select the subjects of the engravings herself, but we know that in the case of the controversial "The Prophecy of Merlin" Thomas Park selected the subject matter.

Called "offensive to decency" by one reader,[61] the engraving features a naked Queen of Beauty, Venus, offering her charmed cup to King Arthur (Figure 4). It is a striking and unusual image to find in a volume of poetry published by a woman in 1802. Before the book had been distributed by the publisher, Park wrote to Anderson about the impending scandal over the engraving, which was generating unkind gossip among the "wits of Edinburgh," who "were complotting to give the fair authoress disquiet & to make the work misprised."[62] In the same month as "The Queen of Beauty" engraving was published in *Tales*, the *Scots Magazine*, with Leyden at the helm, published an unsigned article warning against visually representing "sublime" beings, and singled out Campbell for criticism.[63] Perhaps fearing another essay naming Bannerman, and this time with a more serious charge of indecency, Park suggested a chivalric response:

As Miss B. is guiltless of offence, it is hard that she should need a champion, but in the cause of her Tales of Chivalry I am ready to commence knight-errant, & will take up the gauntlet of opprobrium in this affair.[64]

The incident, no doubt painful to the poet, becomes an opportunity for masculine jests suggesting that the age of chivalry is not dead; it also reveals that Park (and Anderson) viewed the world of publishing as essentially masculine, where fair authoresses venture at their peril, and must be rescued by heroic male patrons.

Park requested that the offensive engraving be removed from copies of *Tales of Superstition* still in the publisher's possession, and it seems a half-hearted effort was made to follow his direction (which may or may not have represented the author's wishes). An examination of 16 copies of *Tales* reveals that in fact only five copies are missing the final engraving, whereas 10 copies include all four.[65] One copy lacks both "The Dark Ladie" and "The Prophecy of Merlin," an important reminder that perhaps the missing engravings were removed because they were desirable, not because they were offensive. These two engravings were the most striking of the four, and readers at any point in the last two

Figure 4 MacKenzie after E. W. Thompson, "The Prophecy of Merlin," from Anne Bannerman's *Tales of Superstition and Chivalry* (1802). Courtesy of the Department of Special Collections, University of California, Davis.

hundred years may have removed the engravings for personal reasons that Park or Bannerman could not have foreseen. But the publishers must have been careful to censor the review copies, because the *British Critic* mentioned only three plates.

Park concluded that the controversy is itself evidence of the lack of a classical education on the part of all those upset (the poet included implicitly):

I really think there is little indelicacy in the design, if no licentious construction be put upon it. – Considered as a Venus anadyomene, which seems to have been the character represented by the artist, – there is no impropriety in the unapparelled piece of statuary he has exhibited; – or considered as the siren of a charmed isle, – there still is little to excite human passion in the display of an ideal sorceress; – at least, there can be little to excite those, who have been accustomed ... to distinguish classical & poetical figures, from those denuded frail ones who traverse the streets, by night. (*Ibid.*)

Classical and poetical figures, then, have no connection to real women, especially those who must live by selling their bodies. Park insists on the traditional masculine (that is, "gentlemanly") distinction between an ideal nude and an actual naked woman, as Lynda Nead described it in *The Female Nude*:

The transformation from the naked to the nude is thus the shift from the actual to the ideal – the move from a perception of unformed, corporeal matter to the recognition of unity and restraint, the regulated economy of art. (14)

Park's letter tries to reaffirm this distinction between ideal and actual woman, the celestial Venus and the terrestrial one. This ideal/actual distinction is always threatened with collapse in Bannerman's volume, and in enforcing this distinction, Park implicitly allies poetic vision with the ideal, arguing that the ideal woman is the appropriate object of (male) vision. The consequences of his idealization for the actual woman poet are of course disastrous.

Bannerman's anxiety over the engraving, to which Park's letter repeatedly alludes, allows for a different interpretation than one of a "fair authoress" shrinking from committing an "offence to decency." Park himself, and not Bannerman, had selected the subject matter – the Queen of Beauty unveiled – a moment that Bannerman's poem never directly represents. To see such an ambiguous and charged moment so starkly and unambiguously displayed counters her poetry's consistent resistance to unveiling truth, and specifically truths embodied in female form. The distinction between the ideal and material aspects of the Queen of Beauty, her dangerously double nature, was policed and fixed through "an unambiguous structure of narrative" according to John Barrell, in order to affirm her role (i.e., that of pleasure) in civil society.[66] This "unambiguous structure of narrative" is precisely what Bannerman undermines in her *Tales*, and what Park and other readers tried to reinforce when they complained of her narratives' obscurity.

The scene the engraving attempts to represent literally shows Arthur encountering a Queen of Beauty who may or may not be unveiled (the poem's description of her as "blushing" suggests she is). But this suggestive unveiled goddess turns out to be deceptive in Bannerman's poem, thwarting the King's, and the reader's, voyeuristic pleasure:

> His lips have drain'd that sparkling cup,
> And he turn'd on her his raptur'd eyes!
> When something, like a demon-smile,
> Betray'd the smooth disguise!   (138)

In Bannerman's poem, the naked body of the ideal goddess is not truth unveiled, but yet another "smooth disguise." The engraving, by fixing in such precise lineaments an apparent unveiling of the divine (and feminine) truth, works against the rest of the *Tales of Superstition and Chivalry*, and their repeated suggestion that truth does not remain truth once it is unveiled.

The visual correspondence between the first and fourth engravings, "The Dark Ladie" and "The Prophecy of Merlin" (Figures 3 and 4), moreover, reveals that the artist relied on the same composition for both subjects. Both engravings show an awe-struck knight kneeling before a supernatural woman with arms raised, bearing a charmed cup. When juxtaposed, the engravings suggest the Dark Ladie veiled and unveiled, the artist's satisfactory denouement of Bannerman's frustrating (anti)narratives of veiled meanings. Also, in "The Dark Ladie" it is the knight who averts his eyes before the Ladie, while in "The Prophecy of Merlin" it is the nude female figure who averts her gaze and assumes a receptive, open posture characteristic of traditional femininity. Even the classical Venus Anadyomene figure used by the artist as the basis for "The Prophecy of Merlin," irrespective of its suggestive relationship to "The Dark Ladie," works against the ballads' evocations of a medieval age of superstition (and the author's intention, referred to in a letter, of illustrating the volume with woodcuts). The palpable tensions between the poet's ballads, the engraver's illustrations, and the patrons' and critics' attempts to make sense of both, reveal the contradictory significations that any published text is heir to. In Bannerman's specific instance, these contradictions, which became visible in Thomas Park's discussion of the scandalous engraving in *Tales of Superstition*, illustrate how Bannerman's poetry moved against the current of contemporary sexual and poetic ideologies.

Park's "gentlemanly" defense of the "Prophecy of Merlin" engraving on classical grounds suggests that he did not perceive these tensions between the poet and her published text. Park saw only a fair authoress's distress at an indecorous engraving, which, given the response of the so-called "wits of Edinburgh," was indeed an appropriate response. But in addition we must also allow for Bannerman's undoubtedly different take on the age of superstition and chivalry, an age which her volume uses to explore and explode contemporary (that is, Romantic) ideals of feminine truth, and the truth of femininity. Park's indulgence in a heroic posture, riding to the rescue of his authoress, is revealed as insensitive at best and cruel at worst when, a few years later, he dismisses Bannerman's reliance on poetic patrons as a hopelessly outdated "loftiness of feeling, which I frankly confess is too Chattertonian to enhance my respect or admiration."[67] Patronage was in fact central to literary publication in 1802,[68] though poets and patrons clearly had a complex and uneasy relationship to this system and the lack of independence (and "manliness") associated with it. For women poets, the problem with patronage was even more vexed, carrying with it suggestions of sexual exchange, as Letitia Landon's controversial career will illustrate.

Park and Anderson were relieved when Bannerman relinquished her attempts to find publishers through their aid, since as they repeatedly confided to each other, she "was not likely to have such personal connexions [*sic*] among the rich and powerful" in London as one would need.[69] Yet Scottish intellectuals like Anderson cultivated the idea of untutored Scottish genius born in poverty, such as Robert Burns, John Leyden, James Hogg, and Thomas Campbell. Campbell and Leyden are particularly apt examples of the sexual inequality women poets faced even in this land of "untutored genius," since both men were part of Bannerman's Edinburgh literary circle, and succeeded in the same system of literary patronage in which she failed.

Anderson lauded Campbell's 1799 *Pleasures of Hope* in the same letters as he did Bannerman's first volume, *Poems* (1800), and Campbell went on to secure a comfortable literary career as editor of the *New Monthly Magazine*, thanks in part to the help of his influential male patrons. His letters reveal a consistent anxiety over his dependence on patrons such as Anderson and the powerful Lord Minto, whose secretary he was and in whose houses he lived.[70] John Leyden, a close friend of Bannerman's and perhaps a romantic interest,[71] was similarly helped by Anderson, briefly given the editorship of the *Scots Magazine*, and finally secured, with Scott's help, the position of assistant surgeon with the East India Company, allowing him to pursue his gift in linguistics (also in the service of Lord Minto).

Campbell's immensely popular *Pleasures of Hope* could not be more different from *Tales of Superstition*, as their titles immediately suggest, and the two poets' divergent careers tell us much about the generic and sexual hierarchies of the early Romantic period. Campbell's poetry affirms the triumph of hope and the Romantic imagination over death, injustice and despair, which is why Hazlitt used him to contrast the anti-Romantic vision of Crabbe in *The Spirit of the Age*. Bannerman's verse "Prologue" in her *Tales of Superstition* invites readers away from precisely the "gay delight" found in the pleasures of hope, and into the "dim regions of monastic night" and "dark recesses" of the Gothic. Campbell's Romantic sexual ideology also complements Bannerman's Gothic and proto-feminist critique of this ideology, for he compares the work of the (Romantic) imagination to that of the sculptor who sculpted an ideal "Queen of Beauty" by unifying the disparate parts of actual women in a single visionary ideal, precisely the figure of the feminized ideal Bannerman challenged in her volume, in particular in her own depiction of a demonic "Queen of Beauty." Campbell even went on to write his own dark lady poem, "The Turkish Lady," in which a grateful Turkish woman leaves her husband and flees with the Christian knight, an endorsement of the Orientalism and dangerous misogyny of this chivalric theme, which Bannerman's "Dark Ladie" had critiqued. Thus these two poets with so much in common offered two consistently different visions of the ideal and the feminine, one successful according to Romanticism's increasingly rigid sexual ideology, the other obscured, as the Gothic itself was obscured in modern literary histories until recently. Even Park's high praise of Bannerman occasionally slipped into faint praise indeed, especially when he labeled her work "gothic":

Is Miss Bannerman printing her ingenious imitations of the gothic ditty, & is T. Campbell proceeding in his career to high poetic fame?[72]

For Bannerman, Park emphasizes the material re-production of popular verse, mere ephemeral printed imitations, whereas he speaks in lofty, immaterial terms of Campbell's "high poetic" aspirations and professional "career." Park's distinction between these two poets, their literary modes, and their careers, amounted to a self-fulfilling prophecy.

That Leyden and Campbell's works have continued to be reprinted and re-anthologized (though probably not read and taught), while Anne Bannerman's have remained in obscurity,[73] demonstrates that poetic patronage at this time in Edinburgh was indeed alive and well, and that like chivalry, it worked to objectify and exclude women even as (and because) it idealized them. The "Prophecy of Merlin" engraving of a nude Venus crystallized the sexual implications for women publishing poetry in this historical moment; that is, that their "poetical figures," their "ideal sorceresses," and even the poets themselves could always be mistaken for public women – prostitutes – and that in the minds of some (male) writers the only appropriate role for women in the production of poetry remained as ideal objects of imagination, there to provide poets and readers with the pleasures of hope.

CONCLUSION: "BLEST BE THE GLOOM"

Blest be the gloom, that wraps each sacred head,
And blest the unbroken sleep, and silence of the dead!
Anne Bannerman, "The Spirit of the Air"

The obscure fate of Anne Bannerman's poetry was the consequence of a complex series of cultural mediations, as Park and Anderson discussed in their letters. "Part of this failure" of *Tales of Superstition*, wrote Park, "& I think, the greater part, is imputable to the want of Miss B's recommending name, to a delay in publishing till the *Tales of Terror* had appeared, and to an injudicious[ly]" large number of copies published.[74] Scott had speculated on the cause of the similar "general depreciation of the *Tales of Wonder*": their inflated price, royal octavo size, and, as with Bannerman's volume, their belated timing. Scott reflected that Lewis "remained insensible of the passion for ballads and ballad-mongers having been for some time on the wane, and that with such alteration in the public taste, the chance of success...was diminished. What had been at first received as simple and natural, was now sneered at as puerile and extravagant."[75] What was true of Lewis's *Tales of Wonder*, then, was more so for Bannerman's *Tales of Superstition*, for as Park noted, they appeared after the parodic *Tales of Terror*. Yet Scott's argument that Gothic ballads were originally valued for being "simple and natural" is unconvincing, since these ballads were self-conscious imitations, deliberately "extravagant," as in the case of Dacre, Coleridge, and especially Lewis, who parodied his own ballads.[76] We need to remember that Scott was anxious in retrospect to excuse his own enthusiasm for extravagant Gothic ballads, and more specifically his participation in *Tales of Wonder*.[77]

Like Scott, Park was a shrewd editor well-versed in the publishing business, and he too had speculated on the adverse effects of the small size of the 1800 *Poems* volume, arguing that varying from the "commodious" large octavo size of Campbell's volume will "thus prevent a potential arrangement with those contemporary classics which have obtain'd a place in every modern library, & which Miss B. is so fully entitled to hold."[78] Park and Scott knew that texts and canons are made up of much more than their linguistic content and aesthetic merit:

The price of a book, its place of publication, even its physical form and the institutional structures by which it is distributed and received, all bear upon the production of literary meaning, and hence all must be critically analyzed and explained.[79]

Thus Jerome McGann argues that criticism must account for these "mediational structures" of production and distribution, because as Park's letter demonstrated, literary works are always "embodied in such structures" (*Ibid.*, 117).

Yet, while Park is happy to discuss the mediational structures of Anne Bannerman's literary marginalization, he is conspicuously silent on how sexual ideology was central to Thomas Campbell's success with *The Pleasures of Hope*. Gender was central to the mediational structures Park discussed: book production, distribution and reception. The engraving scandal, her lack of London connections and education, and the central question of her poetry's "masculine" energy in many reviews demonstrate, as do the works of so many other women poets of the Romantic period, the uphill battle women faced in publishing in this period when, nevertheless, hundreds of women poets flourished.

The association of her poetry with Lewis's *Tales of Wonder* and the parodic *Tales of Terror* seems to have been particularly damaging (as the reviews noted), both because of the Gothic ballad's general "depreciation," and because of all types of Gothic, the "school of Lewis" was the most inappropriate for a woman writer to be associated with, as reviewers of Dacre's novels repeatedly complained. Dacre's bold association of her novels with Lewis's had worked in her favor, because her writing consciously adopted the pornographic effects for which *The Monk* was infamous. Bannerman, on the other hand, had not capitalized on the sexual scandal that "The Queen of Beauty" generated, suggesting a different approach to the Gothic. Furthermore, the *Tales of Superstition*'s anonymous publication in 1802 no doubt fueled speculation as to the volume's relationship to Lewis's maligned volume of the previous year. The *British Critic* noted that: "This beautiful little book belongs, as its title implies, to the family of Tales of Wonder," and warned that its fancy "is fancy perverted to the purpose of raising only horror."[80] And the British Library's copy of Bannerman's *Tales* bears a telling inscription on the flyleaf – "By Monk Lewis" – anecdotal evidence of Bannerman's affinity with the leading writer of the so-called male Gothic, an association that in this instance appears to have backfired.

The anonymous author of "On Novels and Romances" in the 1802 *Scots Magazine* (edited by Leyden) complained of two chief dangers associated with Gothic romances, the first exemplified by *The Mysteries of Udolpho*, the second by *The Monk*. These dual dangers rehearse the familiar distinctions between Gothic obscurity and explicitness, or terror and horror, female and male Gothic, but in so doing clarify for us the difficulties of women publishing poetry in this dangerous genre. The first failing of Gothic romances was their narrative obscurity: "the imagination will not allow of being always on the stretch; as we expect to see, the different occurrences in narration, stated clearly, and with openness, as they naturally rise one from the other, we cannot but feel dissatisfied, when we perceive any part concealed for the purpose of holding the mind in suspense."[81] Bannerman is guilty of such deliberate concealment, specifically through seductive female figures (more so than Radcliffe in her novels), because Bannerman's ambiguous use of the supernatural is never explained and her narratives typically offer no closure. The second, greater danger of the Gothic is its use of "a language ... most indecent and improper," as in *The Monk*. "What then would be our surprise, were we to understand, that this work has been read by a young and beautiful female...?"[82] asks the *Scots Magazine* in the same year as Bannerman published her *Tales*. And, as we saw in chapter 4, the author of this essay went on to echo Bienville's warning about the specific medical dangers such writing posed to young women, prone to "extravagant" desires – nymphomania. Bannerman avoided the explicitness of Lewis's (and Dacre's) eroticism and revealed supernaturalism, yet, as we have seen, she remained tainted by her association with the ballads in *The Monk* and *Tales of Wonder*, having clearly read both and perpetuated this tradition of "literary abortions."[83]

While Park and Anderson understood the complex factors involved in literary meaning, success, and failure, the most important criterion in both of their assessments of Bannerman's career remained her gender, and its incompatibility with that of a poet. The problem finally lay in "her having received an education above her condition" and her stubborn resistance to returning to this condition.[84] The issue here is not class but gender, for when disenfranchised poets such as Leyden (the son of a shepherd) and Campbell (the son of a merchant) received educations above their station, this reinforced the myth of the democratic effects of the "exceptional" Scottish educational system, which supposedly resulted in nearly universal literacy in the late eighteenth century. Yet historians have begun to question this myth of widespread Scottish literacy, in part due to the large gender gap on which the myth depends.[85] For example, Anna Seward sharply distinguished between the commendable "self-educated bard" Robert Bloomfield, son of a shoe-maker and author of *The Farmer's Boy* (also published by Bannerman's publishers, Vernor and Hood), and Bannerman, for "the sensible, interesting, and unaffected worth" of this "self-educated bard" and others like him, such as Stephen Duck, cannot be compared "with the stilted abortions of Miss Bannerman's volume."[86] Both her gender and her class (as the daughter of a street ballad singer) limited Anne Bannerman's professional opportunities, but only the former was incompatible with a serious poetic vocation in the eyes of her patrons.

Leyden and Campbell did not have to rely solely on poetry for financial support, as Bannerman did, or at least tried to do. Letitia Landon and Felicia Hemans were the first British poets, female or male, to accomplish this. Landon wrote of the great difficulties she faced as a professional writer, learning "how little . . . a young woman can do without assistance" from male patrons (*Blanchard*, 1: 55). "Could you," she asks a friend, "have hunted London for a publisher; endured all the alternate hot and cold water thrown on your exertions; bargained for what sum they might be pleased to give; and, after all, canvassed, examined, nay quarrelled over accounts the most intricate in the world?" (*Ibid.*). Landon's publishing success in London came with unwanted sexual scandals, leading to her hasty marriage, self-exile and early death. Bannerman's publishing difficulty in Edinburgh remains an instructive example of the fate many other women poets faced in the Romantic period, casualties of what Clifford Siskin has termed "the Great Forgetting" of women writers, which made possible the Great Tradition: women were "excluded not by the increasingly porous distinction of gentility, but by the newly valorized professional criterion of earned expertise – a criterion that, for the work of writing, was increasingly regulated . . . by the burgeoning institutions of criticism."[87] Park and Anderson envisioned Campbell and

Leyden as fellow professional writers, editors, and critics, and Bannerman, ultimately, as a governess with an opulent imagination, printing her "ingenious imitations" of Gothic verse.

Historicist scholarship continues to investigate the role played by critics, anthologizers, editors, and textual production itself in shaping our understanding of the literature of the Romantic period. Combined with the rediscovery of women writers and the significance of the Gothic, this far-ranging reevaluation invites interest in little-known writers like Bannerman, who explored the illusions of a feminized ideal, and of an ideal woman, and showed both to be destructive. Bannerman's poetry thus challenges the Romantic ideology of imagination, and the increasingly naturalized definitions of "woman" at the turn of the nineteenth century, and in so doing illustrates the centrality of gender in shaping modern critical constructs such as Romanticism and Gothic.

CHAPTER 6

"Life has one vast stern likeness in its gloom": Letitia Landon's philosophy of decomposition

And when, amid no earthly moans,
Down, down that town shall settle hence,
Hell, rising from a thousand thrones,
Shall do it reverence.

Edgar Allan Poe, "The City in the Sea"

INTRODUCTION: LANDON'S CORPOREAL POETICS

The poetry of Letitia Landon (1802–38) has attracted much recent criti-cal attention, which typically emphasizes the destructive degree to which Landon herself inhabited the persona of heartbroken, beautiful femi-ninity, and the conflicted status of "poetess." Yet, as Angela Leighton has also noted, there remains in Landon's work a sense of world-weary Byronic cynicism and a preoccupation with evil that "points... to hidden forces in human nature, even in female nature – forces which, 'unsanc-tified by religion,' might sweep the soul out of its picture-book passivity into real chaos and crime."[1] Landon's poetics of the beautiful are in fact mirrored by a poetics of despair that originate in the body and its dangerous powers, a corporeal poetics that goes far beyond the critique of the beautiful that Anne Mellor, Glennis Stephenson, Leighton, and others have located in her poetry.

Mellor, to note one influential interpretive example, argues that "[b]y equating the essence of woman with her body (the specular object of beauty) Landon defined the kind of knowledge women could possess" (*RG*, 120). But we need not limit women's bodies to their function as ob-jectified Beauty in a specular economy. Landon may have been "trapped in the social discourse of her day,"[2] as we all probably are, but that social discourse, particularly that of the body, included far more than the sexual ideology of love and beauty. By "confining her heroines' consciousness to what they can experience through the body, *on* earth," Mellor argues,

Landon denies these heroines a "conviction of an afterlife; when love dies, they die" (*RG*, 120). What interests me is precisely what we can say about this materialism, beyond its implications for a discourse of beauty. Landon's stubborn materialism, rather than making her an essentialist when it came to gender, made her quite the opposite – a social critic and writer keenly aware of the inessentialness of all categories, both ideal and material, upon which modern gender conceits rest.

The despair in Landon's writings is often embodied in unstable and destructive bodies, which have been consistently downplayed or overlooked by modern scholars. Landon scholarship consistently focuses on the same early poems, most notably "The Improvisatrice" (1824), "Erinna" (1827), "The Lost Pleiad" (1829), and "A History of the Lyre" (1829), and on the themes of female (hetero)sexuality, love, and poetic identity. Rather than focusing on these undeniably self-destructive currents in Landon's early poetry, I locate an alternative poetics in Landon's later works, one which instead of embodying the beautiful to self-destructive ends, reveals destruction and decay as the inescapable condition of all social and proper bodies.

There are thus at least two accounts of poetry and the poet in Landon's works, only one of which has been explored (Landon's fascination with and tragic enactment of Corinne's fate). A second, deeply skeptical poetics of Landon's later career maintains her earlier critique of the patriarchal limits placed on the woman poet and her impossible choice between love and fame, but does so by distrusting all poetic language and transcendence. We can glimpse this skepticism even in early works, for example in "The Minstrel's Monitor," published in *The Improvisatrice* (1824). The speaker alludes to her/his impending tragic fate as poet and lover, a common gesture in Landon's work; yet beneath the poet's routine broken-hearted pose lies a deeper pessimism:

> Dark as its birth-place so dark is my spirit,
> Whence yet the sweet waters of melody came;
> 'Tis the long after-course, not the source, will inherit
> The beauty and glory of sunshine and fame.
>
> (*LPW*, 232)

The speaker reads her/his fate in the river, which s/he compares both to the flow of her heart and of her song, yet the first line tells us that it is the origin, not merely the tragic course, of poetry and love that is their undoing: "Silent and dark as the source of yon river." Landon's explorations of the darkness of origins works against what Marjorie Levinson aptly termed William Wordsworth's "great escape," illustrated in his famous substitution of his actual vantage point downstream of Tintern Abbey and its "poverty and pollution," with his reconstructed vantage point "a few miles above Tintern Abbey." It is therefore not Landon's familiar critique of the deadly consequences of heterosexual romance that I am interested in, but rather her equally significant, yet more subtle, poetics of the silent and dark that confound Romantic idealism at its source.

This chapter first examines Landon's figures of the prophetess, enchantress, and mermaid in their literary context, in order to establish in her work an unacknowledged and disturbing model of the female poet that allies her poetic powers with those of destruction and death. Landon's important revisions of these fatal women traditions are interesting in their own right, demonstrating Romantic-era women's willingness to question the definition of the proper woman as benevolent and nonviolent. The extent to which fatal women feature in Landon's works has been downplayed by modern criticism that focuses on and highlights the self-destructive Sappho/Corinne figures in her works.[3] Her popular novel *Ethel Churchill*, for example, featured a woman who poisoned both her lover and her husband, and both "The Venetian Bracelet" and "The Enchantress," to name but two more of her major works, feature heroines who kill. But like her mermaids, e.g., Melusine in "The Fairy of the Fountains," Landon's fatal women are typically beautiful, idealized figures. While Landon does dwell on the agonies of passion and the intricacies of sensation they experience (for she knew her Hume, as Isobel Armstrong points out[4]), it is not these eroticized dimensions of the corporeal and of the femme fatale in Landon's work that this chapter focuses on.

As I have argued throughout this study, we need to look beyond sexual and maternal bodies, even human bodies, for evocations of embodiment in Romantic-period women's writings. In Landon's case, an innovative and significant exploration of the corporeal emerges if we look beyond her representations of the female body, and to her representations of the larger social body and its dangerous encounter with death and decay. The second half of this chapter therefore examines the role of decay and death in Landon's poetics within the larger contemporary context of public health debates regarding waste, burial and death. What may appear to modern readers as Landon's metaphysical and cynical "fatalism" is in fact an engagement with these debates over the dangers posed to middle-class bodies by the miasma emanating from the decaying matter in urban slums and graveyards. My aim is not to demonstrate that Landon's writings reflect larger social issues, which goes without saying, but to use this public health context to recast familiar gendered dichotomies between surface/depth, and life/death, typically located in her writings, by highlighting how the miasmatic discourse in Landon's poetry disturbs the boundaries between such categories. The threat of decomposition undermines all such dichotomies, particularly that of surface/depth, by demonstrating how both categories are in the process of perpetually collapsing into one another, and exhaling a poisonous "influence" that spreads this disturbance to other bodies, like the plague that decomposition bears. In the early decades of the nineteenth century, Britain faced a sanitary crisis of unprecedented proportions as a result of the overcrowding of dead and decaying bodies and sewage. The new sanitary science that arose to meet this crisis of unchecked decomposition and disease developed a miasmatic theory of "filth" as a dangerous, class-specific menace, a discourse that permeated Romantic-period periodicals, popular culture, and Letitia Landon's poetics.

The ever-present threat of miasmatic influence in Landon's works is part of a larger anxiety about the body, as her narrator repeatedly lamented in *Ethel Churchill*: "it is the world's worst curse, that the body predominates over the mind" (III: 197). This inescapable threat of disease and decay, as well as pleasure – the "world's worst curse" of the body – is put to many uses in Landon's works, and should not be reduced to her identification of the public social sphere with corruption, artificiality, and "baseness." One of the most valuable uses of this corporeal "curse" in Landon's works is its stubborn insistence on the material, corporeal, and historical specificity of literary production, a significant political aspect of Landon's poetics that has been neglected.

"A history of how and where works of imagination have been produced, would be more extraordinary than even the works themselves," wrote Landon in *Ethel Churchill* (II: 163); Landon's concern with decay and disease was part of her contribution to such a history, which has yet to be written. In addition, Landon's corporeal poetics of decomposition challenges the popular charge that "L.E.L. insists on art as an overflow of the female body."[5] By revealing inherent corruption and decay at the heart of all origins, even female ones, Landon undermines the essentializing distinction between patriarchal surface (culture) and prediscursive female depth (nature).

ENCHANTRESS AND MERMAID IN LITERARY CONTEXT

The Sirens offer knowledge.

Cicero, *De Finibus*

In "The Prophetess" (1838), Landon's Prophetess bemoans her alienation from human society and morality ("I am alone – unblessing, and unblest!"), and summons spirits to give her a vision of the future:

> I see the distant vision I invoke.
> These glorious walls have bow'd to Time's dark yoke.
> I see a plain of desert sand extend,
> Scatter'd with ruins where the wild flowers bend,
> And the green ivy, like a last sad friend.
>
> Low are the marble columns on the sand,
> The palm trees that have grown among them
> As if they mock'd the fallen of the land.
>
> . . .
>
> Life has one vast stern likeness in its gloom,
> We toil with hopes that must themselves consume –
> The wide world round us is one mighty tomb.
>
> (*LPW*, 345)

Landon's "The Prophetess" is representative of a strong current in her work, one that repeatedly insists that "Life has one vast stern likeness in its gloom." And it is not merely human life and art, its transient memorials and accomplishments, that have a vast stern likeness in the gloom: woman, too, defined by her gentleness and longing for love, has a stern likeness, the femme fatale. Like Shelley's traveler in "Ozymandias," to which Landon's poem responds, the Prophetess teaches that human work and art are powerless against destruction: "First, toil – then, desolation and decay." But, unlike Shelley's poem, Landon's does not suggest the (albeit ironic) possibility that poetry or truth survives the desolation and decay, instead suggesting as in her poem "The Caves of Elephanta" (1835) that Power and Nothingness alone withstand time:[6]

> Two senses here are present; one of Power,
> And one of Nothingness; doth it not mock
> The mighty mind to see the meaner part,
> The task it taught its hands, outlast itself?
>
> . . .

> The mighty shrine,
> Undeified, speaks force, and only force,
> Man's meanest attribute.   (*LPW*, 293)

Her rhetorical question about the ultimate impotence of the Wordsworthian "mighty mind" is one of many such subtle critiques of Wordsworth found throughout Landon's work, a critique that places Landon's poetics at the heart of Romantic-period debates over idealism and role of the poet.

The prophesy of decay and destruction seems almost actively willed on the part of the Prophetess, for she repeatedly stresses her alienation and despair, saying that "Wholly and bitterly am I forlorn," and "I am alone! – unblessing, and unblest!" Landon's Prophetess and mermaids, like Anne Bannerman's femmes fatales, do not merely recount events they foresee, but seem actively to call down the destruction, offering neither blessing nor pity, and thereby identify themselves with a tradition of artist as destroyer, rather than creator.[7]

Landon's poems of supernatural seductresses are unusual because they conspicuously adopt and seem to celebrate a tradition of poet as destroyer erroneously assumed to be inherently misogynist. Barbara Fass's *La Belle Dame sans Merci and the Aesthetics of Romanticism* considers the legendary Belle Dame as an archetypal supernatural seductress in men's Romantic writings, yet, once again, these functions of the femme fatale in the male imagination are not necessarily helpful when we consider the works of women. Fass argues that the Romantic Enchantress figure exists "in two distinct groups of tales, one depicting the fatal seduction of a mortal, the other portraying the suffering of the enchantress" (27–28). Keats's *Lamia* is a rare example of an ambivalent fusion of both versions of the tale. For Fass, all the female figures in both strands of the Enchantress legend (whether evil seductress or her virtuous mortal rival, or the suffering enchantress) represent conflicting aspects of the male poet's imagination: she may be the poet's muse, or his poem, but never a poet in her own right. Yet, in Landon's poems, the enchantress is a poet figure who is to be both pitied and feared, an ambiguous figure like Keats's Lamia (and Bannerman's earlier femmes fatales), only raised to a new level of gendered awareness because written by a woman poet, to represent a woman poet. If, as Terence Hoagwood has argued, Keats's *Lamia* offers a critique of precisely the ideal/material, or poetry/society dichotomy that many critics continue to reinscribe onto the poem, then Landon redirects Keats's critique of idealism through a consciously gendered perspective, much as Bannerman had done with Coleridge.[8]

The frequent appearance of female semi-monstrous figures in Landon's poetry, such as mermaids, nymphs, and sirens, is significant, for they offer us an alternative model of the Romantic woman poet, a poet who may be broken-hearted, but who uses her song to destroy. Such a poet places little faith in Romantic poetry as a means of finding transcendent truths, since her siren poets repeatedly reveal vast empty spaces, deserts, and scenes of decay. As Landon's narrator says in "A Nereid Floating on a Shell":

> They say, sweet daughter of the sea,
> Thy look and song are treachery;
> Thy smile is but the honey'd bait
> To lure thy lover to his fate.
> I know not, and I care still less;
> It is enough of happiness
> To be deceived.   (*LPW*, 216)

Certainly this passage represents Landon's ironic treatment of love and beauty as women's defining qualities; yet this passage simultaneously represents an ironic treatment of Romantic poetry, one in which the woman poet as seductive and destructive siren represents Landon's deep suspicion of Romantic ideology, and her exploration of the destructive, not merely self-destructive, aspects of being a (female) poet.

Landon understood the significance of the shift from classical siren to Christian mermaid. Although in many of her poems, as in "Nereid Floating on a Shell," the siren seems to promise beauty and pleasure (which is the Christian reinterpretation of the siren's dangerous temptation), Landon also knows that in classical times the siren's song promised knowledge, as in her "Song of the Sirens":

> Whatso'er beside is done
> In earth's confines know we well.
> These to thee, Laertes' son,
> Shall our witching numbers tell.
>   (*LPW*, 320)

Landon's lengthy footnote explains the sirens' function in *The Odyssey*, and connects the voice of the sirens to that of the epic poet himself: "*we*, say the Sirens, but it is Homer, the one Homer, who speaks" (*LPW*, 320). One cannot ask for a clearer connection between the voice of the siren and that of the poet. Although Landon will also use the Christian associations of the siren as sexual temptress or suffering victim, this classical understanding that the siren offers knowledge needs to be reintegrated into our readings of such fatal women. Similarly, the enchantress figures so prevalent in Landon's works need to be considered in light of classical interpretations of Circe, the great enchantress herself, before she too became merely a sexually dangerous and monstrous figure. As Judith Yarnall has argued in *Transformations of Circe*, in pre-Christian accounts, Circe gave Odysseus valuable knowledge that allowed him to return home.[9] Yet the truth Landon's sirens and enchantresses offer is a disturbing one, one that undercuts the value of all truth, and reveals that "The Tree of Knowledge is not that of Life."

"The Byron of our poetesses"

Called the "Byron of our poetesses" and the "female Byron" by Frederic Rowton in his important 1848 anthology, *The Female Poets of Great Britain*, Landon in her prolific career forged significant links to Byron's career and his poetics.[10] Landon assumed Byron's role as the most popular and influential British poet of her generation, and did so in part by capitalizing on the Orientalist motifs and postures, and the satirical wit, that Byron had popularized.[11] Landon is "a second-order Byron," argues Jerome McGann, because she develops "Byron's social self consciousness . . . to a higher level of abstraction."[12] Yet this is precisely why a Byronic poetess is a contradiction in terms, for the poetess is valued for her heart-breaking sincerity and impeccable femininity. If we accept this popular version of Landon as poetess, destroyed by the opposition between love and fame, her becoming the "female Byron" would be a crippling "resurrection: the eagle reborn butterfly," as one disappointed nineteenth-century French critic lamented.[13] So how could this excessively feminine poetess, if one trusted modern critiques, have seemed a Byronic poetess, and even the "female Byron," to Rowton?

In calling Landon the "female Byron," Rowton was engaged in an important and long-standing debate among nineteenth-century critics and writers, a debate over the relationship of women poets to their male contemporaries. In Rowton's Victorian estimation of women poets, they possessed a separate but equal kind of genius; this is entirely understandable, and by now familiar, to those interested in the fate of nineteenth-century British women poets, particularly in the rise of the feminine "poetess" and her ostensibly exclusive focus on heart and home. Rowton defends his celebration of women's poetic genius in terms remarkably similar to those of modern Romanticist scholars: "I am quite prepared to grant that the mental constitutions of the sexes are different; but I am not at all prepared to say that 'difference' means 'inferiority.' "[14] Lack of education and their domestic duties, argues Rowton, mean that female poets necessarily differ from male poets, in terms of their observations, sensibilities, voices, subject matter, and genres, since women understandably write about the private realm of the quotidian and the emotions. Yet he is quick to insist that the male English poets have their female counterparts:

Have we not a Byron in Miss Landon, a Cowper in the Countess of Winchelsea, a Spenser in Mrs. Tighe, a Goldsmith in Mrs. Grant, a Johnson in Hannah More, a Wycherly in Mrs. Centlivre, a Collins in Mrs. Radcliffe, a Coleridge in Mrs. Browning, a Wordsworth in Mary Howitt, a Scott (and more) in Joanna Baillie? (*Ibid.*, xlix).

Thus, there is a poetess for every major poet, according to Rowton's complementary model, a model which in significant ways mirrors modern complementary models of Romantic women poets. Yet just what does it mean for Letitia Landon to be the Byron of our poetesses? What can a poetess possibly have in common with Byron, that most masculine of poets?

When Rowton used these Byronic terms to describe Landon, he was actually disputing with Hartley Coleridge, who in "Modern English Poetesses" in the 1840 *Quarterly* proclaimed that Caroline Norton "is the Byron of our modern poetesses" (376).[15] In his discussion of Caroline Norton, in contrast, Rowton dismisses the *Quarterly's* comparison of Norton to Byron, because "Byron's strains resemble the vast, roaring, wilful Waterfall, rushing headlong over desolate rocks, with a sound like the wail of a lost spirit: Mrs. Norton's, the soft full-flowing River, margined with flowers, and uttering sweet music."[16] In other words, Byron is a Romantic poet, Norton a poetess, and the suggestion is that the poetess cannot be Byronic (and probably by extension, cannot be Romantic, an anticipation of the arguments of Marlon Ross and Anne Mellor). Yet, according to this complementary logic, if Landon is a "female Byron," her poetry must also resemble the demonic "wail of a lost spirit" that characterized the dangerous allure of Byron for Rowton; she must be Romantic, Byronic, and thus no poetess.

Rowton had been right to foreground the correspondences between the lives of Landon and Byron: "both acquired world-wide fame in youth; both were shamefully maligned and misrepresented; both became gloomy and misanthropical under falsehoods asserted of them; both died young, and abroad" (*Female Poets*, 424). It was the similarity of their despair, however, that led Rowton finally "to speak in terms of rebuke and repudiation" (*Ibid.*, 430). "There is an evil spirit in such sentiments which should be bidden behind us," he says of Landon's melancholy and world-weary pessimism, for they "frequently led [her] into most erroneous views and sentiments" (*Ibid.*, 430, 429). This Byronic Landon is a dangerous figure in Rowton's eyes, as she was in the eyes of many contemporaries, and this danger accounts in part for her popularity, as it had for Byron's. As a woman, of course, Landon had more to risk in such traffic with the "evil spirits" of skepticism and despair, and perhaps more to gain.

Rowton wanted to fit Landon in his complementary model of the Romantic poetess, wherein all male poets have a poetess counterpart, yet his "rebuke and repudiation" of Landon reveals the inadequacy of that complementary model, then and now. In his final estimation Landon is a poet, a Byronic one at that, whose dangerous skepticism and despair unravel the hybrid "Byron of our poetesses." Similarly, the complementary modern model of the poetess inherited from such Victorian critics is currently used too sweepingly to describe Landon's prolific and generically diverse body of work. Rowton's rebuke of Landon attests to Landon's more complex status as a Romantic, even a Byronic, poet, in addition to her early capitalization on the poetess persona. And, according to Susan Wolfson, hybrid epithets like "the female Byron" work "as much to feminize Byron as to Byronize Landon, in effect to create a double-gendered poet,"[17] an important reminder of the unintended effects of complementarity.

"The Enchantress"

> The Book of Love is long and boring.
> Stephin Merritt, "The Book of Love"

"The Enchantress" is Landon's most self-consciously Byronic text, published in *Heath's Book of Beauty for 1833*, her most self-consciously Byronic volume.[18] Landon wrote the entire contents of the *Book of Beauty*, a lavishly illustrated giftbook, focusing on the female characters of Scott's and Byron's popular works. In "The Enchantress," which no critic to date has discussed, Landon develops a Promethean, distinctly Luciferan, model of poetic identity and self-creation. She accomplishes this by rewriting the biblical fall, and the birth of a poet, in a distinctly (proto)feminist and yet also Byronic way. She draws attention to the dangerous misogyny of Byron's heroes, their idealization and destruction of women, but does so while exploring the desirable possibilities of such a Luciferan role for the woman poet, not for the "poetess." Landon had satirized Byron (and Wordsworth) in numerous texts, for example in her prose tale "Experiments; or, The Lover from *Ennui*" (also in the *Book of Beauty*).

In "Experiments," the melodramatic and spoiled Lord Cecil, modeled partly on Byron himself and largely on heroes like Lara and Harold, lives on "ennui and credit," runs up great debts in his ancestral estate, and finally flees to Italy in search of oriental romance. He comes running back to English provincial life and women after his eastern fantasy lover, Gulnare, is revealed to be obese and tattooed beneath her mysterious veils. Lord Cecil's problem, Landon's satire makes clear, is his naive reading of Byron and Moore (and by extension, of Landon): "Cecil read Lord Byron – the Giaour and the Corsair were only interrupted by Lalla Rookh. He went to bed and dreamt of the maids 'Who blushed behind the gallery's silken shades'" (238). The orientalist fantasies of womanhood that Landon deflates in "Experiments" implicitly include her own, particularly in her earlier works favored by modern critics. Cecil's return to "the Abbey, his uncle's seat" in England, and his faithful dog and cousin/fiancée, completes his chastening education, which readers of the self-consciously orientalist *Book of Beauty* are also intended to undergo. "Experiments" is also a retelling of Maria Edgeworth's Irish tale *Ennui* (1809), itself an important critique of waning aristocracy, though Landon updates her tale by focusing on the commodification of aristocratic romance found in Byronic orientalism.[19] The real objects of Landon's satire are naive readers who mistake orientalist fiction for fact, yet Landon also parodies Byron's ennui and desire for cultural and sexual experiment. Landon published this and other satires in a costly and lavishly illustrated giftbook format, a format known for such flights of orientalist fancy, thus embedding in the book itself an ironic self-awareness about why her works (and Byron's) sell so well.[20]

Of course, Landon was drawn to Byron's heroines and heroes not only in order to satirize their conventions or capitalize upon their publishing success. In addition to her overlooked critiques of Byron (and Wordsworth, as we will see), we need also consider Landon's ongoing development of a female poetic identity that both incorporates and demystifies the destructive elements of the Byronic hero, often by creating

femme fatale poet figures who defy classification either as projections of
misogynist imagination or as inversions of the abandoned poetess.

For example, "The Enchantress" develops a Satanic heroine based on
Byron's Manfred, while simultaneously redressing Byron's silencing of
Astarte. Landon allows her Enchantress, known as Medora, to succeed
where all other Magi such as Manfred have failed. The Enchantress
tells of how she became an immortal by studying as a Magus, eventually
taking an immortal spirit as a lover and ascending with him into the
heavens, where she drank an elixir of immortality with tragic results:

> I said to him, "Give me an immortality which must be thine." Worlds rolling
> on worlds lay beneath our feet when we stood beside the waters of life. A joyful
> pride swelled in my heart. I, the last and weakest of my race, had won that prize
> which its heroes and its sages had found too mighty for their grasp. (*WL*, 11: 174)

Unlike the biblical Eve who ate of the tree of knowledge, but was unable
to eat of the tree of life before she was cast out of Eden, Landon's Eve
figure already possesses knowledge and therefore knows to eat of the
tree of life (here the waters of life), succeeding where her predecessors,
the male Magi, Adam, and Eve, have failed (see Genesis 3:22). Landon
effectively rewrites the Judeo-Christian fall, granting her Eve the fruit
both of eternal life and of knowledge, which, as with Byron, ultimately
produces an even greater despair. As the "last and weakest of [her]
race" and the only female Magus, the Enchantress embodies Landon's
ambition to outstrip her male predecessors as Promethean poet, most
importantly Byron (whose *Heaven and Earth* she alludes to).[21]

The price of this immortality is, of course, too great:

> Slowly I turned to where my once-worshipped lover was leaning. The same
> change had passed over both. Our eyes met, and each looked into the other's
> heart, and there dwelt hate – bitter, loathing, and eternal hate. I had changed
> my nature; I was no longer the gentle, up-looking mortal he had loved. I had
> changed my nature; he was no longer to me the one glorious and adored being.
> (*WL*, 11: 174)

The immortal spirit, her lover, while initially standing for the fire-spirit
(or Lucifer, or the "Sons of God") who seduced Eve, now clearly stands
for her mate Adam, whom she no longer adores and worships.[22] The
woman's ascent into immortality, read as poetic immortality, and her
pursuit of knowledge at any cost, destroys her illusions of love, and casts
her out of the protected category woman, for, as she repeatedly says: "I
had changed my nature." The word order is significant, for it is not just
her nature that has changed, but the Romantic "I" that has changed

its nature, in a moment of triumphant (some may say masculinist) self-creation. Simultaneously, this pursuit of immortality also transforms her into a Romantic poet, one who, like Manfred, is painfully aware of her conflicted status:

I was immortal; and what was this immortality? A dark and measureless future. Alas, we had mistaken life for felicity! What was my knowledge? it only served to show its own vanity; what was my power, when its exercise only served to work out the decrees of an inexorable necessity? I had parted myself from my kind, but I had not acquired the nature of a spirit. I had lost of humanity but its illusions, and they alone are what render it supportable. (*WL*, 11: 174)

Like Lucifer, Manfred, and Cain, Landon's Enchantress sees humanity's necessary illusions for what they are, and is thus, like Manfred, "Half dust, half deity, alike unfit / To sink or soar" (1. ii. 40–41). Thus two parallel fortunate falls can and should be located in Landon's tale: one critiques the ideology of love, for the Enchantress is disabused of her illusions of love, like Sappho and Corinne before her; the other fortunate fall critiques, as other high Romantic texts do, poetry's claim to transcendent truth, even while deeply desiring this truth.

In her overdetermined use of Byronic allusions, and particularly in her heroines's names, Landon addresses specific concerns with Byron's representation of his most famous heroines. We never learn the Enchantress's true identity, but her tale of forbidden knowledge and "sciences untaught" link her directly to Astarte, Manfred's partner in these occult pursuits. After she acquires the forbidden powers of the waters of Life, the Enchantress reaches out to alleviate human misery: in an effort to "bind myself by human ties," she possessed the dying body of Medora, daughter of Count Manfredi, whose two names identify her as a composite of Byron's long-suffering heroines (*WL*, 11: 175). Like Byron's Astarte, then, the Enchantress has both Manfred's immortal longings, forbidden knowledge, and disillusionment, as well as the pity and tenderness which he lacked, and loved in Astarte (*Manfred*, 11. 108–14). That this Byronic Enchantress reaches down to assume the life of a dying Medora, out of pity for her and her suffering parents, shows how Landon's fascination with the Satanic overreacher is bound to her understanding that this kind of forbidden knowledge, at least in Byron's poetry, is attained largely at the expense of women.

Landon takes her self-conscious response to the Byronic hero even further in a parallel plot throughout "The Enchantress": the Enchantress agrees to help a poor nobleman, Leoni, to win the hand of his cousin,

Lolah, by granting his wish for wealth. After gaining both wealth and his wife, Leoni grows bored with hearth and home, craves "variety," and squanders their money gambling. The couple are accused of gaining their wealth through trafficking with demons, and flee the threat of the Inquisition. The Enchantress kills Leoni when he breaks his oath by revealing her supernatural aid, and Lolah drowns herself rather than live without him. A mysterious memorial appears where the lovers died, inscribed with one word, the final one in Landon's tale: "SUBMISSION!" Satan's last hope for pardon (which "disdain forbids" him (*PL*, IV. 80)), "submission" is also what the long-suffering and defeated Lolah embodies. Thus Landon's conclusion could be at once a chastening corrective to Byronic Satanism, and an acute insight into the misogyny that underlies it. Lolah is a composite of Byron's (and Landon's) most devoted, passive, and selfless heroines, essentially a "second-order Byronic heroine," who amplifies through her exaggerated passivity the ambivalent misogyny in Byron's eastern tales. In the manuscript version of "The Enchantress," moreover, Lolah is a palimpsest for several Byronic heroines: named Leila (from *The Giaour*) throughout the manuscript, the original name that appears beneath Leila is Francesca, yet another ghostly victim (in *The Siege of Corinth*) of the Byronic hero.[23]

Landon takes these three "ghostly presences" of the Byronic hero, as Caroline Franklin[24] calls them (Leila, Astarte, and Francesca), and places them at the center of her retelling of *Manfred*. Medora's death in *The Corsair* is also avenged, for the Enchantress used her dearly bought powers to assume Medora's identity, choosing to become the long-suffering Medora, Byron's most passive heroine, rather than remain an alienated overreacher like Manfred. Leila and Francesca, too, are avenged, no longer ghostly counterparts of the heroes; here their two names designate the human heroine at the center of Landon's tale, whose suffering as the wife of the Byronic Count is unrewarded, yet no longer shrouded in mystery, and no longer merely the idealized occasion of the Byronic hero's brooding meditations. In Landon's version of the Byronic hero, the motivation for Leoni's quest for more knowledge and power is greed and superficiality, not the ennobling metaphysical yearnings that Byron bestows upon his heroes – the immortal longings are reserved for the heroine Medora. Thus, inseparable from this attention to the Byronic heroines as victims of a misogynist ethos, is Landon's evident fascination with the possibilities of the Byronic hero for the woman poet. Because Landon works more closely and deliberately with the poetic materials of her male contemporaries than the other writers discussed so far, her revisions of femmes fatales like the Enchantress allow us to see more clearly the value of such figures to Romantic women writers.

In "The Enchantress" and in other works, Landon is closest to Byron when she sees his genius for what it is: both destructive, and, when *not* taken on its own terms, surprisingly promising for women writers. It is both these aspects of Landon that Rowton glimpsed when he warned that "There is an evil spirit in such sentiments which should be bidden behind us." Landon's profound pessimism emerged in her characteristic ill-fated, passive heroines like Lolah, upon whom modern critics have focused almost exclusively in their assessment of her work and its limitations. But this despair also emerged in Landon's bold Promethean poet figures, like the Enchantress, figures who aspire to and acquire the loftiest of Romantic powers, only to discover "the fatal truth," as the Enchantress confessed, "that my lot is but an awful solitude, without duties or affections – those ties and blessings of humanity" (*WL*, 11: 175). Landon's complex revisions of Byronic conceits have much to teach us about her self-fashioning as Romantic poet, and about how even what are at first glance the most crippling and misogynist of femme fatale figures were refashioned by women writers for distinctly (proto-)feminist ends.

"The Fairy of the Fountains"

Landon's poem "The Fairy of the Fountains" is one of the earliest poetic reworkings by a woman of the Melusine legend, the suffering enchantress/mermaid in search of a Christian soul, and as such marks another important contribution of a woman poet to this femme fatale tradition.[25] Published in *Fisher's Drawing Room Scrap Book for 1835*, after Landon's trip to Paris, the poem is evidence of Landon's extensive reading in French literature and history. The most influential Romantic rendering of the mermaid myth was in fact Staël's, whose *Corinne* was inspired by an 1804 production of *The Nymph of the Danube*.[26] But La Motte Fouqué's novella *Undine*, published in English in 1818 and read by Keats, is the best-known direct literary rendering of this medieval French romance, and serves as a helpful contrast to Landon's work. Barbara Fass argues that Fouqué, unlike Keats in *Lamia*, fails to create a complex Undine because she too readily accepts the constricted status of human woman, becoming "a docile and even dull housewife."[27] Harriet Emma Burton's "Ondine; The Ocean Bride" (1833/35?)[28] is an excellent example of a woman's celebration of this traditional version of Undine as sentimentalized femininity, yearning for the legitimacy of Christian marriage and a Christian soul.

This transformation of Fouqué's Undine from supernatural figure to domestic housewife mirrors the shift in the definition of woman in the eighteenth century. From the dangerously capricious and willful character (or characterlessness) of woman maligned by Swift and Pope, to the selfless, virtuous femininity at the heart of the ascendant bourgeois order, Undine in one sense embodies the rise of the domestic woman, and the sacrifices she makes in order to obtain a Christian soul, and with it a new position of moral authority.

For Fass, Undine serves as a projection of the nineteenth-century (male) artist's imagination: the lesson she teaches is that Romantic aesthetics are ultimately alienating and alienated from human society. But clearly women poets were also interested in the mermaid and the aesthetic dilemma she represented, as well as the sexual politics she obviously embodied, given her transformation from supernatural to "natural" woman. In the mermaid poems of Bannerman and Landon, it is the mermaid herself who is the artist, and neither a male beloved nor a female rival is necessary to complete the analogy. Landon's "Fairy of the Fountains" can be thus read as an account of the woman poet in the Romantic period, much as Fouqué's *Undine* traces the shift bourgeois woman underwent during the same period. In Fouqué's *Undine*, the text nowhere explicitly critiques the mermaid's crippling transformation into devoted wife (though it certainly leaves such a reading open). While Harriet Emma Burton overtly celebrates Ondine's single-minded (and ill-fated) devotion in her poem, Landon shows the mermaid unsuccessfully resisting a series of painful exiles, the aesthetic dilemma of the Romantic woman poet who is exiled not once like the male poet, but twice.

Central to Landon's poem is Melusine's relationship to her fairy mother, as the first lines make clear: "Why did she love her mother's so? / It hath wrought her wondrous wo."[29] The poem begins with Melusine's memory of a primal scene, where she effectively sees her mother violated by her father when he discovers her monstrous mermaid body. Her mother's first words, "'Tis not at my choice!," suggest both that she has been violated somehow, and that her mermaid nature is a curse from which she wishes to be released, as in the traditional Undine legend. Melusine's mother is thus Fouqué's Undine, an earlier generation of mermaid poet who renounces her powers, and advises her readers and her daughter to

> Keep thou then a timid eye
> On the hopes that fill yon sky;
> Bend thou with a suppliant knee,
> And thy soul yet saved may be;-
>   (*LPW*, 295)

Daughter and mother are exiled because of the father's transgression and, like the Lady of Shalott, languish on "a drear and desert plain," while they see "far off, a world more fair / Outlined on the sunny air" (*LPW*, 295). But Melusine refuses to accept this exile, claiming a hero's traditional right to his inheritance:

> "It is my right;
> On me let the task devolve:
> Since such blood to me belongs
> I shall seek its own bright sphere;
> I will well avenge the wrongs
> Of my mother exiled here."
>   (*LPW*, 295)

She is punished by becoming a heroine, a transformation Landon indicates by changing her name once she is cursed by the mother, from "Melusina" at the start of the poem, to the legendary fairy "Melusine," by which the medieval mermaid is known. Her fairy mother curses and exiles her, so that Melusine effectively repeats her mother's example, damned to become the suffering enchantress who needs but ultimately loses the love of a mortal man and thus suffers eternally.

Melusine is born into one exile and dies in another, thus she cannot claim a maternal plenitude, or unalienated wholeness, as origin – she is already alienated and self-divided, as her unfemale, inhuman body indicates. She is exiled both from the father's public sphere and from the mother's private sphere: "Banish'd from her mother's arms, / Banish'd by her mother's charms / With a curse of grief and pain." Landon's Melusine, unlike Fouqué's, joins the ranks of Byron's Manfred and Cain, cursed to be her own proper hell ("Must she be her own dark tomb?" asks Landon (*LPW*, 295)), the quintessentially modern subject for whom subjectivity is subjection. And, because Melusine is twice exiled, twice subjected, she is also at once the distinctly female poet and modern female subject, whose Oedipal vengeance upon the father may succeed temporarily, but who is ultimately defeated by becoming her own mother, the suffering enchantress who languishes for men (as Landon wrote in "Life Surveyed," "to yield is to resemble").

In this poem and in others, and in her verse drama *The Ancestress* (1829), Landon shows a deep distrust of the mother/daughter bond, one which places her in striking contrast to Hemans, for whom this bond was potentially a heaven on earth. Cynthia Lawford's recent revelations that the unmarried Landon probably had three children (who seemed not to have lived with her), render even more pronounced the complicated, even painful, relationship that Landon had with the institution of motherhood.[30] Yet it is important to note that while Landon rejects any nostalgia for motherhood, she simultaneously rejects the Oedipal struggle with the father. Like "The Fairy of the Fountains," *The Ancestress* (a reworking of Grillparzer's *Ahnfrau*, itself a version of "The Bleeding Nun") shows two curses at work in the world, in effect bringing together the so-called female and male Gothic. One curse is that of the father, and tries to dispossess the son of his rightful inheritance; the other is a curse of the mother, the Ancestress, whose presence threatens to taint the daughter with her excessive sexuality and vampyric immortality.[31] The Ancestress (like Melusine's mother) proves more powerful than the father, for, while the hero and heroine seem to be released from the curse of the father, and the hero temporarily regains his inheritance, the Ancestress returns at the end of Landon's play to reveal the incestuous secret at the heart of the family, and brings the castle down on all the inhabitants in an implosive moment like that which destroys the House of Usher. The father is ultimately powerless before the mother, as the hero himself laments before dying: "Is there no rescue in my father's house"? (*LPW*, 126). And, as in "The Fairy of the Fountains" and "The Bleeding Nun" (popularized in *The Monk* and *Zofloya*), the heroine in effect becomes her monstrous Ancestress. Landon notes that in the original play by Grillparzer the hero "falls in love, as unwittingly as Oedipus, with his sister; kills his father... and finally dies in the embrace of his ghostly Ahnfrau, whom he mistakes for Bertha," the heroine (*LPW*, 127). Neither the paternal nor the maternal sphere holds any hope for Landon, and she shows how each destroys the other by displacing it, leaving her female characters without nostalgia and with no "bright sphere" to recuperate.

"The Fairy of the Fountains" and *The Ancestress* offer a sophisticated and antisentimental sexual politics, which illustrate the dangers of idealizing the mother/daughter bond in particular, and "femininity" in general. *Romance and Reality* (1831) follows this same narrative trajectory which lies at the heart of Landon's gender critique. The innocent heroine inherits only the curse of the Abbess, on whose usurped grounds her family hall was built – "sickness... shall take thy maidens in the bower" (*RR*, II: 208). Thus another one of her "romanticist" heroines (as she puts it), again "The Last Survivor of her Family," inherits her ancestress's curse, and her house is destroyed along with her bloodline (*RR*, II: 191; III: 332). The Romantic heroine's death in *Romance and Reality* and *The Ancestress* embodies for Landon the death of Romanticism and its quests, and, because of the maternal curse at the heart of each narrative, the death of woman as a privileged term for life-giving benevolence. Landon's own strained relations with her mother, whose house she had left by 1823 in order to live independently (as well as her as-yet unknown relationship with her own illegitimate children), marked an important departure from the model of the proper woman of her mother's generation, and that of her poetic predecessors and contemporaries who rarely lived alone and single as she did.

Maria Jane Jewsbury, Landon's friend, and, like her, an accomplished poet and prolific periodical critic, was an exception, in that her poetry's fiery energy and her unconventional single life (and early death in India) shares significant affinities with Landon's.[32] Landon's "Fairy of the Fountains" reflects Jewsbury's influence in a way that reveals the female poet at the heart of Melusine's rebellion. In "The History of An Enthusiast" (1830), Jewsbury fictionalizes the struggles faced by the Romantic women of genius, namely Hemans, Landon, Corinne, and above all Jewsbury herself. Her heroine Julia is a visionary poet driven by "the burning hope of self-emancipation," and desire for "a more brilliant sphere,"[33] like Melusine. And, like the Enchantress, she desires "immortal knowledge," to feed "to the very full on the fruit of that tree now forbidden" (*Ibid.*, 50). While her heroine predictably is denied the love of a man, she nevertheless avoids the fate of death so common in Hemans and Landon, and sails for Italy broken-hearted, defiantly quoting Shelley and publishing "mad verses" that echo *Don Juan*. Her scandalized contemporaries predict that "if she completes all by travelling alone, she will be a second Mary Wolstonecroft [*sic*], and... we shall have another version of 'Letters from Norway'" (*Ibid.*, 169–70). "Like the Shelleyan hero," writes Norma Clarke, "Julia accepts alienation. Instead of retreating to sickness, retirement, domesticity, and death, she goes forward into an unknown, uncharted new life."[34] Precisely what Melusine tries to do but cannot, and the reason she cannot, as Landon sees it, is her mother's curse. Landon's poet Melusine is also alienated and exiled, but she is exiled within what is recognizably the claustrophobic sphere of her mother's world, only stripped of the comfort associated with "her mother's arms," a double defeat that exhausts all Romantic consolations of heroic exile as Percy Shelley or Byron would have understood them.

Ironically, in her sketch of Jewsbury in *Romance and Reality*, Landon takes issue with "The History of an Enthusiast" for precisely the same reason that critics, then and now, take issue with Landon's own heroines:

> I cannot help thinking, though, in her first story (the History of the Modern Corinne) she has fallen into the common and picturesque error, of making her woman of genius peculiarly susceptible of love – a fact I greatly doubt. (RR, 1: 143)

This is Landon at her most self-conscious and ironic, well aware of the contradictions that inform and constrict her own writing and that of her contemporaries. *Romance and Reality* itself dispatches another such heroine to sickness, "live burial" in a convent, and death, all due to her unrequited love for a Shelleyan Romantic hero. Landon's sympathies throughout the novel, however, are not with this heroine, but with the urbane and worldly Lady Mandeville, an older woman who sees through the Romantic follies of the people and poets of her day. Lady Mandeville's sparkling critical commentary on contemporary (Romantic) literature and society are examples of Landon's overlooked and considerable skills as a social and literary critic.

Melusine's living death as her mother, then, emerges as a skeptical response both to Jewsbury's more Romantic attempt to rescue Corinne, and to Landon's own earlier tales of "wom[e]n of genius peculiarly susceptible of love." In "Fairy of the Fountains" she gives us the tragic (because inescapable) ideological prehistory, long before the fatal lover arrives on the scene, that makes possible Corinne's defeat: it is love for the mother (perhaps for femininity), and not for the male lover, that dooms Melusine and thus the woman of genius.

Melusine also offers an important and (proto-)feminist revision of the Lady of Shalott's lack of self-consciousness and agency in Tennyson's 1832 poem. The Lady of Shalott "knows not what the curse may be" that imprisons her in her tower, and her rebellion is sparked by the dubious attractions of Lancelot. Landon clarifies the nature of this curse for the Lady, Mariana, and all such embowered figures, including most of her own early heroines. Landon also dispenses with the narcissism of Tennyson's "The Mermaid" (1830), wherein the speaker dreams that "*I would be a mermaid fair; / I would sing to myself the whole of the day*," and all because the creatures of the sea, particularly "the mermen under the sea / Would feel their immortality / Die in their hearts *for the love of me*."[35] This is precisely Melusine's curse, to become the Mermaid that Tennyson dreams of, feeding off the love of others in an underworld. No heroine of Landon's, certainly not Melusine, ever indulges the illusion that everything revolves around this "love of me." The early heroines certainly yearn for this unattainable love, but they do not celebrate it as the source of their freedom (it is, rather, the cause of their deaths). In Tennyson's poem, moreover, the Mermaid's sexual freedom remains inseparable from the economy of heterosexual love (as she repeats four times, everything acts "for the love of me") which is her greatest pleasure, a narcissism that Landon's "Fairy of the Fountains" (like Wollstonecraft's *Rights of Woman*) reinterprets as the curse of women's limited sphere.[36] Melusine's heroic quest is fired by "the burning hope of self emancipation" from this sexual economy of the separate spheres which Tennyson imagines as the Mermaid's ultimate fantasy: "then the king of them all would carry me, / Woo me, and win me, and marry me."

LANDON'S MERMAIDS IN HISTORICAL AND SCIENTIFIC CONTEXT

Landon's interest in mermaids was part of a larger cultural fascination with mermaids and their scientific and sexual significance as indeterminate beings, in terms of both sex and species. In the autumn of 1822, when Landon was living in Old Brompton, a suburb of London, a fabricated mermaid was exhibited in a coffee house in the Strand, and was the subject of a front-page article, complete with a graphic illustration, in *The Mirror of Literature*. The disputed ownership of the mermaid resulted in a Chancery suit, in which the judge argued that "whether man, woman, or mermaid, if the right to property was clearly made out, it was the duty of the court to protect it."[37] The mermaid was also examined by William Clift, the Conservator of the Hunterian anatomy collection at the Royal College of Surgeons, at the request of its owner; the serious medical and legal attention granted the mermaid reveal the danger, or challenge, such unclassifiable creatures posed for specialists in taxonomy and anatomy.[38] London had seen many previous mermaids and mermen displayed (in 1738, 1775, 1794, 1820, 1822 (twice), 1824, and 1836), and would continue to see them, until the 1961 British Museum exhibit of two fake seventeenth-century mermaids.[39] Jerdan's *Literary Gazette* and *The Times* also discussed the mermaid exhibits of 1822 and 1824, attesting to the extent of popular interest in mermaids. In fact, the mermaid account and woodcut in the *Literary Gazette* were published on the same page and

directly next to Landon's "The Castillan Nuptials."[40] Even more numerous than the exhibits were the accounts of mermaid sightings or captures
published in Britain, several of which occurred virtually every decade of
the eighteenth and nineteenth centuries, in such periodicals as the *Scots
Magazine*, *Gentleman's Magazine*, *The Times*, and the *Shipping Gazette*, as well
as numerous books.[41]

A striking disjunction emerges when one compares these contemporary accounts of mermaid sightings and exhibitions with literary
renderings of mermaids such as Landon's "Fairy of the Fountains,"
Bannerman's ode "The Mermaid," and John Leyden's traditional ballad
"The Mermaid." The mermaids reported in eighteenth- and nineteenth-
century periodicals and travel books are almost always described as sea
monsters, and almost never as beautiful, much less seductive, women
with long hair, combs, and melodious voices. Descriptions of sightings
focused on the mermaids' scaly appendages, fins, gills, and their dis-
coloured bodies. In the case of the famous 1822 exhibit described in *The
Mirror of Literature*, the anatomical detail, along with the grotesque illustration, emphasized the monstrous incongruity of the creature: "three to
four hundred people every day pay their shilling each to see a disgusting sort of compound animal, which contains in itself everything that
is odious and disagreeable."[42] Mermaids, like giraffes, hermaphrodites,
dwarfs, and giants, "were part of a range of apparent exceptions that
might, if they were genuine and if they were properly understood, help define the limits of biological possibility."[43] The classification debates over
mermaids and other anomalous monsters revealed, on the one hand, science's ability to co-opt anomalies into its taxonomies, thereby reinforcing
their boundaries, and, on the other hand, popular resistance against this
scientific hegemony (Ritvo, "Professional Scientists," 287). This struggle
between taxonomic order and anomalous disorder between species is
related to the similar struggle between the one-sex and two-sex models, and the seductive and bourgeois orders, discussed throughout this
study. The mermaid embodied the same "antitaxonomic energies" Terry
Castle located in the fabulous creatures portrayed in the eighteenth-
century masquerades, and her persistence throughout at least the first
half of the nineteenth century attests to the extent to which categories of
human and female were still disputed in popular, poetic, scientific, and
even legal contexts.

Early nineteenth-century mermaid sightings dwelled on the corporeal monstrousness, the unnatural combination[44] of characteristics that
characterized the sea "creatures," whereas poets such as Landon and

Bannerman were tellingly uninterested in the corporeal distortions of the mermaid. Leyden's ballad "The Mermaid,"[45] based on the traditional Gaelic ballad of "Macphail of Colonsay, and the Mermaid of Corrivrekin" and published in *Minstrelsy of the Scottish Border*, tells of the mermaid who imprisons a mortal man in her crystal cave, but cannot compete with his mortal lover, and is ultimately abandoned. Leyden's mermaid possessed the literary trappings of beautiful hair, comb, and song that mermaid sightings dispensed with, but Leyden also, unlike Bannerman and Landon, emphasized the significance of the mermaid's sexualized body, her excessively physical, as opposed to emotional or spiritual, desire:

> His hand she to her bosom press'd–
> 'Is there no heart for rapture here?
> These limbs spring from the lucid sea,
> Does no warm blood their currents fill,
> No heart-pulse riot, wild and free,
> To joy, to love's delirious thrill?'
> *(Minstrelsy*, IV: 295)

Leyden's suffering mermaid is thus not the would-be Christian Undine who desires an immortal soul, for she suffers because she loses the sexual love, not the soul, of a mortal man to a mortal rival. Bannerman's mermaid also marked a striking contrast to this suffering Undine, as we saw in chapter 5, for, rather than being cursed, she chose to assume the mermaid's "terrific form" in order to destroy men and their ships, and the only pleasures her mermaid described were those of vengeance and destruction.

Landon's "Fairy of the Fountains" distances the mermaid from her sexualized body, and heightens her symbolic qualities as a suffering Romantic outcast. Since "the witnesses [of mermaids] ... made no attempt to reconcile the sea-creatures they had seen with the merman and mermaid of legend,"[46] we should perhaps ask why Landon made no attempt to reconcile her mermaids with those of mermaid sightings and exhibits. Why does her account de-emphasize the corporeal disruption the mermaid embodies, and attempt instead to mythologize and idealize Melusine? In Jean d'Arras's medieval romance *Melusine*, the mermaid's body had been associated with her abundant enjoyment of sexual pleasure, a lusty quality that was treated sympathetically by both Melusine's husband and the poet.[47] The (inconsistently) antifeminist Victorian Eliza Lynn Linton, in her tale "The Countess Melusine" (1861), modernized the mermaid's weekly seclusion in her blue-and-silver boudoir in an explicitly sexual (and entirely human) way, one which I believe influenced Braddon's *Lady Audley's Secret* (1862); it was in this boudoir that Melusine exchanged sex for money, like the "angry mermaid" Lady Audley in Braddon's novel, and like the courtesans of old (who were sometimes called "mermaids" in the Elizabethan era).[48] But Landon's Melusine is not the sexual predator of Linton's tale and Braddon's novel, nor the even more sympathetic sexual subject of Leyden and D'Arras.

Landon acknowledged that she had revised the original legend in her prose introduction. Her most significant departure is in omitting Melusine's children, who "all were in some way disfigured and monstrous,"[49] the original cause for the husband's suspicion and discovery in traditional accounts such as Thoms's *Lays and Legends*, Landon's acknowledged source. In omitting Melusine's monstrous children, like omitting the Ancestress's incest, Landon reinscribes the proper bourgeois body, *homo clausus*, and stabilizes the dangerous incongruity of Melusine's body, its excessive sexuality and monstrous offspring, by referring to her serpentine body in decorative and distinctly Keatsian language. This may also be another significant displacement of maternity, characterizing it as a secret deformity or sin, particularly compelling in a poem overtly concerned with the heroine's struggle to define a new role for herself, distinct from that of her mother. Here is Landon's description of Melusine's serpent body:

> What below that form appears?
> Downwards from that slender waist,
> By a golden zone embraced,
> Do the many folds escape,
> Of the subtle serpent's shape.–
> Bright with many-colour'd dyes
> All the glittering scales arise,
> With a red and purple glow
> Colouring the waves below!
>
> (*LPW*, 298)

Compare this to the description of the fake mermaid exhibited in London in 1822:

The spinous processes of the cervical and dorsal vertebrae project in that distinct and regular order, down to the lower part of the breast, that we find in the human subject; when they gradually lose themselves on entering the natural form of the lower portion of the body of a fish. The scapula and the arms ... furnish us with an exact representation of those of a delicate female ... Immediately under the breasts, the fishy form commences, by two large fins on its belly...it then tapers off and terminates in the tail of a fish, not unlike that of a salmon.[50]

Landon's beautiful description of "the subtle serpent's shape" evokes the idealized sensuality of Keats's *Lamia* (1820), which Landon had read and admired;[51] a more important similarity between their poems, however, is that they both open "an alienated and critical perspective on the process of idealization itself."[52] In the "curse of grief and pain" that Melusine inherits from her mother, we find evidence of Landon's growing materialism (which is not accompanied by a sexual explicitness), for the "world's worst curse," she wrote in the year she died, is "that the body predominates over the mind" (*EC*, III: 197). Working within the Undine tradition in which a woman cursed with a monstrous body desperately seeks a soul, Landon reveals, perhaps unintentionally, the powers of this body over the soul, and that to discount the powers of the body is to resort to "half-knowledge; and theory that lacks the correction of practice, is as the soul without the body" (*EC*, I: 8).

In place of the traditional legend's focus on sexual pleasure, and the mermaid exhibit's focus on deformity, Landon offers a different take on the corporeal significance of Melusine, associating her with the under-world and the grave, "a thing of dark imaginings." In Part II of "Fairy of the Fountains," after she has been cursed by her fairy mother to become a mermaid every seventh day, Melusine is enshrined "Like a statue, pale and fair" as the femme fatale who seduces and marries the mortal Ray-mond, who "feels that he could die / For the sweetness of her sigh." In short, her curse, like that of her mother, is to become "The Mermaid" that Tennyson and Fouqué dreamed of. Like all fairy brides, Melusine is inherently dangerous because she is utterly Other, and in Landon's ver-sion of the legend, she bears the otherness of the grave and the corpse, to which her secret bower and secret body are likened:

> Dark and still like some vast grave,
> Near there yawns a night-black cave.
> O'er its mouth wild ivy twines
> There the daylight never shines.
> Beast of prey or dragon's lair,
> Yet the knight hath enter'd there....
> He sees a sudden light appear,
> Wan and cold like that strange lamp
> Which amid the charnal's damp
> Shows but brightens not the gloom
> Of the corpse and of the tomb.
> (*LPW*, 298)

Landon transmutes the monstrousness of the incongruous mermaid body
into the monstrousness of the living corpse, and hints that Melusine's
bower is in reality the grave to which she must return, like the vampyre
she resembles.[53] Melusine has the "damp and heavy" hair of the dead,
and the "hectic blushes" and "fever'd cheek" of pestilent fever, again
associated with the vampyre's plague. I am not arguing that Melusine
is "truly" a vampyre, any more than I am interested in tracing Landon's
permutations of the traditional legend for their own sake. Rather than
searching, as her lovers do, for the symbolic truth of Melusine's body,
or of her secret sexuality, I want to show how Landon's poem, despite its
elision of the corporeal incongruities of the mermaid legend, nevertheless resists reinscribing the female body as the secret, repressed object of
Melusine's curse. Melusine's secret body, while described in decorative
poetic language, and while inextricably linked to maternity and heterosexuality (as the curse of menstruation and reproductive sexuality, for
example), still bears a disturbing resemblance to the corpse and its
disturbance of any such sexual categories.

Landon had linked female criminality to the living corpse as early as
The Improvisatrice (1824), where the heroine of the song "The Charmed
Cup" descends into a wizard's cave to procure her deadly charm, and
begins to resemble a corpse:

> On that face
> Was scarcely left a single trace
> Of human likeness: the parch'd skin
> Show'd each discolour'd bone within;
> And, but for the most evil stare
> Of the wild eyes' unearthly glare,
> It was a corpse, you would have said,
> From which life's freshness long had fled.

One could read Landon's "Fairy of the Fountains" as a revision of the
misogyny at the heart of Male Gothic, which in Anne Williams's formulation "expresses the horrors... that 'the female' (the mother) is 'other,' forbidden, and dreadfully, uncannily powerful, a monster that the nascent
self must escape" (*Art of Darkness*, 135). Clearly death and femininity are
intimately related constructs, as Elizabeth Bronfen has argued in *Over Her
Dead Body*. Yet one limitation of both Williams's and Bronfen's accounts
is their neat alliance of all things other, all things repressed, and all things
corporeal, with the female.

Reading the corpse as quintessentially female because abject, as
Williams does, for example, deprives the corpse of its most disturbing qualities, which have to do with its revelation of "seething life," in
Bataille's words, rather than with a repressed female or maternal body.[54]
Reading the mermaid and the corpse, on the other hand, as points in the
history of the body where corporeal categories, like all bodies, decom-
pose, allows us to examine the history of the definition of "the female" as
well. My argument is not that Landon feared and demonized the body,
even the specifically female body, by associating it with death and disease,
but that her work shared Bataille's insight that "death will proclaim my
return to seething life."[55]

In "The Funeral," first published as "Windleshaw Abbey" in the same
volume as "The Fairy of the Fountains," Landon violates one of the period's poetic taboos by discussing death and funerary rites in uncomfort-
ably realistic terms, much as she did in deathbed scenes in *Ethel Churchill*
and *Romance and Reality*:

> See the velvet pall hangs over
> Poor mortality's remains;
> We should shudder to discover
> What the coffin's space contains.
> Death itself is lovely – wearing
> But the colder shape of sleep;
> Or the solemn statue bearing
> Beauty that forbids to weep.
> But decay – the pulses tremble
> When its livid signs appear:
> When the once-loved lips resemble
> All we loathe, and all we fear.
> Is it not a ghastly ending
> For the body's godlike form,
> Thus to the damp earth descending,
> Food and triumph for the worm?
> ("Windleshaw Abbey," 53)

Landon does not even bother entertaining spiritual doubts regarding the
afterlife of the soul, but instead focuses wholly on the body and its decay,
a more dangerous object of contemplation. We are all "Hastening to the
worm's possession" says Landon, anticipating Poe's conqueror worm by
nearly a decade. Poetry, as the most Romantic aspiration of our "godlike
form," shares its inevitable fate as "food and triumph for the worm."
Melusine's imprisonment as the femme fatale in her grave/bower,

considered together with Landon's numerous expressions of anxiety regarding burial and decay, corresponds to Poe's recurrent fear of live
burial. In Landon's case, this preoccupation with decay undoes the last
sacred site in post-Enlightenment thinking – not god, but "the body's
godlike form." This radical skepticism allows for no essential bodies,
certainly no "female body," as a privileged site of beauty, truth, or purity.
Thus, the persistent melancholy and despair in Landon's works, in addition to imploding the cult of femininity as modern critics have argued,
also point to her understanding that the proper body and its metaphysical consolations (among them, the truth of sex, and the naturalness of
health and purity) are inextricably bound to death and disease in the
most profound ways.

"A home already half a grave": poetry and putrescence

Water, with its rich symbolic associations, allowed Landon to engage
with the larger cultural discourses of public health and its precarious
purity, a context in which her frequent reflections on decay should be
read. The opening of "The Enchantress" offers an extended meditation
on water and its symbolic significance:

WATER – the mighty, the pure, the beautiful, the unfathomable – where is thy
element so glorious as it is in thine own domain, the deep seas. What an infinity
of power is in the far Atlantic, the boundary of two separate worlds, apart like
those of memory and of hope! (*WL*, II: 169)

It is the infinite and inhuman water of the deep seas that interests Landon,
that her mermaids inhabit and inevitably must return to, even though
during Landon's time the water at issue was anything but pure, beautiful,
and unfathomable. The domestic social world mirrored in these waters
appears precariously placed and fundamentally unsound, because in
Landon's works the thresholds between these two worlds, water and
land, are never stable:

The silence of a summer night is now mirrored on [the Mediterranean's] bosom,
where the bright stars are mirrored, as if in its depths they had another home
and another heaven. A spirit, cleaving air midway between the two, might have
paused to ask which was sea, and which was sky. The shadows of earth and
earthly things, resting omenlike upon the waters, alone showed which was the
home and which the mirror of the celestial host. ("The Enchantress," *WL*, II:
169)

It is in the social world of love, where these female figures interact with, and are often betrayed by, mortal lovers, that women embody normative ideas of love that prove fatal. Distinct from what happens on land, however, is the undersea world in which these mermaids prophesy the future of humankind: vast deserts and measureless caverns, images of emptiness that these figures inhabit, and that, it is implied, the human social world also inhabits, unawares.

Water was one of the most urgent public-health issues of Landon's day, linked to the London outbreak of Asiatic cholera in 1831–32, and her imagery of a dark world beneath the waters and its uneasy relationship to the domestic world above needs to be examined in this social and medical context. I am particularly interested in reading Landon's underwater world and mermaids in such a way as to resist a more familiar move that locates in such images of submersion of the secret self or body the repression of the prediscursive, "natural" female body. The narrative of the "The Fairy of the Fountains" dramatizes this quest for what Foucault termed the truth of sex, as well as a quest for the secret female body. Landon understood this quest better than most, being herself the object of intense public speculation regarding her sexual status. Working against this repressive hypothesis of a submerged truth are the contemporary associations of water and fountains with disease and death, which link the secret body of Melusine not to the promised truth of sex, but to everpresent death and decay.

Landon's landscapes are littered with fountains, which provide the threshold between the inhuman world and the human, between death and life, and it is near fountains that her enchantresses typically seduce and destroy their lovers.[56] This identification of fountains as thresholds between the human and the supernatural is a traditional one, and associating women with such thresholds, as seductive nymphs, obviously can rob these fatal women of "subjective intention" (to recall Mary Ann Doane's point) by reducing them to agents of larger supernatural or unconscious forces. Scott's *Bride of Lammermoor* (1819), which Landon knew well,[57] is one such traditional reduction of one woman's violence to supernatural agency, or fate, ending in her descent into madness and silence. Scott likens Lucy Ashton to the legendary "murdered Nymph of the Fountain" in such a way that her attempt at murder becomes a fulfillment of fate rather than the result of her own agency, something Hardy's *Tess of the D'Urbervilles* would attempt to restore. Thus fountains and their deadly nymphs are traditional literary motifs, yet it is the heightened political and philosophical significance of water purity and water-borne disease during Landon's lifetime that makes her revisions of these motifs so valuable.

Landon's use of fountains to represent a doubling between land and sea, life and its likeness in the gloom, is paralleled by her doubled femmes fatales – the Enchantress, Melusine, and the Prophetess are all fundamentally doubled figures, half human and half serpent in Melusine's case, no longer mortal though appearing to be so in the case of the Enchantress and Prophetess.[58] One could argue that such conflicted natures represent women's "doubleness of vision," their ability to remain "elsewhere," as Irigaray, Cixous, and other feminist theorists have argued. Yet this conflicted nature need not imply that these female figures are exiled from the prelapsarian plenitude of the chora, the woman-centered world of romance beneath the water.

While Landon's texts could be used to sustain such an (essentializing) psychoanalytical reading, I want to suggest that beneath, or rather beside, this fundamental, gendered doubling of surface and depth, illusion and reality, symbolic and semiotic, one finds a landscape radically different – distrustful of any such binary distinctions, a landscape in which the deep truth is imageless, inhuman, and certainly unfemale. The rhetoric of mask and veil, so popular with women writers in general and with Landon in particular,[59] serves as a good example for my contention that in Landon the illusion/truth distinction, especially as it relates to women, is displaced by a larger, pervasive epistemological pessimism that makes questions of surface/depth, illusion/truth in her poetry almost beside the point.

In "The Mask," published in the *Book of Beauty for 1833*, Landon makes the familiar point that the broken-hearted woman putting on a happy face does so because of societal expectations:

> The mask and veil which thou dost wear
> Are of thyself a part;
> No mask can ever hide thy face
> As that conceals thy heart.
> Thy smiles, they sparkle o'er thy brow,
> Like sunbeams to and fro;
> But no one in their light can read
> The depths that lurk below.   (*WL*, II: 181)

Landon points out that this need for social masks, especially for women, is the subject's own strategy of self-monitoring and therefore, tragically, constitutive of the female subject herself, instead of an externally imposed control. We can interpret this image of unknowable depth literally as the quintessential modern dream of subjectivity (especially female subjectivity) as latent depth, Matthew Arnold's "buried life," or the unconscious. Instead of reading this depth as the deep subject, however, I suggest we can read it as Shelley's deep truth, one that ultimately rejects the rhetoric of latent truth for one of imageless truth, as in his poems "Lift not the Painted Veil" and "Mont Blanc." Moreover, these "depths that lurk below" that so often appear in Landon's poems also need to be examined in the context of the contemporary debate over the proper meaning and treatment of a literal "buried life": death, decay, and waste.

The anxiety over authentic subjectivity, ubiquitous in nineteenth-century British literature and a mainstay of its modern criticism, in Landon mirrors a larger problem:

> Alas! what depths of wretchedness
> The human soul can know!
> How bitterly the waters taste,
> Which seem in light to flow!
> For love and hope, those leaves which give
> Their sweetness to the wave,
> Flung with no blessing, lose their charm,
> And find the stream their grave!
> ("The Mask," *WL*, II: 182)

This stream is already a grave not because of a vague pessimism, "essentialism," or fatalism on Landon's part, but because during her lifetime water purity and contamination were thought to be literally a matter of life and death in London. London's rapid expansion and development in the early part of the nineteenth century made it the largest city in the world, with a population of over one million by 1830.[60] While only 20 percent of the English and Welsh lived in cities at the beginning of the nineteenth century, by mid century the majority did so.[61] This rapid urban expansion produced health problems of pressing concern, and Landon's poems that reveal that "the wide world round us is one mighty tomb" show an unshrinking understanding of life's uncomfortable closeness to death and decay, one comparable to that of Poe, whose work she influenced.[62]

The Thames was in more than one sense a grave, from the decomposing bodies it periodically produced, to the industrial and human waste that regularly poured into it. London's sewage ran untreated into the Thames during Landon's lifetime, and the Thames was also the main source of the city's drinking water, which few people in the 1820s and 1830s even had piped directly into their houses. The pollution of London's water source was frequently and graphically lamented, as in John Hogg's *London as It Is* (1837):

When we consider that this fluid enters into the preparation, or even the com-position of nearly all our food, and when we reflect that all the abominations of this Augean Babylon are constantly sliding into it, knowing as we do that the same body of water keeps its position in and near London, without going far above or below it, we must come to the conclusion, that we are sapping the very foundation of our constitutions by daily drinking of this foul stream. (361)

I refer to this contemporary discussion of London's "foul stream," not so as to reduce Landon's frequent associations of streams with graves, or of homes with graves, to covert mimetic representations, a kind of early "condition of England" poetry. Rather, we need to remember that the public health connotations surrounding water and graves that Landon's contemporaries were well aware of, necessarily give her writings a wider social scope, beyond a concern with the ill-fated poetess destined to die broken-hearted. Thus, in "The Altered River" (1829), she likens the river's destined contamination by industry and soil (aka night-soil, or sewage) to the impending tragic fate of the "young poet":

> In vain, – thy waters may not rest,
> Their course must be away.
> In yon wide world, what wilt thou find?
> What all find – toil and care:
> Your flowers you have left behind
> For other weight to bear.
> The heavy bridge confines your stream,
> Through which the barges toil,
> Smoke has shut out the sun's glad beam,
> Thy waves have caught the soil.
> (*LPW*, 240–1)

Landon does more than capitulate to the ideology of the beautiful, or rehearse a nostalgia for Wordsworthian pastoralism.[63] Instead, this poem demonstrates that the will to purity central to Romanticisms such as Wordsworth's is unsustainable and "In vain": "Bend thou, young poet, o'er the stream – / Such fate will be thine own; / Thy lute's hope is a morning dream, / And when have dreams not flown?"

Evocations of impending decay in Landon's works should be read both figuratively *and* literally, as in the opening setting of a ruined convent and its "long-forgotten graves" in her poem "Roland's Tower":

How like this is
To the so false exterior of the world!
Outside, all looks so fresh and beautiful;
But mildew, rot, and worm, work on beneath,
Until the heart is utterly decay'd.   (*LPW*, 25)

Glennis Stephenson reads this as "one of Landon's frequent reflections on the hypocrisy of society" (*Letitia Landon*, 77); it is simultaneously one of Landon's frequent reflections on the exigency and centrality of material decay, a materialist social critique that has remained unexamined.

The dead versus the living: the politics of miasma

During Landon's lifetime, Britain witnessed an important shift in sanitary ideology, which can be loosely described as a shift from a miasmatic theory of disease that blamed epidemic diseases on the dangerous exhalations of decomposing bodies and sewage, to a bacteriological theory increasingly favored after the 1860s, which isolated specific organisms rather than a general poisonous atmosphere, as the source of contagious disease.[64] During the first few decades of the nineteenth century, the miasmatic "sanitary science" enjoyed much public discussion and debate in prominent journals such as the *Westminster Review*, the *Edinburgh Review*, and the *Quarterly Review*. Until the late Victorian period these scientific and popular works on the sanitation question invoked arguments regarding divine providence and nature's intentions regarding the treatment of decay and waste.[65] Untreated sewage ran directly into the Thames until well into the Victorian period, prompting the first cholera epidemic in Britain in 1831–32 (which killed 31,000 people), as well as those of 1848, 1854, and 1866,[66] and contributing to the periodic outbreaks of typhoid.

The technological challenges that so much untreated urban sewage and so many decomposing bodies posed for nineteenth-century sanitarians were accompanied by a moral challenge of potentially horrifying dimensions, one which undermined the very "naturalness" of purity and health, both physical and moral. The disturbing medical analogies of and connections between putrefaction and disease, in addition to the anxiety of agricultural economists that urban sewage was not reentering the natural cycle of fertilization when it was disposed of in the Thames, led the Victorians to question the place of humanity in the "natural" order.[67] The sanitation reforms began in earnest with Edwin Chadwick's investigations of London's slums in 1838–39 and his landmark *Report . . . on an*

Inquiry into the Sanitary Condition of the Labouring Population of Great Britain of 1842, and culminated in the establishment of the General Board of Health in 1848. Yet, during Landon's lifetime, the miasmatic theory of disease that Chadwick was to put into practice was widely debated in popular British journals, and it invoked, as did Landon's poetry, doubts about the natural status of corporeal health and purity.

Southwood Smith's numerous essays advocating a new "sanitary science" in the 1825 *Westminster Review* are representative of the miasmatic theory of disease; Smith, like Edwin Chadwick, argued that disease originated from the gaseous emanations from "filth," that is, sewage, decomposing animal bodies, and general decaying matter. The miasmatic theory of disease thus rejected as inhumane the quarantine measures suggested by contagionists such as Charles MacLean,[68] and instead advocated the removal of "filth" from metropolitan centers, ventilation, and drainage (the movement of slaughterhouses and graveyards from the city centers to the outskirts in the early Victorian period was one result of this sanitation movement). The *Quarterly Review* published an article in 1831 outlining home defense measures against the coming cholera plague, and expressed frustration at the unending debates between the two warring medical camps while the epidemic came closer.[69] The dozens of articles and reviews debating the miasmatic and contagionist theories of disease, and suggesting a wide variety of preventative measures, published in such widely read, popular journals during the 1820s and 1830s, were addressed to a general, not a medical, audience. We can safely assume that Landon would have been aware of this large-scale health debate (especially since it was also conducted in the periodicals to which she frequently contributed),[70] and we know that she had first-hand experience with the sanitary conditions at issue. The extensive coverage of the cholera epidemic in periodicals places Landon's poetry, with its focus on decay and death, squarely in the midst of a public-health crisis.

One essay in the *Westminster Review*, "Gatherings from Graveyards: The Dead *versus* the Living," is representative of the graphic and Gothic descriptions of the dangers posed to the middle classes by the miasmatic exhalations from slums and graveyards:

The burial-ground is the most decided place of maleficent influence. To the necessary degradation of the air by the living, is wantonly and unnecessarily added, the decomposition of the dead, whose gaseous products in the open country would be directly neutralized by mixing immediately with the surrounding atmosphere ... which in a city lie accumulating and lurking at the base of the walls which confine them, rise slowly into the upper air, or rather disperse themselves horizontally into the streets, alleys, houses, and finally into the lungs of the people. In the city there is no living laboratory of vegetable organism to convert the poison of the dead into the healthy tissues of life, but it floats about freely, and becomes to animal life, when combined with it, the cause of disease, decrepitude, and death.[71]

The dangers of death and its miasmas were class-specific in sanitary literature, for it was the rising, lurking, dispersing bodies of the working classes that, whether living or dead, threatened to creep out of the slums and into the neighborhoods, homes, and even the bodies of the middle classes, thus breaking down social and class boundaries in the most profound way – at the corporeal level. Chadwick's own *Supplementary Report on the Results of a Special Inquiry into the Practice of Interment in Towns* (1843) concentrated on the dangers posed to the middle classes by the working-class dead, thus extending his 1838–39 Poor Law inquiries from the living to the dead. In addition to cataloguing the physical dangers posed by the burial practices among the urban poor, most notably keeping the body in the house for an extended period, Chadwick, quoting a clergyman, warns against the "moral evils" which are "yet more deplorable" (44):

With the upper classes, a corpse excites feelings of awe and respect; with the lower orders, in these districts, it is often treated with as little ceremony as the carcase in a butchers shop . . . when the respect for the dead, that is, for the human form in its most awful stage, is gone, the whole mass of social sympathies must be weakened – perhaps blighted or destroyed? At any rate, it removes that wholesome fear of death which is the last hold upon a hardened conscience. They have gazed upon it so perpetually, they have grown so intimate with its terrors, that they no longer dread it. (45–6)

Working-class promiscuity here continues after death, in their "having grown so intimate" with the terrors of decomposition. This promiscuous blurring of the lines between life and death, embodied in miasma, is capable of unleashing pestilent "crime, like sores," as Chadwick put it (45), upon the middle-class social body at large.

The miasmatic theory of the dangers of putrescence influenced significantly Landon's concept of nature and woman's nature. I examine Landon's poetics in this context not so as to reduce her work to a reflection of a "larger" scientific dispute, but to demonstrate the dangers of focusing exclusively on Landon's gender and gendered poetic identity to the exclusion of such scientific and political contexts. Such scientific discourses as the miasmatic theory in women's poetry radically undermined, even while they tried to uphold, the very possibilities of nature's benevolence and purity, and, by extension, the embodiment of these

bourgeois ideals in the stable, sexed body of "woman." Landon's repeated references in early poems such as "Erinna" (1827) to a doubled
world, to an unknown world beneath the sea or in the ruined past lend
themselves to feminist readings that rely on a binary formulation emphasizing an essential, prediscursive female wholeness that is lost or contaminated by the world of "man," in both senses of the word. Charlotte
Spivack, for example, writes of Landon's "hidden world below" as part of
nineteenth-century women poets' general interest in a poetic world "not
affected by confinement or construction."[72] Landon's use of the world-
in-ruins motif lends itself to readings that locate an essentialist ideal as
her work's nostalgic center; Anne Mellor, for example, sees Landon as
perpetuating essentialist notions of femininity because she "identifies
a woman's movement from the private to the public sphere with the
progress of a disease, with pestilence and death" (*RG*, 119).

Yet Landon's use of pestilence, corporeal decay, and death has greater
significance beyond its figurative implications for the middle-class poetess. These motifs in her work radically undermine the redeeming role of
nature, particularly Wordsworthian nature, and of the natural woman,
and reveal in their place a primary corporeal decay at the heart of human life. Her "hidden world below" introduces into idealized Romantic
landscapes the literal hidden world beneath London's streets, as *London as
It Is* described it: "It is no uncommon thing at present for public sewers of
great size to pass across, and under, houses in all directions; from which
the effluvia often escapes, to the great annoyance of the inhabitants, to
say nothing of the detriment caused to their health" (212).

Landon's materialism and Wordsworth's idealism: a critique of "half-knowledge"

I wake from daydreams to this real night.
    James Thomson ("B.V."), "The City of Dreadful Night" (1874)

Oh! Give me back the past that took no part
In the existence it was but surveying;
That knew not then of the awakened heart
Amid the life of other lives decaying.
    Letitia Landon, "Three Extracts from the Diary of a Week" (1837)

One of Landon's poems from her novel *Ethel Churchill*, "Life Surveyed,"
serves as an epigraph to Lady Marchmont's letter describing her growing
disillusionment with London high society (she will later murder her husband and lover, and become "insane"). But, more importantly, this poem

rereads William Wordsworth's idealized nature, and reveals the material decay Wordsworth tried to transcend:

> Not in a close and bounded atmosphere
> Does life put forth its noblest and its best;
> 'Tis from the mountain's top that we look forth,
> And see how small the world is at our feet.
> There the free winds sweep with unfettered wing;
> There the sun rises first, and flings the last,
> The purple glories of the summer eve;
> There does the eagle build his mighty nest;
> And there the snow stains not its purity.
> When we descend, the vapours gather round,
> And the path narrows: small and worthless things
> Obstruct our way: and, in ourselves, we feel
> The strong compulsion of their influence.
> We grow like those with whom we daily blend:
> To yield is to resemble.   (*EC*, I: 255)[73]

"Life Surveyed" is much more than a commentary of the hypocrisy of Georgian court society (the novel's setting), for it is saturated with terms and concerns (e.g., ventilation and atmospheric influence) that had public health connotations specific to the 1830s. Landon's ironic treatment of the landmark Romantic experience of transcendence on a mountain top demonstrates that the "purity" and "glories" of such transcendent visions are only possible through active denial of the ultimately inescapable ills of the material, and in this case distinctly urban, world and its "close and bounded atmosphere." Landon's response to Wordsworthian transcendence is also distinct from that of Charlotte Smith, who in poems like *Beachy Head* (1807) and *The Emigrants* (1793) typically moved from scenes of sublime transcendence to scenes of social suffering, insisting that the former never abandon the latter. Landon, unlike Smith and Wordsworth, is a committed urban poet, one who has yet to be recognized as such. Her evocations of nature sought and lost should always be read while keeping in mind that "nature" for Landon is always "remembered," as Adorno and Horkheimer say of Enlightenment subjects.

Landon's "Life Surveyed" evokes the rhetoric of the miasmatic theory of disease to a remarkable extent, drawing attention to the poisonous atmosphere as "the vapour gathers round" and to its dangerous "influence." Representative articles on the miasmatic theory, such as "Gatherings from Graveyards" in the *Westminster Review*, discussed the problems of urban interment and sewage in terms identical to Landon's, warning of the "Low and moist places" where miasma collects, particularly when streets are not straight but obstructed (204) (Landon herself had warned that "the vapour gathers round, / And the path narrows: small and worthless things / Obstruct our way"):

Although London is but a small speck in the vast aerial ocean above and around it, and although it occupies but a few feet of vertical elevation in an atmosphere which is said to rise many miles, yet it is found practically that flowing through its sinuous streets, and pent up in the countless little cells where its myriads toil like clusters of coral-insects at the bottom of the sea, the air, by constant inspiration...is polluted and deteriorated faster than it can be purified. ("Gatherings from Graveyards," 203–4)

The reviewer's distinction between the "vast aerial ocean above," and the poisonous climate issuing from sewers and graves one finds upon earthly descent, is a common one in such sanitation articles, as well as in Landon's writings. Published in the same year as *Ethel Churchill*, Hogg's *London as It Is* catalogued in great detail the effects of narrow, crooked streets, poor ventilation, and miasma in similar terms:

Vapours of animal and vegetable matter mingle with it [the atmosphere] mechanically, and the presence or absence of these give character to the salubrity of places. The air on elevated situations is most free from these impurities, but the close atmosphere of cities and towns is most of all contaminated by them. (183)

Landon had in fact introduced such a discourse of poisonous atmosphere and poor ventilation at the beginning of *Ethel Churchill*, where the rural poet Walter Maynard arrives in a gloomy and smoky London and is immediately affected: "the very atmosphere is dull and close. Its gloomy influence is on all" (*EC*, 1: 161). Like the stanza from "Three Extracts from the Diary of a Week" (1837) that serves as epigraph for this section, Landon's later poetry, such as "Life Surveyed," is that of the "awakened heart / Amid the life of other lives decaying."

The death and decay that threaten and frequently overwhelm Landon's visions of idyllic domestic happiness, or her poetess's flights into the sublime "vast aerial ocean above," owe much more to contemporary awareness of death's influence on life, than to her "essentialist" association of the masculine public sphere with pestilence. The above-quoted article "Gatherings from Graveyards" went on to argue that "[t]he burial-ground is the most decided place of maleficent influence" (205), much as Landon had noted the dangerous "influence" of material decay, for in her words, "We grow like those with whom we daily blend." Hers is thus a specific "influence," not a simplistic rejection of artificial urban life for an idealized pastoral purity, for it is the dead and decaying with whom the living were feared to blend, as "Gatherings from Graveyards" lamented: "the...gases...eliminated...from the thousands of dead bodies in London, which become mixed with the air, and are breathed by the people, incorporated with their blood, and thus the very putrefactions of the dead become parts of the living" (207). To "grow like those with whom we daily blend," then, is to grow to resemble the (living) dead and the laboring classes, so that, as in her poem "The Factory" (1835), London becomes "a living grave" where the "moral atmosphere" of toiling children "makes of many an English home / One long and living tomb" (*LPW*, 278–80).

Also published in 1835, two years after the Factory Act, Catherine Grace Godwin's poem "The Reproving Angel: A Vision" propels the poet seeking inspiration through a series of scenes of physical suffering, relying on the same public health discourse as Landon had, in a visionary context. From the Lazar-house (for quarantined victims of epidemics), to prison, to slave markets and mines, Godwin's angel reproves the poet's "fantastic griefs" and instead dwells on physical descriptions that utilize the contemporary sanitary discourse to urge reform, warning of "heavy vapours, fetid and impure, / Rife with jail-fever" (*Poetical Works*, 129). We are more familiar with such middle-class concern over urban poverty, disease, and "immorality" in the "condition of England" novels from the 1840s onward, as in Dickens' warning in *Bleak House* about the dangerous mobility of Tom-all-Alone's slum residents, living and dead, and their material threat to the indifferent middle classes.[74] Yet even in the 1820s and 1830s, before the "condition of England" novels wholeheartedly took up the causes of the Victorian public-health and social-justice movements, earlier versions of these sanitarian discourses are visible in Landon's writings, so that we can locate in her works, even when set in distant times and places, an engagement with the most important political and medical issues of her day.

In her poem "Fountain's [*sic*] Abbey," the magnificent ruins of the Abbey (the center of which is marked by a fountain) represent the persistent ruins of human illusions and their consolations, as well as the ruins of Romanticism and its shrine, Tintern Abbey: "How many, too heartsick to roam, / Still longer o'er the troubled wave, / Would thankful turn to such a home – / A home already half a grave" (*LPW*, 310).[75] As Melusine knew full well, all homes are already half a grave in Landon's poems, because they stand in uneasy relation to a vast stern likeness in the gloom. The proximity, or rather, the identity of home and grave is a recurring theme in Landon's works, most strikingly illustrated by the repeated wish not to be buried in a city graveyard found throughout her works: "Here, [in the urban graveyard] all is harsh and artificial: the palpable weight of human care seems upon the thick atmosphere. The very dead are crowded together, and crushed beneath the weight of those weary-looking stones" (*EC*, 83). This concern with urban interment found throughout *Ethel Churchill* and many other works, was an important public-health issue at the time the novel was written, and not in the eighteenth century when it was set. *London as It Is* exemplifies the urgency of writings on interment from this period: "What rank hot-beds then of poisonous effluvia must the London burying-grounds be! and yet the practice of packing the dead in these confined enclosures is pertinaciously adhered to the present day" (236). In her poem "Scenes in London: The City Churchyard" (1822), Landon had contrasted the city and its graveyard with an idealized pastoral landscape in such a way that, as in the above quote from *Ethel Churchill*, distinctions between the city and the grave dissolve: "Here Poesy and Love come not – It is a world of stone" (*LPW*, 309).

Wordsworth's essay "On Epitaphs," published in Coleridge's *The Friend* in 1810, and appended to the 1814 *Excursion* (which Landon had quoted in *Ethel Churchill*) evoked a nostalgia for pastoral purity that sanitarians often shared. Edwin Chadwick quoted "On Epitaphs" in his study on urban interment, which described the horrific "effects of putrescent animal matter on healthy bodies" and mourned the picturesque graveyards that Wordsworth had written about:

when death is in our thoughts, nothing can make amends for the want of the soothing influences of nature, and for the absence of those types of renovation and decay which the fields and woods offer to the notice of the serious and contemplative mind. (Wordsworth, as qtd. in Chadwick, *A Supplementary Report*, 143)

The extent to which Wordsworth's "soothing influences of nature" deliberately denied the "defiling" influences of aggressive industrialization that most English people, rural and urban, had to live with has been explored at length. In Landon's work, in contrast with Wordsworth's, nature is neither soothing nor even ultimately accessible, but rather is typically experienced as an everpresent threat of a perpetual material decay and intense sensual pleasure which her works insist are central to the life of the imagination.

While Landon's nature does influence human subjects, it often does so in an infernal miasmatic inversion of Wordsworth's concept of nature's benevolent and purifying influence. In "Rydal Water and Grasmere, The Residence of Wordsworth," Landon's homage to the "influence of a moral spell" found in Wordsworth's sacred Grasmere is, as in "Life Surveyed," undermined through reintroducing the same contrast between pure nature and urban decay on which Wordsworth's "high endeavour" depended, and demonstrating that his purified nature simply does not exist, much as one might wish it to. Landon's ironic praise of Wordsworth's cult of the (male) child and his "solemn creed" of a spiritualized nature is in fact deeply patronizing:

> A solemn creed is thine, and high,
> Yet simple as a child,
> Who looketh hopeful to yon sky
> With eyes yet undefiled.
>
> (*LPW*, 340)

In Landon's poetic landscape, unlike in Wordsworth's, eyes and the nature they behold are always already "defiled," much as Melusine is born already exiled and self-divided. As she wrote in "Caldron Snout," "I turn'd to childhood's once glad scenes / And found life's last illusions flown. / Ah! those who left their childhood scenes / For after years of toil and pain / Who but bring back the breaking heart / Should never seek those scenes again" (*LPW*, 290). Though one could project a prelapsarian domestic bliss into her work, perhaps one centered on a displaced female presence, Landon's works are particularly resistant to such a move: they themselves obsessively rehearse this nostalgia in order to repeatedly demonstrate its hopelessness and helplessness in the face of a primary material decay that reveals all prelapsarian origins to be "Silent and dark as the source of yon river" ("The Minstrel's Monitor").

Landon in fact voiced what Wordsworth's poems everywhere reveal but actively deny: "I know too well that I cannot work out my own ideal, but I deeply feel that it is the beautiful and the true" (Preface, *EC*, 1: viii). Landon's homes are already half graves because their domestic purity was always already threatened from within. From the cellars in which the dead of the poor were sometimes buried, to their overflowing cesspools and graveyards, to their lack of running water, much less clean water, these would-be domestic sanctuaries were the sites of extraordinarily low life expectancy,[76] disease, poverty, and misery during Landon's lifetime, and her works repeatedly demonstrate that homes and graves, like surface and depth, literally collapse into one another. In *The Ancestress*, this collapse of the home into the grave is a literal implosion, as in Poe's "House of Usher," while in "The Prophetess" it is the prophecy of desolation that unites the Prophetess's idyllic "ancestral city" with the decay it would transcend. Thus Landon's numerous laments for Wordsworthian rural idylls,[77] and for the "pure poetry" only they can produce, should be read as deeply ironic critiques. This nostalgic voice is certainly not Landon's only one, for, as she wrote in a letter while visiting Aberford, she was a confirmed city-dweller: "I would not take five thousand a year to settle down in the country. I miss the new books, the new faces, the new subjects of conversation" (*Blanchard*, 1: 81).

Landon's works of social criticism (in novels and prose) and satire have been largely ignored by modern critical accounts, and, as a result, her distinctly urban outlook has been overlooked, and her poetics distorted. In an important exception to this critical neglect of Landon's prose, Tricia Lootens suggests that "[o]ne way to rethink the works and reception of L.E.L. as a woman poet, then, is to read her primarily as something other than a woman. Another is to read her as something other than a poet."[78] Ironically, Landon's prose may also be the key to reassessing her role in the poetess tradition that *Corinne* initiated, since, as Kari Lokke has recently argued, prose writers like Mary Shelley and Margaret Fuller "are more sharply critical of Staël's definition of the female artist" than poets are.[79] Contemporary reviews of Landon's novels are an important starting point of such a reappraisal, for they frequently acknowledged her developing critical voice, which broadened her concerns beyond those of love and femininity. Found throughout her later prose and poetry, Landon's urban sensibility places her squarely in the camp of Byron and the eighteenth-century salon culture which intrigued her. Her satire of Wordsworth, "Grasmere Lake. A Sketch, by a Cockney!," published anonymously in 1834, is, I believe, one of Landon's estimated hundreds of unsigned essays. Like her (signed) "Experiments" satire of Byron, "Grasmere Lake" warns against reading for truth in Romantic (in this case, pastoral) poetry. "Oh! that I had never read Cowper's Task, or Thomson's Seasons,"[80] laments the narrator, who has retired to Grasmere to enjoy the fantasy of rural simplicity disseminated (and profitably so) by its most famous resident. Wordsworth had published his own *Guide to the Lakes*,[81] one among many, and Landon's narrator is the unfortunate victim of this early tourist industry. This

Cockney would-be Wordsworth wants to "live poetically" in the Lake District, but finds such a life deadly dull:

walking tires me, fishing makes me swear, and I catch cold by going on the water: as to shooting, that is quite out of the question, unless, in my extremity, I shoot myself – and I don't want to die; I only want to live, and live poetically. If I had but taken a house near the high-road, I should at least have seen the stages pass; or if there were even an apothecary in the neighbourhood, or an officer on half-pay, or a curate, I might sometimes get to dine with them, and not be doomed to watch my shadow on the wall. (46)

"Grasmere Lake" is accompanied by an engraving, "Grasmere Lake & Village, Westmorland," by G. Pickering, a stereotypically pastoral prospect of Wordsworth's village, whose rural virtues Landon's Cockney persona undercuts in the accompanying text. The Lake District was already being marketed as a fantasy of English pastoralism through guidebooks such as Wordsworth's, and similar engravings and poems in periodicals. Landon brilliantly exposes the fabrication of English Romantic pastoralism through this literary marketplace, and revives the Cockney versus Lake School rivalry in the process. The narrator concludes with a challenge to the poets of this Romantic pastoralism:

I have done a great deal for the poets; is there not one among them to do something for me? I entreat them to recollect that I have read them, which is a great deal; I have bought them, which is still more; and I have reduced their theory to practice, which is most of all. They owe me a recompense, and I have a plan in my head. I want one of them to come and commit suicide in my garden, and leave a paper behind requesting to be interred in that very spot...My house would then be put down in the guide-books, and all travelers informed "that it would be very desirable for them to go a little out of their way, to see the beautiful monument erected to the memory of the well-known and unfortunate Mr. , so celebrated for his genius, his misfortunes, his death." I might then hope to see a little company. (47)

No wonder that Landon published this story anonymously, as I suggest, given that Wordsworth still lived, but published her satire of Byron under her own name.

As a "Cockney," Landon also published (in the same year as "Grasmere Lake") "A Calendar of the London Seasons," a substantial signed essay celebrating the virtues of urban life and aesthetics, and another refutation of the Lake School in the name of a revised Cockney aesthetics. "I am a Cockney, heart and soul, in every thing but 'that bitter boon my birth,'" Landon writes in her essay.[82] "Linmouth" (1833) is another variation on the theme, with Landon beginning her poem with the customary celebration of a country retreat, only to turn to the city and the social:

> There's more for thought in one brief hour
> In yonder busy street,
> Than all that ever leaf or flower
> Taught in their green retreat. (39)

The prose note undercuts the idealization of nature and the countryside ("copy-book cant," she says) even more emphatically: "This is just another branch of that melodramatic morality which talks of rural felicity, and unsophisticated pleasures" (*Ibid.*, 40). More importantly, Landon insists that "nature" is a constructed category:

The country is no more left as it was originally created, than Belgrave Square remains its pristine swamp. The forest has been felled, the marsh drained, the enclosures planted, and the field ploughed. All these, begging Mr. Cowper's pardon, are the works of man's hands; and so is the town – the one is not more artificial than the other. (*Ibid.*, 40)

Cowper is typically named in such instances, but it is Wordsworth, still living and still a publishing force to be reckoned with, who is the immediate object of her critique. The praise of manual industry and progress marks Landon as an early Victorian, but in her Romantic context it marks her as a writer keenly aware of the material and social nature of poetic production – one who values genius above sincerity ("surely genius, intellectual goodness and greatness, are far nobler emanations of the Divine Spirit than mere honesty") and art above nature ("We talk of the beauties of nature, I must own I am more pleased with those of art").[83] Like Byron and Blake, Landon is a Romantic poet who does not worship nature, because to do so, as McGann argues, would be to commit "a serious intellectual error."[84] "Nature" for Landon is undeniably inaccessible, remembered, imagined – whether in the country or in the city. Bodies, in particular female bodies, are similarly products of history and culture; the urban health crises that Landon confronted, as well as her own ill health and debilitating literary labors, were also in part "the works of man's hands."

Landon's insistence on the material, explicitly corporeal, conditions of literary production cannot be contained by the argument, made separately yet similarly by Mellor, Stephenson, and Leighton, that "L.E.L. insists on art as an overflow of the female body,"[85] and that therein lies the downfall (as well as the spectacular epiphanies) of her poetesses.

In *Ethel Churchill*, the downfall of the poet Walter Maynard is a testament to the body's triumph over and consumption of the mind (and its mind/body binary), and the inability of the imagination to transcend the material; as Landon wrote, "I believe there is nothing that causes so strong a sensation of physical fatigue as the exercise of the imagination" (*EC*, II: 26). Walter Maynard's initials, WM, suggest the abbreviation for William, and *Ethel Churchill* is on one level Landon's retelling of Wordsworth's rise as a poet, if he had had to support himself in London, as she had, solely through writing. This critique of Wordsworth's "great escape" is part of a larger social critique central to the novel; F. J. Sypher's Introduction to the facsimile edition of *Ethel Churchill* praises "the strong current of social criticism that is conspicuous in this novel and in other works of Landon's" (*EC*, 1: 11), and William Howitt's memoir of L.E.L. published in 1840 likewise praised the novel's "clear perception of the fearful social condition of this country, and the fervent advocacy of the poor" in Landon's works.[86] Victorian critics found much to praise in Landon's social critique (and were simultaneously concerned by her lack of piety), though this might be surprising today when renewed interest in Landon often portrays her works as self-absorbed and essentially escapist.

Landon's detailed work plan before embarking for Africa reinforces this social direction found in her later works. In a letter to Bulwer Lytton she enumerated an ambitious "list of the works which I am desirous of publishing during the next two years":

1st a novel of modern life called "Lady Anne Granard, or, Keeping Up Appearances"...
2 a romance called "Charlotte Corday." I have not done more than just sketch out the plan – and write a chapter or two.
2 [*sic*] Two volumes of travels in the country I am about to visit, including the history of the slave trade of which I shall [have] the opportunity of collecting so many curious facts...
3 My tragedy...
4 A critical work in three vols – to be called "Female Portrait Gallery in Modern Literature"...It has long been my favourite project and one for which I have collected a vast mass of material.[87]

Landon's work plan gives a more accurate picture of her writing than do most modern accounts. Her social criticism comes to the fore here, in her literary criticism on women in literature, the novel on modern manners, and her projected history of the slave trade. Even the unfinished romance on Charlotte Corday, perhaps the sole such British novel since

Helen Craik's *Adelaide de Narbonne with Memoirs of Charlotte de Cordet*, evokes that "dialectic of 'Romance and Reality' "[88] that governed Landon's imagination.

Landon's social critique works not only through its representations of poverty and hypocrisy, but also, more subtly, through her demonstration of the body's exigencies, and her use of Wordsworth's idealism against itself. The Preface of *Ethel Churchill* announces that the novel was "written when in very wretched health," and the novel repeatedly calls attention to the suffering body of its author:

> the history of the circumstances under which most books are written would be a frightful picture of human suffering. How often is the pen taken up when the hand is unsteady with recent sickness, and bodily pain is struggled against, sometimes in vain! (*EC*, III: 100)

To Bulwer Lytton, she was even more forthcoming about *Ethel Churchill*: "all its associations are painful. I was ill, and a sort of illness which entailed much physical suffering... [I was] miserable in every way. It is to me a sort of Newgate Calendar of the last few months."[89]

In Landon's novel, the poet Walter Maynard dies an early death in poverty, sickness, and anonymity, a victim of "the world's worst curse, that the body predominates over the mind" (*EC*, III: 197). Landon dispels any nostalgia for the poet writing in the lonely garret like the legendary Chatterton, a favorite of the male Romantics. Instead, she emphasizes the physical privations and commercial obligations that such a Romantic scene of writing demands, for she herself worked and lived in such a garret: "The life of the most successful writer has rarely been other than of toil and privation; and here I cannot but notice a singularly absurd 'popular fancy' that genius and industry are incompatible. The one is inherent in the other" (*EC*, I: 163). This "singularly absurd" distinction is a quintessentially Romantic one, particularly a Wordsworthian one, and Landon explodes this Romantic notion of disinterested solitary genius by insisting on the identity of production and poetry inherent in the very definition of poet as maker.[90] Like Mary Robinson in "The Poet's Garret," Landon argues that all poetry, not merely her own, is inseparable from (though not reducible to) the commercial and material context in which it was produced, down to the poet's bodily health. Landon labored to support herself in London by writing for most of her short life; she did not enjoy Wordsworth's relative financial independence nor his rural upbringing; thus her repeated echoes of what Levinson terms Wordsworth's "getting-spending anxieties" and his "acts of exclusion" of industrialization from idyllic rural landscapes, are instances of repetition with a critical difference: they mark Landon's departure from and critique of Wordsworth's desire "to preserve something [he] knows is already lost" and his denial of this very knowledge.[91] If, as Marjorie Levinson argues, through Wordsworth's acts of exclusion in "Tintern Abbey," the "conditions of Wordsworth's historiography, have no room to surface" (*Ibid.*, 2), then Landon's poetry, in its conflicted and repeated insistence on the corporeal costs and pleasures of the imagination, reintroduces a significant material, that is, corporeal, dimension of poetry. And the corporeal dimension of poetic production is inseparable from the commercial reproduction, distribution, and commodification of this poetical work; thus Jerome McGann's illuminating reassessment of Landon and her demystification of poetry's relationship to the market applies directly to her demystification of disembodied poetics: "Identifying itself as a commodified form, her poetry forecloses that final (romantic) illusion of art: that it lives in a world elsewhere."[92] The "conditions of Wordsworth's historiography," of Romantic historiography, are then precisely what Landon brings to the surface (and/or into which she embeds the imagination) when she insists that "[a] history of how and where works of the imagination have been produced, would be more extraordinary than even the works themselves" (*EC*, 11: 163).

Landon offers a theory of poetic of composition in *Ethel Churchill* that rehearses and critiques Wordsworth's in "Tintern Abbey," the "Intimations Ode," and his prefatory essays to the *Lyrical Ballads*. Like Poe's "The Philosophy of Composition,"[93] which brilliantly undermined the Romantic conventions of his own poems by revealing their debts to commercial and practical concerns, what I term Landon's philosophy of decomposition undermines high Romantic conventions by insisting on the corporeal dimension of poetry, a gesture which goes far beyond equating poetry with the outpourings of the female body, or *l'écriture féminine*: "Composition," writes Landon in her last novel,

like everything else, feels the influence of time. At first, all is poetry with the poet; his heart is full of emotions eagerly struggling for utterance; everything suggests the exercise of his own sweet art ... Gradually this profusion exhausts itself, the mind grows less fanciful, and poetry is rather a power than a passion. Feelings have hardened into thoughts, and the sensations of others are no longer almost as if they had been a matter of experience. The world has become real, and we have become real along with it. (*EC*, 11: 157–58)

Landon's theory of composition follows Wordsworth's in his "Essay, Supplementary to the Preface" with the young poet first experiencing poetry as a "passion," then as a "power" after his irrevocable loss of sympathy and unity with nature. But Wordsworth's philosophy of composition is, as is often noted, dependent on transcending the body, for, as he wrote in "Tintern Abbey," we cannot "see into the life of things" until "the breath of this corporeal frame / And even the motion of our human blood / Almost suspended, we are laid asleep / In body, and become a living soul." Landon's repeated references to the often hidden corporeal suffering, as well as the distinctly sexual pleasure, that accompanies poetic production enact a direct critique of Wordsworthian poetic creation, a critique made even more pronounced by her ironic incorporation of Wordsworthian idealism in her philosophy of composition. Like Dacre, Landon explores the dangerous material properties of imagination, corporeal properties that Wordsworth tried to put to sleep.

Quoting Wordsworth's *The Excursion* (1814), Landon concludes her revisionary passage on the decay of the poet's vision with the possibility that "Still, the 'vision and the faculty divine' are never quite extinguished" (*EC*, II: 158); yet the consumptive death of the Wordsworthian poet in volume three confirms, as her chapter title suggests, "The Usual Destiny of the Imagination." While Wordsworth was a major influence on Landon, she nevertheless thought him "[t]he most passionless of writers" (*Blanchard*, 150). Wordsworth, says Lady Mandeville (Landon's voice of urbane wisdom) in *Romance and Reality*, "is the most poetical of philosophers. Strange, that a man can be so great a poet, and yet deficient in what are poetry's two grand requisites, – imagination and passion" (II: 118). Lady Mandeville's sympathies are clearly with Byron, "our poet of passion" (*RR*, III: 181). According to Landon's poetics, a passionless poet can only produce "half-knowledge," a disembodied poetry of the living soul, and indeed she aptly sums up Wordsworth's genius as that of the "moral sublime" (*RR*, II: 119). Recall the earlier quotation from *Ethel Churchill* where Landon described the half-knowledge of theory without practice "as the soul without the body" (I: 8). Landon's word order is significant, for the soul without the body is precisely the state that allows Wordsworth to "see into the life of things." This immaterial immortality is not what Landon is after, though this Wordsworthian idealism is precisely what Walter Maynard sees in the country graveyard before he departs for London: "Poetry is the immortality of earth" (*EC*, I: 54). His radically different impressions of nature and death upon his arrival in the London graveyard, a synecdoche for the city as a whole, attest to the mortality of his half-knowledge, and that of the "mighty mind."

Landon's letters reinforce even more clearly her insistence on the connections between poetry and production, mind and body: "I have been both bodily and intellectually industrious. I have written poetry 'by the pound;' I have eaten fruit enough to stock a stall in Covent-garden" (qtd. in *Blanchard*, 11: 61). Producing poetry and consuming fruit "by the pound," in both senses of the word, is an unusual declaration for a Romantic woman poet, celebrating the fleshly and the unabashedly commercial without the rhetoric of sin and guilt that would become commonplace in Victorian women's poetry (for example, in Christina Rossetti's "Goblin Market"). Judging poetry by such material criteria is precisely what Wordsworth, who admitted in private correspondence that he wrote *Lyrical Ballads* hoping to make a profit, denigrated in his note to "The Thorn": Words "ought to be weighed in the balance of feeling and not measured by the space they occupy upon paper."[94] Weighing and consuming words (like fruit) by the pound, in contrast, implies a healthy acknowledgment of poetry's complicity in the market.

Landon certainly does not celebrate the disease and toil that are the body's inheritance. But, by insisting on the eventual triumph of corporeal decay over both poetry and pleasure, and repeatedly introducing corporeal suffering in the midst of Wordsworthian celebrations of nurturing nature, Landon offers us an embodied poetics that resists essentializing gestures even while it attests to the body's powers to disturb the mind/body dichotomy. Like Elaine Scarry in *The Body in Pain*, Landon reveals that the opposite of pain is not pleasure, but imagining. As her chapter title describing the poet's death in *Ethel Churchill* implies ("The Usual Destiny of the Imagination"), Romantic imagination decays along with the body from which it obsessively imagines its escape.

CONCLUSION

A magnificent landscape trenched with dark drains.
Charlotte Brontë, description of Zenobia Percy

Landon's consistent focus on love lost and her idealization of domestic affections unattained, of homes that are already graves, are part of her conflicted critique of domesticity and romantic heterosexual love, as Leighton, Mellor, Stephenson, and others have demonstrated. Yet, again,

parallel to this gendered critique of love is Landon's point that poetry
is always elsewhere, like the stars mirrored in water, "as if in its depths
[it] had another home and another heaven" ("The Enchantress," *LPW*,
169). And this elsewhere is not Irigaray's *ailleurs*, outside hom(m)osexual
exchange, but an uncanny and material elsewhere, life's "mighty tomb,"
that is always with us.

Felicia Hemans's poetry also seems to celebrate social and moral conventions while simultaneously marking their insubstantiality, according
to Jerome McGann, and his reading of Hemans is in this sense also
applicable to Landon:

Hemans' works understand that they are haunted by death and insubstantiali-
ties. And like Tennyson's *Idylls of the King*, her work is a vision of the doom of an
order of values which it simultaneously, and paradoxically, celebrates as a solid
and ascendant order of things. (*Poetics of Sensibility*, 187)

It is important to remember that in Landon's works the dissolution of
this ascendant order is accomplished, as in Percy Shelley's and Anne
Bannerman's, by the prophecy of poetry, often sung from the bottom of
the sea by siren poets. The "malificent influence" of death and decay
that rises from the grave and the sewer, like that of poetry that rises from
beneath dead cities and seas, poses a social threat that Bannerman and
Landon were clearly interested in associating with women poets:

> 'Tis a strange mystery, the power of words!
> Life is in them, and death. A word can send
> The crimson colour hurrying to the cheek,
> Hurrying with many meanings; or can turn
> The current cold and deadly to the heart....
> A word is but a breath of passing air.
> ("The Challenge," *EC*, III: 231)

The dangerous ability of poetic language to permeate and disturb boundaries, to spread "crime, like sores" through perpetually questioning, destroying, recasting, reimagining, is allied to nature's destructive powers that poets like Landon, Bannerman, and Dacre explored in order
to undermine Romantic transcendence and its sentimentalization and
feminization of the "natural." Wordsworth warned against this "awful"
power of language as "counter-spirit" in his third "Essay on Epitaphs":
"Language, if it do not uphold, and feed, and leave in quiet, like the
power of gravitation or the air we breathe, is a counter-spirit, unremit-
tingly and noiselessly at work, to subvert, to lay waste, to vitiate, and

to dissolve."[95] This "language so violently denounced," writes Paul de Man, "is all language including his [Wordsworth's] own language of restoration."[96] This language is that of the dangerous imagination that dissolves the poet's self-presence and spirit in sensation, and deprives him of the immortality that epitaphs, like his poems, desperately try to "uphold, and feed, and leave in quiet."

Poetic language shares with miasma a curious threshold status as counter-spirit and counter-matter, where the very criteria for materialization, for what counts as material, are perceptible and therefore come into question. The material dimension of poetic "influence" and "inspiration" binds them, because of their shared corporeal dimension, to miasma and the deadly effects of its influence and inspiration. Isobel Armstrong reminds us that the metaphor of poetic influence, and of "an air" as breath, in women's poetry is "literally an 'influence,' a flowing in, the air of the environment that sustains life";[97] to this insight we should add an acknowledgment of the disruptive properties of air, influence, breath, and nature. The material ground of poetry I have explored is thus not an empirically and historically stable Real (e.g., nature as an "environment that sustains life") but the shifting ground where the real and ideal, or the living and the dead, converge.

Questioning the shifting boundaries and properties of the material in the context of early nineteenth-century sanitation and disease, and of the relationship of imagination to the body, does not disembody or depoliticize these boundaries, but, on the contrary, highlights their political contingency and volatility. As Judith Butler has argued, to problematize the material is neither to presume nor to negate materiality: "This unsettling of 'matter' can be understood as initiating new possibilities, new ways for bodies to matter" (*Bodies*, 30). The sanitarians of Landon's day debated and were interested in the anomalous status of miasma, in the way it insinuated itself into and out of bodies, and in its role in what they saw as a gruesome class struggle between the living and the dead, a displaced version of that other class struggle in which they were engaged. Their "unsettling" of matter would become, in the 1840s, part of a larger political effort of the middle-classes to investigate and control the living conditions and "moral character" of the working classes.[98] Miasma demanded that the sanitarians and their readers question the veracity of *homo clausus*, the stable, hygienic bourgeois body, and the nature of "influence" and "inspiration," as in this 1822 article, "Contagion and Quarantine," from the *Quarterly Review*:

Is contagion absorbed occasionally through the surface of the body, or are the lungs its only inlet? . . . Some physiologists indeed doubt whether, while the outer skin is whole and entire, it be at all permeable to the most minute and subtle matter from without; and whether every thing, both salutary and noxious, does not find its way into the system . . . it is urged that infectious effluvia . . . may possess the power of penetrating through the scarf-skin and thus impregnate the body. (552)

The author dispelled these frightening speculations that "subtle matter from without" could penetrate and impregnate the (suggestively ungendered) body, and predicted that the then-distant plague of Asiatic cholera would not infect England: "it does not seem probable that the metropolis of England can ever receive from the shores of the Levant a sufficient measure of contagious miasmata to cause the existence or prevalence of positive plague" (*Ibid.*, 553).

Mary Shelley imagined precisely this unthinkable catastrophe in *The Last Man*, published in 1826 and begun in 1824 while the cholera swept towards Europe. In 1831, while Landon was living in London, the cholera epidemic struck England, and claimed over 30,000 lives by 1832. More people died of tuberculosis or influenza than cholera, but cholera had a social and psychological impact out of proportion with its mortality rate, striking as it did so quickly, horrifically, and mysteriously. It was known as a "disease of society" because it was directly linked to poverty and therefore exacerbated the already contentious class relations of 1832 (30 cholera-related riots erupted in 1832 in Britain), causing widespread "cholera mania."[99] Landon's writings about "ruined worlds" and the "pestilence" of the public sphere thus occurred amidst a broad continuum of scientific and lay thinking on the nature of contagion and corporeal ruin, and a widespread anxiety over the vulnerability of the middle-class home and body to "the evil coming upon us in its most frightful form," as the *Quarterly Review* put it in 1831.[100]

In *Ethel Churchill*, Landon subtly illustrates the disruptive corporeal and moral influence of the dead upon the living. In addition to the motives of pride and vengeance that Lady Marchmont has for murdering her unfaithful husband and lover, the novel leaves open the possibility that it was her contact with the corpse of her beloved uncle, and her lingering in the graveyard, that led to her madness and murderousness. Landon also dwelled on the unpleasant effects of the corpse on the heroine in *Romance and Reality*, in another unveiling of decay (not poetic death) beneath the pastoral childhood idyll (II: 21–29). Sanitarians often warned of the moral dangers posed by "continuing to deposit the dead in the midst of the living," for "contagion is frequently found to extend from the body after death. It was remarked in 1832 that the persons who had been engaged in placing in coffins those who had died of Cholera, and even those who had only followed the corpse to the grave, were, in very many instances, the next victims of the disease."[101] In *Ethel Churchill*, Lady Marchmont's uncle had died of a sudden "fever," a general term for diseases such as cholera, typhoid, typhus, and influenza. Her beloved uncle's death is the catalyst for Lady Marchmont's descent into madness and murder, and Landon subtly likens her moral derangement and aggression to a contagious disease caught at the graveside. After seeing the corpse of her uncle, Lady Marchmont's face "was like that of a corpse, with a strange unnatural spot of red burning on either cheek, and the large eyes fixed and gazing, but with no expression" (*EC*, II: 310). After performing "each of the mournful rites preceding interment" (*EC*, II: 313), including the screwing down of the coffin lid, Lady Marchmont prepares the poison (her murder weapon) in her uncle's laboratory, again bearing the "red spot" of pestilence, and visits his grave: "The misty moonlight that struggled through the black masses of gathering vapours, scarcely sufficed to guide her steps as she passed, languid and lingering, along the narrow path" (*EC*, II: 330). This deadly miasmatic influence of dark, gathering vapours is implicitly linked to the powers of poetry (as is Lady Marchmont's alchemical sorcery, her "potent spells"), for Landon's description of Lady Marchmont echoes William's invitation to Dorothy at the conclusion of "Tintern Abbey":

> Therefore let the moon
> Shine on thee in thine solitary walk;
> And let the misty mountain winds be free
> To blow against thee.   (lines 135–38)

In Wordsworth's poem, Dorothy's "mind / Shall be a mansion for all lovely forms," but in Landon's text, with the miasmatic "black masses of gathering vapours" through which the moonlight struggles to shine, the female figure inherits from the winds not Wordsworth's "cheerful faith that all which we behold / Is full of blessings," but a contrary awareness that there is "a perpetual warfare going on between the outward and the inner world. Nothing is really what it appears to be" (*EC*, III: 24).

In this final volume of the novel, Landon's intermittent didactic, and often patronizing, speeches against the ills and immorality of poverty increase in number, and even extend to the dead, as in "Gatherings from Graveyards."[102] Landon's evocations of miasmatic influence and decay problematize the identity and stability of the female body by questioning the stable boundaries between other categories of bodies – living versus dead, poor versus middle class – so that her "hidden world below" remains neither hidden nor below, and certainly not a female "elsewhere." One of the most interesting and extreme versions of the "perpetual warfare going on between the outward and the inward world" takes place far beyond the world of "social hypocrisy" – in the graveyard, where bodies and their environment lose all integrity and distinctness. There, Lady Marchmont, like other "dark goddesses"[103] in Landon's works, begins to physically resemble the corpses that surround her, unleashing what Chadwick most dreaded – "crimes, like sores."

A poetics of decomposition and decay, distinct from that of ruins and fragmentation, has yet to be articulated within the context of nineteenth-century poetic and scientific discourses. Yet, as I have argued in my chapter on Dacre and now Landon, the threat of decay posed by the dead or undead is erroneously dismissed as implicitly misogynist, or at the very least not of interest to women writers, who are too often assumed to have favored concepts of nature as maternal, benevolent wholeness. I thus close with Landon's poem "The Phantom" (1836), for here we see a celebration of the undead lover similar to Dacre's, which also draws on the scientific rhetoric of urban waste's miasmatic influence. "The Phantom" also uses the same metaphor of coral insects that we saw in "Gatherings from Graveyards" ("pent up in the countless little cells where its [London's] myriads toil like clusters of coral-insects at the bottom of the sea"), both texts being indebted to Lyell's *Principles of Geology* (1830–33):

> I come from my home in the depth of the sea,
> I come that thy dream may be haunted by me; . . .
> And dark is the cavern wherein I have slept,
> There the seal and the dolphin their vigil have kept;
> And the roof is incrusted with white coral cells,
> Wherein the strange insect that buildeth them dwells.
> There is life in these shells that are strew'd o'er the sands,
> Not fill'd but with music as on our own strands;
> Around me are whitening the bones of the dead,
> And a starfish has grown to the rock overhead.
>
> (*LPW*, 310)

Wordsworth's dream of the shell and the stone in Book 5 of *The Prelude* is here exploded before his poem is even published, for in place of his prophetic, musical shell, representing imagination's potential power of salvation, Landon gives us a landscape strewn with cells that are both homes and graves of "strange insects," filled with both living and dead creatures, not with the music we attribute to life and death.[104]

Although Landon's mermaids typically lack the material incongruity emphasized in contemporary accounts of mermaids's monstrous bodies, her poetry remains deeply engaged with embodiment. In "The Phantom," Landon's interest in miasmatic influence, in the exigencies of material embodiment, is combined with her fascination with mermaids. The poem, while ostensibly about an immaterial phantom, emphasizes the material decay and instability of the lover's body in a watery grave, and the connection between the dead and the living: the phantom speaks to her beloved, "I come to thee now, my long hair on the gale/... is dark with the sea damps, and wet with the spray" (*LPW*, 310)). The natural order's boundary between the living and the dead is a permeable one in Landon's work, as it was in Dacre's. This boundary is assuredly the most sacred, for on it rest all other social boundaries, as Edwin Chadwick's 1842 study of burial practices feared:

when the respect for the dead, that is, for the human form in its most awful stage, is gone, the whole mass of social sympathies must be weakened – perhaps blighted and destroyed? At any rate, it removes that wholesome fear of death which is the last hold upon a hardened conscience. (46)

Landon's poetry, like Dacre's, demonstrates not a "wholesome fear of death," but rather, an unwholesome fascination with it and its powers to disturb social relationships among the living. "Terror by the hearth stood cold," wrote Landon on the Gibraltar plague, "and rent all natural ties."[105] We too should remember that "the image ... a society evolves of the relationship between the living and the dead is, in the final analysis, an attempt ... to conceal, embellish or justify the actual relationships which prevail among the living."[106] Landon's philosophy of decomposition has much to tell us about the pervasive cultural significance of public-health debates during the late Romantic period, and their impact on Romantic ideologies of the natural and the female.

Landon's Prophetess asked, "A few fair flowers around their colours fling, / But what does questioning their sources bring? / That from corruption and from death they spring." Prophetesses and poetesses, like the fair flowers they resemble, all give way to "desolation and decay" not because "their lifeblood is infected by the fatal plague of ambition and vanity,"[107] but because "from corruption and from death they spring." The Prophetess's "sweet dreams" lie in a "dark grave of unbelief," by no means a still grave, as do the Romantic ideals of poetess, femininity, redemptive nature, and original plenitude, replaced in Landon's works by the insubstantial, the shadowy, even the miasmatic. Like the natural order that at the beginning of the nineteenth century temporarily supplanted the order of seduction, Landon's poetry, despite its affinities with this ascendant "natural" order, simultaneously moves beneath it and against it, celebrating the insubstantial that is at once material, the "vast stern likeness in its gloom."

Notes

1. Hoeveler, *Romantic Androgyny*; Andriano, *Our Ladies of Darkness*; Fass, *La Belle Dame sans Merci*. On the Victorian period and after see: Stott, *The Fabrication of the Late Victorian Femme Fatale*; Allen, *The Femme Fatale*; Dijkstra, *Idols of Perversity*. Additional works on the *femme fatale* will be noted in subsequent chapters.
2. Ezell, *Writing Women's Literary History*. Such modern anthologies begin with Gilbert and Gubar's *Norton Anthology of Literature by Women* (1985).
3. Nancy Armstrong makes this point regarding the history of the novel in *Desire and Domestic Fiction*.
4. Much of this scholarship builds upon Michel Foucault's pioneering work on the history of the body and of sexuality, particularly in his three volume *History of Sexuality*, *Discipline and Punish*, and *Herculine Barbin*. See for example: Sawicki, *Disciplining Foucault*; Diamond and Quimby, eds., *Feminism and Foucault*; Ramazanoglu, ed., *Up Against Foucault*; McKay, *Foucault and Feminism*; Stanton, ed., *Discourses of Sexuality*.
5. Birke, *Feminism and the Biological Body*; Grosz, *Volatile Bodies*; Haraway, *Simians, Cyborgs, and Women*; Herdt, ed., *Third Sex, Third Gender*; Judith Butler, *Gender Trouble* and *Bodies That Matter*; Arthur and Marilouise Kroker, eds., *The Last Sex*; Bordo, *Unbearable Weight*; Wittig, *The Lesbian Body* and *The Straight Mind*; Scarry, *The Body in Pain*.
6. Laqueur, *Making Sex*, 154, 174.
7. Schiebinger summarizes that "the great public dramas of the eighteenth century – the struggle for enfranchisement and the abolition of slavery – exposed the Janus-face of *nature* destined to plague democratic orders for the next two hundred years: inclusion in the polis rested on notions of *natural* equalities, while exclusion from it rested on notions of *natural* differences" (*Nature's Body*, 9–10, orig. emphasis). See also Schiebinger's *The Mind Has No Sex?*
8. Jill Matus's *Unstable Bodies* shows how Victorian scientific and literary texts alike anxiously questioned the stability of the supposedly natural two-sex system, focusing on instances of sexual "slippage" and unnatural embodiment, and thereby provides a much-needed rigorous examination of the instability

of sexual difference in the Victorian period. Other works that focus on the body in nineteenth-century British literature and culture include: Vrettos's *Somatic Fictions*; Michie's *The Flesh made Word*; Wiltshire's *Jane Austen and the Body*; Haley's *The Healthy Body*; Bruhm's *Gothic Bodies*. Eighteenth-century studies include: Kelly and von Mucke, eds., *Body and Text in the Eighteenth Century*; Roberts and Porter, eds., *Literature and Medicine in the Eighteenth Century*; Stafford, *Body Criticism*.

9. Moscucci, *Science of Woman*, 28. See also Blackwell, ed., *Science and Sensibility*.

10. Foucault's work on the body initiates his second, genealogical phase, beginning with *Discipline and Punish: The Birth of the Prison*, and his important essay, "Nietzsche, Genealogy, History." The *History of Sexuality* and *Herculine Barbin* continue this genealogical work. Foucault's essay on "Nietzsche, Genealogy, History" offers a concise version of his idea of "docile bodies" imprinted by power, which some see as overemphasizing passivity and denying agency: "The body is the inscribed surface of events (traced by language and dissolved by ideas), the locus of a dissociated Self (adopting the illusion of a substantial unity), and a volume in perpetual disintegration. Genealogy, as an analysis of descent, is thus situated within the articulation of the body and history. Its task is to expose a body totally imprinted by history and the process of history's destruction of the body" (148). All of the cited essay collections on Foucault and feminism offer helpful overviews of the Foucauldian issues of interest to feminist theory. For a good overview of Foucault and literary studies, see During, *Foucault and Literature*.

11. Ramazanoglu and Holland, "Women's sexuality," in Ramazanoglu, ed., *Up Against Foucault*, 260. Numerous other essays rejecting Foucault's usefulness for feminism can be found in the collections cited above. See for example: MacKinnon, "Does Sexuality Have a History?" in Stanton, ed., *Discourses of Sexuality*; Soper, "Productive Contradictions," in Ramazanoglu, ed., *Up Against Foucault*; McNay's *Foucault & Feminism* and Grosz's *Volatile Bodies*. The latter two nevertheless find much value in Foucault's work despite their criticism of his emphasis on the body's passivity and his failure to acknowledge fully the force of gender in his theory of the body.

12. Foucault, *Power/Knowledge*, 142.

13. Martin, "Feminism, Criticism, and Foucault," 15.

14. Foucault, "Power and Sex," 123; Foucault, qtd. in Sheridan, *Michel Foucault*, 219.

15. Bordo, "Feminism, Foucault," 192–93.

16. Martin, "Feminism, Criticism, and Foucault," 13. This notion of women's "doubleness" is widespread in feminist and literary theory; a particularly good example is Teresa de Lauretis, *Technologies of Gender*.

17. Armstrong, *Desire and Domestic Fiction*, 23.

18. Like Gilbert and Gubar in *Madwoman in the Attic*, Margaret Homans emphasizes women writers' "anxiety of authorship" because of the masculine "aspects of literary tradition that made it difficult and even undesirable for such women to think of themselves as potential poets" (*Women Writers*, 8); see

also her subsequent book, *Bearing the Word*. Ross, in *The Contours of Masculine Desire*, and Mellor, in *Romanticism and Gender*, also emphasize the differences between canonical male poets' concepts of poetic identity and those of their female contemporaries. In Mellor's subsequent book, *Mothers of the Nation*, she expands her notion of women's poetic identity to distinguish between "the female poet" and "the poetess." Gender-complementary studies of the (female) Gothic also abound, and are typically psychoanalytical: Anne Williams, *Art of Darkness*; Hoeveler, *Gothic Feminism*; Day, *In the Circles of Fear and Desire*; Andriano, *Our Ladies of Darkness*, and Massé, *In the Name of Love*; as well as Ellis's Marxist *The Contested Castle*.

19. Notable examples of increasingly canonical women's texts include the journals of Dorothy Wordsworth (Homans and Mellor), the poems of Felicia Hemans and the early poems of Letitia Landon (Ross and Mellor), the novels of Mary Shelley (Poovey and Mellor), and the poems of Christina Rossetti and Emily Dickinson (Homans, and Gilbert and Gubar).

20. Foucault, "Nietzsche, Genealogy, History," 148.

21. See Craciun and Lokke, eds., *Rebellious Hearts*.

22. Sade, "DISCOURS PRONONCE à la fête décernée par la Section des Piques" (1793), 121 (my translation).

23. Poovey goes on to argue that women writers found paradoxical ways to express their socially suppressed desires and experiences regarding their sexuality. My argument looks beyond sexuality as the defining indicator of corporeal experience.

24. See also Weil's *Androgyny and the Denial of Difference*, where she argues that images of the androgyne function to eclipse and absorb the feminine in the universality of the masculine.

25. See for example: Irigaray, *This Sex Which is Not One*; Gayatri Spivak, "Displacement and the Discourse of Woman"; Alcoff, "Cultural Feminism versus Post-Structuralism"; Poovey, "Feminism and Deconstruction"; Schor, "Dreaming Dyssymetry." Riviere's early "Womanliness as Masquerade" remains an influential discussion of gender and masquerade; on eighteenth-century literary contexts, see also Castle's *Masquerade and Civilization* and Craft-Fairchild's *Masquerade and Gender*.

26. Doane, *Femmes Fatales*, 2–3.

27. Hart, Fatal Women, 141.

28. On Corday as a femme fatale, see Craciun, "The New Cordays," in eds., Craciun and Lokke, *Rebellious Hearts*.

29. McGann, *Poetics of Sensibility*, 111.

30. Bannerman was part of a Whig literary circle, though she wrote against the French Revolution in her *Epistle from the Marquis de La Fayette to General Washington*. Dacre married a well-known Tory and named her son after William Pitt. Landon described herself as a Tory, but towards the end of her career grew interested in questions of social justice and reform. Though she did marry the Governor of Cape Coast Castle, who was under investigation for participating in the outlawed slave trade, she also planned to write a

history of the slave trade, so her politics are by no means clear. None of them addressed the rights of women in any specific sense, as Robinson and Wollstonecraft had.

31. Schiebinger *The Mind Has No Sex?*, chap. 8.

1 THE SUBJECT OF VIOLENCE: MARY LAMB, FEMME FATALE

1. *Mrs. Leicester's School*, published anonymously, contained seven stories by Mary and three by Charles; Mary likewise wrote the majority (14) of the adaptations in *Tales from Shakespeare*, as well as of *Poetry for Children*. Her name did not appear on any of the title pages of the first editions.

2. See Homans, *Women Writers* and *Bearing the Word*; Mellor, *Romanticism and Gender*.

3. Foucault, *The History of Sexuality*, vol. 1; Foucault, *Discipline and Punish*.

4. Massé, *In the Name of Love*, 238.

5. Spivak, "Three Women's Texts"; Armstrong, *Desire and Domestic Fiction*.

6. Armstrong and Tennenhouse, "Introduction," *Violence of Representation*, 7.

7. My argument regarding the "use value" of Lamb's violence is informed by Bataille's important essay, "The Use Value of D.A.F. de Sade."

8. De Lauretis, "The Violence of Rhetoric," 250.

9. Derrida, "The Violence of the Letter," in *Of Grammatology*, 127.

10. Wordsworth, "Written after the Death of Charles Lamb" (*WW*, IV: 275).

11. Aaron, "A Modern Electra," 10.

12. Leslie Friedman elaborates on the prevalence of this theme in her dissertation on Lamb: "In each of Mary Lamb's stories in *Mrs. Leicester's School*, the little girl who narrates has been abandoned by her parents before being sent to the school," and in all but two of her stories it is "the mother alone who is guilty" ("Mary Lamb," II: 427).

13. Marsden, "Letters on a Tombstone," 36.

14. *Ibid.*, 34.

15. *WCML*, III: 377. Lucas suggests that this poem is Mary's but offers no evidence.

16. Aaron writes that "In many of her stories for *Mrs. Leicester's School* she appears to be struggling, in covert ways, both to tell the tale of her relation with her mother, and resolve the tensions it created" (*Double Singleness*, 125).

17. Friedman, "Mary Lamb," II: 443.

18. Aaron suggests the name derives from a character in Mary Hays's *Letters and Essays* (*Double Singleness*, 51). Sallust is mentioned in the Lambs's poem "The Sister's Expostulation on the Brother's Learning Latin," the authorship of which is in dispute. See also Aaron, " 'On Needlework.' "

19. Sallust, *Jugurthine War*, 192–93. Sallust's Sempronia was the wife of D. Junius Brutus (Consul in 77 BCE). For a second classical Sempronia, one rumored to have been involved in her famous Gracchi brothers' revolutionary conspiracy, see the entry in Lemprière's *Classical Dictionary*.

20. Hussey, "Fresh Light on the Poems of Mary Lamb," 9. Hussey examined early editions of Mylius's *First Book of Poetry* (1810), in which several of the Lambs's poems were reprinted (some with author's initials); he suggests that "The Coffee Slips" and "A Sister's Expostulation on the Brother's Learning Latin" are by Mary, not by Charles as Lucas suggests; Hussey does not discuss "The Beasts in the Tower."

21. Mrs. Gilchrist, quoted in Hussey, *Ibid.*, 5.

22. Mrs. Gilchrist's *Mary Lamb* follows the *Morning Chronicle* and its elision of the murder almost verbatim (23), as does Ross in *The Ordeal of Bridget Elia* (24), and Ashton and Davies in their *I had a Sister* (32). Katherine Anthony's account in *The Lambs* is the most forthright, though she links Lamb's violence to the "archaic fury" (44) of natural forces such as the storms accompanying the autumnal equinox of 21 September, the day before the murder; Anthony also links Lamb's violence to the fourth anniversary of the French republic, also 21 September (43). More recently, Mary Blanchard Balle, in "Mary Lamb" offers the most detailed discussion of Lamb's "diagnosis" of bipolar disorder, and argues that "[m]ost psychiatric authorities agree that Mary suffered from the major effective disorder commonly known as manic-depressive" (8), though she does not cite any; it certainly seems that literary scholars working on Mary Lamb agree on this diagnosis. Meaghan Hanrahan Dobson offers a detailed and valuable feminist examination of Lamb's theory and practice of writing, and an important response to Aaron's *Double Singleness*, in "(Re)considering Mary Lamb."

23. Woof, "Writers," part 1, 50.

24. *Monthly Review* 64 (1811), 102.

25. W. Carew Hazlitt lists this poem as one of those written by Mary in *Mary and Charles Lamb* but Lucas suggests "The Beasts in the Tower" might be one of the few poems in the volume by Charles, because the poem contains an allusion to Blake's "The Tyger," which we know Charles admired, and according to Lucas means that Charles must have written it (*WCML*, III: 496). I do not find this deduction convincing, because we simply do not know Mary Lamb's thoughts on Blake or his poem, and even if we did, this would not be sufficient evidence to make a definitive attribution. Regardless of this poem's authorship, we can see that both Mary and Charles tried to rationalize and make sense of Mary's act of murder in this and other works.

26. Aaron, *Double Singleness*, 111.

27. 3 Oct. 1796 (*LCML*, 1: 47).

28. Qtd. in Charles Lamb's letter to Coleridge, 17 Oct. 1796 (*LCML*, 1: 52).

29. Friedman, "Mary Lamb," 11: 419.

30. Foucault, "Tales of Murder," in *I, Pierre Rivière*.

31. Anthony points out this connection in *The Lambs*, 43.

32. Landry, "Figures of the Feminine," 108, 107.

33. See the caption to Figure 2, Fuseli's "Woman with Stiletto, Man's Head with Startled Expression," for details on the drawing's three inscriptions. The verso of this drawing is also inscribed, again in an unknown

hand: "Nothing could afflict Mr. F." See Brown, *Ashmolean Museum Oxford*, 300–1.

34. *WCML*, v: 37. Lucas suggests that "Salome" was composed 1808–9.
35. "Helen" was published in Charles Lamb's *John Woodvil* (1802), was probably composed in 1800, and is reprinted in McGann's *New Oxford Book of Romantic Period Verse*, 227.
36. Barton, *A New Year's Eve*, 37–44.
37. Nietzsche, *The Gay Science*, 126, orig. emphasis.

2 VIOLENCE AGAINST DIFFERENCE: MARY WOLLSTONECRAFT,
MARY ROBINSON AND WOMEN'S STRENGTH

1. Sade, "DISCOURS PRONONCE" (1793), 121 (my translation); see Craciun, "The New Cordays."
2. Staël, "On Women Writers" (1800), *An Extraordinary Woman*, 201.
3. Hunt, "The Unstable Boundaries of the French Revolution," 13.
4. Gutwirth, *Twilight of the Goddesses*, 383. For a Marxist dissenting opinion on the effects of such female allegories, see Doy, "Women and the Bourgeois Revolution of 1789."
5. Landes, *Women and the Public Sphere*, 12.
6. Rogers, "The View from England," 360–61.
7. I share Dorinda Outram's desire (regarding Madame Roland) to resist the "historiography of women which is either overmedicalized or overmaternalized" (*The Body and the French Revolution*, 132).
8. Robinson, *Letter*, 18, orig. emphasis; first published under the pseudonym Anne Francis Randall.
9. Robinson echoes Rousseau's *Social Contract*: man's "first law is to see to his own preservation" (*Political Writings*, 86). Charlotte Smith had used a similar phrase in *The Young Philosopher* (1798): "Self-preservation, which has been called the first law of nature" (11). In their meditations on the historical role that physical strength played in sexual inequality, Robinson, Smith, Wollstonecraft, and Aikin are all in dialogue with Rousseau's *Social Contract* (1762) and *Discourse on Inequality* (1755), which did not consider inequality in terms of gender.
10. *Trial of Miss Broderick*, (1795) 13. At the conclusion of Robinson's example, the lady returns to the sentimental tradition from which she had strayed, retiring to a convent and dying of longing for her dead lover.
11. "Tabitha Bramble" to Robert Dundas, 23 Jan. 1794.
12. Butler, *Gender Trouble*, 7.
13. Similarly, the anonymous author of *The Female Aegis, or, the Duties of Women* (1798) affirms the necessity of women being permitted to develop "a strong constitution" through exercise, inasmuch as this physical strength will "communicate to [the mind's] powers an accession of strength" and allow women to forbear with "steady spirits" and a "strong and alert mind" (31–32).

14. Castle, *Masquerade and Civilization*, 103.
15. Kates, "D'Eon Returns to France," 186. Wollstonecraft mentions d'Eon in her *Rights of Woman*, listing her as one of the exceptional women, along with the likes of Sappho and Macaulay, who transcend the limitations of their gender and therefore do not serve as models for average (middle-class) women (*VRW*, 77). Robinson used d'Eon as an example of the double standard applied to women's accomplishments, since, when d'Eon "was discovered to be a WOMAN, the highest terms of praise were converted into, 'eccentricity, absurd and masculine temerity, at once ridiculous and disgusting'" (*Letter*, 71).
16. Scholars who maintain that travesty and transsexualism reinforce the patriarchal sexual binary include Janice Raymond in *The Transsexual Empire*, Diane Dugaw in *Warrior Women*, and Catherine Craft-Fairchild in *Masquerade and Gender*. These critics share a reliance on a biological sexual dimorphism while calling for the separation of gender identity from such binary biological difference. Modern challenges to this belief in a stable and stabilizing sexual dimorphism include the work of Michel Foucault, Thomas Laqueur, Judith Butler, and Gilbert Herdt.
17. Kaplan, "Wild Nights," 41.
18. *Ibid.*, 39.
19. Poovey, *Proper Lady*, 76.
20. Bordo, "Feminism, Foucault," orig. emphasis, 185.
21. We should, however, keep in mind Claudia Johnson's important point that "the centrality of maternity in Wollstonecraft's political thought has been exaggerated" (*Equivocal Beings*, 215 n. 3).
22. Poovey, *Proper Lady*, 79.
23. Kelly, *Revolutionary Feminism*, 108, 110.
24. Nancy Armstrong argues that, in the eighteenth century, conduct books shifted their focus from the aristocratic man to the middle-class woman, grounding the bourgeois ideology of self-transformation in the middle-class female body: "This transformational power still seems to arise from within the self and to affect that self through strategies of self-discipline, the most perfect realization of which is perhaps anorexia nervosa. What we encounter in books of instruction for women, then, is something on the order of Foucault's productive hypothesis that continues to work upon the material body unencumbered by political history because that body is the body of a woman" (*Desire*, 95).
25. See, for example, "Woman in an Uncultivated State" and "[Woman] in Civilized Society," in *The Female Aegis*.
26. Examples include the female creature in *Frankenstein*, the Bleeding Nun in *The Monk*, Victoria in Charlotte Dacre's *Zofloya*, Vashti in Brontë's *Villette* and Bertha in *Jane Eyre*; I argue this point in greater detail in the chapter on Dacre.
27. Wollstonecraft quotes from Rousseau's *Emile* (*WMW* 4: 437).
28. *VRW*, 35, 11, 39; emphasis added.

29. Polwhele, *The Unsex'd Females*, 14–15, 20–22.
30. Taylor, *Rights of Brutes*, 10–11, orig. emphasis. In their pseudonymous parody *A Sketch of the Rights of Boys and Girls* (1792), Light and Lookabout also highlight the presumed absurdity of boys and girls engaging in the same physical exercise (17). For excerpts from these and many other responses to *Rights of Woman*, see my *Routledge Literary Sourcebook for Wollstonecraft's A Vindication of the Rights of Woman*.
31. Bisset, *Modern Literature*, as qtd. in Claudia Johnson, *Equivocal Beings*, 11.
32. Silliman, *Letters of Shahcoolen* (1802), 26–27.
33. Gallagher argues this point persuasively in "The Body Versus the Social Body."
34. Macaulay's belief that children not be brought up "to be devourers of animal substances," for example, is based on her understanding that the cruelty involved in consuming animal flesh perpetuates a system of human oppression that denatures human sympathy: "It is a diet only fit for savages; and must naturally tend to weaken sympathy which Nature has given man, as the best guard against the abuse of the extensive power with which she has entrusted him" (*Letters on Education*, 38, 39).
35. Rogers, "Fat is a Fictional Issue"; see also Flynn, "Running out of Matter."
36. See Weil, *Androgyny and the Denial of Difference*; Hoeveler, *Romantic Androgyny*; and Mellor, "Blake's Portrayal of Women." For a positive reading of andro-gyny in male Romantic writing, see Stevenson, *Romanticism and the Androgynous Sublime*.
37. "From every quarter I have heard exclamations against masculine women: but where are they to be found? If by this appellation men mean to inveigh against their ardour in hunting, shooting, and gaming, I shall most cordially join in the cry" (*VRW* 8). Hays similarly urged women to increase their "masculine" intellectual and physical "virtues" (like horseback riding), but denounced women who took part in masculine "vices" like cruelty and war: "Let women then leave to the other sex, such barbarous amusements, as that of hunting poor innocent creatures to death! let them in the name of humanity leave such, to the other sex, whose misfortune perhaps it is, in the present imperfect state of society, to be obliged to assist in the destruction of their own species" (*Appeal to the Men of Great Britain*, 181–82).
38. Sade, *The Complete Justine*, 520–21.
39. Carter, *The Sadeian Woman*, 105–6. The feminist debate on Sade is far ranging, dynamic, and ongoing, and outside the scope of this project. Briefly, feminists who are doubtful of Sade's usefulness to feminist projects include Nancy Miller, Andrea Dworkin, and Luce Irigaray.
40. Curran, " 'The Cenci,' " 75.
41. *Sadeian Woman*, 110.
42. *Ibid.*, 109.
43. *Gender Trouble*, 33.
44. Norberg, "Making Sex Public."

3 "THE ARISTOCRACY OF GENIUS": MARY ROBINSON AND MARIE ANTOINETTE

1. Hunt, *The Family Romance of the French Revolution* and "The Many Bodies of Marie Antoinette." On the pamphlets, see Thomas, *La Reine scélérante* and Revel, "Marie-Antoinette in Her Fictions."
2. Hunt, *Politics, Culture and Class*, 104.
3. Outram, *The Body and the French Revolution*, 127.
4. Landes, *Women and the Public Sphere*, 149.
5. *Ibid.*, 151. Williams mentioned the closing of women's clubs, which she attributed to the Jacobins' unwillingness to agree with their "modest requisitions" (*LF*, 11. 3: 139–40).
6. Letter critiquing Philip's *Necrology* (*Anti-Jacobin* [Jan. 1800] 94).
7. Landes, *Women and the Public Sphere*, 141.
8. Hunt, "The Many Bodies of Marie Antoinette," 123.
9. *The Accusation, Trial... of Marie Antoinette*, 2. Numerous such accounts of the trial and execution were published in Britain in 1793, e.g.: *Trial at Large of Marie Antoinette*; *The Genuine Trial of Marie Antoinette*; *Procès de Marie Antoinette*.
10. Hunt, "The Many Bodies of Marie Antoinette," 123.
11. Rev. of *Le Plutarque des Jeunes Desmoiselles – The Young Ladies' Plutarch* (1806), in *The Anti-Jacobin* 23 (1806), 475.
12. Hunt, "The Many Bodies of Marie Antoinette," 123.
13. Burke, *Further Reflections*, 22.
14. On the bourgeois cultural revolution and its rejection of court culture, see Kelly, *Women, Writing, and Revolution* and *Revolutionary Feminism*. On earlier uses of the Empire of Beauty, see Jones, *Gender and the Formation of Taste*.
15. Wollstonecraft, *A Historical... View of the French Revolution*.
16. In contrast, Ferguson argues that Yearsley "embraces the oppression of Catholic monarchs" because of her growing conservatism and patriotism (*Eighteenth-Century Women Poets*, 73). Landry, on the other hand, argues that Yearsley's contradictory political, poetic, and class positions prefigure the radicalism of the Owenites (*Muses of Resistance*, chap. 4).
17. Landry, *Muses*, 169.
18. *Ibid.*, 169.
19. Landry writes that "[i]t is hard not to see in the frontispiece to *The Rural Lyre* a representation of Yearsley herself as both "The British Muse" and *British Liberty*" (*Ibid.*, 173).
20. Yearsley, *An Elegy on Marie Antoinette*.
21. See also Robinson's poems "A Fragment, Supposed to be Written near the Temple, On the Night Before the Murder of Louis the Sixteenth," and "Marie Antoinette's Lamentation, in her Prison of the Temple," and her unsigned essay "Anecdotes of the late Queen of France" in which she recounts her meeting with Marie Antoinette as in her *Memoirs*.

22. Examples of the satirical, sometimes pornographic, writings published about Robinson include: *Poetical Epistle from Florizel to Perdita* (1781) and *The Mistress of Royalty* (1814). A number of satirical prints of Robinson are reprinted in Steen's *The Lost One*.

23. See McGann, *Poetics of Sensibility*.

24. Castle, "Marie Antoinette Obsession," 14, 25. Judith Pascoe's important *Romantic Theatricality* makes a similar observation regarding Robinson's encounter with Marie Antoinette, in which "the prince becomes an object of exchange" in an "exclusively female marketplace," though she concludes that while "It is possible to read this...as a lesbian interchange with the Prince of Wales serving as a triangulated object of desire...I prefer to dwell on the parallel between the fetishistic aspects of this scene and my introductory discussion of Sarah Siddons" (122).

25. Piozzi, *Thraliana*, II: 740. On eroticism between women in eighteenth-century fiction, see Moore, *Dangerous Intimacies* and Donoghue, *Passions Between Women*.

26. Castle, "Marie Antoinette Obsession," 13–14.

27. In addition to McGann's important discussion of Robinson and Sappho, see also Perry, "The British Sappho."

28. Saint-Amand, "Adorning Marie Antoinette."

29. Rev. of *Monody*, 115.

30. Rev. of *Monody*, 304 (orig. emphasis). The volume nevertheless was very well reviewed, even in the reviews cited here, as well as in the *British Critic* and *Analytical Review*.

31. Burke, *Further Reflections*, 25.

32. On Robinson's politics, see Adams, "Chapter IV: Mrs. Mary Robinson."

33. Furniss, *Edmund Burke's Aesthetic Ideology*, 257.

34. McGann, *Poetics of Sensibility*.

35. Pascoe, *Romantic Theatricality*, 123.

36. In his *Appeal from the New to the Old Whigs* (1791), Burke argued that "A true natural aristocracy is not a separate interest in the state, or separable from it." Qualities of this natural aristocracy include: "To be bred in a place of estimation, to see nothing low and sordid from one's infancy...to be led to a guarded and regulated conduct, from a sense that you are considered as an instructor of your fellow-citizens in their highest concerns, and that you are a reconciler between God and man" (qtd. in O'Brien, *The Great Melody*, 447).

37. In 1790, Tom Paine similarly explained to Edmund Burke the new sense in which the Revolutionaries employed the word aristocracy: "The Term Aristocrat is used here [Paris], similar to the word Tory in America; – it in general means an Enemy to the Revolution, and is used without that peculiar meaning formerly affixed to Aristocracy" (*Correspondence of Edmund Burke*, VII: 68).

38. Letter to Elizabeth Montagu, 20 January 1797 (Huntington Library, MS M O 6777).
39. Rev. of *Walsingham*, in *The Anti-Jacobin* 1 (1799), 161.
40. Walsingham also articulates Robinson's concept of an aristocracy of genius: "Mental distinctions there certainly are" (III: 262). Sir Sidney, who will become Walsingham's lover once s/he is revealed to be a woman, agrees: "Perish all distinctions, but those, which originate in mental superiority!" (II: 16). Walsingham also praises the *philosophes* in a quote the *Anti-Jacobin* singled out in its review: "had not such men as Rousseau and Voltaire existed, the earth had still been shackled by tyranny and superstition" (III: 264).
41. When pressed by her hypocritical husband regarding aristocratic superiority (he asks: "You acknowledge some *distinctions* in society, then?"), Martha insists that "I respect superior talents, when they are converted to laudable uses by the polish of education" (*ND* II: 244; orig. emphasis). The "aristocracy of wealth" was one of the phrases that the *British Critic* found particularly insulting; the phrase was also used by Wollstonecraft in *French Revolution* and Shelley in *Queen Mab*. On the connections between the Duchess of Devonshire and Robinson's Duchess of Chatsworth, see Sharon Setzer, "Romancing the Reign of Terror."
42. Cook, *Epistolary Bodies*, 10.
43. *Thomas Paine Reader*, 277. Helen Maria Williams agreed that the "glorious event," the French Revolution, "has surely been the work of literature, of philosophy, of the enlarging views of mankind" (*LF*, I. 2: 70).
44. See Goodman, *Republic of Letters*, chap. 6.
45. "Present State of the Manners, Society, &c . . . of the Metropolis of England" *Monthly Magazine* (Aug. 1800), 36. This four-part essay (hereafter "Present State") is signed "M.R.," and Robinson refers to her authorship of it in a letter quoted in Pascoe's edition of Robinson's *Selected Poems* (30).
46. "Present State" (Oct. 1800) 220.
47. Pigott, *The Female Jockey Club*, 195.
48. "Present State" (Oct. 1800) 220. Robinson praised individual bluestockings like Carter, Dacier, Montagu, More, and Piozzi in her *Letter*, and critiqued their political conservatism in her *Modern Manners* (London, 1793).
49. Goodman, *Republic of Letters*, 105.
50. Cafarelli, "The Common Reader." On male Romantic writers' displacement of femininity in their models of authorship, see Hofkosh, *Sexual Politics and the Romantic Author*. On Robinson as a professional author, see Fergus and Thaddeus, "Women, Publishers, and Money, 1790–1820." For William Hazlitt's anxious attack on the "privileged order in letters," see his "On the Aristocracy of Letters."
51. Cafarelli, "The Common Reader."
52. For example: "There never were so many monthly and diurnal publications as at the present period; and to the perpetual novelty which issues from the

press may in great measure, be attributed the expansion of mind, which daily evinces itself among all classes of the people" ("Present State" [Nov. 1800] 305).

53. Hunt, *Family Romance*, 94.

54. Marlon Ross, Sonia Hofkosh, Jerome McGann, and Margaret Homans, among others, have variously discussed male Romantics' anxieties over their lack of masculine authorial autonomy in feminine genres and in a marketplace in which women had considerable buying power.

55. Campbell, *Complete Poetical Works*, 360–61; Wolcot, *Works*, III: 219–20. See also Dallas, "The Thoughts of Marie Antoinette," *Miscellaneous Works*, I: 298–99.

56. "The noblest work of God" refers to an "honest man," in Pope's *An Essay on Man*, Epistle IV. Robinson's *Letter* also praises Marie Antoinette in the same terms as does the *Monody*, with similar echoes of the Queen's Satanic pride: "this extraordinary WOMAN, whose days had passed in luxurious splendour; whose will had been little less than law! Behold her hurled from the most towering altitude of power and vanity; insulted, mocked, derided, stigmatized, yet *unappalled* even at the instant when she was compelled to endure an ignominious death!" (orig. emphasis, 27).

57. The association of Satan with the morning star can be traced to Christian interpretations of Isaiah 14:12: "How art thou fallen from heaven, O Lucifer, son of the morning! how art thou cut down to the ground" (King James Version).

58. Charlotte Smith, "Written in September 1791, during a remarkable thunder storm" (*Poems*, 53). For an insightful discussion of the significance of this sonnet for Smith's poetics and politics, see Lokke, " 'The Mild Dominion of the Moon.' "

59. *Monody* 26, 10.

60. *Monody*, 24–25; *PL*, I. 612–15. The cedar metaphor possibly also alludes once again to Isaiah: "Yea, the fir trees rejoice at thee, and the cedars of Lebanon, saying, Since thou art laid down, no feller is come up against us" (14:8).

61. *Monody* 24; *PL*, II. 464–65. In *Ainsi Va le Monde*, Robinson concludes with a similarly feminized Promethean figure of the "Goddess" Freedom, and also uses the electric metaphor for liberty popular with Williams (and later Percy Shelley): "Thy temple glitters with Promethean fire. / The sacred Priestess in the centre stands, / She strews the sapphire floor with flowery bands. / See! From her shrine electric incense rise; / Hark! 'Freedom' echoes thro' the vaulted skies. / The Goddess speaks! O mark the blest decree, – / TYRANTS SHALL FALL – TRIUMPHANT MAN BE FREE!" (16).

62. The allusion is to *Paradise Lost* and Isaiah 14:12–15, which continues regarding Lucifer: "For thou hast said in thine heart, I will ascend into heaven, I will exalt my throne above the stars of God: I will sit also upon the mount of the congregation, in the sides of the north: / I will ascend above the heights

of the clouds; I will be like the most High. / Yet thou shalt be brought down to hell, to the sides of the pit."

63. Smith, *Emigrants*, II. 173–74; *PL*, III. 91–92. Day used the same Satanic allusion to describe Marie Antoinette, "Hurl'd from her throne, from all the soul prefers," as "Supreme in woe, as glory heretofore" ("Evening. An Elegy. Finished on Reading the Melancholy Separation of the Dauphin from the Queen of France," (1796) in *Poems*, 112–16).

64. See: Praz, "The Metamorphoses of Satan," in *Romantic Agony*; Huckabay, "The Satanist Controversy"; Gross, "Satan and the Romantic Satan"; Wittreich, *The Romantics on Milton*; Schock, "*The Marriage of Heaven and Hell*."

65. Cafarelli, writing on Radcliffe and Milton, concurs that "[w]omen writers of the Romantic era, struggling to overturn their historical exclusion, seem less to have feared influence than sought to declare affinities" with Milton ("How Theories of Romanticism exclude Women," 88). The novels of Radcliffe, Shelley, and Emily Brontë have been examined in light of their Miltonic, specifically Satanic, elements (i.e., their villains): see Gilbert and Gubar's *Madwoman* and Ellis's *Contested Castle*.

66. Anon., "Ode on Liberty, Recited at the Meeting, in honour of the Anniversary of the French Revolution, held at the Mitre Tavern, Aldgate, on Saturday, July 14, 1792," first published in the *Morning Chronicle*, 17 July 1792, and reprinted in Scrivener, ed., *Poetry and Reform*, 38–40.

67. Southey, "July Thirteenth. Charlotte Corde Executed for Putting Marat to Death" (1798); Lux, *Charlotte Corday* (1793). See Craciun, "The New Cordays."

68. "Impromptu, By. Mr. Tasker, On Reading Mrs. ROBINSON's Poems," dated 1793 (*European Magazine* 25 (1794), 140). A different poetic tribute by Tasker is included in Robinson's 1806 *Poetical Works*.

69. See Tracy, "The Mobbed Queen."

70. She asks: "Why are women excluded from the auditory part of the British senate? The welfare of their country, cannot fail to interest their feelings; and eloquence both exalts and refines the understanding" (*Letter*, 89). On eighteenth-century women's political representation, see Chalus, "Women, Electoral Privilege" and my *Routledge Literary Sourcebook* to the *Rights of Woman*.

71. Sawicki's *Disciplining Foucault* was one of the earliest interrogations of Foucault's critique of power and genealogy from a feminist perspective; her argument regarding Foucault's formulation of power as productive, not merely oppressive, is particularly valuable for feminism: "It is just as important to use Foucault against himself, and against the use of his work to undermine the very struggles he claimed to support, as it is to criticize dangerous tendencies within feminism. But it would also be a mistake to assume uncritically feminist political theories and practices developed in the context of patriarchal capitalism ... In the final analysis, we have here another example of the double bind characteristic of every situation of oppression. Identity formation is both strategically necessary and dangerous" (108).

72. Gilmartin, *Print Politics*, 25, 24.
73. "Gallery of Literary Characters. No. XLI. Miss Landon," 433.
74. Colley, *Britons*, 268.
75. Baudrillard, *Seduction*, 1. See also Castle, *Masquerade and Civilization* and Craft-Fairchild, *Masquerade and Gender*.
76. Cullens, "Mrs. Robinson," 269. See also Setzer, "The Dying Game."

4 UNNATURAL, UNSEXED, UNDEAD: CHARLOTTE DACRE'S GOTHIC BODIES

1. Summers's publications include: *The Gothic Quest* (Fortune Press, 1938); *A Gothic Bibliography* (Fortune Press, 1941); *The Vampire, His Kith and Kin* (1929); *The History of Witchcraft and Demonology* (1926); *The Marquis de Sade* (1920).
2. "Books on Sex Matters," *The Times* (13 March 1935), 11. For a brief account of the Fortune Press case, see Craig, *The Banned Books of England*, 92–93.
3. "Professor Defends 'Obscene' Books, One by Clergyman Authority on Witchcraft," 7. According to *The Daily Telegraph*, there were "over 100 volumes" that the court considered, making the likelihood good that *Zofloya* was among them ("Books Seized by Police," 6).
4. For a full account, see *Montague Summers: A Bibliography*, by Timothy D'Arch Smith. Summers makes no mention of the Fortune Press scandal in his autobiography, *The Galanty Show*.
5. Sade, "Reflections on the Novel," 116.
6. Most of the biographical information on Dacre in the modern introductions to her works (e.g. by Summers, Reiman, Varma, Knight-Roth) contain significant inaccuracies. The information presented in this chapter is based in part on Ann Jones's account in *Ideas and Innovations*. Wu's introduction to Dacre also provides some new sources and information (*Wu*, 358–63), as do my "Charlotte Dacre" and Introduction to *Zofloya*. Extended discussions of Dacre in her own right can be found in: Jones, *Ideas and Innovations*; Miles, *Gothic Writing*; Hoeveler, *Gothic Feminism*; Knight-Roth, *Charlotte Dacre and the Gothic Tradition*; Dunn, "Charlotte Dacre"; and Wilson, "Female Pseudonymity."
7. Reiman, "Introduction," *Hours of Solitude*, by Charlotte Dacre, vii; Iain McCalman, *Radical Underworld*, 38.
8. In her *Memoirs*, Robinson mentions John King as one of the disreputable influences on her husband (48). The rumored affair was reported in the anonymous *Letters from Perdita to a Certain Israelite* (1781). The fictional letters cover the period between September and November 1773, and suggest that Robinson prostituted herself with King in order to gain his financial support. *The Scourge* suggested that King was Robinson's first infidelity and that he forged the letters in order to blackmail Robinson (1 [1811], 1–27; 13). Dacre's poem, "To the Shade of Mary Robinson," is discussed later in this chapter, and reprinted in *Zofloya*, ed. Craciun. See also Wu's introduction to Dacre's poetry for a brief discussion of Robinson's possible affair with King (*Wu*, 358–63).

9. King, *Oppression Deemed no Injustice*, (1798?), 60. King describes how "the stigma of bankruptcy had always terrified me: I had made strenuous efforts to avoid it," but nevertheless had to sell his "library which had been [his] chief consolation" (*Ibid.*, 53), and which presumably had made Dacre's education possible. Further accounts of his trials can be found in *The Times*, 29 Nov. 1794 (3) and 9 March 1797 (3).

10. In *Mr. King's Apology; or a Reply to His Calumniators* [*With Respect to a Charge of indecent behaviour brought against him by Anna Taylor and Maria Towers*] (1798) King discusses his support of the Treason Trial defendants, and of religious tolerance. In 1793 he published a speech in the *Morning Herald* that prompted Paine to reply that "You have gone back from all you ever said" (*Mr. King's Speech, at Egham, with Thomas Paine's Letter to Him*, 9th edn [1793], 8). In *Letters from France* (1802), clearly intended to compete with Williams's successful series, King wrote in negative terms of Williams in particular, and of the British Club, Holcroft, and Stone. In contrast, McCalman argues that King "supported Jacobinism throughout the 1790s" (*Radical underworld*, 38).

11. King's account of the incident appears in *Mr. King's Apology* (1798), where he reprints the recantation the women signed on 23 July 1798. The incident was reported in the *Morning Chronicle*, and King alludes to its widespread publication elsewhere. An anonymous response to King's defense implies that King had flogged and sodomized the two women against their will, and had offered a small amount of money in token payment (*The Real Calumniator Detected: Being Candid Remarks on Mr. King's Apology* (1798)). King claimed that, following his series of financial disasters, the two women sought to blackmail him, and then lost their nerve, withdrawing their charges three days after making them. The account of King in *The Scourge* had suggested that he beat his first wife, Charlotte Dacre's mother.

12. Charlotte and Sophia King, *Trifles from Helicon* (1798). All of the poems labeled as Charlotte's reappear in Charlotte Dacre's *Hours of Solitude* (1806).

13. "Two years in durance, in poverty, no means of subsistence, I am obliged to write for bread . . . without metaphor, my situation is literally as I describe it" (King, *Oppression Deemed no Justice*, 60).

14. Apparently her husband, Nicholas Byrne, "was a zealous Pittite and . . . a passionate champion of law and order . . . His great mistake as an editor was to conduct the Morning Post as a servile party organ" (Herd, "The Strange Case of the Murdered Editor," 47). Dacre's husband was murdered in his office in 1832 or 1833 (after Dacre's death) under mysterious circumstances that may have been connected to his outspoken Toryism and opposition to the Reform Bill.

15. Nicholas and Charlotte Byrne had three children, William, Charles, and Mary in 1806, 1807, and 1809, respectively, who were all baptized much later in 1811 (Jones, *Ideas*, 226).

16. Published in *The Morning Post*, 27 Jan. 1806. In her poem "Mr F[o]x," Dacre lampoons the radical leader (*The Morning Post*, 17 July 1806).

17. According to the archives of the House of Longman, the first edition of *Zofloya*, printed in May 1806, sold 754 copies by February 1807. In addition, *The Morning Post* of 28 June 1806 announced that a dramatic piece from *Zofloya* was expected in the following season (see Varma's introduction to the Garland edition of *Zofloya*, xxvi). *The Daemon of Venice* contains colored illustrations, possibly by Rowlandson, though I do not believe it to be written by Dacre (the chapbook is reprinted in *Zofloya*, 278–98). *Zofloya* was translated into French in 1812 by Mme. de Viterne (Paris, Barba).

18. Dacre's influence on P. B. Shelley is discussed by Behrendt in his Introduction to Shelley's *Zastrozzi and St. Irvyne*, Hughes in "Shelley's *Zastrozzi and St. Irvyne*," and Peck in "Shelley's Indebtedness in *Zastrozzi*."

19. Rev. of *The Libertine* (*Monthly Magazine* suppl. vol. 23 [30 July 1807] 645). *The Libertine* was translated into French in 1816 by "Mme. Elizabeth de B[on]" and was first published in four volumes by Cadell and Davies.

20. In *Virtue in Distress*, Brissenden demonstrates a strong continuity between the critiques of sensibility found in Richardson, Sade, and Austen (see esp. part 1, chaps. 1 and 5). Sade was a great admirer of Richardson, and his *La Nouvelle Justine* ruthlessly attacks Rousseau's *La Nouvelle Héloïse*, as does Dacre's *The Passions*. Brissenden notes many similarities between the doubled female figures in *Sense and Sensibility* and *Justine* and *Juliette*. Dacre's doubled female characters in *Zofloya* and *The Passions* demonstrate a similar critique of Rousseauesque sensibility, in particular his construction of the virtuous, submissive woman.

21. Adorno and Horkheimer, *Dialectic of Enlightenment*, 119.

22. Reed, in *Demon Lovers and Their Victims*, makes the feminist, though reductive, argument that the male demon lover popular in ballads for centuries is a trans-historical manifestation and instrument of men's oppression of women through rape and murder. Works on the demon lover in male-authored fiction which explore the psychosexual function of the (usually female) demon lover for the male imagination include: Praz, *The Romantic Agony*; Andriano, *Our Ladies of Darkness*; Fass, *La Belle Dame sans Merci*; Grudin, *The Demon-Lover*; Senf, *The Vampire in Nineteenth-Century English Literature*; and Kurth-Voigt, "'La Belle Dame sans Merci.'" Kiessling, in "Demonic Dread," provides a helpful survey of the three separate traditions – Judeo-Christian, Early Germanic, and Celtic – from which early nineteenth-century demon lovers were derived. Kiessling argues that these multiple origins account for the contradictory, both destructive and positive, associations with this figure. Auerbach's *Woman and the Demon* differs significantly from most works on the demon lover in that she focuses on the feminist potential of the Victorian myths of demonic and angelic women. While my project is indebted to Auerbach's focus on metamorphosis between cultural types (e.g. demonic and angelic women) and on "a woman with a demon's gifts'" (9), her "archaeological" methodology and its reliance on a universal and unconscious Victorian mythology differs from my own, which does not attempt to reconstruct a collective unconscious or mythos.

23. On Byron and Dacre, see McGann, " 'My Brain is Feminine' " and Summers, "Byron's Lovely Rosa."
24. Byron, *Poems* 1: 253. The *Monthly Literary Recreations*' association of Dacre ("Rosa Matilda") with the Della Cruscans (and Mary Robinson) is characteristic of her reception: "for... an affected sensibility and glitter of imagery, they [the Della Cruscans] gave up energy of thought and diction, manly feelings, and even sense; such were the Laura Marias, the Robinsons, Jerninghams, Edwins of later years, and such the Rosa Matildas, the Hafiz, and other newspaper writers of the present day" ("An Essay, whether the Present Age can, or cannot be Reckoned among the Ages of Poetical Excellence," 172).
25. This is the subtitle to "Grimalkin's Ghost; or, the Water Spirits," a parodic extravagance reminiscent of Lewis's ballads in *The Monk*. Similarly, "The Elfin King; or, the Scoffer Punished. *After the manner of some modern poets*" alludes to the ballads of Lewis and Coleridge. "Death and the Lady. In Imitation of the Old English Ballads" and her translation of Burger's "The Lass of Fair Wone" likewise highlight their relation to earlier traditions.
26. DeLamotte, *Perils*, 121.
27. Published anonymously in Lewis's *Tales of Wonder* (1801); qtd. from McGann, *New Oxford Book of Romantic Period Verse* (219–22). Another example of the demon lover growing immense upon disclosing its supernatural nature occurs the traditional ballad "The Demon-Lover," in circulation since the seventeenth century and published in Leyden and Scott's *Minstrelsy of the Scottish Border* (1802–3).
28. In the Bleeding Nun episode in Lewis's novel, Lewis emphasizes Raymond's growing resemblance to a corpse as he becomes clammy, cold, lifeless, mute, and even impotent in the Medusal gaze of the Nun: "struck by something petrifying in [the Nun's] regard," his "nerves were bound up in impotence, and [he] remained in the same attitude inanimate as a statue" (*Monk*, 170).
29. Scholars who make this argument include Mario Praz, Devendra Varma, Peter Grudin, Joseph Andriano. Sedgwick reads the male Gothic's focus on illicit sexuality and paranoia as symptomatic of heterosexist culture's homophobic panic: "The Gothic novel crystallized for English audiences the terms of a dialectic between male homosexuality and homophobia, in which homophobia appeared thematically in paranoid plots" (*Between Men*, 92).
30. Miles, *Gothic Writing*, 188.
31. Burke, *Sublime and Beautiful*, 65.
32. Horace Walpole had thus described Wollstonecraft in his letters. Laqueur notes that the "hyena... was long thought to be hermaphroditic" (*Making Sex*, 19).
33. Porter, "Mixed Feelings," 7. Laqueur also argues that in the eighteenth century, "compared to earlier periods, there was certainly open hostility to nonreproductive sexuality" ("Sexual Desire," 198).
34. Spacks, "Ev'ry Woman is at Heart a Rake," 38.

35. M. D. T. Bienville's *Nymphomania, or, A Dissertation Concerning the Furor Uterinus* (London, 1775), was first printed (in French) in Amsterdam, 1771. For a feminist account, see Groneman's "Nymphomania."
36. Rousseau, "Nymphomania, Bienville," 103.
37. Although literature and medicine have little overlap today, Roberts and Porter remind us that "the Enlightenment [was] . . . an exceptionally fruitful period in the interplay of literature and medicine," in which, "[r]ather than C. P. Snow's 'two cultures,' there was . . . 'one culture' " (Roberts and Porter, "Introduction," *Literature and Medicine*, 3, 2).
38. *Monk*, 308.
39. *Nymphomania*, 174 (orig. emphasis).
40. Foucault, *Madness*, 149 (orig. emphasis).
41. *Ibid.*, 150.
42. Dacre, "The Mistress to the Spirit of Her Lover," *Hours*, 11: 31–33 (emphasis added); both versions of this poem are reprinted in *Zofloya*, 269–71.
43. *Nymphomania*, 78. For an important contribution to theories of the sublime and gender, see Pipkin, "The Material Sublime of Women Romantic Poets."
44. Rousseau, "Towards a Social Anthropology," 15.
45. Foucault, *Madness*, 89. Martin, in *Mad Women in Romantic Writing*, discusses the Romantic period's conflation of the categories woman and insane.
46. In Dacre's *The Passions*, one of the characters meditates for several pages on the nature of the sublime experience (a familiar occurrence in her works), discussing Longinus and specific qualities of Burke's sublime, such as terror, immensity, distance, and indistinctness: "indistinctness . . . is a character of the sublime. The clouds rest on the highest mountains . . . The mind's eye . . . catches a glance of some mysterious form – imagination pursues it till sense almost totters, and the idea becomes lost. A blue vapour ascends from the lakes like the smoke of subterranean fire . . ." (1: 37).
47. Dacre's *Hours of Solitude* also contains examples of this more traditional interpretation of the demon lover as destructive masculinity, such as "Death and the Lady," and "The Skeleton Priest; or, The Marriage of Death," where the woman is told that as *"the wife of the tomb,"* her marriage is in reality "A bond of destruction" and a "murderous compact" (reprinted in *Zofloya*, 274–75). What is destructive about Dacre's demon lovers here and in *Zofloya* is not their sexual desires but their desire to marry and thus legally control their wives.
48. Lewis, *Monk*, 178.
49. Foucault, *History of Sexuality*, 154.
50. Foucault, *Power/Knowledge*, 142.
51. This gesture of embracing the phantom or revenant lover recurs throughout her poetry, for example, in "How Canst Thou Doubt?": "Then thus let us live, and in death die together, / Embracing, embrac'd, let the light'ning consume; / Our spirits shall range thro' the fields of pure ether, / Our ashes together repose in the tomb" (*Hours*, 11: 30). "The Lover's Vision" is closest to the Mistress poems in this respect: " 'Oh, thou!' I cried, And stretch'd

my longing arms – 'Oh, why in life didst thou withhold thy charms? Why, shadowy bride, While I am living clay, Speak'st thou of heav'n, yet leadest not the way? Let me, bright saint, no more despair, But take my soul away, And mix with thine in death, oh, spirit fair!' " (*Hours*, 1: 52). See also "The Sovereignty of Love" (*Hours*, 1: 127).

52. Violence had two meanings in the Romantic period, referring both to violent action against an object (the modern meaning of the word), and to inner violence against the subject's self-possession and stability. For an overview of these dual meanings, see "Violence" in Williams's *Keywords*.

53. To back up a step further, the question of whether travesty is subversive is a part of a larger anthropological debate on the subversive nature of spectacle, the carnivalesque and masquerade; Marx, Clifford Geertz, and Rene Girard are among those who saw in temporary reversals of order an ultimately normalizing effect, either because dangerous elements are exorcized through a safety-valve mechanism, or because the desired social behavior is highlighted through the negative example.

54. We should be careful, however, not to assume that this audience was overwhelmingly female, since Fergus and Jacobs have documented that men made up a significant portion of circulating library novel-reading patrons (Fergus, "Eighteenth-Century Readers"; Jacobs, "Anonymous Signatures").

55. Reprinted in *Zofloya*, 298.

56. "On Novels and Romances," *Scots Magazine* (June 1802), 470–74.

57. *Literary Journal* (1806); reprinted in *Zofloya*, 267.

58. *Literary Journal, Ibid.*, 267.

59. Lewis had similarly manipulated the terms of this debate over the dangers of novel reading by naming the Bible as the most morally dangerous text, a gesture deemed blasphemous and (self-)censored in later editions of *The Monk*. A 1792 children's-rights parody of Wollstonecraft's *Rights of Woman* similarly used the Bible to make a satirical (though overtly conservative) point regarding the dangers of reading: Launcelot Light and Laetitia Lookabout, *A Sketch of the Rights of Boys and Girls*, 43.

60. Bienville also considers the possibility that a young woman may come across his own volume, but assures us that after reading *Nymphomania*, a woman "would feel the fragility of her nature; she would respect, and even cherish the principles which could certainly preserve her from that impending wreck to which the sex are, by reason of their imbecility, exposed" (vii). Though Dacre also focuses on the "impending wreck" facing sexually transgressive women, her dramatization of this wreck is a critique of the impossible double bind sexually active women are placed in, not a meditation on women's "imbecility."

61. It is important to note that their positions on the Romantic woman subject are in some respects quite different, though both are gender-complementary. Mellor contrasts their positions by stating that she rejects Homans' argument that Dorothy Wordsworth's " 'poetic identity' was silenced by her adherence to her brother's equation of unspeaking nature

with the female" (*RG*, 144). Mellor instead models Dorothy Wordsworth's subjectivity according to the poet's own metaphor in her "Floating Island" poem ("my life became / A floating island"), arguing that Wordsworth's concept of subjectivity eluded scholars such as Homans because it rejected the male Romantic model of the stable, controlling subject and instead affirmed a subject "that is interactive, absorptive, constantly changing, and domestic" (*RG*, 156). Both Mellor and Homans's models of women's subjectivity, however, are complementary to what they separately identify as "male subjectivity."

62. Weimar's account of Appollonia resembles negative characterizations of bluestocking salonnières. For example, Nathaniel Wraxall described Elizabeth Montagu as possessing "great natural cheerfulness, and a flow of animal spirits; loved to talk, and talked well on almost every subject; [she] led the Conversation, and was qualified to preside in her Circle, whatever subject of discourse was started: but her manner was more dictatorial and sententious, than conciliating or diffident. There was nothing feminine about her; and though her opinions were usually just, as well as delivered in language suited to give them force, yet the organ which conveyed them, was not soft or harmonious . . . Notwithstanding the defects and weaknesses that I have enumerated, she possessed a masculine understanding, enlightened, cultivated, and expanded by the acquaintance of Men, as well as of Books" (qtd. in Heller, "Bluestocking Salons," 71–72).

63. Yaeger, "Toward the Female Sublime," 211.

64. Burke, *Sublime and Beautiful*.

65. As qtd. in Barker-Benfield, *Culture of Sensibility*, 353.

66. After Godwin's publications of Wollstonecraft's *Memoirs* in 1798, her feminist politics were intimately and unfortunately connected with the sexual "scandals" in her own life, as critics such as Polwhele made it clear. One unfortunate incident of which Godwin reminded readers involved the Kingsborough family for which Wollstonecraft was governess, the daughter of which eloped with her married uncle, who was himself murdered by her family. After the shocking trial, "the *European Magazine* explained it as a result of Wollstonecraft's 'system of education' " (Barker-Benfield, *Culture of Sensibility*, 369). Bienville's Berton in *Nymphomania* has a similar function of initiating young middle-class women into sexual immorality with hints of lesbianism, though Bienville is unable to give his readers any insight as to why she would want to do this, whereas Dacre gives us many good reasons (e.g., power, pleasure, revenge).

67. John Wiltshire makes a similar point regarding *Sense and Sensibility*, "a novel pervaded by forms of homosocial desire": "In this novel the repartee between potential lovers that makes *Pride and Prejudice* so exhilarating is displaced into contests of wit and cunning between sisters and rivals, between women" (*Jane Austen*, 60).

68. Lanser has recently argued that class played a crucial role in determining whether eighteenth-century women's intimate friendships were represented

as genteel romantic friendships or as unnatural sapphism; even within this continuum, however, Lanser notes that "what is most striking about the public representation of female friendship in the long eighteenth century is precisely its embodiment" ("Befriending the Body," 183). For fuller discussions of lesbianism in the eighteenth century see Donoghue's *Passions Between Women* and Moore's *Dangerous Intimacies*.

69. Irigaray is one of many feminists who make this point regarding the feminist value of Sade's female libertines in " 'Frenchwomen,' Stop Trying" (*This Sex Which Is Not One*), though of course other feminists disagree with this position, among them Jane Gallop, Alice Laborde, Angela Carter, and myself.

70. *New Annual Register* 27 (1806), 372–73.

71. Anne Williams's definition of "female Gothic," the most elaborate and persuasive thus far, similarly cannot apply to any of Dacre's novels. For Williams, in the female Gothic: readers share the narrative perspective of the heroine; the supernatural is explained; the plot ends in marriage, a "happy ending"; the "female Gothic heroine experiences a rebirth" into "a world in which love is not only possible but available" (*Art of Darkness*, 102–3). Dacre also does not fit Hoeveler's model, for reasons that I delineate in this chapter. I disagree with Hoeveler's characterization of *Zofloya* (and of Wollstonecraft's *Rights of Woman*) as embodying a clear "ideology" or moral: "The ideology goes something like this: if women fail to be effectively educated by their mothers, if they fail to embrace their proper feminine roles as docile, passive, and dependent on ... patriarchy, then we will all witness women as monstrous as Victoria ... This particular maternal ideology ... merely exaggerates in its extremely crude form the celebration of the mother and the centrality of the mother's role as educator that Wollstonecraft had advocated" (*Gothic Feminism*, 152–53).

72. *Monthly Literary Recreations* 1 (1806), 80 (orig. emphasis).

73. Kelly, *English Fiction*, 106.

74. Milner makes this important point regarding the novel's original use of the demon lover motif in *Le Diable dans la littérature française* (290); Milner praises the novel in positive terms rarely seen since Swinburne: "Comment ce roman plein d'originalité et de sombre poésie ne rencontra-t-il qu'indifférance en ce temps où les plus médiocres productions du genre noir étaient assurées du succès?" (288).

75. Miles, *Gothic Writing*, 188.

76. Picquenard's *Zoflora* is set before and during Haiti's rebellion after the French Revolution of 1789, and features a selfless Creole slave, Zoflora, the epitome of virtue in distress, who is persecuted and nearly raped by sadistic (white and black) fathers and would-be lovers. Zoflora eventually falls in love with a "good white man" (as she refers to him), the novel's hero, for whose love she twice offers to sacrifice her life.

77. *General Review of British and Foreign Literature*, vol. 1 (London: D. Shury, 1806) 590–93.

78. *The Literary Journal* n.s. 1 (June 1806), 632.
79. See Foucault's Introduction to *Herculine Barbin*.
80. Butler, *Gender Trouble*, 7.
81. Carter, *Sadeian Woman*, 79. Some of the most dynamic Sade scholarship in the last twenty years has been produced by feminists. See, for example, Laborde's "The Problem of Sexual Equality" and Hunt's edited volume, *The Invention of Pornography*.
82. On Gothic spectacles of pain, see Bruhm's *Gothic Bodies*.
83. Carter, *Sadeian Woman* 37. For further discussions of Dacre and pornography, see my Introduction to *Zofloya*, and, more recently, Gamer's "Genres for the Prosecution."

5 "IN SERAPH STRAINS, UNPITYING, TO DESTROY": ANNE
BANNERMAN'S FEMMES FATALES

1. All references to poems from the 1800 volume will refer to the reissued 1807 *Poems. A New Edition* (cited as *AB*), because it contains poems not in the 1800 edition. References to the 1802 *Tales* will refer to the original 1802 *Tales* edition because central to my discussion are the specifics of this volume's production, including the engravings; the 1807 *Poems* omits two of the ballads from *Tales* and all four engravings, and revises the remaining eight ballads. In addition to these three volumes, Bannerman also probably wrote the verse *Epistle from the Marquis de La Fayette, to General Washington* (1800), and published poems in the *Monthly Magazine, Poetical Register, Edinburgh Magazine, The Casket* (1829), *The Laurel* (1830), and in Joseph Cooper Walker's *Essay on the Revival of the Drama in Italy* (1805).
2. This is the only known extant letter from Bannerman; letter to Mr. Hood, 17 Oct. 1804, British Library, Evelyn Papers 4, vol. 1: 12.
3. Parish registry entry for Anne Bannerman, 31 October 1765, Edinburgh. Bannerman was the daughter of William Bannerman and Isobel Dick.
4. Anderson to Dr. James Currie (Burns's biographer) 28 June 1800 (Mitchell Library). Anderson's correspondence remains the most easily accessible source for information on Bannerman; see his correspondence with Bishop Percy in *Correspondence of Thomas Percy and Robert Anderson*, many of which were included in John Nichols's *Illustrations of Literary History*.
5. Percy to Anderson, 28 September 1804 (NLS MS 22.4.10).
6. Anderson to J. Cooper Walker, 4 Dec. 1805 (Edinburgh University MS La II 598). Bannerman visited Park and his family in Hampstead in 1811, and he wrote to Anderson of his "sincere gratification to hear her establishment is so comfortable. May her strengthened health enable her to receive every enjoyment from it" (15 April 1811, NLS MS 22.4.10).
7. Grant, *Memoir*, III: 162.
8. Baird, *Annals of Duddingston*, 467, 464–65.
9. Lady Beresford to Mrs. Walker, 11 Jan. 1830. A search of Portobello death registers and graveyards has not turned up any sign of Bannerman, who

was probably buried in an unmarked pauper's grave since she died in debt and probably could not afford an entry in the death register. See below for more details on her later years.

10. Burke's *A Philosophical Enquiry into . . . the Sublime and the Beautiful* (1757) offered a highly influential argument that obscurity is one of the most powerful sources of the sublime (see part 2, sections 3–4 and part 4, sections 14–18).

11. Review of *Tales* in *Critical Review* second series 38 (May 1803), 110; review of *Tales* in *Poetical Register of 1802* (1803), 431. *The British Critic*, which like the *Monthly Mirror* identified Bannerman as the author, wrote that *Tales* "does very considerable honour to the fair writer, who has devoted her time to the cultivation of her poetical talents" (102), even though like the other reviewers it did not care for the poems' Gothic sensibility, though it "strongly recommended" the poems to those who do. The positive review of *Tales* in the *Poetical Register* also expressed a dissatisfaction with her poems' "obscurity": "The author . . . has often left so much to be imagined by the reader that he is turned aside from the general beauty of the poem to discover the connection or the meaning of particular parts" (431–32). Thomas Park for one praised "The Dark Ladie"'s obscurity: "The Dark Ladie is . . . characteristic & most judicious its obscurity at the close" (Park to Anderson, 12 July 1800, NLS MS 22.4.10).

12. "The Festival of St. Magnus" and "The Black Knight of the Water" were omitted from the 1807 volume.

13. Seward, *Letters*, 5: 336, 338. The Della Cruscan comparison is from a review Seward quotes at length. "Palpable obscure" comes from Milton's *PL*, 11. 406.

14. Park to Anderson, 10 Oct. 1812 (NLS MS 22.4.10). Park copied Seward's letter in a letter to Anderson, who had requested to see it, and asked that it be destroyed, but it was not. Unlike Bannerman and Charlotte Smith (whom Seward also attacked), Seward was a staunch advocate of the "legitimate" sonnet.

15. Terming Bannerman's anticlosural obscurity "abortions" certainly suggests a hostility towards her refusal to complete normative narratives of femininity in her poetry. But the term "abortive" was also commonly used to attack the Della Cruscans and in particular the Gothic, thus placing Seward's attack within this larger critical context. For example, *The Satirist* derided Scott's *Marmion* in 1808 for its "indistinct throes of abortive horror" (qtd. in Robertson, *Legitimate Histories*, 53). In Gifford's satiric attack on Robert Merry in *The Baviad*, it is the Della Cruscans' synaesthetic sensibilities that are "Abortive thoughts that right and wrong confound" (qtd. in McGann, *Social Values*, 75).

16. Seward, letter quoted in Park to Anderson, (1812, NLS MS 22.4.10).

17. In *Romantic Agony* (274 n. 17), Praz singles out the following lines from Coleridge's "Introduction to the Tale of the Dark Ladie" as the inspiration for Keats's "La Belle Dame sans Merci": "There came and looked him in the face / An Angel beautiful and bright; / And how he knew it

was a Fiend, / This mis'rable Knight! / ... And how she nurs'd him in a cave; / And how his madness went away, / When on the yellow forest leaves / A dying man he lay" (*STC*, II: 1056–57).

18. "Introduction to the Tale of the Dark Ladie" has received very little critical attention, considering that Coleridge saw it as part of his set of "mystery" poems, including "Kubla Khan," "The Ancient Mariner," and "Christabel."

19. Curran, *Poetic Form*, 137.

20. Coleridge first published "An Introduction to the Tale of the Dark Ladie," with a brief introductory letter, in *The Morning Post* (1799); Coleridge's poem was also published in the February *Edinburgh Magazine*, edited by Bannerman's friend Anderson, and Bannerman's poem appeared in March 1800 (pp. 218–20), signed "B." "B" also published "Sonnet" in the *Monthly Magazine* (3 [March 1797], 218), as well as "The Distressed Cottagers" (vol. 13 [1802], 353–54); these poems may be hers, but neither appears in her published volumes. Bannerman may also be the author of "On the Death of Dr. Darwin" and an untitled poem (Ah! long fare-well") also signed "B." in the *Scots Magazine* (May 1802, 423; July 1802, 595), edited by her friend John Leyden. We know that she did publish in the *Monthly Magazine*, however, because Leyden noted in 1798 that she was publishing in that periodical as "Augusta" (letter to Thomas Brown, NLS MS 3380). "Augusta" published "A Night Scene," a traditional Gothic poem about a woman lingering at the grave of her dead lover, which did not appear in her volumes (*Monthly Magazine* 3 [April 1797], 298); three other poems by "Augusta" published in the *Edinburgh Magazine* in 1798 were revised and republished in Bannerman's 1800 *Poems* ("Sonnet. To the Owl," "Sonnet," and "To the Nightingale"). Under her own name she also published five poems in the *Edinburgh Magazine*, including her popular "Verses on an Illumination" and "Ode. – The Spirit of the Air" (1800), and six in the *Poetical Register* (1801–1803). It is also probable that Bannerman published as "A.B." in the *Edinburgh Magazine*; a manuscript poem signed "A.B." appears in a letter of Bannerman's close friend William Erskine (who wrote to Cadell and Davies on her behalf in 1799); the poem is titled "Elegy Written by the Grave of a French Prisoner–June 1795," and he indicates that the poet is female (Erskine to Robert Lundie, 28 Jan. 1796, NLS MS 1675). "A.B." published three additional poems in the *Edinburgh Magazine*, though they were not included in any of Bannerman's volumes: "Verses on the Death of General Washington," 16 (1800), 141 (Anderson possibly alludes to this poem in a letter – see notes below); "To the Genius of Britain" 22 (1803), 55; "To the memory of James Beattie L.L.D." 22 (1803), 366–68.

21. Sedgwick, *Coherence of Gothic*, 147, 146. Luce Irigaray has written extensively on the veil as a metaphor for woman's "duplicity" in the hom(m)osexual system of exchange (see *Speculum of the Other Woman*, *This Sex Which is Not One*, and *An Ethics of Sexual Difference*). For a challenging response to Irigaray's use

of veils, see Anne-Emmanuelle Berger, "The Newly Veiled Woman." Lady Mary Wortley Montague's popular *Turkish Letters* discussed veiling in positive terms, and specifically double veils, earlier in the eighteenth century.

22. Moorman, *William Wordsworth*, 1: 490.

23. Hazlitt, for example, wrote that "the effect of the general story is dim, obscure, and visionary" (*The Examiner* [2 June 1816], 349). Tom Moore's devastating extended review of the *Christabel* volume was the worst, calling the poet guilty of "incoherence" and "extravagance," and possessing "not a ray of genius" (*Edinburgh Review* 27 [Sept. 1816], 66).

24. *Monthly Review* 2nd series 29 (June 1799), 204; *British Critic* 14 (Oct. 1799), 365; *Critical Review* 2nd series 24 (Oct. 1798), 200.

25. Magnuson, *Reading Public Romanticism*, 103.

26. Bannerman's scholarly notes quote both Drayton himself, and Selden's notes to the *Polyolbion*; Selden's note to Drayton's brief mention of Seäm reads: "In the *Seam* (an isle by the coast of the French Bretagne), nine virgins were priests of a famous oracle. Their profession, or religion, consisted in arbitrarily metamorphosing themselves, charming the winds (as of later times the witches of Lapland and Finland), skill in predictions, &c" (qtd. in Bannerman's 1807 *Poems*, 188). Her notes demonstrate that she received some form of education, and that she was well versed in the influential early Romantics – Rousseau, Goethe, Schiller, Smith, Baillie, Scott.

27. A translation of Schiller's "The Ideal" (signed "J.B.") appeared in the *Poetical Register of 1801* (published in 1802, pp. 205–8), the same issue that included Bannerman's "The Exile" and "Sonnet, at the Sepulchre of Petrarch." "The Ideal" was also published in the *Monthly Magazine* (1799). Schiller's poem "Hero and Leander" was translated in the *Poetical Register of 1803*, which also included several poems by Bannerman. Bannerman also quoted and cited Schiller in her poem "To the Nightingale, from Rousseau" (*AB*, 216). Scott discussed the transmission of German Romantic literature to eighteenth-century Scotland, beginning in 1788, in his "Essay on Imitations of the Ancient Ballad"; see also Frederic Ewen, *The Prestige of Schiller in England*.

28. Nietzsche, Preface to the second edition, *The Gay Science*, 38.

29. *Ashfield*, 226–27. Browne nevertheless wrote visionary poems celebrating the imagination and the sublime in similar ways as did Bannerman (see *Ashfield*, 227–36).

30. Female figures who curse are also found in Byron's *Cain* and *Manfred* (and in his 1816 poem "The Incantation," which is the excerpted curse from *Manfred*), Shelley's "Julian and Maddalo," Coleridge's "Christabel," and Lewis's "The Grim White Woman" (in *Tales of Wonder*).

31. Probably an allusion to the traditional ballad of the captive poet of the fairy queen, Thomas the Rhymer, and his tower at Ercildoune.

32. Shelley, "[Lift not the Painted Veil]."

33. The question is Hölderlin's, from his elegy "Bread and Wine."

34. Rajan, *Dark Interpreter*, 86.

35. *Prometheus Unbound*, 11. iv. 123.
36. (*AB*, 20 orig. emphasis). Bannerman quotes from *The Rambler* no. 187, "The history of Anningait and Ajut concluded," a continuation of "Anningait and Ajut, a Greenland history" in *The Rambler* (no. 186). John Leyden's traditional ballad "The Mermaid" was published two years after Bannerman's "The Mermaid," in *Minstrelsy of the Scottish Border* (1802–3).
37. Penny, *Poems*, 115.
38. Not all women's poems that speak in the voice of the mermaid accomplish this; for example, Radcliffe's "The Sea-Nymph" presents a less interesting though more playful account of a mermaid's frolics in her undersea world, one which celebrates her power of song (her "potent voice" [*Poems of Ann Radcliffe*, 61]), a song that, however, does not call its own status into question. Jessie Stewart's ("Adeline") "The Sea-Nymph" is closer to Bannerman's poem than to Radcliffe's in the way her speaker delights in the sublimity of her own powers: "Round many a proud unshaken height, / That props the blue vault of the sky, / I revel in the beamy light / That sports in boundless liberty" (*Poetical Register of 1804* [1806] 58–61).
39. Hemans, "The Voice of Spring" (*Ashfield*, 177–78). See also Hemans's "The Voice of the Wind" (1828) *Ashfield*, 183–84. Bannerman's storm poems are most directly indebted to Joanna Baillie's *Poems* (1790), where Baillie explored human passions through her descriptions of Gothic atmospherics, as in "Thunder" and "Wind."
40. Goldsmith, *Unbuilding Jerusalem*, 220.
41. Bannerman cites as her immediate inspiration for the poem James Ridley's *Tales of the Genii*, which went through numerous editions in the late eighteenth century, and also notes that, despite the similarities with Darwin's *The Botanic Garden*, "The Genii" was written six months prior to the publication of that work. The *British Critic*'s favorable review of *Poems* contained a long excerpt from "The Genii" as an example of its "brilliant passages" (16 [1800], 141).
42. Storms were particularly popular as a theme in Scottish literature of the Romantic period. James Hogg, in his essay "Storms," first published in *Blackwood's* (1819), explored the social and poetic functions of storms in Scotland and, at the end of his essay, Hogg quotes a poem, the first stanza of which reads: "Who was it reared those whelming waves? / Who scalp'd the brows of old Cairngorm, / And scoop'd these ever yawning caves? / 'Twas I, the Spirit of the Storm!" (19).
43. Robinson's well-known correspondence with Coleridge in periodicals like the *Morning Post* includes the first published references to "Kubla Khan," which Coleridge wrote in 1798 but did not publish until 1816. Specifically, Robinson's "To the Poet Coleridge" alluded to "Kubla Khan" (which she had seen in manuscript) and was published in the 17 Oct. 1800 *Morning Post*. Bannerman's *Poems*, including "The Genii," were published earlier that same year, and thus cannot echo Robinson's allusions to "Kubla Khan" (on Coleridge and Robinson, see Pascoe's Introduction to Robinson's *Selected Poems*).

44. Moir, *Sketches*, 17.
45. My argument regarding the use value of Bannerman's violence is informed by Bataille's essay, "The Use Value of D.A.F. de Sade."
46. There are good indications to suggest that Bannerman is the author of the *Epistle*, though it has been attributed at times to her and at other times to George Hamilton. In a letter to J. C. Walker, Anderson refers to Bannerman's "verses on Washington" as "elegant" (20 June 1800, Edinburgh University MS La II 598). The two 1800 volumes – *Poems* and the *Epistle* – were both published by Mundell in Edinburgh and Longman's in London, and appear listed next to one another in the Longman archives, in Park's letters, and in reviews. In the *Archives of the House of Longman*, the first mention of the two volumes may even be linked by an "&" ("Bannerman's Poems [&?] / Lafayette's Epistle") though the record is not clear (A1 Reel 1 Item 83). Bannerman probably published "Verses on the Death of General Washington" in the *Edinburgh Magazine* (16 [1800], 141), signed "A.B." This poem may be the "verses on Washington" to which Anderson referred, or perhaps it is further indication of Bannerman's interest in the subject.
47. The best-known Romantic-period exploration of this theme is DeQuincey's "On Murder, Considered as One of the Fine Arts." See Black, *The Aesthetics of Murder* and McDonagh, "Do or die."
48. Bannerman's poetry is also used as an epigraph in "Melrose Abbey: a Tale" written by "M.S.A.," probably Anderson's daughter and Bannerman's friend, Margaret Susannah Anderson (*Edinburgh Magazine* 16 [1800], 472). William Preston's "An Epistle to Robert Anderson, M.D., On Receiving from him a Present of Various Poetical Works" (1807) contains a long passage referring to Bannerman's 1800 and 1802 volumes, and in particular to her "Verses on an Illumination": "The tuneful maid I hail from winding Forth, / Who female sweetness joins to manly worth, / And, while her muse the guilty laurel sings, / By blood-stain'd myriads wreath'd for frantic kings, / Humanely wise, beholds with temperate ray, / The dazzling things that lead the crowd astray. / Undaunted, now, she roams the wizard cave, / She scales the crag where deafening billows rave, / Or hears, at midnight hour, the mutter'd spell / Convoke the shrouded dead, and forms of hell" (168).
49. Park to Anderson, 9 Dec. 1801, NLS MS 22.4.10. The poems by Adeline mentioned appeared in the *Poetical Register* of 1801 and 1802 (published 1802 and 1803); Adeline also conducted a poetic correspondence in this same periodical with Rev. Henry Boyd, a friend of the Anderson circle and author of a famous translation of Dante. For information about "Adeline," see Anderson's correspondence with Percy in *The Percy Letters*. Stuart Curran has also suggested that Bannerman influenced the Shetland poet Dorothea Primrose Campbell, author of many supernatural poems.
50. Baillie to Bannerman, 9 June 1800.
51. See Daniel Robinson, "Reviving the Sonnet."
52. Original emphasis; review of *Poems*, in *Critical Review*, second series 31 (April 1801), 438–38. This review quoted "The Spirit of the Air" in full as an

example of Bannerman's lofty thought, and also lauded "The Genii" and "Verses on an Illumination."

53. Anderson to Dr. James Currie (Robert Burns's biographer) 28 June 1800 (Mitchell Library).

54. Anderson to J. C. Walker, 4 Dec., 1805 (Edinburgh University MS La II 598).

55. Anderson to J. C. Walker, March 1807 (Edinburgh University MS La II 598); Anderson is echoing Park here, who had written to Anderson earlier that month with the same sentiment. Only two of her poems are known to have been published after 1807: "They only may be said to possess a child for ever who have lost one in infancy" in *The Casket* (1829), and "The Exile" (first published 1800) in *The Laurel* (1830); subscribers to *The Casket* included Lady Frances Beresford, Joanna Baillie, Lady Byron, and E. L. Bulwer.

56. In addition to the praise from Anderson, Scott, and Park, Joseph Cooper Walker, in his *An Historical and Critical Essay on the Revival of the Drama in Italy* (for which Bannerman contributed two translations of Poliziano and Allamanni, reprinted in 1807) wrote that her poetry "displayed a richness of fancy, an energy of thought and expression, and a strength and brilliancy of colouring which has not often been surpassed" (ix–x).

57. Bannerman, "The Spirit of the Air" (*AB*, 9).

58. Bath, quoted in King and Lokke, " 'The Choicest Gift of Genius,' " 40–44. On women and transcendence, see Lokke, "The Mild Dominion of the Moon."

59. The inability of current models of Romantic genius to account for Bannerman's work leads Andrew Elfenbein to claim, without evidence, that "the link between female genius and homoeroticism was at the center of her writing" ("Lesbianism," 934). It is certainly true that her female figures "cannot be contained within . . . heterosexual conventions" (*Ibid.*, 950), but labeling her genius "lesbian genius" leaves the problem with current models intact by simply creating this new category of lesbian genius: current gendered models of Romanticism often prematurely establish rigid distinctions between female and male writers, and typically privilege a relatively narrow range of women writers. The true value of Romantic women poets such as Bannerman and Charlotte Smith, whom Elfenbein dismisses as a mere "sonneteer" of "bland sensibility" (950), will remain obscured by such projections of current critical needs onto their work, projections which reify the gendered limits they rightly set out to challenge.

60. Park to Anderson, Jan. 1802, NLS MS 22.4.10. In this same letter Park suggested titling the volume *Metrical Legends; or Tales of Other Times*, though clearly, in going with *Tales of Superstition and Chivalry*, Bannerman is writing in the tradition of Lewis's *Tales of Wonder* (1801), an allusion partly to blame for her volume's poor reception.

61. Park to Anderson, 29 Nov. 1802, NLS MS 22.4.10. The engraving is dated 12 Oct. 1802, and appears on page 124 of *Tales*. All four engravings are by McKenzie after E. W. Thomson, spelled Thompson in the last two

engravings. The first two, "The Dark Ladie" and "The Penitent's Confession," are dated 1 June 1802, and the latter two, "The Murcian Cavalier" and "The Prophecy of Merlin," are dated 12 Oct. 1802.

62. Park to Anderson, 29 Nov. 1802, NLS MS 22.4.10.

63. "On the Choice of Subjects for Engravings."

64. Park to Anderson, 29 Nov. 1802, NLS MS 22.4.10.

65. There are at least 22 extant copies of *Tales* held in libraries internationally.

66. Barrell, " 'The Dangerous Goddess,' " 120.

67. Park to Anderson, 15 Feb. 1806, NLS MS 22.4.10.

68. *The Scots Magazine*, ed. by John Leyden in 1802, published an essay on the subject, "Strictures on Literary Patronage," which warned male writers that "above all things...your virtuous independence is not to be sacrificed... your honour, as men, is to be preserved entire" (810). On the persistence of both public and private means of literary patronage in the Romantic period, see Griffin, *Literary Patronage in England*. On the tensions created by the growing professionalization of poetry in Scotland, see Murphy's *Poetry as an Occupation* and Siskin's *The Work of Writing*.

69. Park to Anderson, 23 May 1803, NLS MS 22.4.10. On London's domination of book production and distribution at this time, see Lincoln, "What Was Published in 1798?" On Robert Burns's and Janet Little's difficulties as socially marginalized Scottish poets, see Davis, "Gender and the Nation."

70. In Campbell's letters to Elizabeth Coates in 1802, he is at pains to point out "that my connection with him [Lord Minto]...is not founded on selfish or dependant [*sic*] expectations – He knows himself whether I have ever sacrificed an atom of my independence to his rank and Aristocracy" (Miller, "Five Recently-Found Letters," 296). Campbell also complained of women writers who "affect[ed] the woman of letters" (*Ibid.*, 291).

71. Leyden's letters and journals reveal that he and Bannerman were close friends from at least the mid-1790s on, and that she and her mother were visited by mutual friends such as William Erskine and Henry Brougham. In 1803, on the eve of his departure from Edinburgh on his way to India, Leyden had a disturbing confrontation with Bannerman that suggests that he and Bannerman had been quite close, perhaps romantically; he confided to their mutual friend William Erskine that Bannerman's "extreme irritability...for considerable time before my departure...rendered it quite impossible for me to keep any terms with her. Her character & temper is in some instances strangely unaccountable; but a few months before my departure, I was almost convinced (at least she strenuously attempted to convince me) that she had accomplished a quarrel...between us. As I could not forgive her for this, I saw her no more till the night of my departure for London...When I saw you [Erskine] my mind was a perfect vortex, and the ideas I had long cherished deep in my soul were too dear to me even to subject them to discussion. I forgot every unpleasant idea & ever attempted to retain only the recollection of Miss. B's good qualities. My whole frame was indeed in a state of great exhaustion" (15 Sept. 1804, NLS MS 971).

After Leyden's death in India in 1811, his brother wrote to Bannerman to request the return of his brother's correspondence, which she had saved from almost certain destruction after Leyden's executor had mysteriously abandoned the manuscripts (Robert Leyden to Anne Bannerman, 7 March 1818 (NLS MS 3381 f.104)).

72. Park to Anderson, 30 Jan. 1801, NLS MS 22.4.10.

73. An electronic edition of *Tales of Superstition and Chivalry* is now available through the British Women Romantic Poets Project at the University of California, Davis (www.lib.ucdavis.edu/English/BWRP/), and a collected edition of both *Poems* and *Tales*, prefaced by my critical introduction, is published in the *Scottish Women Poets* series edited by Stephen Behrendt and Nancy Kushigian (Alexander Street Press). Ashfield's *Romantic Women Poets Vol. II* also reprints five poems by Bannerman.

74. Park to Anderson, 23 May 1803, NLS MS 22.4.10. Park had actually suggested delaying publication (to October 1803) in July 1802, when the book had been ready, except for the engravings (Park to Anderson, 30 July 1802, NLS MS 22.4.10).

75. Scott, "Essay on Imitations of the Ancient Ballad," 49–50. The *British Critic*'s review of *Tales of Wonder* is one example of critics's general lack of enthusiasm for reasons Scott referred to: "A guinea is charged for two thin volumes, which might, and which ought, to have been comprised in one; and not a third of the contents will be found to be original composition." Lewis's original ballads are called "exceedingly stupid," and the volume as a whole "trifling, puerile, and unfair" (*British Critic* 16 [1800], 681). It is no surprise, then, that the *British Critic* also did not like Bannerman's *Tales*.

76. For example, in *Tales of Wonder*, Lewis included a self-parody, "Giles Jollop the Brave" immediately after "Alonzo the Brave," his most famous and highly regarded poem. He also included this self-parody in some editions of *The Monk*. On Lewis's ballads, see: Irwin, *M.G. "Monk" Lewis*, chap. 6; Conger, *Matthew Lewis*; Parreaux, *The Publication of The Monk*. On the mistaken suspicion that Lewis was the author of *Tales of Terror*, see Church, "A Bibliographical Myth."

77. Friedman reminds us that "strange as it may seem, Scott, who was a master of ballad lore from boyhood, did not take to writing ballads as a result of collecting and studying the Border ballads, but rather as a consequence of his enormous admiration for the German artistic imitations of the ancient style with their love of supernatural terrors" (*Ballad Revival*, 287); see in particular Friedman, "Comic, Romantic and Gothic Ballad Imitations," chap. 9, and Murphy, *Poetry as an Occupation*, chap. 4. On the Romantic ballad revival, see also Curran, *Poetic Form*, chap. 6.

78. Park to Anderson, 20 March 1800, NLS MS 22.3.11.

79. McGann, *Social Values*, 117.

80. Rev. of *Tales* in *British Critic* 21 (1803), 78. The *Critical Review* also noted the similarity to *Tales of Wonder* (second series 38 [May 1803], 110). The *Critical Review* also compared Bannerman's ballads to those of Leyden, Scott, and William Wordsworth.

81. "On Novels and Romances," part 1 of 2, 474.
82. *Ibid.*, part 2 of 2, 546, 548.
83. *Ibid.*, part 1 of 2, 473.
84. Anderson to Joseph Cooper Walker, 4 Dec. 1805, Edinburgh University MS La II 598.
85. For example, only 11 percent of women in Cambuslang, near Glasgow, could write in 1746, as opposed to 60–72 percent of men (Anderson, *Education and the Scottish People*, 16).
86. Seward, *Letters*, v: 338.
87. Siskin, *Work of Writing*, 218, 222.

6 "LIFE HAS ONE VAST STERN LIKENESS IN ITS GLOOM": LETITIA LANDON'S PHILOSOPHY OF DECOMPOSITION

1. Leighton, *Victorian Women Poets*, 69.
2. Mellor, *RG*, 120.
3. With the exception of Jerome McGann and Tricia Lootens, most modern scholars engage with Landon in terms of the "poetess" construction she supposedly embodies, relying heavily on Landon's biography and on the heroines of her early poetry. Blain argues regarding "Landon's female subject" that her "self-alienation is . . . fueled by anger inturned and masochistically paraded as acceptance of inevitable abandonment" ("Letitia Elizabeth Landon," 41). Peterson argues that "a poetess like Landon came to exemplify a debased or inferior form of Romanticism" that later poets like Barrett Browning transcended ("Rewriting *A History*," 117). Greer follows this familiar pattern of reducing Landon to the feminine "poetess," whose works are saturated by "an impossible idealism of love" and nothing more: "L.E.L. did put herself into her poetry – she had nothing else to put in it" (*Slip-Shod Sybils*, 284, 309). See also Stephenson, who argues that Landon was ultimately defeated by her embodiment of femininity and the "poetess" role (*Letitia Landon*), and Francis, who finds Landon's problematization of femininity in her Corinne poems more subversive ("Letitia Landon"). The best accounts of Landon are McGann's (in *Poetics of Sensibility* and his Introduction to Landon's *Selected Writings*) and Lootens's ("Reviving the Legend").
4. Armstrong, *Victorian Poetry*, 326.
5. Leighton, *Victorian Women Poets*, 61.
6. Landon also echoes Byron: "There is the moral of all human tales; / 'Tis but the same rehearsal of the past, / First Freedom, and then Glory – when that fails, / Wealth, vice, corruption, – barbarism at last. / And history, with all her volumes vast, / Hath but *one* page" (*Childe Harold's Pilgrimage*, IV. 108). Her quote that gives this chapter its title also echoes *Childe Harold*: "Making the sun like blood, earth a tomb / The tomb a hell, and hell itself a murkier gloom" (IV. 25).
7. Stephenson notes that "[i]t was Landon . . . who was initially responsible for popularizing the links between poetess and prophetess in the early

nineteenth century" (*Letitia Landon*, 102). Not all prophetesses in Romantic women's poetry share this affinity with the destruction they foresee: see Abdy's "The Dream of the Poetess" (1836) and West's "Sonnet" (1796) on Cassandra (*Ashfield*, 224–25; 154). See also Evadne's prophecy in *The Last Man* by Mary Shelley, whose considerable influence on Landon has yet to be explored.

8. Hoagwood, "Keats and Social Context."

9. See esp. Yarnall, *Transformations of Circe*, chap. 1.

10. Rowton, "Laetitia Elizabeth Maclean," in *Female Poets*, 424–25. In his memorial essay on Landon, Howitt also compared her to Byron: "We have not forgotten the electric shock which the death of Byron, falling in his prime and in a noble cause, sent through Europe: nor the more expected, but not less solemn and strongly recognized departure of Sir Walter Scott: but neither of these exceeded that with which the news was received of the sudden decease of this still young and popular poetess" ("L.E.L.," 5). The *Literary Gazette's* review of *The Improvisatrice* famously heralded Landon as the heir to Byron's genius, but these comparisons to Byron resulted in the inevitable backlash and charges of imitation and puffery, as in the "Noctes Ambrosianæ": "NORTH. I ran over the book [*The Improvisatrice*] – and I really could see nothing of the originality, vigour, and so forth, that they chatter about. Very elegant, flowing verses they are – but all made up of Moore and Byron" (Wilson, "Noctes Ambrosianæ" (1824)).

11. On Byron's debts to a previous generation of women writers, see Behrendt, "The Gap that is Not a Gap."

12. McGann, *Poetics of Sensibility*, 146.

13. LeFevre-Deumier, *Célébrités anglaises*, 242 (my translation).

14. Rowton, *Female Poets*, 1.

15. In his review of Norton's *The Dream* (1841), Poe also affirmed that "Mrs. Norton is the Byron of our female poets" (*Complete Works* 101).

16. Rowton, *Female Poets*, 410.

17. Wolfson, *Figures in the Margin* (forthcoming).

18. Note that, as with other giftbooks (such as *Fisher's Drawing Room Scrap Book*), the *Book of Beauty* appeared in December of the previous year to that indicated on the title page, so that the *Book of Beauty for 1833* appeared late in 1832; I have used the title page dates throughout to avoid confusion. The *Book of Beauty* includes a number of poems and prose tales that draw overtly on Byron's texts: "The Enchantress," "Gulnare," "The Choice," "Experiments; or, The Lover from *Ennui*." A number of the nineteen engravings also depict Landon's heroines whose names and stories derive from Byron's best-known poems, and the List of Plates notes that these "illustrate Lord Byron's Poems": "Medora," "Lolah," "Laura," "Donna Julia," "Gulnare." In addition to engravings of "Lolah" and "Medora," "The Enchantress" is also illustrated by an engraving of the Enchantress herself, drawn by W. Boxall and engraved by J. Thomson.

19. I am grateful to Marilyn Butler for drawing my attention to Edgeworth's tale. Landon also discussed Edgeworth in *RR*, 1: 194–96.

20. Landon demonstrates the same self-awareness of the market's shaping of her literary form in "The Chinese Pagoda" (1833), where, instead of writing a poem to accompany an expensive engraving, Landon writes a poem about how difficult it is to write a poem illustrating someone else's engraving.

21. Landon's description of the Enchantress as "the last and weakest of [her] race" echoes Japhet's description of Anah as "The last and loveliest of Cain's race" in Byron's *Heaven and Earth* (1. iii. 386). Landon here speculates about the sequel to *Heaven and Earth*, which Byron had contemplated writing himself: Anah and the angel escape the flood and effectively repeat the Fall, with a difference (she gains both immortality and knowledge).

22. There exists a tradition of interpreting Genesis in which Eve mated with fire-spirits (or fallen angels, "The Sons of God"), one possible account of the birthright of Cain. A related interpretative tradition, of which Byron and Landon make use, tells of how the flood was sent to punish humanity because of the "unnatural" love between the Daughters of Man (specifically of Cain's lineage) and the Sons of God (see Genesis 6, and chap. 63 and "Noah's Vision" in *The Book of Enoch* (1821), ed. Laurence).

23. Landon, "The Enchantress," British Library Add. MS 44887.

24. Franklin argues that Byron's Leila in *The Giaour* (who also drowned, like Lolah), as well as Astarte and Francesca, are "viewed entirely from the vantage point of" their deaths, existing "only as a ghostly presence in the consciousness of the hero" (*Byron's Heroines*, 39, 40).

25. Landon cites William Thoms's *Lays and Legends of Various Nations* (1834) as the direct source for her poetic revision. Thoms's brief "Story of Melusine" differs from Landon's poem in that she omits Melusine's two fairy sisters Melior and Palatine, as well as Melusine's deformed children, and generally gives Melusine a much more assertive and sterner demeanor. The relationship between Melusine and her mother is also more complex and made central in Landon's poem.

26. See Goldberger's Introduction to *Corinne*, xxviii. My thanks to Kari Lokke for this reference.

27. Fass, *La Belle Dame*, 57.

28. Burton's "Ondine" (1833), appears to predate Landon's 1835 poem (although the publication date of Burton's volume may actually be 1835). Burton writes in direct opposition to Landon, thus her "Ondine" is predictably the suffering enchantress who longs for a Christian soul and marriage: "Hast thou not sworn to make me thine, / By sacred altar and rite divine? / Hast thou not sworn to be mine own? / And now wouldst thou leave thine Ondine alone? / Star of my worship, and life of my heart, / Think what a death it would be – to part!" (*White Rose*, II: 18). Landon's Melusine's quest is for justice and self-possession, significantly different from Ondine's traditional feminine quest for marriage. Burton wrote directly against Landon's dangerous example, as she made clear in her

poem "The Ivy-Wreath": "Then, Landon, wear thy rose of red, / Entwined with myrtle boughs; /...But, ivy-wreath! sweet type of truth, / And woman's constancy! Years cannot dim thy faith of youth – / Mayst thou my emblem be!" (*White-Rose*, 11: 48–49).

29. Landon's use of "mother's" instead of "mother" in this opening line is puzzling. The first published version in *Fisher's*, for which Landon presumably saw proofs, prints the line with "mother's," and McGann and Riess follow this version in their Broadview edition. Subsequent Victorian editions of Landon, such as the *LPW* that I usually quote, amend the line to read "Why did she love her mother so?" which makes more immediate sense. I use the first published version following McGann and Riess, on the assumption that Landon perhaps intended the possessive form, even though this spelling creates more (not entirely undesirable) ambiguities regarding Melusine and her mother.

30. Lawford suggests that the father of Landon's apparent three children was most likely William Jerdan, the *Literary Gazette* editor. Jerdan, twenty years older than Landon, lived next door to the Landons in Brompton, where he met Landon, launched her literary career, and began an affair with her that seems to have lasted for over a decade. According to Lawford, the three children were: Ella Stuart (born 1822 or 1823), Fred Stuart (possibly born 1826), and Laura Landon (born 29 June 1829). Landon had long suffered public rumors and insults regarding her relationships with Jerdan, Maclise, Forster, and Lytton, but this is the first substantiated account of such a sexual relationship (Lawford, "Diary").

31. The Ancestress is distinctively vampyric because she, like Elizabeth Bathory, desired beauty and eternal youth enough to commit an unholy act in order to possess them: "for the sake of lasting loveliness / Her soul was forfeit to the evil power, / Who tempted her with beauty" (*LPW*, 121). As in the traditional, implicitly incestuous, account of vampyres who must destroy their own families, the Ancestress's sin curses her whole race, and she herself becomes an undead wanderer until her own family line dies out, something she must bring about herself. This aspect of her damnation (haunting the familial castle) she also shares with the Melusine of medieval legend. Only her descendant Bertha can see her until the very end, and the Ancestress's presence has a transformative effect on Bertha, making her progressively less interested in the bland domestic joys which made her so ideally feminine, and instead inspiring in her the desire for worldly pleasures and passions, which Bertha likens to "those lands, where I have read, / Beneath an outward show of fairest flowers / The soil has veins of subterranean flame, / Whose fiery sparkles start to sudden life / When we least dream of them" (*LPW*, 126).

32. Landon and Jewsbury both wrote poems about each other, and Landon includes a positive sketch of Jewsbury in *Romance and Reality* (1: 140–43).

33. Jewsbury, "The History of an Enthusiast," *The Three Histories*, 79. Julia rails against "this dull, dreary and most virtuous domestic life!" (78), because

such scenes "suggest to me ideas of imprisonment – they shut out the world, the beautiful world beyond, the breathing world of society where mind is king" (78). Jewsbury's "To L.E.L." characterized Landon in terms Landon would later use to describe Melusine: "As . . . a child from fairy land / Into the desert brought: / Forgetting there the visions / That make of childhood part; / And singing songs of fairy land, / Without the fairy heart" (Landon, *Selected Writings*, 372).

34. Clarke, *Ambitious Heights*, 86.
35. Tennyson, "The Mermaid." This poem is included in Hunt's "The Sirens and Mermaids of the Poets" (1836).
36. Armstrong reads Tennyson's mermaid poem, in contrast, as a celebration of the mermaid's amoral sexuality "in a world free of any economy but the pleasure principle" (*Victorian Poetry*, 47).
37. Quoted in Ritvo, "Professional Scientists," 277). This celebrated exhibit is also discussed by Thompson in *Mystery and Lore of Monsters* (chap. 13), Gwen Benwell & Arthur Waugh in *Sea Enchantress* (chap. 7), and Richard Altick, *Shows of London* (303). See also "The Natural History of the Mermaid" in Richard Carrington, *Mermaids and Mastodons*.
38. See Ritvo, "Professional Scientists," 277–78.
39. Benwell and Waugh, *Sea Enchantress*, 122–26; Altick, *Shows*, 303.
40. *Literary Gazette* (28 Sept. 1822) 616. Another notice respecting the mermaid exhibit is found on 19 Oct. 1822 in the *Literary Gazette*, and Landon's "Songs on Absence" appears on the following page (664).
41. The number of sightings published in Britain are far too numerous to mention here, but were most numerous in the early nineteenth century (1806, 1809, 1811, 1812, 1814, 1819, 1827, 1830, 1833).
42. *Mirror of Literature*, No. 11, 9 Nov. 1822, 17. The story was continued in the 16 Nov. 1822 issue.
43. Ritvo, "Professional Scientists," 284.
44. Combination is also a political term referring to organized popular resistance, as well as other kinds of political/economic organizations. Nancy Armstrong offers a compelling account of how a backlash against the reform movement and its combinations helped shape the discourse of monstrosity in Victorian literature (see chap. 4 in *Desire*).
45. Published in Scott's *Minstrelsy of the Scottish Border* (1802–3) which Leyden co-edited. Leyden's verse dedication (to Lady Charlotte Campbell) to the poem distinguishes between the siren's and the poet's art, flattering Campbell that if she sings his verse, "the listening throng, / Rapt by the siren, would forget the song!" and that this spellbinding effect would be "not the poet's, but the siren's art" (284). Bannerman (who was Leyden's friend) and Landon, on the other hand, explicitly equate the siren's and the poet's art.
46. Benwell and Waugh, *Sea Enchantress*, 120.
47. D'Arras's Melusine laments her change in fortune as a loss of pleasures and privilege, not of a Christian soul: " 'And al they that myght come to my presence had grete Joye to behold me / and fro this tyme foorth they shal

dysdayne me & be ferefull of myn abhomynable figure / and the lustes & playsirs that I was wonnt to haue shal be reuertid in tribulacions & grieuous penitences.' And thenne she bygan to say with a hye voyce: 'Adieu, my lustis & playsirs' "; her husband continues to love and desire her after discovering her monstrous body, but the curse banishes her from him forever (*Melusine* (1387), [chap. xlvi] 319–20).

48. Linton writes, "The most carefully guarded secret of all was the ultimate purpose of this blue-and-silver boudoir off the drawing room" ("The Countess Mélusine," 331–43); this secret is revealed as part of Melusine's extensive swindling scheme, as in *Lady Audley's Secret*.

49. Baring-Gould, "Melusina," 131.

50. *Mirror of Literature* (9 Nov. 1822), 18.

51. Landon praised Keats's *Lamia* in a letter *c*. 1822 (*Critical Writings*, 182–84).

52. Hoagwood, "Keats," 694.

53. In "The Fairy of the Fountains" Melusine is "Doom'd to wander and to pine," but, in Thoms's version, Melusine is even more vampyric (and similar to the Ancestress) because she must "fleet about the earth in pain and suffering, as a spectre, until the day of doom: and that only when one of her race was to die at Lusignan would she become visible" (Thoms, *Lays*, 87).

54. Williams's reading of *Dracula* is a case in point, suggesting that we might "conclude that the conflict between human and vampire is tacitly a struggle between a reigning patriarchal culture and an ancient female nature" (*Art of Darkness*, 130). Williams's reading of otherness as the female, like Kristeva's on which it is based, relies on a prediscursive, prepatriarchal female ("ancient female nature").

55. Bataille, *Erotism*, 57.

56. Landon wrote that "all the associations of a fountain are poetical" because fountains are "the entrance" into the world of romance (*EC*, ii: 148–49).

57. See Landon, "Lucy Ashton," in "The Female Portrait Gallery," no. 14 (*Blanchard*, ii: 142–43). Landon admired this character so much that she wrote an additional episode for the novel, titled "An Evening of Lucy Ashton's," in which Lucy is told the story of a woman revenant. Also published in *The Book of Beauty* (1833), "An Evening of Lucy Ashton's" bears an uncanny resemblance to Bannerman's "The Dark Ladie," for Lucy hears a tale of a young lady seduced/raped, abandoned, and murdered by an arrogant knight. The dead woman returns in the guise of another woman, pledges the knight with a glass of wine, turns into a skeleton, and kills her killer.

58. For different feminist readings of the significance of doubling for the femme fatale, see Hoeveler's *Romantic Androgyny*, Auerbach's *Woman and the Demon*, and Gilbert and Gubar's *Madwoman in the Attic*.

59. Landon's use of masquerade and theatrical subjectivity has been commented on at length by Stephenson, Mellor, Pascoe, Isobel Armstrong, and Leighton.

60. Hobsbaum, *Age of Revolution*, 168.
61. Wohl, *Endangered Lives*, 3.
62. Poe referred to Landon in his essays, poems, and letters, and her influence is perceptible in poems like "Al Aaraaf," "A Dream," "Israfel," and "The Valley of Unrest." In particular, see his reviews of Blanchard's *Life and Literary Remains of L.E.L.* and Norton's *The Dream* (*Complete Works*, 195–96; 100–5) and his poem "An Acrostic" (*Complete Poems*, 149). In his review of *Life . . . of LEL*, Poe praised "the *passionate purity* of her verse" (orig. emphasis, 195–96). His reviews show a thorough knowledge of the leading women poets of the age, including a particular appreciation for Hemans.
63. Riess notes that Landon's poem alludes to Wordsworth's "Lines Written Near Richmond, Upon the Thames," and that it shatters "the image of a benevolent Nature from which the poet may intuit divine truths" ("Laetitia Landon," 823).
64. Such a clear-cut distinction between miasmatic and germ, or "contagionist" theories of disease is oversimplistic, and, while an accurate description on a general level, does not do justice to the complex diversity of opinion among the miasmatic school. The issue of quarantine measures distinguished the two ends of the spectrum more clearly, with sanitarians finding quarantine ineffective and cruel, and contagionists advocating and implementing it in order to stop what they believed was a contagious disease. The most significant aspect of the shift from miasmatic to germ theories of disease in nineteenth-century Britain is the loss of moral and religious debates in the new, rigidly professionalized, germ theories of disease (Hamlin, "Providence and Putrefaction"). Women's significant participation in the sanitation movement also fell off when, at the end of the nineteenth century, disease was reduced to particular germs only identifiable by (male) scientists in laboratories, and combated by paid (male) municipal health inspectors (see Williams, "The Laws of Health").
65. See Hamlin, "Providence and Putrefaction."
66. Death counts vary: 31,000 is Durey's figure, which most other studies approximate, e.g., Briggs, Wohl (Durey, *The Return of the Plague*). 16,437 is Altick's rather low estimate for England and Wales in *Victorian People* (44). Hodgkinson estimates 50,000 in her Introduction to *Public Health in the Victorian Age*, vol. 1. Hodgkinson also notes that by "the 1860s there had also been four epidemics of typhoid," also transmitted in part through contaminated water, and "the disease was endemic and accounted for about 20,000 deaths a year" (Introduction, [n.p.]). Unless otherwise indicated, the subsequent references to nineteenth-century public health articles will be from Hodgkinson's facsimile collection, with original pagination.
67. See Hamlin, "Providence and Putrefaction," 383.
68. There does not appear to be any relation between Charles MacLean, who wrote numerous books on contagion, and George MacLean, Landon's eventual husband.
69. Ferguson, "Directions to the Privy Council in the Case of Pestilence."

70. To give the example of but one journal, the *New Monthly Magazine*, to which Landon frequently contributed: the *NMM* followed the medical debates surrounding the spread of "cholera morbus" thoroughly in 1831 and 1832, the year of the epidemic in London. It discussed in detailed essays the nature of the disease, such as "Cholera Morbus: What is its nature? In what matter ought it to be treated? And is it likely to visit the British Islands?" by David Uwins. In September 1831, under "Political Events," it published the preventative measures suggested by the Privy Council (507), repeating them in December, 1831, highlighting the importance of "Free and continued admission of fresh air to all parts of the house and furniture" (517). "It is impossible to impress too strongly the necessity of extreme cleanliness and free ventilation," reaffirmed the *NMM* in that issue (517). Each month in 1831 and 1832, the *NMM* provided news on the spread of the disease throughout Europe and the East, and on debates over public health policies (and quarantine and contagion) at home. The *NMM* objected to the graphic and "lugubrious detail" of the cholera coverage in *The Gazette* (*NMM* 32 (1831), 490), and warned that quarantine and the resulting paranoia "is utterly useless in stopping the progress of the disease, and that it may do harm by creating an imaginary security" (*NMM* 32 (1831), 490). In 1832 it began also to publish mortality statistics according to parishes, and also information on the Privy Council's measures to help cope with the financial burden of burying the bodies.
71. "Gatherings from Graveyards: The Dead *versus* the Living," an essay on Dr. G. A. Walker's *Gatherings from Graveyards* (1839), first published in the *Westminster Review* 1842 (Hodgkinson, *Public Health*, 11 (205)).
72. Spivack, " 'The Hidden World Below,' " 54.
73. The title "Life Surveyed" is given in the reprint of the Ethel Churchill fragments in Blanchard; the poem's title in the novel was "Courtiers."
74. See also Gallagher's "The Bio-Economics of *Our Mutual Friend*."
75. Landon used the same expression in her poem "Valley of Linmouth: North Devon": "here I will find for myself a cave, / Half a home, and half a grave" (*LPW*, 315).
76. At mid-century, life expectancy in Britain was 18 to 25 in industrial areas, and "40 for the country as a whole" according to Hodgkinson ("Introduction," [n.p.]). Asa Briggs places the average age of death in 1840 at 29 ("Public Opinion," 138).
77. See also her poem "Home" (1824): "I stood upon a mountain height, and look'd / Into the vale below / ... I sought my home; I sought, and found a city" (*LPW*, 48). In "The Wishing Gate" (*Fisher's* (1834), 44) Landon responds in a similar way to Wordsworth's "The Wishing-Gate," published in *The Laurel* (1830).
78. Lootens, "Receiving the Legend," 246.
79. Lokke, "Sibylline Leaves," 172.
80. "Grasmere Lake" 45–47, published in the 1834 *Fisher's*. Landon's Preface suggests that she wrote both the poetry (as is widely known) and prose

for this particular volume: "The same motive which caused me to give a continued story, instead of separate sketches, to the Indian Views, has also led me to accompany some of the English landscapes in a different style."

81. First published anonymously as the introduction to another's work in 1810, Wordsworth published his popular *Guide to the Lakes* in *The River Duddon* volume in 1820, and in many subsequent editions.

82. Landon, "A Calendar," 425. Landon was a confirmed Tory, so it does not seem likely that she is using Cockney as a means of associating herself politically with the earlier Cockney School of Hunt and Keats.

83. Landon, "Linmouth," 40; "Boscastle Waterfall and Quarry," 22. These statements are in Landon's prose notes to each poem, both published in the same volume of *Fisher's* (1833).

84. McGann, *Byron and Wordsworth*, 25.

85. Leighton, *Victorian Women Poets*, 61.

86. Howitt, "L.E.L.," 7. Shepard also praised *Ethel Churchill* for this reason: "There is less of the ideal, more of the actual; less of the poet's inner and abstract life, with more of the outward world's experience and ways;" (*Characteristics of the Genius . . . of L.E.L.*, 115). Shepard nevertheless warns of the dangers of Landon's "fatalism," which denies the power of Christianity: "her views and estimate of life, with its affections and pursuits, are correct, inasmuch as she represents life unsanctified by religion, – affections whose element is earthliness, and pursuits unredeemed by the hope and prospect of eternity" (165).

87. Landon, letter to Edward Bulwer Lytton [1837], Hertfordshire Archives & Local Studies, MS D/EK c1/88–101.

88. McGann, Introduction to Landon's *Selected Writings*, 11.

89. Landon, letter to Edward Bulwer Lytton [1837], Hertfordshire Archives & Local Studies, MS D/EK c1/88–101.

90. Leighton cites Mary Coleridge as a contrast to what is supposedly Landon's identification of poetry as feeling, not industry: "Poetry is, by its very derivation, *making*, not feeling" (Coleridge, qtd. in *Victorian Women Poets*, 64).

91. Levinson, *Wordsworth's Great Period Poems* 20–21, 37.

92. McGann, *Poetics of Sensibility* 170.

93. McGann also likens Poe to Landon: "Landon approaches writing in the same spirit as Poe does," both having learned from Byron "that they lived in a world of signs and conventions" (*Poetics of Sensibility*, 146).

94. Wordsworth, *Literary Criticism*, 13.

95. *Ibid.*, 126.

96. de Man, *Rhetoric of Romanticism*, 80.

97. Armstrong, *Victorian Poetry*, 326. Armstrong offers a fascinating discussion of "visionary materialism" in the works of James Thomson ("B.V."). For an important statement on the material properties of inspiration, see Derrida's essay on Artaud in *Writing and Difference* ("La parole soufflée").

98. See Childers, "Observation and Representation."
99. Durey, *Return of the Plague*, 157. Cholera was famously dubbed a "disease of society" by *The Economist* in 1849 (during the second epidemic); see Briggs "Cholera and Society." In 1832 Landon referred to it as the "common disease" in a characteristically sardonic letter to Croker: "I take it for granted that you are not affected by the common disease; very well for common people all to be affected alike; we, I flatter myself, are above being seized with the vulgar generalities of colds, choleras and influenzas" (Rutgers University Library, John Symington Collection). See also Landon's poem "The Cholera" (1832), in which she comments on the deadly properties of breath (cholera was not confirmed as a water-borne disease until significantly later): "There's a curse on the blessed sun and air: / What will ye do for breath? / For breath, which was once but a word for life, / Is now but a word for death" (*Oriental Observer*, 18 July 1832). My thanks to Máire ní Fhlathúin for bringing this poem to my attention.
100. Ferguson, "Directions to the Privy Council," 266.
101. Hogg, *London as It Is*, 236–37.
102. E.g., "The difference that began in the cradle continues to the tomb. The bare coffin, a few boards hastily nailed together, is flung into the earth; the service is hurried over, the ground trodden down, and the next day the children are playing upon the new grave, whose tenant is already forgotten. So much for the equality of human existence" (*EC*, III: 36).
103. "The ancients gave the balance of life to a dark goddess, who, following in the track of fortune, as the shadow follows the sunshine, enforces bitter repayment for our few and transitory delights. Nothing is good, but evil comes thereof" (*EC*, I: 5).
104. Lydia Sigourney, the prolific American poet (and the source of Poe's closing lines to "The City in the Sea"), was also intrigued by Lyell's revelations of the coral "insects" and the ruins they left behind; see her poem "The Coral Insect." See also Landon's "The Volcano of Ki-rau-e-a" (*Fisher's* (1832), 24). On Romanticism and the sea, see Auden's *The Enchafèd Flood*.
105. "Gibraltar. Scene During the Plague" (1836) (*LPW*, 330). In "The Cholera," Landon makes a similar point: "Wo for affection! when love must look / On each face it loves with dread- / Kindred and friends! when a few brief hours / And the dearest may be dead!" (see fn. 99 above)
106. Levi-Strauss, *Tristes Tropiques*, 272.
107. Mellor, *RG*, 120.

Bibliography

MANUSCRIPTS

"Address from the British at Paris to the National Convention, 1792," British Library, Liverpool Papers, MS 38351 f.281.

Anderson, Robert, correspondence, National Library of Scotland, MS 22.4.10, 22.3.11; Edinburgh University MS La II 598; Mitchell Library, Glasgow.

Baillie, Joanna, letter to Anne Bannerman, 9 June 1800, private collection.

Bannerman, Anne, letter to Mr. Hood, British Library, Evelyn Papers 4, vol. 1: 12.

Erskine, William, correspondence, National Library of Scotland, MS 3112, 1675.

Landon, Letitia Elizabeth, letter to Edward Bulwer Lytton [1837], Hertfordshire County Archives, MS D/EK c1/88–101.

Landon, Letitia Elizabeth, letter to T. Crofton Croker [1832], James Symington Collection, Rutgers University Library.

Leyden, John, papers at the National Library of Scotland, MS 971, 3380, 3381.

Leyden, Robert, letter to Anne Bannerman, 7 March 1818, National Library of Scotland, MS 3381.

Robinson, Mary (as "Tabitha Bramble"), letter to Robert Dundas, 23 January 1794, Public Record Office NAS RH2/4/74.

Williams, Helen Maria, letter to Elizabeth (Robinson) Montagu, January 20, 1797, Huntington Library, MS MO6777.

BOOKS AND ARTICLES

Aaron, Jane, *A Double Singleness: Gender and the Writing of Charles and Mary Lamb*, Oxford: Clarendon, 1991.

" 'On Needle Work': Protest and Contradiction in Mary Lamb's Essay," in Mellor (ed.), *Romanticism and Feminism*, 167–84.

"A Modern Electra: Matricide and the Writings of Charles and Mary Lamb," in *Reviewing Romanticism*, ed. Philip Martin and Robin Jarvis, Basingstoke: Macmillan, 1992.

Abrams, M. H. (ed.), *English Romantic Poets: Modern Essays in Criticism*, New York: Galaxy Books/Oxford University Press, 1960.

The Accusation, Trial, Defence, Sentence and Execution of Marie Antoinette, Edinburgh: J. Elder, T. Brown, and Walter Berry, 1793.

Adams, M. Ray, "Chapter IV: Mrs. Mary Robinson, a Study of Her Later Career," in *Studies in the Literary Backgrounds of English Radicalism*, Lancaster, PA: Franklin and Marshall College Press, 1947, 104–29.

"Helen Maria Williams and the French Revolution," in *Wordsworth and Coleridge: Studies in Honor of George McLean Harper*, ed. Earl Leslie Griggs, 1939, New York: Russell and Russell, 1962, 87–117.

Adorno, Theodor and Max Horkheimer, *Dialectic of Enlightenment*, trans. John Cumming, New York: Continuum, 1993.

Aikin, Lucy, *Epistles on Women*, London: Joseph Johnson, 1810.

Alcoff, Linda, "Cultural Feminism versus Post-Structuralism: The Identity Crisis in Feminist Theory," in *Culture/Power/History*, ed. Nicholas Dirks, Geoff Eley, and Sherry Ortner, Princeton University Press, 1994, 96–122.

Alexander, Meena, *Women in Romanticism*, Totowa, NJ: Barnes and Noble, 1989.

Allen, Virginia M., *The Femme Fatale: Erotic Icon*, Troy, New York: Whitson, 1983.

Altick, Richard, *The Shows of London*, Cambridge, MA: Belknap Press of Harvard University Press, 1978.

Victorian People and Ideas, New York: Norton, 1973.

Anderson, R. D., *Education and the Scottish People 1750–1918*, Oxford: Clarendon, 1995.

Andriano, Joseph, *Our Ladies of Darkness: Female Daemonology in Male Gothic Fiction*, University Park: Pennsylvania State University Press, 1993.

Anthony, Katherine, *The Lambs: A Study of Pre-Victorian England*, London: Hammond, Hammond, & Co., 1948.

Antoinette d'Autriche, ou Dialogues entre Catherine de Médicis et Frédégonde reine de France, aux Enfers, London, 1789.

Applewhite, Harriet and Darlene Levy (eds.), *Women and Politics in the Age of Democratic Revolution*, Ann Arbor: University of Michigan Press, 1990.

Archives of the House of Longman, 1794–1914, Cambridge: Chadwyck-Healey, 1978, Microfilm.

Archives of the Royal Literary Fund, 1790–1918, compiled by Nigel Cross, London: World Microfilms Pub., 1982.

Armstrong, Isobel, *Victorian Poetry: Poetry, Poetics and Politics*, London: Routledge, 1993.

"The Gush of the Feminine: How Can We Read Women's Poetry of the Romantic Period?" in Feldman and Kelley (eds.), *Women Romantic Writers*, 13–32.

Armstrong, Nancy, *Desire and Domestic Fiction: A Political History of the Novel*, Oxford University Press, 1987.

Armstrong, Nancy and Leonard Tennenhouse (eds.), *The Violence of Representation: Literature and the History of Violence*, London: Routledge, 1989.

Ashfield Andrew (ed.), *Women Romantic Poets 1770–1830: An Anthology*, Manchester University Press, 1995.

Women Romantic Poets Vol. II: 1788–1848, Manchester University Press, 1998.

Ashton, Helen and Katherine Davies, *I had a Sister: A Study of Mary Lamb, Dorothy Wordsworth, Caroline Herschel, Cassandra Austen*, London: Lovat Dickson, 1937.

Auden, W. H., *The Enchafèd Flood: or The Romantic Iconography of the Sea*, Charlottesville: University Press of Virginia, 1979.

Auerbach, Nina, *Woman and the Demon: The Life of a Victorian Myth*, Cambridge, MA: Harvard University Press, 1982.

Bade, Patrick, *Images of Evil and Fascinating Women*, New York: Mayflower Books, 1979.

Baillie, Joanna, *Plays on the Passions*, ed. Peter Duthie, Peterborough: Broadview, 2001.

Baird, William, *Annals of Duddingston and Portobello*, Edinburgh: Andrew Elliot, 1898.

Balle, Mary Blanchard, "Mary Lamb: Her Mental Health Issues," *Charles Lamb Bulletin* n.s. 93 (1996), 2–11.

Bannerman, Anne, *Epistle from the Marquis de La Fayette to General Washington*, Edinburgh: Mundell and Son; London: Longman and Rees, and J. Wright, 1800. [Published anonymously. Bannerman's authorship of this poem is conjectural.]

   Poems, Edinburgh: Mundell and Doig; London: Longman and Rees, 1800.

   Poems, A New Edition, Edinburgh: Mundell, Doig and Stevenson, 1807.

   Tales of Superstition and Chivalry, Edinburgh: Vernor and Hood, 1802.

Baring-Gould, Sabine, "Melusina," in *Curious Myths of the Middle Ages*, 1866, ed. Edward Hardy, New York: Crescent Books, 1987, 129–33.

Barker-Benfield, G. J., *The Culture of Sensibility: Sex and Society in Eighteenth-Century Britain*, University of Chicago Press, 1992.

Barrell, John, " 'The Dangerous Goddess': Masculinity, Prestige, and the Aesthetic in Early Eighteenth Century Britain," *Cultural Critique* 12 (Spring 1989), 101–31.

Barrington, E., *The Exquisite Perdita*, New York: Dodd, Mead, and Company, 1926.

Bartky, Sandra Lee, *Femininity and Domination: Studies in the Phenomenology of Oppression*, London: Routledge, 1990.

Barton, Bernard, *A New Year's Eve*, London: John Hatchard and Son, 1828.

Bataille, Georges, *Erotism: Death and Sensuality*, San Francisco: City Lights, 1986.

   Literature and Evil, trans. Alastair Hamilton, London: Calder and Boyars, 1973.

   "The Use Value of D.A.F. de Sade," in *Visions of Excess: Selected Writings, 1927–1939*, trans. Ann Stoekl, Minneapolis: University of Minnesota Press, 1985, 91–102.

Battersby, Christine, *Gender and Genius: Towards a Feminist Aesthetics*, London: Women's Press, 1989.

Baudrillard, Jean, *Seduction*, trans. Brian Singer, New York: St. Martin's Press, 1990.

Beauvoir, Simone de, *Must We Burn De Sade?*, trans. Annette Michelson, New York and London: Peter Nevill, 1953.

Behrendt, Stephen, "The Gap that is Not a Gap: British Poetry by Women, 1802–1812," in *Romanticism and Women Poets: Opening the Doors of Reception*, ed. Harriet Kramer Linkin and Stephen Behrendt, Lexington: University Press of Kentucky, 1999, 25–45.

Behrendt, Stephen, Introduction, *Zastrozzi and St. Irvyne*, by Percy Bysshe Shelley, Oxford University Press, 1986.

Benjamin, Walter, *Illuminations*, ed. Hannah Arendt, trans. Harry Zohn, New York: Schocken Books, 1976.

Benwell, Gwen and Arthur Waugh, *Sea Enchantress: The Tale of the Mermaid and Her Kin*, New York: Citadel Press, 1965.

Berger, Anne-Emmanuelle, "The Newly Veiled Woman: Irigaray, Specularity, and the Islamic Veil," *Diacritics* 28.1 (1998), 93–119.

Bienville, M. D. T., *Nymphomania, or a Dissertation Concerning the Furor Uterinus*, trans. E. Sloane Wilmot, London, 1775; reprinted with Tissot's *Onanism* as *Onanism / Nymphomania*, New York: Garland, 1985.

Birke, Lynda, *Feminism and the Biological Body*, New Brunswick: Rutgers University Press, 2000.

Black, Joel, *The Aesthetics of Murder: A Study in Romantic Literature and Contemporary Culture*, Baltimore, MD: Johns Hopkins University Press, 1991.

Blackwell, Marina (ed.), *Science and Sensibility: Gender and Scientific Enquiry, 1780–1945*, Oxford: Blackwell, 1991.

Blain, Virginia, "Letitia Elizabeth Landon, Eliza Mary Hamilton, and the Genealogy of the Victorian Poetess," *Victorian Poetry* 33 (1995), 31–51.

Blain, Virginia, Patricia Clemens, and Isobel Grundy (eds.), *The Feminist Companion to Literature in English*, New Haven, CT: Yale University Press, 1990.

Blake, William, *The Poetry and Prose of William Blake*, ed. David V. Erdman, Garden City, NY: Doubleday and Co., 1965.

Blakemore, Steven, *Crisis in Representation*, Madison, NJ: Fairleigh Dickinson University Press, 1997.

Blakey, Dorothy, *The Minerva Press, 1790–1820*. London: printed for the Bibliography Society at the University Press, Oxford, 1939.

Blanchard, Laman, *Life and Literary Remains of L.E.L.*, 2 vols., London, 1841.

Blanchot, Maurice, *The Space of Literature*, trans. Ann Smock, Lincoln: University of Nebraska Press, 1982.

Bloom, Harold, *The Visionary Company: A Reading of English Romantic Poetry*, 1961; Garden City, NY: Anchor Books, 1963.

The Book of the Old Edinburgh Club for the Year 1909, vol. 11, Edinburgh: T. and A. Constable, 1909.

"Books on Sex Matters," *The Times* (13 March 1935), 11.

"Books Seized by Police," *Daily Telegraph* (11 October 1934), 6.

Bordo, Susan, *Unbearable Weight: Feminism, Western Culture, and the Body*, 1993; Berkeley: University of California Press, 1995.

   "Feminism, Foucault, and the Politics of the Body," in Ramazanoglu (ed.), *Up Against Foucault*, 179–202.

Boucé, Paul-Gabriel (ed.), *Sexuality in Eighteenth-Century Britain*, Totowa, New Jersey: Barnes and Noble for Manchester University Press, 1982.

Braddon, Mary Elizabeth, *Lady Audley's Secret*, 1862; New York: Penguin Books/Virago Press, 1985.

Briggs, Asa, "Cholera and Society in the Nineteenth Century," in *The Collected Essays of Asa Briggs*, Urbana and Chicago: University of Illinois Press, 1985, II: 153–76.

"Public Opinion and Public Health in the Age of Chadwick," in *The Collected Essays of Asa Briggs*, II: 129–52.

Brissenden, R. F., *Virtue in Distress: Studies in the Novel of Sentiment from Richardson to Sade*, New York: Barnes and Noble, 1974.

Bronfen, Elisabeth, *Over Her Dead Body: Death, Femininity, and the Aesthetic*, London: Routledge, 1992.

Brown, David Blayney, compiler, *Ashmolean Museum Oxford: Catalogue of the Collection of Drawings*, vol. 4: *The Earlier British Drawings*, Oxford: Clarendon, 1982.

Bruhm, Stephen, *Gothic Bodies: The Politics of Pain in Romantic Fiction*, Philadelphia: University of Pennsylvania Press, 1995.

Burke, Edmund, *Correspondence of Edmund Burke*, ed. Alfred Cobban and Robert Smith, Chicago University Press, 1967.

Further Reflections on the Revolution in France, ed. Daniel Ritchie, Indianapolis: Liberty Fund, 1992.

A Letter from Mr. Burke, to a Member of the National Assembly, Oxford: Woodstock, 1990.

A Philosophical Enquiry into the Origin of Our Ideas of the Sublime and the Beautiful, ed. James Boulton, University of Notre Dame Press, 1968.

Reflections on the Revolution in France, and on the Proceedings in Certain Societies in London, relative to that Event, 1790; ed. Thomas Mahoney, New York: Liberal Arts Press, 1955.

Burney, Fanny, *The Wanderer; or, Female Difficulties*, 1814; ed. Margaret Anne Doody, Robert Mack, and Peter Sabor, Oxford University Press, 1991.

Burton, Harriet Emma, *The White-Rose Wreath*, London: Hatchard, [1833/35?].

Butler, Judith, *Bodies That Matter: On the Discursive Limits of "Sex,"* London: Routledge, 1993.

Gender Trouble: Feminism and the Subversion of Identity, London: Routledge, 1990.

Butler, Marilyn, *Jane Austen and the War of Ideas*, Oxford University Press, 1975.

Romantics, Rebels and Reactionaries, Oxford University Press, 1981.

Byron, George Gordon, Lord, *Lord Byron – The Complete Works*, ed. Jerome J. McGann, 7 vols., Oxford: Clarendon, 1980–93.

Cafarelli, Annette Wheeler, "The Common Reader: Social Class in Romantic Poetics," *Journal of English and Germanic Philology* 96 (1997), 222–46.

"How Theories of Romanticism exclude Women: Radcliffe, Milton, and the Legitimization of the Gothic Novel," in *Milton, the Metaphysicals, and Romanticism*, ed. Lisa Low and Anthony John Harding, Cambridge University Press, 1994, 84–113.

Cameron, Deborah and Elizabeth Frazer, *The Lust to Kill: A Feminist Investigation of Sexual Murder*, New York University Press, 1987.

Campbell, Thomas, *The Complete Poetical Works*, vol. Juvenilia, New York and Toronto: Oxford University Press, 1907.

The Pleasures of Hope, Edinburgh: Mundell and Sons, 1799.

The Poetical Works of Thomas Campbell, Philadelphia: Crissy and Markley, [n.d.].

Carrington, Richard, *Mermaids and Mastodons: A Book of Natural and Unnatural History*, New York: Rinehart and Co., 1957.

Carter, Angela, *The Sadeian Woman and the Ideology of Pornography*, New York: Pantheon, 1978.

The Casket, A Miscellany, Consisting of Unpublished Poems, ed. Mrs Blencowe. London: John Murray, 1829.

Castle, Terry, *The Female Thermometer: 18th-Century Culture and the Invention of the Uncanny*, Oxford University Press, 1995.

Masquerade and Civilization: The Carnivalesque in Eighteenth Century English Culture and Fiction, Stanford University Press, 1986.

"Marie Antoinette Obsession," *Representations* 38 (1992), 1–38.

Chadwick, Edwin, *A Supplementary Report on the Results of a Special Inquiry into the Practice of Interment in Towns*, London: W. Clowes and Sons, 1843.

Chalus, Elaine, "Women, Electoral Privilege and Practice in the Eighteenth Century," in *Women in British Politics 760–1860*, ed. Kathryn Gleadle and Sarah Richardson, Houndsmills: Macmillan, 2000, 19–38.

Childers, Joseph, "Observation and Representation: Mr. Chadwick Writes the Poor," *Victorian Studies* 37 (1994), 405–32.

Church, Elizabeth, "A Bibliographical Myth," *Modern Philology* 19 (1921–22), 307–14.

Clarke, Norma, *Ambitious Heights: Writing, Friendship, Love: The Jewsbury Sisters, Felicia Hemans and Jane Carlyle*, London: Routledge, 1990.

Coleridge, Hartley, "Modern English Poetesses," *Quarterly Review* 66 (1840) 374–418.

Coleridge, Samuel Taylor, *The Complete Poetical Works of Samuel Taylor Coleridge*, ed. E. H. Coleridge, Oxford: Clarendon, 1912.

Colley, Linda, *Britons: Forging the Nation 1707–1837*, New Haven, CT: Yale University Press, 1992.

Conger, Syndy M., *Matthew Lewis, Charles Maturin, and the Germans*, Salzburg: Institut für Englische Sprache und Literatur, Universität Salzburg, 1977.

"Sensibility Restored: Radcliffe's Answer to Lewis's *The Monk*," in Graham (ed.), *Gothic Fictions*, 113–49.

"Contagion and Quarantine," *Quarterly Review* 27 (1822), 552, reprinted in Hodgkinson (ed.), *Public Health in the Victorian Age*.

Cook, Elizabeth Heckendorn, *Epistolary Bodies: Gender and Genre in the Eighteenth-Century Republic of Letters*, Stanford University Press, 1996.

Copley, Stephen and John Whale (eds.), *Beyond Romanticism: New Approaches to Texts and Contexts 1780–1832*, London: Routledge, 1992.

Craciun, Adriana, "Charlotte Dacre," *An Encyclopedia of British Women Writers*, ed. Paul and June Schlueter, New Brunswick: Rutgers University Press, 1998, 188–9.

" 'I Hasten to be Disembodied': Charlotte Dacre, the Demon Lover, and Representations of the Body," *European Romantic Review*, 6 (1995), 75–97.

"Introduction: Charlotte Dacre and the Vivisection of Virtue," *Zofloya; or, The Moor*, by Charlotte Dacre, Peterborough: Broadview, 1997, 9–32.

"The New Cordays: Helen Craik and British Representations of Charlotte Corday, 1793–1800," in Craciun and Lokke (eds.), *Rebellious Hearts*, 193–232.

Craciun, Adriana, (ed.), *A Routledge Literary Sourcebook on Wollstonecraft's A Vindication of the Rights of Woman*, London: Routledge, 2002.

Craciun, Adriana and Kari Lokke, "British Women Writers and the French Revolution 1789–1815," in Craciun and Lokke (eds.), *Rebellious Hearts*, 3–32.

Craciun, Adriana and Kari Lokke (eds.), *Rebellious Hearts: British Women Writers and the French Revolution*, Albany: State University of New York Press, 2001.

Craft-Fairchild, Catherine, *Masquerade and Gender: Disguise and Female Identity in Eighteenth-Century Fictions by Women*, University Park: Pennsylvania State University Press, 1993.

Craig, Alec, *The Banned Books of England*, London: Allen and Unwin, 1962.

Craik, Helen, *Adelaide de Narbonne, with Memoirs of Charlotte de Cordet*, 4 vols., London: Minerva Press, 1800.

Cullens, Chris, "Mrs. Robinson and the Masquerade of Womanliness," in Kelly and Mücke (eds.), *Body and Text in the Eighteenth Century*, 266–89.

Curran, Stuart, *Poetic Form and British Romanticism*, Oxford University Press, 1986.

" 'The Cenci': The Tragic Resolution," in *Percy Bysshe Shelley: Modern Critical Views*, ed. Harold Bloom, New York: Chelsea House, 1985.

"The 'I' Altered," in Mellor (ed.), *Romanticism and Feminism*, 185–207.

"Mary Robinson's *Lyrical Tales* in Context," in Wilson and Haefner (eds.), *Re-visioning Romanticism*, 17–35.

"Women Readers, Women Writers," in *Cambridge Companion to British Romanticism*, ed. Stuart Curran, Cambridge University Press, 1993, 177–95.

Dacre, Charlotte, *Confessions of the Nun of St. Omer*, 1805, 3 vols., New York: Arno Press, 1972.

George the Fourth, London: Hatchard, 1822.

Hours of Solitude. A Collection of original Poems, now first published, 1805; 2 vols. in 1, New York: Garland, 1978.

[The Libertine] Angelo, comte d'Albini, ou les Dangers du vice, par Charlotte Dacre Byrne connue sous le nom de Rosa Matilda, traduit de l'anglais par Mme. Elisabeth de B***, 3 vols., Paris: A. Bertrand, 1816.

The Libertine, 1807; 4 vols., New York: Arno Press, 1974.

The Passions, 1811; 4 vols., New York: Arno Press, 1974.

[Charlotte King and Sophia King], *Trifles from Helicon*, London: James Ridgway, 1798.

Zofloya; or, the Moor: A Romance of the Fifteenth Century, ed. Adriana Craciun, Peterborough: Broadview, 1997.

Zofloya; or, the Moor: A Romance of the Fifteenth Century, 1806; 3 vols., New York: Arno Press, 1974.

Zofloya, ou le Maure, histoire du XVeme siècle, traduite de l'anglais par Mme. de Viterne, 4 vols., Paris: Barba, 1812.

Dallas, Robert, *Miscellaneous Works*, London: Longman, Hurst, Rees, Orme and Brown, 1813, vol. 1 of 7.

D'Arras, Jean, *Melusine*, 1387; ed. A. K. Donald, London: Early English Text Society, by Kegan Paul, Trench, Trubner, 1895.

Davidoff, Leonore and Catherine Hall, *Family Fortunes: Men and Women of the English Middle Class, 1780–1850*, University of Chicago Press, 1987.

Davis, Leith, "Gender and the Nation in the Work of Robert Burns and Janet Little," *SEL* 38 (1998), 621–45.

Day, Esther Milnes, *Poems and Fugitive Pieces, by Eliza*, Edinburgh and London: Cadell and Davies, 1796.

Day, William Patrick, *In the Circles of Fear and Desire: A Study of Gothic Fantasy*, University of Chicago Press, 1985.

DeLamotte, Eugenia, *Perils of the Night : A Feminist Study of Nineteenth-Century Gothic*, Oxford University Press, 1990.

De Lauretis, Teresa, *Technologies of Gender: Essays on Theory, Film, and Fiction*, Bloomington: Indiana University Press, 1987.

"The Violence of Rhetoric: Considerations of Representation and Gender," in Armstrong and Tennenhouse (eds.), *The Violence of Representation*, 239–58.

Deleuze, Gilles, *Masochism: Coldness and Cruelty*, New York: Zone, 1991.

De Man, Paul, *The Rhetoric of Romanticism*, New York: Columbia University Press, 1984.

The Dæmon of Venice. An Original Romance, London: Thomas Tegg, 1810.

De Quincey, Thomas, "On Murder, Considered as One of the Fine Arts," in *Selections Grave and Gay from Writings Published and Unpublished*, Edinburgh: James Hogg, 1854, vol. 4.

Derrida, Jacques, *Of Grammatology*, trans. Gayatri Spivak, Baltimore, MD: Johns Hopkins University Press, 1976.

Writing and Difference, trans. Alan Bass, University of Chicago Press, 1978.

Diamond, Irene and Lee Quimby (eds.), *Feminism and Foucault: Reflections on Resistance*, Boston: Northwestern University Press, 1988.

Dijkstra, Bram, *Idols of Perversity: Fantasies of Feminine Evil in Fin-de-Siècle Culture*, Oxford University Press, 1986.

Doane, Mary Ann, *Femmes Fatales: Feminism, Film Theory, Psychoanalysis*, London: Routledge, 1991.

Dobson, Meaghan Hanrahan "(Re)considering Mary Lamb: Imagination and Memory in *Mrs. Leicester's School*," *Charles Lamb Bulletin* n.s. 93 (1996): 12–21.

Donoghue, Emma, *Passions Between Women: British Lesbian Culture 1668–1801*, London: Scarlet Press, 1993.

Doy, Gen, "Women and the Bourgeois Revolution of 1789," in *Femininity and Masculinity in Eighteenth-Century Art and Culture*, ed. Gill Perry and Michael Rossington, Manchester University Press, 1994, 184–203.

Duff, David, *Romance and Revolution*, Cambridge University Press, 1994.

Dugaw, Diane, *Warrior Women and Popular Balladry, 1650–1850*, Cambridge University Press, 1989.

Dunn, James, "Charlotte Dacre and the Feminization of Violence," *Nineteenth-Century Literature* 53:3 (1998), 307–27.

Durey, Michael, *The Return of the Plague: British Society and the Cholera, 1831–2*, Dublin: Gill and Macmillan, 1979.

During, Simon, *Foucault and Literature: Towards a Genealogy of Writing*, London: Routledge, 1992.

Elfenbein, Daniel, "Lesbianism and Romantic Genius: The Poetry of Anne Bannerman," *ELH 63* (1996), 929–57.

Ellis, Kate Ferguson, *The Contested Castle: Gothic Novels and the Subversion of Domestic Ideology*, Urbana: University of Illinois Press, 1990.

Erdman, David, "Byron's Mock Review of Rosa Matilda's Epic on the Prince Regent: A New Attribution," *Keats–Shelley Journal* 19 (1970), 101–17.

"An Essay, whether the Present Age can, or cannot be Reckoned among the Ages of Poetical Excellence," *Monthly Literary Recreations*, no. xv (September 1807).

Ewen, Frederic, *The Prestige of Schiller in England 1788–1859*, New York: Columbia University Press, 1932.

Ezell, Margaret, *Writing Women's Literary History*, Baltimore, MD: Johns Hopkins University Press, 1993.

Fass, Barbara, *La Belle Dame sans Merci and the Aesthetics of Romanticism*, Detroit: Wayne State University Press, 1974.

Feldman, Paula and Theresa M. Kelley (eds.), *Women Romantic Writers: Voices and Countervoices*, Hanover: University Press of New England, 1995.

Felman, Shoshona, "Re-reading Femininity," *Yale French Studies* 62 (1982), 19–44.

The Female Aegis; or, The Duties of Women from Childhood to Old Age, and in Most Situations of Life, Exemplified, 1798; New York: Garland, 1974.

Fergus, Jan, "Eighteenth-Century Readers in Provincial England" *Papers of the Bibliographical Society of America* 78 (1984), 155–213.

Fergus, Jan and Janice Farrar Thaddeus, "Women, Publishers, and Money, 1790–1820," *Studies in Eighteenth-Century Culture* 17 (1987), 191–207.

Ferguson, Frances, "Sade and the Pornographic Legacy," *Representations* 36 (1991), 1–21.

Ferguson, Moira, *Eighteenth Century Women Poets: Nation, Class, and Gender*, Albany: State University of New York Press, 1995.

Ferguson, Robert, "Directions to the Privy Council in the Case of Pestilence," *Quarterly Review* 46 (1831), reprinted in Hodgkinson (ed.), *Public Health in the Victorian Age*, vol. 1.

Fleenor, Julian E. (ed.), *The Female Gothic*, Montreal: Eden Press, 1983.

Flynn, Carol Houlihan, "Running out of Matter: The Body Exercised in Eighteenth-Century Fiction," *The Languages of Psyche*, ed. G. S. Rousseau and Roy Porter, Berkeley: University of California Press, 1990, 147–85.

Fordyce, James, *Sermons to Young Women*, 1766; 3rd American edn, Philadelphia, 1809.

Foucault, Michel, *Discipline and Punish: The Birth of the Prison*, trans. Alan Sheridan, New York: Vintage, 1979.

 The History of Sexuality: Volume I: An Introduction, trans. Robert Hurley, New York: Vintage, 1980.

 "Introduction," in *Herculine Barbin: Being the Recently Discovered Memoirs of a Nineteenth-Century French Hermaphrodite*, by Herculine Barbin, trans. Richard McDougall, Brighton, Sussex: Harvester Press, 1980, vii–xvii.

 I, Pierre Rivière, having Slaughtered my Mother, my Sister, and my Brother . . ., ed. Michel Foucault, trans. Frank Jellinek, 1975; Lincoln: University of Nebraska Press, 1982.

 Madness and Civilization: A History of Insanity in the Age of Reason, trans. Richard Howard, New York: Vintage, 1973.

 "Nietzsche, Genealogy, History," in *Language, Counter-Memory, Practice: Selected Essays and Interviews*, ed. Donald Bouchard, trans. Donald Bouchard and Sherry Simon, Ithaca, NY: Cornell University Press, 1977, 139–64.

 "Power and Sex," in *Michel Foucault: Politics, Philosophy, Culture: Interviews and Other Writings 1977–1984*, ed. L. Kritzman, London: Routledge, 1988.

 Power/Knowledge: Selected Interviews and Other Writings, 1972–1977, ed. C. Gordon, Brighton: Harvester, 1980.

 "A Preface to Transgression," in *Language, Counter-Memory, Practice: Selected Essays and Interviews*, ed. Donald Bouchard, trans. Donald Bouchard and Sherry Simon, Ithaca, NY: Cornell University Press, 1977.

Francis, Emma, "Letitia Landon: Public Fantasy and Private Sphere," *Essays and Studies: Romanticism and Gender*, ed. Anne Janowitz, London: D. S. Brewer, 1998, 93–115.

Friedman, Albert, *The Ballad Revival: Studies in the Influence of Popular on Sophisticated Poetry*, University of Chicago Press, 1961.

Friedman, Leslie Joan, "Mary Lamb: Sister, Seamstress, Murderer, Writer," Diss., Stanford University, 1976, 2 vols.

Furniss, Tom, *Edmund Burke's Aesthetic Ideology*, Cambridge University Press, 1993.

Gallagher, Catherine, "The Bio-Economics of *Our Mutual Friend*," in *Fragments for a History of the Human Body*, ed. Michel Feher, New York: Zone, 1989, part 3, 344–65.

 "The Body Versus the Social Body in the Works of Thomas Malthus and Henry Mayhew," in Gallagher and Laqueur (eds.), *The Making of the Modern Body*, 83–106.

Gallagher, Catherine and Thomas Laqueur (eds.), *The Making of the Modern Body*, Berkeley: University of California Press, 1987.

"Gallery of Literary Characters. No. XLI. Miss Landon," *Fraser's Magazine* 8 (1833), 433.

Gamer, Michael, "Genres for the Prosecution: Pornography and the Gothic," *PMLA* 114 (1999), 1043–54.

"Gatherings from Graveyards: The Dead *versus* the Living," essay on Walker's *Gatherings from Graveyards* (1839), in the *Westminster Review* 1842, reprinted in Hodgkinson (ed.), *Public Health*, vol. 2.

The Genuine Trial of Marie Antoinette, Late Queen of France, London: J. S. Jordan, J. Mathews, and T. Boosey, 1793.

Gilbert, Sandra and Susan Gubar, *The Madwoman in the Attic*, New Haven, CT: Yale University Press, 1979.

Gilbert, Sandra and Susan Gubar (eds.), *Norton Anthology of Literature by Women*, New York: Norton, 1985.

Gilchrist, Mrs, *Mary Lamb*, London: W. H. Allen, 1883.

Gilmartin, Kevin, *Print Politics: The Press and Radical Opposition in Early Nineteenth-Century England*, Cambridge University Press, 1996.

Godwin, Catherine Grace, *Poetical Works of the Late Catherine Grace Godwin*, ed. A. Cleveland Wigan, London: Chapman and Hall, 1854.

Goldberger, Avriel, Introduction, *Corinne, or Italy*, by Germaine de Staël, New Brunswick: Rutgers University Press, 1987.

Goldsmith, Steven, *Unbuilding Jerusalem: Apocalypse and Romantic Representation*, Ithaca, NY: Cornell University Press, 1993.

Goodman, Dena, *The Republic of Letters: A Cultural History of the French Enlightenment*, Ithaca, NY: Cornell University Press, 1994.

Graham, Kenneth (ed.), *Gothic Fictions: Prohibition/Transgression*, New York: AMS Press, 1989.

Grant, Anne, *Letters from the Mountains, Being the Real Correspondence of a Lady Between the Years 1773 and 1807*, 3 vols., 2nd edn, London: Longman, Hurst, Rees & Orme, 1807.

Memoir and Correspondence of Mrs. Grant of Laggan, 3 vols., London: Longman, Brown, Green and Longmans, 1933.

Greer, Germaine, *Slip-Shod Sibyls: Recognition, Rejection and the Woman Poet*, Harmondsworth: Penguin, 1995.

Griffin, Dustin, *Literary Patronage in England, 1650–1800*, Cambridge University Press, 1996.

Groneman, Carol, "Nymphomania: The Historical Construction of Female Sexuality," *Signs* 19 (1994), 337–67.

Gross, Kenneth, "Satan and the Romantic Satan: a Notebook," in *Re-membering Milton: Essays on Texts and Traditions*, ed. Mary Nyquist and Margaret Ferguson, New York: Methuen, 318–41.

Grosz, Elizabeth *Volatile Bodies: Toward a Corporeal Feminism*, Bloomington: Indiana University Press, 1994.

"Bodies and Knowledges: Feminism and the Crisis of Reason," in *Feminist Epistemologies*, ed. Linda Alcoff and Elizabeth Potter, London: Routledge, 1993, 187–215.

"Contemporary Theories of Power and Subjectivity," in *Feminist Knowledge: Critique and Construct*, ed. Sneja Gunew, London: Routledge, 1990, 59–120.

Grudin, Peter, *The Demon-Lover: The Theme of Demoniality in English and Continental Fiction*, New York: Garland, 1987.

Gutwirth, Madelyn, *The Twilight of the Goddesses: Women and Representation in the French Revolutionary Era*, New Brunswick: Rutgers University Press, 1992.

"The Rights and Wrongs of Women: The Defeat of Feminist Rhetoric by Revolutionary Allegory," in *Representing the French Revolution*, ed. James Hefferman, Hanover, NH: University Press of New England, 1992.

Hale, Sarah Josepha, *Three Hours; or, The Vigil of Love*, Philadelphia: Carey and Heart, 1848.

Haley, Bruce, *The Healthy Body in Victorian Culture*, Cambridge, MA: Harvard University Press, 1978.

Hamlin, Christopher, "Providence and Putrefaction: Victorian Sanitarians and the Natural Theology of Health and Disease," *Victorian Studies* 28 (1985), 382–411.

Hanley, Keith and Raman Selden (eds.), *Revolution and English Romanticism*, Hertfordshire: Harvester Wheatsheaf and St. Martin's, 1990.

Haraway, Donna, *Simians, Cyborgs, and Women*, London: Free Association, 1991.

Hart, Lynda, *Fatal Women: Lesbian Sexuality and the Mark of Aggression*, Princeton University Press, 1994.

Hays, Mary, *Appeal to the Men of Great Britain in Behalf of Women* (1798), ed. Gita May, New York: Garland, 1974.

Hazlitt, William, "On the Aristocracy of Letters," in *Table Talk: Essays on Men and Manners*, ed. William Carew Hazlitt, London: George Bell, 1876, 284–97.

Heller, Deborah, "Bluestocking Salons and the Public Sphere," *Eighteenth-Century Life* 22.2 (1998), 59–82.

Herd, Harold, "The Strange Case of the Murdered Editor," in *Seven Editors*, London: Allen and Unwin, 1952, 40–56.

Herdt, Gilbert (ed.), *Third Sex, Third Gender: Beyond Sexual Dimorphism in Culture and History*, New York: Zone, 1994.

Hertz, Neil, "Medusa's Head: Male Hysteria Under Political Pressure," *Representations* 4 (1983), 25–55.

Hickok, Kathleen, *Representations of Women: Nineteenth-Century British Women's Poetry*, Westport, CT: Greenwood Press, 1984.

"'Intimate Egoism': Reading and Evaluating Noncanonical Poetry by Women," *Victorian Poetry* 33 (1995), 13–30.

Hoagwood, Terence Allan, "Keats and Social Context: *Lamia*," *SEL* 29 (1989), 675–97.

Hoagwood, Terence and Rebecca Jackson, Introduction, *Sappho and Phaon*, by Mary Robinson, Delmar, NY: Scholar's Facsimiles and Reprints, 1995, 3–11.

Hobsbaum, E. J., *The Age of Revolution: Europe 1789–1848*, London: Weidenfeld and Nicolson, 1962.

Hodgkinson, Ruth (ed.), *Public Health in the Victorian Age: Debates of the Issue from Nineteenth Century Critical Journals*, 2 vols., Westmead, England: Gregg International Publishers, 1973.

Hoeveler, Diane Long, *Gothic Feminism: The Professionalization of Gender from Charlotte Smith to the Brontës*, University Park, PA: Pennsylvania State University Press, 1998.

Romantic Androgyny: The Women Within, University Park, PA: Pennsylvania State University Press, 1990.

Hofkosh, Sonia, *Sexual Politics and the Romantic Author*, Cambridge: Cambridge University Press, 1998.

Hogg, James, "Storms," in *The Shepherd's Calendar*, ed. Douglad Mack, Edinburgh University Press, 1995.

Hogg, John, *London as It Is*, 1837; ed. Lynn Hollen Lees and Andrew Lees, New York: Garland, 1985.

Holford, Margaret, "Lines Suggested by a Portrait of the Unfortunate Queen of France," in *The Poetical Album and Register of Modern Fugitive Poetry*, ed. Alaric Watts, London, 1828, 255–56.

Homans, Margaret, *Bearing the Word: Language and Female Experience in Nineteenth-Century Women's Writing*, Chicago University Press, 1986.

Women Writers and Poetic Identity, Princeton University Press, 1980.

"Keats Reading Women, Women Reading Keats," *Studies in Romanticism* 29 (1990), 341–70.

Howells, Coral Ann, *Love, Mystery, and Misery: Feeling in Gothic Fiction*, London: The Athlone Press, University of London, 1978.

Howitt, William, "L.E.L.," *Fisher's Drawing Room Scrapbook for 1840* (1839), 5–8.

Huckabay, Calvin, "The Satanist Controversy of the Nineteenth Century," in *Studies in English Renaissance Literature*, ed. Waldo McNeir, Baton Rouge: Louisiana State University Press, 1962, 197–210.

Hughes, A. M. D., "Shelley's *Zastrozzi* and *St. Irvyne*," *Modern Language Review* 7 (1912), 54–63.

Hunt, Leigh, "The Sirens and Mermaids of the Poets," *New Monthly Magazine* 47 (1836), 273–82.

Hunt, Lynn, *The Family Romance of the French Revolution*, Berkeley: University of California Press, 1992.

Politics, Culture, and Class in the French Revolution, Berkeley: University of California Press, 1984.

"The Many Bodies of Marie Antoinette: Political Pornography and the Problem of the Feminine in the French Revolution," in *Eroticism and the Body Politic*, ed. Lynn Hunt, Baltimore, MD: Johns Hopkins University Press, 1991.

"The Unstable Boundaries of the French Revolution," in *A History of Private Life: Vol. 4*, ed. Michelle Perrot, trans. Arthur Goldhammer, Cambridge, MA: Harvard University Press, 1990.

Hunt, Lynn (ed.), *The Invention of Pornography: Obscenity and the Origins of Modernity 1500–1800*, New York: Zone, 1993.

Hussey, Cyril, "A Fresh Light on the Poems of Mary Lamb," *Supplement to the Charles Lamb Bulletin*, 213 (Jan. 1972), 1–12.

Irigaray, Luce, *This Sex Which Is Not One*, trans. Catherine Porter, Ithaca, NY: Cornell University Press, 1985.

Irwin, Joseph James, *M.G. "Monk" Lewis*, Boston: Twayne, 1976.

Jacobs, Edward, "Anonymous Signatures: Circulating Libraries, Conventionality, and the Production of Gothic Romances," *ELH* 62.3 (1995), 603–29.

Jacobus, Mary, Evelyn Fox Keller, and Sally Shuttleworth (eds.), *Body/Politics: Women and the Discourses of Science*, London: Routledge, 1990.

Janes, Regina, "On the Reception of Mary Wollstonecraft's *A Vindication of the Rights of Woman*," *Journal of the History of Ideas* 39 (1978), 293–302.

Jewsbury, Maria Jane, *The Three Histories*, London: F. Westley, 1830.

"John King," *The Scourge* 1 (1811), 1–27.

Johnson, Claudia, *Equivocal Beings: Politics, Gender, and Sentimentality in the 1790s*, Chicago University Press, 1995.

Jones, Ann, *Ideas and Innovations: Best Sellers of Jane Austen's Age*, New York: AMS Press, 1986.

Jones, Chris, "Helen Maria Williams and Radical Sensibility," *Prose Studies* 12 (1989), 3–24.

Jones, Robert, *Gender and the Formation of Taste in Eighteenth-Century Britain*, Cambridge University Press, 1998.

Jones, Vivien, "Femininity, Nationalism, and Romanticism," *History of European Ideas* 16 (1993), 299–305.

"Women Writing Revolution: Narratives of History and Sexuality in Wollstonecraft and Williams," in Copley and Whale (eds.), *Beyond Romanticism*, 178–99.

Jones, Vivien (ed.), *Women in the Eighteenth Century: Constructions of Femininity*, London: Routledge, 1990.

Jump, Harriet, "'No Equal Mind': Mary Wollstonecraft and the Young Romantics," *The Charles Lamb Bulletin* n.s. 79 (1992), 225–38.

Kaplan, Cora, "Wild Nights: Pleasure/Sexuality/Feminism," in *Sea Changes: Essays on Culture and Feminism*, London: Verso, 1986, 31–56.

Kates, Gary, "D'Eon Returns to France: Gender and Power in 1777," in *Body Guards: The Cultural Politics of Gender Ambiguity*, ed. Julia Epstein and Kristina Straub, London: Routledge, 1991.

Keats, John, *The Poems of John Keats*, ed. Jack Stillinger, Cambridge, MA: Harvard University Press, 1978.

Kelly, Gary, *English Fiction of the Romantic Period 1789–1830*, London and New York: Longman, 1989.

Revolutionary Feminism: The Mind and Career of Mary Wollstonecraft, London: Macmillan, 1992.

Women, Writing and Revolution, 1790–1827, Oxford: Clarendon, 1993.

"Revolutionary and Romantic Feminism: Women, Writing, and Cultural Revolution," in Hanley and Selden (eds.), *Revolution and English Romanticism*, 107–30.

Kelly, Veronica and Dorothea von Mucke (eds.), *Body and Text in the Eighteenth Century*, Stanford, CA: Stanford University Press, 1994.

Kiessling, Nicolas, "Demonic Dread: The Incubus Figure in British Literature," in *The Gothic Imagination: Essays in Dark Romanticism*, ed. G. R. Thompson, Pullman, WA: Washington State University Press, 1974, 22–41.

King, Jane and Kari Lokke, " 'The Choicest Gift of Genius': Working with and Teaching the Kohler Collection," *Approaches to Teaching British Women Poets of the Romantic Period*, eds. Stephen Behrendt and Harriet Kramer Linkin, New York: MLA, 1997, 40–44.

King, John, *Letters from France*, London: William Burton for M. Jones, [1802].

Mr. King's Apology; or a Reply to His Calumniators (With Respect to a Charge of indecent behaviour brought against him by Anna Taylor and Maria Towers), London, 1798.

Mr. King's Speech, at Egham, with Thomas Paine's Letter to Him on It, and Mr. King's Reply, 9th edn, Egham: C. Boult, [1793].

Oppression Deemed no Injustice Towards Some Individuals, London, [1798?].

Knight-Roth, Sandra, "Charlotte Dacre and the Gothic Tradition," Diss., Dalhousie University, 1972.

Kroker, Arthur and Marilouise Kroker (eds.), *The Last Sex: Feminism and Deviant Bodies*, New York: St. Martin's Press, 1993.

Kurth-Voigt, Lieselotte, "La Belle Dame sans Merci: The Revenant as Femme Fatale in Romantic Poetry," in *European Romanticism*, ed. Gerhart Hoffmeister, Detroit: Wayne State University Press, 1990, 247–67.

Labbé, Jacqueline, "Selling One's Sorrows: Charlotte Smith, Mary Robinson, and the Marketing of Poetry," *Wordsworth Circle* 25, 68–71.

Laborde, Alice, "The Problem of Sexual Equality in Sadean Prose," in *French Women and the Age of Enlightenment*, ed. Samia Spencer, Bloomington: Indiana University Press, 1984.

Lamb, Mary, *Mary and Charles Lamb: Poems, Letters, and Remains*, ed. W. Carew Hazlitt, London: Chatto & Windus, 1874.

The Letters of Charles and Mary Anne Lamb, ed. Edwin W. Marrs, Jr, Ithaca, NY: Cornell University Press, 1975–78.

The Works Of Charles and Mary Lamb, ed. E. V. Lucas, London: Methuen, 1903–5.

"On Needlework," (Signed "Sempronia"), *New British Ladies' Magazine* 1 (1815), 257–60.

Landes, Joan, *Women and the Public Sphere in the Age of the French Revolution*, Ithaca, NY: Cornell University Press, 1988.

Landon, Letitia Elizabeth, *Critical Writings by Letitia Elizabeth Landon*, ed. F. J. Sypher, Delmar, NY: Scholars' Facsimiles and Reprints, 1996.

Ethel Churchill: or, the Two Brides, 1837; ed. F. J. Sypher, 3 vols. in 1, Delmar, NY: Scholars' Facsimiles and Reprints, 1992.

Heath's Book of Beauty for 1833, London: Longman, Rees, Orme, Brown, Green and Longman [1832].

Miscellaneous Poetical Works of L.E.L., with minor revisions, London: Saunders and Otley, 1835.

The Poetical Works of L.E. Landon, Boston: Phillips, Sampson and Co., 1856.

Poetical Works of Letitia Elizabeth Landon "L.E.L.", A Facsimile Reproduction of the 1873 Edition with an Introduction and Additional Poems, ed. F. J. Sypher, Delmar, NY: Scholars' Fascimiles and Reprints, 1990.

Romance and Reality, 3 vols., London: Henry Colburn and Richard Bentley, 1831; reprinted in facsimile, ed. F. J. Sypher, Delmar, New York: Scholars' Facsimiles and Reprints, 1998.

Selected Writings, ed. Jerome McGann and Daniel Riess, Peterborough: Broadview, 1996.

The Works of L.E. Landon, 2 vols., Boston: Phillips, Sampson, and Co., 1857.

The Zenana and Minor Poems of L.E.L., ed. Emma Roberts, London, 1839.

"Boscastle Waterfall and Quarry," *Fisher's Drawing-Room Scrap Book for 1833* (London [1832]), 22.

"A Calendar of the London Seasons," *New Monthly Magazine* 40 (1834), 425–33.

"A Chinese Pagoda," *Fisher's Drawing Room Scrapbook for 1833* (London [1832]), 50.

"The Female Portrait Gallery," reprinted in Blanchard (ed.), *Life and Literary Remains of L.E.L.*, vol. 2.

"Grasmere Lake. A Sketch, By a Cockney!" *Fisher's Drawing Room Scrapbook for 1834* (London [1833]), 45–47 [unsigned].

"Linmouth," *Fisher's Drawing-Room Scrap Book for 1833* (London [1832]), 39–40.

Landry, Donna, *The Muses of Resistance: Laboring-Class Women's Poetry in Britain, 1739–1796*, Cambridge University Press, 1990.

"Figures of the Feminine: An Amazonian Revolution in Feminist Literary History," in *The Uses of Literary History*, ed. Marshall Brown, Durham: Duke University Press, 1995, 107–28.

Lanser, Susan, "Befriending the Body: Female Intimacies as Class Acts," *Eighteenth-Century Studies* 32.2 (1999), 179–98.

Laqueur, Thomas, *Making Sex: Body and Gender from the Greeks to Freud*, Cambridge, MA: Harvard University Press, 1992.

"Orgasm, Generation, and the Politics of Reproductive Biology," in Gallagher and Laqueur (eds.), *The Making of the Modern Body*, 1–41.

"Sexual Desire and the Market Economy During the Industrial Revolution," in Stanton (ed.), *Discourses of Sexuality*, 185–215.

The Laurel; Fugitive Poetry of the XIXth Century, London: J. Sharpe, 1830.

Laurence, Richard (ed.), *The Book of Enoch the Prophet*, Oxford University Press, 1821.

Lawford, Cynthia, "Diary," *London Review of Books* (21 Sept. 2000), 36–37.

LèFevre-Deumier, Jules, *Célébrités anglaises. Essais et études biographiques et littéraires. James Thomson. Anne Radcliffe. George Psalmanazar. Elisabeth Landon. Christopher North*, Paris, 1895.

Leighton, Angela, *Victorian Women Poets: Writing Against the Heart*, Charlottesville: University Press of Virginia, 1992.

Letters from Perdita to a Certain Israelite, and his Answers to Them, London: J. Fielding, 1781.

Levinson, Marjorie, *Wordsworth's great period poems*, Cambridge University Press, 1986.

Lévi-Strauss, Claude, *Tristes Tropiques*, trans. John and Doreen Weightman, New York: Pocket Books, 1977.

Levy, Darline Gay, Harriet Branson Applewhite, and Mary Durham Johnson (eds.), *Women in Revolutionary Paris 1789–1795: Selected Documents Translated with Notes*, Chicago: University of Illinois Press, 1980.

Lewis, Matthew G., *The Monk*, 1796; New York: Grove, 1981.

Tales of Wonder, 2 vols., London: W. Bulmer; J. Bell, 1801.

Leyden, John, "The Mermaid," in *Minstrelsy of the Scottish Border*, ed. T. F. Henderson, Edinburgh and London: William Blackwood, 1902, vol. 4.

Light, Launcelot and Laetitia Lookabout, *A Sketch of the Rights of Boys and Girls*, London: J. Bew, 1792.

Lincoln, Andrew, "What Was Published in 1798?," *European Romantic Review* 10.2 (1999), 137–51.

Linton, Eliza Lynn, "The Countess Mélusine," *Temple Bar* 24 (Feb. 1861), 331–43.

Lokke, Kari, "Charlotte Smith and Literary History: 'Dark Forgetfulness' and the Intercession of Saint Monica," *Women's Studies* 27 (1998), 259–80.

"'The Mild Dominion of the Moon': Charlotte Smith and the Politics of Transcendence," in Craciun and Lokke (eds.), *Rebellious Hearts*, 85–108.

"Sibylline Leaves: Mary Shelley's *Valperga* and the Legacy of *Corinne*," in *Cultural Transformations in the Romantic Age*, ed. Gregory Maertz, New York: State University of New York Press, 1998, 157–73.

Lonsdale, Roger (ed.) *Eighteenth-Century Women Poets*, Oxford University Press, 1990.

Lootens, Tricia, "Receiving the Legend, Rethinking the Writer: Letitia Landon and the Poetess Tradition," *Romanticism and Women Poets: Opening the Doors of Reception*, ed. Harriet Kramer Linkin and Stephen Behrendt, Lexington: University Press of Kentucky, 242–59.

Macaulay, Catherine, *On Burke's Reflections on the French Revolution*, intro. by Jonathan Wordsworth, Poole: Woodstock Books, 1997.

Letters on Education (1790), facsimile edn, introduction by Gina Luria, New York: Garland, 1974.

MacKinnon, Catharine, "Does Sexuality Have a History?" in Stanton (ed.), *Discourses of Sexuality*, 117–36.

Magnuson, Paul, *Reading Public Romanticism*, Princeton University Press, 1998.

Malchow, H. L., *Gothic Images of Race in Nineteenth-Century Britain*, Stanford, CA: Stanford University Press, 1996.

Marsden, Jean, "Letters on a Tombstone: Mothers and Literacy in Mary Lamb's *Mrs. Leicester's School*," *Children's Literature* 23 (1995), 31–44.

Martin, Biddy, "Feminism, Criticism, and Foucault," in Stanton (ed.) *Discourses of Sexuality*, 3–19.

Martin, Philip, *Mad Women in Romantic Writing*, Brighton, Sussex: Harvester Press, 1987.

Massé, Michele A., *In the Name of Love: Women, Masochism, and the Gothic*, Ithaca, NY: Cornell University Press, 1992.

Matus, Jill, *Unstable Bodies: Victorian Representations of Sexuality and Maternity*, Manchester University Press, 1995.

Mayo, Robert, "The Contemporaneity of the *Lyrical Ballads*," *PMLA* (1954), 486–522.

McCalman, Iain, *Radical Underworld: Prophets, Revolutionaries, and Pornographers in London, 1795–1840*, 1988; Oxford: Clarendon, 1993.

McDonagh, Josephine, "Do or Die: Problems of Agency and Gender in the Aesthetics of Murder," in *New Feminist Discourses*, ed. Isobel Armstrong, London: Routledge, 1992, 222–37.

McGann, Jerome, *Byron and Wordsworth*, University of Nottingham Press, 1999.

The Poetics of Sensibility: A Revolution in Literary Style, Oxford: Clarendon, 1996.

The Romantic Ideology: A Critical Investigation, Chicago University Press, 1983.

Social Values and Poetic Acts, Cambridge, MA: Harvard University Press, 1988.

"The Beauty of the Medusa," *Studies in Romanticism* 2 (1972), 3–25.

"Byron and the Anonymous Lyric," *Byron Journal* 20 (1992), 27–45.

"Byron and the Lyric of Sensibility," *European Romantic Review* 4 (1993), 71–83.

"Introduction," Landon, *Letitia Landon: Selected Writings*, ed. McGann and Riess, 11–31.

" 'My Brain is Feminine': Byron and the Poetry of Deception," in *Byron, Augustan and Romantic*, ed. Andrew Rutherford, Houndsmills, Basingstoke: Macmillan, 1990, 26–51.

McGann, Jerome (ed.), *The New Oxford Book of Romantic Period Verse*, Oxford University Press, 1994.

McKay, Lois, *Foucault and Feminism: Power, Gender and the Self*, Cambridge: Polity Press, 1992.

Mellor, Anne K., *Mothers of the Nation: Women's Political Writing in England, 1780–1830*, Bloomington: Indiana University Press, 2000.

Romanticism and Gender, London: Routledge, 1993.

"Blake's Portrayal of Women," *Blake: An Illustrated Quarterly* 16 (1982–83), 148–55.

"Why Women Didn't Like Romanticism: The Views of Jane Austen and Mary Shelley," in *The Romantics and Us*, ed. Gene Ruoff, New Brunswick: Rutgers University Press, 1990.

Mellor, Anne K. (ed.), *Romanticism and Feminism*, Bloomington: Indiana University Press, 1988.

Melzer, Sara and Leslie Rabine (eds.), *Rebel Daughters: Women and the French Revolution*, Oxford University Press, 1992.

"The Mermaid," *The Mirror of Literature, Amusement, and Instruction* 2 (9 Nov. 1822), 17–19, and 3 (16 Nov. 1822), 35–38.

Metz, Nancy Aycock, "Discovering a World of Suffering: Fiction and the Rhetoric of Sanitary Reform 1840–1860," *Nineteenth Century Contexts* 15 (1991), 65–81.

Michie, Helena, *The Flesh Made Word: Female Figures and Women's Bodies*, Oxford University Press, 1987.

Miles, Robert, *Gothic Writing 1750–1820: A Genealogy*, London: Routledge, 1993.

Miller, J. Hillis, *Fiction and Repetition: Seven English Novels*, Cambridge, MA: Harvard University Press, 1982.

Miller, Mary Ruth, "Five Recently-Found Letters by Thomas Campbell," *Modern Language Review* 83.2 (April 1988), 287–96.

Miller, Nancy K., " 'I's' in Drag: The Sex of Recollection," *The Eighteenth Century: Theory and Interpretation* 22 (1981), 47–57.

"Juliette and the Posterity of Prosperity," *L'Esprit créateur* 15 (1975), 413–24.

Milner, Max, *Le Diable dans la littérature française: de Cazotte à Baudelaire, 1772–1861*, vol. 1, Paris: Librairie José Corti, 1960.

Milton, John, *Paradise Lost* [the 12-book edition], ed. Scott Elledge, New York: Norton, 1975.

The Mirror of Literature, Amusement and Instruction, No. II, 9 Nov. 1822.

The Mistress of Royalty; or, the Loves of Florizel and Perdita, London: P. Egan, 1814.

Moers, Ellen, "Female Gothic," in *The Endurance of Frankenstein*, ed. George Levine and U. C. Knoepflmacher, Berkeley: University of California Press, 1982.

Moir, David, *Sketches of the Poetical Literature of the Past Half-Century*, Edinburgh: Wm. Blackwood, 1851.

Moore, Lisa, *Dangerous Intimacies: Toward a Sapphic History of the British Novel*, Durham, NC: Duke University Press, 1997.

Moorman, Mary, *William Wordsworth: A Biography. The Early Years 1770–1803*, 2 vols., Oxford: Clarendon, 1957.

Moscucci, Ornella, *The Science of Woman: Gynaecology and Gender in England 1800–1929*, Cambridge University Press, 1990.

Murphy, Peter, *Poetry as an Occupation and an Art in Britain 1760–1830*, Cambridge University Press, 1993.

Myers, Sylvia Harcstark, *The Bluestocking Circle: Women, Friendship, and the Life of the Mind*, Oxford: Clarendon, 1990.

Nead, Lynda, *The Female Nude: Art, Obscenity and Sexuality*, London: Routledge, 1992.

Nichols, John (ed.), *Illustrations of Literary History of the Eighteenth Century*, vol. 7, London: JB Nichols and Son, 1848.

Nietzsche, Friedrich, *On the Genealogy of Morals / Ecce Homo*, trans. and ed. Walter Kaufmann. New York: Vintage, 1989.

Preface to the Second Edition, *The Gay Science*, trans. Walter Kaufmann, New York: Vintage, 1974.

Norberg, Kathryn, "Making Sex Public: Félicité de Choiseul-Meuse and the Lewd Novel," *Going Public: Women and Publishing in Early Modern France*, ed. Elizabeth Goldsmith and Dena Goodman, Ithaca, NY: Cornell University Press, 1995, 161–75.

Obituary of Anne Bannerman, *Blackwood's Edinburgh Magazine* 27 (Jan. 1830), 135.

O' Brien, Conor Cruise, *The Great Melody: A Thematic Biography and Commented Anthology of Edmund Burke*, London: Sinclair-Stevenson, 1992.

Oliver, Kelly, *Womanizing Nietzsche: Philosophy's Relation to the "Feminine,"* London: Routledge, 1995.

"On Novels and Romances," signed "W.W.," part 1 of 2, *Scots Magazine* (June 1802), 470–74.

"On Novels and Romances," signed "W.W.," part 2 of 2, *Scots Magazine* (July 1802), 545–48.

"On the Choice of Subjects for Engravings," *Scots Magazine* 64 (Oct. 1802), 825–28.

Outram, Dorinda, *The Body and the French Revolution*, New Haven, CT: Yale University Press, 1989.

Paine, Thomas, *Thomas Paine Reader*, ed. Michael Foot and Isaac Kramnick, Harmondsworth: Penguin, 1987.

Parreaux, André, *The Publication of The Monk: A Literary Event 1796–1798*, Paris: M. Didier, 1960.

Pascoe, Judith, *Romantic Theatricality: Gender, Poetry, and Spectatorship*, Ithaca: Cornell University Press, 1997.

"Mary Robinson and the Literary Marketplace," in Feldman and Kelley (eds.), *Women Romantic Writers*, 252–68.

Paulson, Ronald, *Representations of Revolution, 1789–1820*, New Haven: Yale University Press, 1983.

"Gothic Fiction and the French Revolution," *ELH* 48 (1981), 545–54.

Peck, Walter Edwin, Appendix A: "Shelley's Indebtedness in *Zastrozzi* to Previous Romances," in *Shelley: His Life and Work*, Boston: Houghton Mifflin, 1927, II: 305–9.

Penny, Anne, *Poems, with a Dramatic Entertainment*, London, 1771.

Percy, Bishop Thomas, *The Correspondence of Thomas Percy and Robert Anderson*, ed. W. E. K. Anderson, vol. 9 of *The Percy Papers*, General eds., Cleanth Brooks and A. F. Falconer, New Haven, CT: Yale University Press, 1988.

Perry, Gill, "The British Sappho: Borrowed Identities and the Representations of Women Artists in late Eighteenth-Century British Art," *The Oxford Art Journal* 18.1 (1995), 44–57.

Peterson, Linda, "Becoming an Author: Mary Robinson's *Memoirs* and the Origins of the Woman Artist's Autobiography," in Wilson and Haefner (eds.), *Re-visioning Romanticism*, 36–56.

"Rewriting *A History of the Lyre*: Letitia Landon, Elizabeth Barrett Browning and the (Re)Construction of the Nineteenth-Century Woman Poet," *Women's Poetry, Late Romantic to Late Victorian*, ed. Isobel Armstrong and Virginia Blain, London: Macmillan, 1999, 115–34.

Picquenard, J. B., *Zoflora, or The Generous Negro Girl. A Colonial Story*, 2 vols., London: Lackington, Allen & Co., 1804.

Pigott, Charles, *The Female Jockey Club, or a Sketch of the Manners of the Age*, London, 1794.

Piozzi, Hester Thrale, *Thraliana: The Diary of Mrs. Hester Lynch Thrale, 1776–1809*, ed. Katharine Balderston, 2 vols., Oxford: Clarendon, 1951.

Pipkin, John, "The Material Sublime of Women Romantic Poets," *SEL* 38 (1998), 597–619.

Poe, Edgar Allan, *Complete Poems*, ed. Thomas Ollive Mabbott, 1969; Chicago: University of Illinois, 2000.

Complete Works, ed. James Harrison, New York: Thomas Crowell, 1903, vol. 10 of 17.

Poetical Epistle from Florizel to Perdita: with Perdita's Answer, 2nd edn, London: J. Stockdale, 1781.

Polwhele, Richard, *The Unsex'd Females: A Poem*, London: Cadell and Davies, 1798.

Poovey, Mary, *The Proper Lady and the Woman Writer*, Chicago University Press, 1984.

"Feminism and Deconstruction," *Feminist Studies* 14 (1988), 51–65.

"Speaking of the Body: Mid-Victorian Constructions of Female Desire," in Jacobus, Keller, and Shuttleworth (eds.), *Body/Politics*, 29–46.

Porter, Roy, "*Mixed feelings: The Enlightenment and Sexuality*," in Boucé (ed.), *Sexuality in Eighteenth-Century Britain*, 1–27.

Praz, Mario, *The Romantic Agony*, trans. Angus Davidson, 1931; New York: Meridian Books, 1956.

Preston, William, "An Epistle to Robert Anderson, M.D., On Receiving from him a Present of Various Poetical Works," *Poetical Register of 1805* (1807) 166–70.

Procès de Marie Antoinette, de Lorraine-d'Autriche, Londres: J. De Boffe, 1793.

"Professor Defends 'Obscene' Books, One by Clergyman Authority on Witchcraft," *Daily Herald* (24 Jan. 1935), 7.

Radcliffe, Ann, *The Italian*, ed. Frederic Garber, Oxford University Press, 1968.

The Poems of Mrs. Ann Radcliffe, London: J. Smith, 1816.

Railo, Eino, *The Haunted Castle*, London: Routledge, 1927.

Rajan, Tilottama, *Dark Interpreter: The Discourse of Romanticism*, Ithaca, NY: Cornell University Press, 1980.

Ramazanoglu, Caroline (ed.), *Up Against Foucault: Explorations of Some Tensions Between Foucault and Feminism*, London: Routledge, 1993.

Ramazanoglu, Caroline and Janet Holland, "Women's Sexuality and Men's Appropriation of Desire," in Ramazanoglu (ed.), *Up Against Foucault*, 239–64.

Raymond, Janice, *The Transsexual Empire: The Making of the She-male*, Boston: Beacon, 1979.

The Real Calumniator Detected: Being Candid Remarks on Mr. King's Apology, London: J. Downes, 1798.

Reed, Toni, *Demon-Lovers and Their Victims in British Fiction*, Lexington: University Press of Kentucky, 1988.

Reiman, Donald, Introduction, *Hours of Solitude*, by Charlotte Dacre, New York: Garland, 1978.

Revel, Jacques, "Marie-Antoinette in Her Fictions: The Staging of Hatred," in *Fictions of the French Revolution*, ed. Bernadette Fort, Evanston, IL: Northwestern University Press, 1991, 111–29.

Richardson, Alan, "Romanticism and the Colonization of the Feminine," in Mellor (ed.), *Romanticism and Feminism*, 13–25.

Richardson, Samuel, *Clarissa: Or, the History of a Young Lady*, London: Penguin, 1986.

Pamela: or, Virtue Rewarded, New York: Norton, 1958.

Ridley, James, *Tales of the Genii, Translated from the Persian*, London: C. Cooke, 1797.

Riess, Daniel, "Laetitia Landon and the Dawn of English Post-Romanticism," *SEL* 36 (1996) 807–27.

Riley, Denise, *"Am I That Name?": Feminism and the Category of "Women" in History*, Minneapolis: University of Minnesota Press, 1988.

Ritvo, Harriet, "Professional Scientists and Amateur Mermaids: Beating the Bounds in Nineteenth-Century Britain," in *Victorian Literature and Culture*, ed. John Maynard and Adrienne Auslander Munich, New York: AMS, 1991, vol. 19.

Riviere, Joan, "Womanliness as Masquerade," in *Formations of Fantasy*, ed. Victor Burgin, James Donald, and Cora Kaplan, London: Methuen, 1986, 36–44.

Roberts, Marie Mulvey and Roy Porter, "Introduction," *Literature and Medicine During the Eighteenth Century*, ed. Roberts and Porter, London: Routledge, 1993, 1–22.

Robertson, Fiona, *Legitimate Histories: Scott, Gothic, and the Authorities of Fiction*, Oxford: Clarendon, 1994.

Robinson, Daniel, "Reviving the Sonnet: Women Romantic Poets and the Sonnet Claim," *European Romantic Review* 6 (1995), 98–127.

Robinson, Mary, *Ainsi va le Monde, Inscribed to Robert Merry*, 2nd edn, London, 1790.

Captivity, a Poem. And Celadon and Lydia, a Tale, London: T. Becket, 1777.

Impartial Reflections on the Present Situation of the Queen of France, by a Friend to Humanity, London: John Bell, 1791.

A Letter to the Women of England, on the Injustice of Mental Subordination, 1799, pub. by *Romantic Circles*, ed. Adriana Craciun, Anne Close, Megan Musgrove, Orianne Smith, www.otal.umd.edu/rc/eleced/robinson/cover.htm, Dec. 1998.

Lyrical Tales, 1800; Oxford: Woodstock, 1989.

Monody to the Memory of the Late Queen of France, London: T. Spilsbury and Son, 1793.

The Natural Daughter, with Portraits of the Leadenhead Family. A Novel, 2 vols., Dublin: printed by Brett Smith, 1799.

Perdita: The Memoirs of Mary Robinson, ed. M. J. Levy, London: Peter Owen, 1994.

Poetical Works, 3 vols. (1806); facsimile edn, London: Routledge/Thoemmes, 1996.

Sappho and Phaon (1796) in Wu (ed.), *Romantic Women Poets*, 184–208.

Selected Poems, ed. Judith Pascoe, Peterborough: Broadview, 2000.

Sight, the Cavern of Woe, and Solitude, London: T. Spilsbury and Son, 1793.

Walsingham; or, the Pupil of Nature. A Domestic Story, 1797; Introduction by Peter Garside, 4 vols., London: Routledge/Thoemmes, 1992.

"Anecdotes of the late Queen of France," *Monthly Magazine* (Aug. 1800), 40–41[unsigned].

"A Fragment, Supposed to be Written near the Temple, On the Night Before the Murder of Louis the Sixteenth," *The European Magazine* 23 (April 1793).

"Present State of the Manners, Society, &c. &c. of the Metropolis of England," *Monthly Magazine* (Aug., Sept., Oct., Nov. 1800).

Rogers, Katherine M., *Feminism and Eighteenth-Century England*, Chicago: University of Illinois Press, 1982.

"The View from England," in *French Women and the Age of Enlightenment*, ed. Samia Spencer, Bloomington: Indiana University Press, 1984, 357–68.

Rogers, Pat, "Fat is a Fictional Issue: The Novel and the Rise of Weight Watching," in *Literature and Medicine During the Eighteenth Century*, ed. W. F. Bynum and Roy Porter, London: Routledge, 1993, 168–87.

Ross, Ernest, *The Ordeal of Bridget Elia*, Norman: University of Oklahoma Press, 1960.

Ross, Marlon, *The Contours of Masculine Desire: Romanticism and the Rise of Women's Poetry*, Oxford University Press, 1989.

"Romantic Quest and Conquest: Troping Masculine Power in the Crisis of Poetic Identity," in Mellor (ed.), *Romanticism and Feminism*, 26–51.

Rousseau, G. S., "Nymphomania, Bienville, and the Rise of Erotic Sensibility," in Boucé (ed.), *Sexuality in Eighteenth-Century Britain*, 95–113.

"Towards a Social Anthropology of the Imagination," in *Enlightenment Crossings: Pre-and Post-modern Discourses: Anthropological*, by G. S. Rousseau, Manchester University Press, 1991, 1–25.

Rousseau, G. S. and Roy Porter (eds.), *Sexual Underworlds of the Enlightenment*, Chapel Hill: University of North Carolina Press, 1988.

Rousseau, Jean-Jacques, *Emile; or, On Education*, trans. Alan Bloom, New York: Basic Books, 1979.

La Nouvelle Héloise, trans. Judith H. McDowell, University Park: Pennsylvania State University Press, 1987.

Rousseau's Political Writings, ed. Alan Ritter and Julia Conaway Bondanella, trans. Julia Conaway Bondanella, New York: Norton, 1988.

Roworth, Wendy Wassyng, "Anatomy is Destiny: Regarding the Body in the Art of Angelica Kauffman," in *Femininity and Masculinity in Eighteenth-Century Art and Culture*, ed. Gill Perry and Michael Rossington, Manchester University Press, 1994, 41–62.

Rowton, Frederic, "Laetitia Elizabeth Maclean," in Rowton (ed.), *The Female Poets of Great Britain*, 424–45.

Rowton, Frederic (ed.), "Introductory Chapter," in *The Female Poets of Great Britain*, reprint, Detroit: Wayne State University Press, 1981, xlvii–lii.

Sade, Donatien Alphonse François, Marquis de, *The Complete Justine, Philosophy in the Bedroom, and Other Writings*, trans. Richard Seaver and Austryn Wainhouse, New York: Grove, 1965.

"DISCOURS PRONONCE à la fête décernée par la Section des Piques, aux mânes de Marat et de Le Pelletier," 1793, in *Oeuvres Complètes du Marquis de Sade*, Paris: Cercle du Livre Précieux, 1967, XI, 119–22.

"Reflections on the Novel," in *The 120 Days of Sodom and Other Writings*, trans. Austryn Wainhouse and Richard Seaver, New York: Grove, 1966.

Saint-Amand, Pierre, "Adorning Marie Antoinette," *Eighteenth-Century Life* 15 (Nov. 1991), 19–34.

"Terrorizing Marie Antoinette," trans. Jennifer Curtiss Gage, *Critical Inquiry* 20 (Spring 1994), 379–400.

Sallust, *The Jugurthine War/Conspiracy of Catiline*, trans. S. A. Handford, Harmonsworth: Penguin, 1963.

Sawicki, Jana, *Disciplining Foucault: Feminism, Power, and the Body*, London: Routledge, 1991.

Scarry, Elaine, *The Body in Pain: The Making and Unmaking of the World*, Oxford University Press, 1985.

Schiebinger, Londa, *The Mind Has No Sex? Women in the Origins of Modern Science*, Cambridge, MA: Harvard University Press, 1989.

Nature's Body: Gender in the Making of Modern Science, Boston: Beacon Press, 1993.

Schiller, Friedrich, "The Ideal," *Monthly Magazine* 12 (Oct 1801), 221–22.

"The Ideal," *Poetical Register of 1801* (1802), 205–8.

Schock, Peter, "*The Marriage of Heaven and Hell*: Blake's Myth of Satan and its Cultural Matrix," *ELH* 60 (1993), 441–70.

The School for Friends: A Domestic Tale, By Miss Dacre, London: Thomas Tegg [n.d.].

Schor, Naomi, "Dreaming Dyssymetry: Barthes, Foucault, and Sexual Difference," *Men in Feminism*, ed. Alice Jardine and Paul Simon, New York: Methuen, 1987, 98–110.

Scott, Sir Walter, *The Bride of Lammermoor*, 1819, London: Everyman, 1991.

"Essay on Imitations of the Ancient Ballad," in *Minstrelsy of the Scottish Border*, ed. T. F. Henderson, vol. 4, Edinburgh and London: William Blackwood, 1902.

Scrivener, Michael (ed.), *Poetry and Reform: Periodical Verse from the English Democratic Press 1792–1824*, Detroit: Wayne State University Press, 1992.

Sedgwick, Eve Kosofsky, *Between Men: English Literature and Male Homosocial Desire*, New York: Columbia University Press, 1985.

The Coherence of Gothic Conventions, New York: Arno Press, 1980.

"The Character in the Veil: Imagery of the Surface in the Gothic Novel," *PMLA* 96 (1981), 255–70.

Senf, Carol, *The Vampire in Nineteenth-Century English Literature*, Bowling Green, OH: Bowling Green State University Popular Press, 1988.

Setzer, Sharon, "The Dying Game: Crossdressing in Mary Robinson's *Walsingham*," *Nineteenth Century Contexts* 22 (2000), 305–28.

"Romancing the Reign of Terror: Sexual Politics in Mary Robinson's *Natural Daughter*," *Criticism* 34 (1997), 531–55.

Seward, Anna, *The Letters of Anna Seward*, vol. 5 of 6, Edinburgh: Constable, 1811.

Shelley, Mary, *The Last Man*, ed. Anne McWhir, Peterborough: Broadview, 1996.

Shelley, Percy Bysshe , *Poetical Works of Percy Bysshe Shelley*, ed. Newell Ford, Boston: Houghton Mifflin, 1975.

Zastrozzi and St. Irvyne, ed. Stephen C. Behrendt, Oxford University Press, 1986.

Shepard, Sarah, *Characteristics of the Genius and Writings of L.E.L.*, London: Longman, Brown, Green, 1841.

Sheridan, Alan, *Michel Foucault: The Will to Truth*, New York: Tavistock, 1980.

Shires, Linda (ed.), *Rewriting the Victorians: Theory, History, and the Politics of Gender*, London: Routledge, 1992.

Sigourney, Lydia, "The Coral Insect," *The Lyre. Fugitive Poetry of the Nineteenth Century*, London: Tilt & Bogue, 1841.

Silliman, Benjamin, *Letters of Shahcoolen* (1802), Introduction by Ben Harris McClary, Gainesville: Scholars' Facsimiles & Reprints, 1962.

Siskin, Clifford, *The Work of Writing: Literature and Social Change in Britain 1700–1830*, Baltimore, MD: Johns Hopkins University Press, 1998.

Small, Helen, *Love's Madness: Medicine, the Novel, and Female Insanity, 1800–1865*, Oxford: Clarendon, 1996.

Smith, Charlotte, *The Poems of Charlotte Smith*, ed. Stuart Curran, Oxford University Press, 1993.

The Young Philosopher (1798), ed. Elizabeth Kraft, Lexington: University Press of Kentucky, 1999.

Smith, Timothy D'Arch, *Montague Summers: A Bibliography*, Wellingborough: Aquarian Press, 1983.

Smith, T. Southwood, "Contagion and Sanitary Laws," *Westminster Review* (1825), reprinted in Hodgkinson (ed.), *Public Health in the Victorian Age* [n.p.].

"Life and Organization," *Westminster Review* (1827), reprinted in Hodgkinson (ed.), *Public Health in the Victorian Age* [n.p.].

"Plague–Typhus Fever–Quarantine," *Westminster Review* (1825), reprinted in Hodgkinson (ed.), *Public Health in the Victorian Age* [n.p.].

"Spasmodic Cholera," *Westminster Review* (1831), reprinted in Hodgkinson (ed.), *Public Health in the Victorian Age* [n.p.].

Snitow, Ann, "Mass Market Romance: Pornography for Women is Different," in *Powers of Desire: The Politics of Sexuality*, ed. Ann Snitow, Christine Stansell, and Sharon Thompson, New York: Monthly Review Press, 1983.

Soper, Kate, "Productive Contradictions," in Ramazanoglu (ed.), *Up Against Foucault*, 29–50.

Spacks, Patricia Meyer, "Ev'ry Woman is at Heart a Rake," *Eighteenth-Century Studies* 8 (1974).

Spivack, Charlotte, " 'The Hidden World Below': Victorian Women Fantasy Poets," in *The Poetic Fantastic: Studies in an Evolving Genre*, ed. Patrick Murphy and Vernon Hyles, New York and Westport, CT: Greenwood Press, 1989, 53–64.

Spivak, Gayatri, "Displacement and the Discourse of Woman," in *Displacement: Derrida and After*, ed. Mark Krupnick, Bloomington: Indiana University Press, 1983.

"Three Women's Texts and a Critique of Imperialism," *Critical Inquiry* 12 (1985), 243–61.

Staël, Germaine de, *Corinne, or Italy*, trans. Avriel Goldberger, New Brunswick: Rutgers University Press, 1987.

"On Literature Considered in Its Relationship to Social Institutions," *An Extraordinary Woman: Selected Writings of Germaine de Staël*, trans. Vivian Folfenflik, New York: Columbia University Press, 1987, 172–208.

Stafford, Barbara, *Body Criticism: Imaging the Unseen in Enlightenment Art and Medicine*, Cambridge, MA: Massachusetts Institute of Technology, 1991.

Stanton, Domna (ed.), *Discourses of Sexuality: From Aristotle to AIDS*, Ann Arbor: University of Michigan Press, 1992.

Steen, Marguerite, *The Lost One: A Biography of Mary (Perdita) Robinson*, London: Methuen, 1937.

Stephenson, Glennis, *Letitia Landon: The Woman Behind L.E.L.*, Manchester University Press, 1995.

Sterrenburg, Lee, "*The Last Man*: Anatomy of Failed Revolutions," *Nineteenth-Century Fiction* 33 (1978), 324–47.

Stevenson, Warren, *Romanticism and the Androgynous Sublime*, Madison: Fairleigh Dickinson University Press, 1996.

Stewart, Susan, "Scandals of the Ballad," in *Crimes of Writing: Problems in the Containment of Representation*, Oxford University Press, 1991.

Stott, Rebecca, *The Fabrication of the Late Victorian Femme Fatale*, London: Macmillan, 1992.

"Strictures on Literary Patronage," signed "A.M.," *Scots Magazine* 64 (July 1802), 807–10.

Studlar, Gaylyn, *In the Realm of Pleasure: Von Sternberg, Dietrich and the Masochistic Aesthetic*, Urbana and Chicago: University of Chicago Press, 1988.

Summers, Montague, "Byron's Lovely Rosa," in *Essays in Petto*, 1928, Freeport: Books for Libraries Press, 1967, 57–73.

"Introduction," *Zofloya; or, The Moor*, by Charlotte Dacre, London: Fortune Press, 1928, v–xxvii.

Swinburne, Algernon Charles, *The Swinburne Letters*, ed. Cecil Y. Lang, vol. 5, New Haven: Yale University Press, 1963.

Tasker, Mr., "Impromptu, By. Mr. Tasker, On Reading Mrs. ROBINSON's Poems," *European Magazine* 25 (1794), 140.

Taylor, Thomas, *A Vindication of the Rights of Brutes*, Gainesville, FL: Scholars' Facsimiles and Reprints, 1966.

Tennyson, Alfred, "The Mermaid," *Poems, Chiefly Lyrical*, London: Effingham Wilson, 1830, 27–30.

Thomas, Chantal, *La Reine scélérante: Marie-Antoinette dans les pamphlets*, Paris: Seuil, 1989.

Thompson, C. J. S., *The Mystery and Lore of Monsters*, New York: Barnes and Noble, 1994.

Thoms, William, *Lays and Legends of Various Nations*, London: G. Cowie, 1834.

Todd, Janet, *Gender, Art, and Death*, New York: Continuum, 1993.

The Sign of Angellica: Women, Writing and Fiction, 1660–1800, New York: Columbia University Press, 1989.

Tracy, Robert, "The Mobbed Queen: Marie Antoinette as Victorian Ikon," *Literature, Interpretation, Theory* 4 (1993), 275–90.

Trial at Large of Marie Antoinette, Late Queen of France, 3rd edn, London: Chapman, 1793.

The Trial of Miss Broderick, for the Wilful [sic] Murder of George Errington, Esq. Before Lord Chief Baron Macdonald, at Chelmsford, on Friday, July 17, 1794, Edinburgh: J. Robertson, 1795.

Ty, Eleanor, *Unsex'd Revolutionaries: Five Women Novelists of the 1790s*, Toronto University Press, 1993.

Uwins, David, "Cholera Morbus: What is its Nature? In what Matter ought it to be Treated? And is it likely to Visit the British Islands?" *New Monthly Magazine* 32 (1831), 13–19.

Varma, Devendra, "Introduction," *The Libertine*, by Charlotte Dacre, 1807; New York: Arno Press, 1974.

"Introduction," *The Passions*, by Charlotte Dacre, 1811; New York: Arno Press, 1974.

"Introduction," *Zofloya; or, the Moor*, by Charlotte Dacre, 1806; New York: Arno Press, 1974, xi–xxx.

"Verses, Addressed to a Female Republican," signed "S.," *The European Magazine* 35 (Jan. 1799), 46.

Vrettos, Athena, *Somatic Fictions: Imagining Illness in Victorian Culture*, Stanford University Press, 1995.

Wakefield, Priscilla, *Reflections on the Present Condition of the Female Sex*, London: Joseph Johnson, 1798; New York: Garland, 1974.

Walker, Cheryl, "In Bluebeard's Closet: Women Who Write with the Wolves," *Literature, Interpretation, Theory* 7 (1996), 13–26.

Walker, Joseph Cooper, *An Historical and Critical Essay on the Revival of the Drama in Italy*, Edinburgh: Mundell and Son, 1805.

Weil, Kari, *Androgyny and the Denial of Difference*, Charlottesville: University Press of Virginia, 1992.

Williams, Anne, *Art of Darkness: A Poetics of Gothic*, Chicago University Press, 1995.

Williams, Helen Maria, *Letters from France*, 8 vols. in 2, Introduction by Janet M. Todd, Delmar, New York: Scholars' Facsimiles and Reprints, 1975.

Williams, Perry, "The Laws of Health: Women, Medicine and Sanitation Reform, 1850–1890," in Marina Blackwell (ed.), *Science and Sensibility*.

Williams, Raymond, *Keywords*, 1976; Glasgow: Fontana/Croom Helm, 1981.

Wilson, Carol Shiner and Joel Haefner (eds.), *Re-visioning Romanticism: British Women Writers, 1776–1837*, Philadelphia: University of Pennsylvania Press, 1994.

Wilson, John, "Noctes Ambrosianæ No. XVI," *Blackwood's Magazine* 16 (16 Aug. 1824), 237–38.

Wilson, Lisa, "Female Pseudonymity in the Romantic 'Age of Personality':
The Career of Charlotte King/Rosa Matilda/Charlotte Dacre," *European Romantic Review* 9 (1998), 393–420.

Wiltshire, John, *Jane Austen and the Body*, Cambridge University Press, 1992.

Wittig, Monique, *The Lesbian Body*, London: Peter Owen, 1975.

The Straight Mind and Other Essays, Boston: Beacon Press, 1992.

Wittreich, Joseph Anthony (ed.), *The Romantics on Milton*, Cleveland: Press of Case Western Reserve University, 1970.

Wohl, Anthony, *Endangered Lives: Public Health in Victorian Britain*, London, J. M. Dent, 1983.

Wolcot, John ("Peter Pindar"), *The Works of Peter Pindar*, London: J. Walker, 1816, vol. 3.

Wolfson, Susan, *Figures in the Margin: The Languages of Gender in British Romanticism*, Philadelphia: University of Pennsylvania Press, forthcoming.

Wollstonecraft, Mary, *A Historical and Moral View of the French Revolution*, 1794; in *The Works of Mary Wollstonecraft*, vol. 6.

A Vindication of the Rights of Woman, 2nd edn, 1792; ed. Carol H. Poston, New York: Norton, 1975.

The Vindications: A Vindication of the Rights of Men / A Vindication of the Rights of Woman, ed. D. L. Macdonald and Kathleen Scherf, Peterborough: Broadview, 1997.

The Works of Mary Wollstonecraft, ed. Janet Todd and Marilyn Butler, 7 vols., London: William Pickering, 1989.

"Letter Introductory to a Series of Letters on the Present Character of the French Nation," in *The Works of Mary Wollstonecraft*, vol. 6.

Woodward, Lionel D., *Une anglaise amie de la Révolution Française: Hélène Maria Williams et ses amis*, Paris: Honoré Champion, 1930.

Woof, Pamela, "Dorothy Wordsworth and Mary Lamb, Writers," part 1, *Charles Lamb Bulletin* n.s. 66 (1989), 41–52.

"Dorothy Wordsworth and Mary Lamb, Writers," part 2, *Charles Lamb Bulletin* n.s. 67 (1989), 82–93.

Wordsworth, William, *A Guide through the District of the Lakes*, introduced by W. M. Merchant, London: Rupert Hart-Davis, 1951.

Literary Criticism of William Wordsworth, ed. Paul Zall, Lincoln: University of Nebraska Press, 1966.

Poetical Works of William Wordsworth, ed. Ernest de Selincourt and Helen Darbishire, Oxford: Clarendon, 1947.

Wu, Duncan (ed.), *Romantic Women Poets: An Anthology*, Oxford: Blackwell, 1997.

Romanticism: An Anthology, 2nd edn, Oxford: Blackwell, 1998.

Yaeger, Patricia, "Toward a Female Sublime," in *Gender and Theory*, ed. Linda Kauffman, Oxford: Blackwell, 1989, 191–212.

Yarnall, Judith, *Transformations of Circe: The History of an Enchantress*, Chicago: University of Illinois Press, 1994.

Yearsley, Ann, *An Elegy on Marie Antoinette of Austria*, Bristol: J. Rudhall, [1795?].

Index

319

CAMBRIDGE STUDIES IN ROMANTICISM

GENERAL EDITORS
MARILYN BUTLER, *University of Oxford*
JAMES CHANDLER, *University of Chicago*